D1263346

SELECTED WRITINGS OF
ABRAM S. HEWITT

SELECTED WRITINGS OF
ABRAM S. HEWITT

Edited by ALLAN NEVINS

With an introduction by

NICHOLAS MURRAY BUTLER

KENNIKAT PRESS, INC./PORT WASHINGTON, N. Y.

Introduction

THE papers here printed are of unusual interest and importance. They record and reflect the intellectual and public activity of a citizen of the first order of ability and influence. They reveal a man who in a manner quite unique combined scholarship with intimate practical knowledge of a great industry, mastery of a great and growing business with public service in both official and unofficial life, and who had as well a power of leadership which was everywhere recognized and hailed by his contemporaries.

Mr. Hewitt used to say that the Creator had not given him adequate boiler capacity to run his engine, meaning that his physical strength was not adequate to the demands which his intellect made upon it. Nevertheless, that engine never ceased its activity during all the years of his long life, and it always functioned on the highest plane of understanding and of unselfish human and public service.

His oration of Sir Henry Bessemer has been acclaimed on both sides of the Atlantic as the ablest and most penetrating interpretation of the contribution which Bessemer made to the steel industry. His various papers and speeches which have to do with that industry are, without exception, masterpieces of understanding and exposition. The same may be said of his political papers. Among these will be found for the first time the fullest and most intimate record of what really took place in the settlement of the disputed presidential election of 1876. This paper will make history. Mr. Hewitt's personal relation to all that happened at that time and his part in shaping it are the outstanding political achievement of his career.

What can be said of his papers on iron and steel and of his political papers may also be most emphatically said of his addresses on other subjects. No citizen of New York in this day and generation should fail to read the illuminating address which Mr. Hewitt delivered at the opening of the Brooklyn Bridge in 1883 or that at the dedication of the new site of Columbia University on Morningside Heights in 1896 or his last Commencement address at Cooper Union in 1902.

It is fortunate indeed that there is here published in orderly fashion this remarkable record of a lifelong intellectual and public activity on the highest plane of excellence and unselfish devotion to the nation's interests and ideals.

NICHOLAS MURRAY BUTLER

*Columbia University
in the City of New York
November 11, 1936*

Contents

Contents

Chronology

1822—Born at Haverstraw, New York, July 31.

1824—Brought by his father John Hewitt to New York City.

1835—Enters Grammar School of Columbia College.

1842—Graduates at head of class from Columbia College.

1843-44—Teaches in Columbia College Grammar School and studies law.

1844—Visits England, France, Germany, and Italy.

1845—Assists Peter Cooper in establishing ironworks at Trenton, N. J.

1847—With Edward Cooper establishes Cooper & Hewitt to manage Trenton Iron Company.

1853-54—With Edward Cooper and Charles Hewitt perfects manufacture of wrought-iron structural beams.

1855—Marries Peter Cooper's daughter Amelia, April 6, in New York City.

1856-57—Gives Bessemer process first American trial at Phillipsburg, N. J.

1858—Assists Cyrus W. Field and Peter Cooper in work of laying Atlantic cable.

1859—As trustee and secretary of Cooper Union plays a major rôle in launching its work.

1861—Undertakes manufacture of gun metal for Union armies.

1862—Visits England and obtains data which permit first successful manufacture of gun metal in America.

1862—Supplies Grant's Fort Donelson expedition with mortar beds.

1865-66—Begins manufacture of steel-topped rails by Mushet-Heath process.

1867—Visits Paris Exhibition and European ironworks as United States Commissioner.

1867-69—Introduces open-hearth (Siemens-Martin) process into United States.

1874—Elected Representative in Congress from New York City.

1876—As Democratic national chairman manages Tilden campaign; president American Institute of Mining Engineers.

1876-77—House Democratic leader in adjustment of disputed election.

1876, 1878, 1882, 1884—Reëlected Representative in Congress.

1886—Elected mayor of New York City against Henry George and Theodore Roosevelt.

1890—Joins Carnegie in tour of the South; president American Institute of Mining Engineers.

1896—Treasurer of the Gold Democratic Party.

1896—Delivers dedicatory address at new Columbia University site.

1898-1902—Completes his work for Cooper Union, placing it on firm foundation.

1903—Dies in New York City, January 18.

Autobiographical Papers

The Shipwreck of the "Alabamian," December 12, 1884[1]

[Hewitt, whose eyesight had failed under the strain of his law studies and his work as teacher in the Grammar School of Columbia College, sailed for Europe with his former college mate, Edward Cooper (son of Peter Cooper) on March 6, 1844. He visited his father's boyhood home in Cannock, Staffordshire; stayed for some time in London, where he made his first English friendships; and spent a busy summer touring France, Germany, Switzerland, and northern Italy. His first publications were newspaper letters on this tour to the New York Democrat, *decidedly radical in tone. Early in October Hewitt and Edward Cooper reached Leghorn. Here they took passage on an American vessel. Their narrow escape from death on the ensuing voyage is related in this paper, probably written by Hewitt, though signed by Edward Cooper as well, and published in the New York press in December, 1844. Its merits of style are notable.]*

The following is an account of the perils of the voyage and final abandonment of this ship, and the rescue of the crew and passengers.

The *Alabamian* sailed from Leghorn for New York on the 10th of October, 1844, with a valuable cargo, consisting of marble, straw, silks, etc. On the 25th of October, before passing the Straits of Gibraltar, she encountered a severe gale of wind, which did no material damage. On the 29th she passed the Straits, and on the 14th of November, in lat. 32° 04', long. 30° 32', off the Western Islands, she met with one of the most terrific gales of wind that had ever been witnessed by any person on board. The ship seemed to be at the point of meeting of two tremendous gales, one from the N. N. E., the other from the N. W. She could carry no sail save the mizzen staysail, covering perhaps fifty square feet, while the sea broke on every side with awful fury. Being an excellent sea-boat, she rode out the gale admirably and suffered very little damage until the wind died away, when we had two fearful seas from the N. N. E. and N. W. We headed to the N. W., and thus one sea was striking on her bows while the other came like the blow of a huge trip hammer upon her counter; added to this, the marble in her lower

1 This account was published in some New York newspaper, probably the *Democrat*, in December, 1844; the editor has been unable to find the issue. Hewitt kept a copy and reprinted it in pamphlet form in 1894.

hold caused her to roll on both sides almost to the water's edge. The continued effect of all these causes was to rack the ship almost to pieces. The whole of the stern was in a state of continual motion, while all the carved ornaments and the bulwarks of the poop-deck were knocked off by the incessant blows which descended upon her. The pumps were kept going about one-third of the time. It was very fortunate that on the day before the mate had succeeded in stopping a steady leak which had existed from the time we left port, or else the labor of the pumps would have been doubled.

It is impossible to convey an idea of the fearful desolation which reigned on every side; and had we not been extremely fortunate in obtaining a fair wind before which we could run, the ship must then have gone down. From this time until we came within about one hundred and twenty miles of New York, we had most delightful weather; and although the ship was very weak and the pumps were nearly half the time in motion, we were looking joyfully forward to a reunion with our friends in fifteen or eighteen hours, when the wind came out N. E., contrary to all the appearances of the skies and the opinion of a Delaware pilot who had boarded us within twenty miles of Cape May. Captain Hitchcock, however, was anxious to get within the Delaware Breakwater; but as the wind was blowing from the N. W., it was impossible. The wind then went round to the N. and N. E. During the entire night of the 10th and all of the 11th of December, the wind blew with tremendous violence. The ocean seemed one vast succession of water volcanoes spouting forth volumes of foam. The pumps were worked every ten minutes. The maintopsail was split on the morning of the 11th, and at seven o'clock next went the mizzen staysail, and nothing was heard amid the howling of the wind and the blows of the waves on the ship but the clinking of the pumps, at which all hands were now employed.

Nature seemed thundering forth a doleful requiem, and we soon lost all hopes of keeping the ship long afloat. So mighty was the power of the sea that one blow in the bows threw the men from the pumps and caused the ship to quiver like a leaf in the wind. The whole stern of the ship and the cabin were working as if they would go to pieces, while the dead-lights were ground about as in a mill. At eight o'clock at night the double pump-break was rigged, and passengers and crew [1] betook themselves to pumping; but still the water gained rapidly. At this time the water was above the keelson; at twelve o'clock our only hope was to keep her afloat till morning. Would that we could do justice to the efforts of the crew to save the ship and the perfect cheerfulness which reigned among them! Slowly passed the hours till daylight

[1] Eighteen men in all.

dawned. A lifetime seemed to be contained in a minute. Part of the crew now got the boats ready for launching: the one a surfboat which might live in almost any sea, the other the longboat, which had been used for a pigpen for ten years, was full of holes in the bottom and in such a state of decay that no person was allowed to tread upon the planks lest the bottom should fall out. At this time the sea was still breaking with fearful violence, although the wind had somewhat subsided. At length morning dawned, and to our great joy a brig was discerned about three or four miles to the windward. We made signals of distress, but no attention was paid to them.

Not a murmur was heard from the crew, and the only exclamation came from the Captain, who, as he saw our chance of deliverance running away from us, said: "God grant that he may never need that aid which he now refuses to afford!" At seven o'clock A. M. on the 12th inst. the crew prepared to launch the boats, while the passengers worked the pumps. The ship was now fast settling by the head. Captain Hitchcock in the noblest manner gave the mate, Mr. Benson, the choice of boats, although he knew that in one there was almost certain life, and in the other almost certain death. Indeed, it would be impossible to do justice to the coolness, intrepidity, and generosity of Captain Hitchcock during the whole of this trying occasion. Mr. Benson chose the surfboat, and to that we owe our preservation. The passengers resolved to accompany the Captain in the longboat; but such was its rottenness that we did not dare to save one particle of clothing beyond what was on our backs. At eight o'clock the longboat, or rather pigpen, was launched; and as the sea was still running fearfully high, the greatest care was observed to prevent her from being dashed to pieces against the ship. We were afraid to jump in, for fear of staving the bottom; but as Providence would have it, a wave brought her alongside, so we all got in safely and were soon clear of the ship.

God alone knows what our feelings were when we thus committed ourselves to the mercy of the raging sea, in perhaps the frailest boat that ever floated with twelve men on the Atlantic. After seeing the mate safely clear, we lay for more than an hour within one hundred and fifty yards of the ship, expecting every instant to see her sink; for when we left her she had ten feet of water forward and seven feet aft and was very much down by the head. No refuge but that of death was now before our eyes; and, cast away as we were in lat. 36° 40', long. 74°, in a spot where no vessel would be likely to traverse, unless driven thither by stress of weather; in the Gulf Stream, where storms and the sea rage with accumulated power; in a boat that we could not press our weight upon, through dread that all that separated us from eternity would stave out beneath our feet, and leaking so badly that continual bailing alone kept her afloat; chilled with the water that had dashed over while on board of the ship, we looked upon death not only as certain, but as a kind of relief from worse evils. We had no sails, but with the aid of the drag she drifted with the current away from the ship, so that at three o'clock we were perhaps five miles distant. The sea ran so high that the ship was hid from view more than half the time.

At this time the men, wearied with their toilsome labors for the last three days, ate some bread; and after a solemn invocation to Him who rules the storm, either to grant us rescue or to smooth our path to that world in which we soon expected to appear, all but the Captain and one passenger reclined as well as they could to sleep. The same thoughts of home and friends and family were passing through the minds of these two, and unbidden tears came from the eyes of both for the first time during the whole of this awful scene, when suddenly, as if in answer to our prayer, the Captain exclaimed, "Sail ho!" The crew started as if struck by an electric shock; and all with joy that knew no bounds saw a ship at the distance of ten miles. We pass over the fearful anxiety of the two hours during which we knew not whether she would see us or not, when every minute seemed an age, till about half-past five o'clock we were safely on board the ship *Atalanta*, Captain George B. Raymond, of New York, where to our great joy we found the mate with the five men who had accompanied him. Indeed, to the exertions of Mr. Benson and his men, under Providence, we owe our deliverance; for in little more than two hours they had pulled more than twenty miles from the ship, so as to board another ship which was not in the horizon of the *Alabamian*.

Mr. Benson, the night before, had been unable to leave his berth from a severe fever; but in the morning excitement gave him strength to accomplish this remarkable feat. To Captain Raymond we never can be sufficiently grateful, and we trust that God will reward the generous conduct of this noble man, who stood from his course, although he had a fair wind. Mariners who know how little southerly wind we have on the coast in winter, can appreciate the sacrifice he thus made. He had resolved, if he had not found us, to proceed to the *Alabamian* (which Providence seemed to have wonderfully kept above water as a guide for him), heave to, and set a light at his masthead so that we might pull to him before morning. Captain Raymond,[1] his officers and crew, did everything to render the eighteen human beings whom they

[1] Hewitt and Edward Cooper presented Captain Raymond with a handsome silver vase, expressing their gratitude for his heroism in "having nobly rescued" the souls aboard the *Alabamian*. After paying for his share of it, Hewitt often said later, he had but $2 left with which to face the world. The vase is now (1936) in the possession of Mr. Erskine Hewitt.

had preserved comfortable; and in one hundred and ten hours we were landed safely in New York, but destitute in everything save thankfulness to God that He in His great mercy had seen fit to preserve us from the awful fate which had impended over us.

ABRAM S. HEWITT
EDWARD COOPER } Passengers

New York, December 18th, 1844

The Stevens Family

TWENTY-FIFTH ANNIVERSARY ADDRESS, FEBRUARY 18, 1897

[*Hewitt always took pride in recalling his connections with the Stevens family, one of the most gifted groups in the history of American engineering. Its founder was John Stevens, who in 1784 bought at auction a large tract on the west bank of the Hudson comprising most of present-day Hoboken. Hewitt's father, John Hewitt, helped John Stevens run his pioneer steamboat the* Polacca *on the Passaic River in 1798. Stevens all but anticipated Fulton in placing the first successful steamboat on the Hudson—his 100-foot steamboat the* Phoenix *was planned in 1806. Debarred from full use of the Hudson by the rights granted his rival, he turned to railroading and was one of the founders of the Pennsylvania system, while his two sons Robert and Edwin A. were founders of the Camden & Amboy. Hewitt, who furnished rails in the forties for the Camden & Amboy, often stayed at the Castle Point (Hoboken) mansion of Robert L. Stevens, the ablest naval architect of his time. It was Robert L. Stevens who invented the modern type of ferry slip, the T-rail, the hook-headed railroad spike, and the first really workable marine tubular boiler; and who introduced the wrought-iron walking-beam, the forced-draught firing system for boilers, the split paddle wheel, and other improvements in navigation. John C. Stevens, a brother, was a founder of the New York Yacht Club. Edwin A. Stevens was perhaps more largely responsible than any other member of the family for the success of the Camden & Amboy; and he founded the Stevens Institute of Technology, bequeathing both money and land for it on his death in 1868.*]

I suppose I am the only person in this room,[1] and one of the very few persons alive, who can say that he has seen and known the entire family from its founder, John Stevens, who was born in 1745, before the Revolution, as well as his children, grandchildren and great-grandchildren, who have gathered round the old ancestral home on the other side of the Hudson River. It may seem strange that anyone should be

[1] The banquet room of the Waldorf-Astoria Hotel; the occasion was the twenty-fifth anniversary dinner of the Stevens Institute. The text is taken from the *Stevens Indicator*, Vol. XIV, No. 2.

here who knew the elder John Stevens, but it so happened that when I was a boy of about six years of age, I was taken by my father to Hoboken for the purpose of being introduced to John Stevens, because at that early age I had witnessed from the wharf at the foot of Jay Street a magnificent steamer, with four ponderous smokestacks, passing rapidly up the Hudson River, and had asked whose steamer it was and where it was going. My father told me that there were two of these boats, the finest in the world, and that they had been built by the Stevens family of Hoboken. I said, "Do you know the Stevens family?" to which he replied, "Yes. I will take you to Hoboken, and let you see the greatest engineer of his time."

And so before 1830, somewhere between 1828 and 1830, I was taken to Hoboken and introduced to John Stevens, who was then a man of eighty-three years of age, but in possession of all his faculties and manifesting the greatest possible interest in this visit from an old friend and a young boy. Familiarly he called my father "John," for both bore the same name, and my father said, "This is my son. I want him to see you and know you," and then they began to talk of old times and particularly of this remarkable story, which was often repeated to me by my father afterwards, or else possibly I should not remember it so well.

My father was the draughtsman and the pattern maker, who had come out from England with a party of machinists to erect the first stationary double-acting condensing engine which was put at work upon the American continent. It was built by Boulton and Watt at the Soho Works, near Birmingham in England, and was brought out and erected at Center Square in Philadelphia for the purpose of supplying that city with water, before the Fairmount Works on the Schuylkill River were erected. In a monograph which I have seen, it is stated that John Stevens saw the first engine that was "built" in America, but he did more than this—he not only saw the first condensing engine that was erected in America, but he had built for himself the first Watt engine which was constructed in America; for that party of men, at the head of whom was an engineer by the name of Smallman—whose name possibly none of you have ever heard—and whose iron founder was a man by the name of Rhodé, the predecessor and instructor of James P. Allaire, who founded the Allaire Works in this city, where many of the engines which were subsequently designed by the Stevens family were built, these men, with my father as draughtsman and pattern maker, erected a new Soho Works at Belleville, N. J., near the old copper mines known usually as the Schuyler mines. There John Stevens came and there he had built the first low-pressure engine that was constructed upon the American continent. He therefore not only saw the first one erected, but he himself ordered and paid for the first condensing double-acting engine that was built upon the American continent.

Of course this interview with John Stevens made a profound impression upon my mind, and on my way home my father said, "Yes, that engine was put in a boat in which I traversed the route from Belleville to New York and back again, John Stevens being the owner, the builder, and the captain of the boat, and Mr. Smallman and Mr. Rhodé and myself being the passengers, and we came to New York in that boat nine years before Fulton put the *Clermont* on the Hudson."

Portions of the engine thus constructed were for a time preserved in the Stevens Institute and must be there still unless they have been placed in the National Museum at Washington; but the boat in which the engine was placed must not be confounded with the one whose model I see here upon the table, built later, in 1804, with a double screw, and which preceded Fulton's boat by four or five years. I only remember that the Belleville boat had a stern wheel, and my father said that Mr. Stevens, during the trip, remarked that wheels should have been placed upon the side, and not at the stern. But upon this ground I shall not further trespass, as I understand the subject has been assigned for a more competent authority to deal with in the course of the evening.

I never saw John Stevens again. My next knowledge of the Stevens family was when I was a student in Columbia College about 1840. We used to play ball upon the college grounds, and the game "base ball" would doubtless be regarded by modern college teams as altogether too tame for the much greater athletic development of this generation. It was a very simple game, and it had one drawback. We often knocked the ball out of the field, and it generally landed in the rear of a house which fronted upon Barclay Street. On one occasion, while we were playing ball, we exhausted our stock, and on searching our pockets we found that there was not money enough in the entire team to buy a new ball from a neighboring toy shop. The result was that I was made a committee of one to go around to Barclay Street and ring the doorbell of the house where most of the balls were known to have disappeared. It was a basement house; I remember it perfectly well.

There came to the door a middle-aged woman with a benevolent face, to whom I explained that we had lost a ball, which was then in the back yard, and asked her to be good enough to let me go in and pick it up. She seemed to hesitate, and while she was hesitating, a gentleman appeared from the room immediately adjoining the hallway, who made a very great impression upon me. I was a diffident boy. I used to blush when I was spoken to, and positively I feel very much inclined to blush now in telling this very simple story in this intelligent presence. He looked at me for a moment very benevolently and said, "So you want a ball." And he added, "Will you be satisfied with one ball?" I said, somewhat embarrassed, "Yes, sir." He smiled, and I may as well say here now, as at any other time, that a more genial, attractive and lovely face I have never seen in this terrestrial sphere. His presence was noble and his manner sympathetic, but on that occasion I was very timid. He turned and said to the woman, "Margaret, go and get the basket." She disappeared but came back in a few moments with a basket of the old-fashioned kind such as eggs used to be carried in, and in this basket were not less than I should say twenty-five or thirty balls. Said he, "Are all these balls yours?" I said, "I suppose that they must be, sir." "Well," said he, "every one of them has broken a window in my music room." "Well," said I, "we didn't do it on purpose." "No," he replied, "I know that. I was a boy myself once, and I have no doubt that I have broken hundreds of windows in my time." Then he added, "Take them, go back, enjoy yourselves, and when you have broken all the windows in my music room, go over to Hoboken and there you will find a fair field in which you can play without breaking any windows." That was the greatest mechanical engineer, the greatest naval engineer, the greatest railroad engineer which the nineteenth century has produced— Robert L. Stevens.

We continued to play ball and to break windows, but I do not remember that any other committee ever ventured to ask for a return of the stray balls. Personally I saw no more of the Stevens family until the year 1846, more than fifty years ago, when Mr. Edwin Stevens sent for me one day and said that the Camden & Amboy R. R. Co. wanted to get two thousand tons of rails and that it was impossible owing to the great scarcity of the article to procure them in time to be laid in that year. He said, however, that he was prepared to pay the cost of importation if my firm would undertake to make the rails at a price which will make the mouth of my friend Carnegie water, or to use the more orthodox Scotch phraseology—"will make him lick his chops with envy"—when I tell him that the price offered was ninety dollars per ton. We had just built a little rolling mill at Trenton for the manufacture of wire. Now wire is very much the reverse of a railroad bar. Mr. Stevens said, "I want you to make two thousand tons of rails, weighing sixty-five pounds to the yard," which was the heaviest rail at that time ever made in the world. I afterward discovered that the pattern, like all the inventions of the Stevens family, was peculiar and somewhat difficult to roll. Nevertheless, I finally agreed to make the attempt, and as a matter of fact we succeeded in delivering two thousand tons of rails, for which we received the sum of one hundred and eighty thousand dollars in hard cash, an amount sufficient at this time to pay for ten thousand tons of rails according to the latest quotations which Mr. Carnegie has just whispered in my ear.

Robert L. Stevens, as you all know, was the designer of what is known as the flange rail. He had it made in Wales at the works of Sir John Guest, and with such expedition that within two years from the

time of undertaking the practical scheme of building the Camden &
Amboy R. R., that railroad was constructed, running, and carrying
passengers and freight with entire success between the cities of New
York and Philadelphia. Robert L. Stevens and his brother Edwin, who
was the business manager of the enterprise, thus performed in two years
a feat which at that time, if you will consider the development of the
mechanical arts, the state of the financial transactions of the world, and
the unknown elements which entered into the problem, was a greater
performance than if any man were to undertake at this time to build
a road from New York to San Francisco in two years. The world never
saw a greater triumph than the construction of that road, and out of its
operation have come all the developments which have culminated in
the modern railway and its wonderful appliances. They had to provide
cars, because there was no model for cars. They were, however, the
proprietors of the Union line, which carried passengers from New York
and Philadelphia. Forty coaches, often in a line, would start from New
Brunswick (on the arrival of one of the Stevens' steamboats) across the
state of New Jersey, drawn by thoroughbred horses to Trenton, where
the old buildings which were constructed by the Stevens family of solid
brick and mortar stand to this day and where the house still remains
in the possession of my family, in which John C. Stevens, who was the
superintendent of the Union line, resided and superintended the business; for the peculiarity of the Stevens family was that whatever they
undertook to do they did themselves. They had subordinates, they had
trusted men, they had tried assistants, but the superintendence of the
work to the minutest part was done by John and Robert and Edwin
Stevens. Together they built railroads, and ferries, and steamboats, and
yachts, and ironclad batteries; and this suggests the first lesson which I
would draw from this necessarily sketchy statement for the benefit of the
young men who are here assembled. It is this, that these three brothers
worked as though they were one man. No one ever heard of any quarrel
or dissension in the Stevens family. They were workmen themselves, and
they were superior to their subordinates only because they were better
engineers and better men of business than any people who up to that
time had undertaken the business of transportation within the limits of
the United States. More than any other men whom I have ever known,
they demonstrated the truth of the saying, "Behold, how pleasant a
thing it is for brethren to dwell together in unity."

But I am asked to speak especially of the founder. I have been
speaking of the founders, John Stevens, the elder, John C. Stevens,
Robert L. Stevens, and Edwin A. Stevens, who were the founders and
pioneers who have made this country what it is—the miracle of the
ages, the admiration of the world. No one who cannot go back as I can
to the time when there were no railways, to the time when there were

no ocean steamers, when there were no telegraphs, no telephones, no armored navies, no access to any point beyond the Mohawk Valley, when the Great West was yet unsettled, when this great Empire was a wilderness—no one who cannot recall this primitive condition of things and did not see it can realize what the Stevens family has done for America.

Tantæ molis erat Romanam condere gentem.[1]

I have said enough of the achievements of this remarkable family, but I have not said enough of the other side of their personality—the lovely, gentle, sweet, and human character which belonged to the father and to the three brothers, of whom I have spoken. I told you that I was a poor and diffident boy, yet when I was brought into contact with them, I never was made to feel that there was any difference either in social standing or in wealth, in years, or even in ability. I was welcomed to Castle Point in my early youth, just as I would be today by the honored mistress of that noble mansion. They did not believe that the acquisition of wealth was sufficient for the development of human nature. They knew that the emotional side of man's nature controls in the long run and that the reason is always the servant of the imagination. Hence when they ran stage coaches, they had fine horses; when they ran boats for profit to Albany, they adorned them with pictures and beautiful objects. The sense of beauty was ever present in everything they did. Their leisure hours were regaled by the charms of art and music. I suppose no connoisseur who ever lived in New York was superior to Robert Stevens in his knowledge of music, and no man ever lived who enjoyed it more. I heard him once tell how when for the first time he heard the angelic notes of Malibran, the golden Gates of Paradise seemed to open and the Heavenly Hosts to be lost in adoration.

It was thus the characteristic of the Stevens family that, while they have always had an eye to main chance, they have never neglected any opportunity either for rational enjoyment or for the improvement of the æsthetic side of the world in which they lived. Therefore it is not surprising that Edwin Stevens, who, as I have said, was first of all a man of business and who as an engineer was doubtless inferior both to his father and his brother, but who was nevertheless no contemptible engineer, for his judgment I assure you on practical matters was as sound as that of any man I ever knew, I say it is not surprising that when he came to make a disposition of the great fortune which had been created by the ability, the foresight, the energy, and the courage of the family, that he made provision for the diffusion of the elementary principles of mechanics and of the extraordinary practical knowledge, which they had acquired through so many difficulties, by the agency of

[1] Virgil's Æneid Book I, line 33. To found the Roman nation was (a thing) of so great labor.

an institution of learning. The less famous engineer became thus the greater benefactor of mankind.

The Stevens Institute was created by Mr. Stevens's will which was signed on the 15th of April, 1867, on the night before the day when Mrs. Stevens and her children came upon the *Great Eastern* with Mr. Stevens for that trip from which he was never to return. It was my good fortune, in fact, it was my understanding with him, that I should accompany him on that trip. He was very anxious to understand the *Great Eastern,* and so was everybody that ever had anything to do with that ship, and I doubt if anybody succeeded. I only refer to it on this occasion because from the time we left New York until we arrived at Brest, the ship was subject to a chapter of accidents of a very amusing character. Mrs. Stevens will remember that it was a matter of wonderment every day what was going to happen next, for everything did happen that nobody wanted to happen during that eventful voyage. But I refer to it now because I had many conversations with Mr. Stevens on the subject of the Stevens Institute. Mr. Peter Cooper, my father-in-law, had founded the Cooper Institute, and it had been in operation for eight years at that time. Mr. Stevens was very anxious to know exactly the methods upon which it was conducted and how far it had fulfilled the expectations of the founder. Of course I explained to him that Mr. Cooper was a mechanic and that he had founded his institution for mechanics; that as the Stevens family were engineers it was natural and fitting in every way that the institution which he proposed to found should be devoted to the education of engineers. I explained to him that all the resources of the Cooper Union were used in giving the education which the mechanic needed and that what was wanted in this country was a higher institution which could start where the mechanic ended and produce the engineers who were to become the leaders of modern enterprise and the captains of industry.

Mr. Stevens entered heartily into this view of the subject, so that I have reason to know that while the language of the will provides for "an institution of learning," President Morton, with the approval of Mrs. Stevens and Mr. Dod and Mr. Shippen, as trustees, merely carried into effect the views which Mr. Stevens entertained as to the objects of the institution and the position which it should occupy in the domain of education.

But I referred to the voyage which we took together for the purpose mainly of showing some of the traits in the character of Mr. Stevens which made him so interesting and so lovable to all his friends. The *Great Eastern* was going out practically in ballast with no cargo, but with passengers who were on their way to visit the great Universal Exposition in Paris, which was in reality one of the wonders of the world. To replace the cargo 4,000 tons of water had been pumped into the space between the outer and the inner shell of the ship, and the water ballast was relied upon to keep her in trim. As a matter of fact, however, someone had neglected to close up the bulkheads, so that the water had free passage from one side of the ship to the other, causing her to reel in a most unpleasant way; and Mrs. Stevens will remember, I think, that we often used to sit in the saloon with the piano vertical over our heads, and I remember once that Mr. Stevens, who was a very good judge of the behavior of a ship, said to me: "I don't think she will reel over, but it looks very suspicious." Besides the water ballast, the ship was subjected to other difficulties. Incidentally, the sheriff had levied upon her as we were leaving the harbor, and we were detained one day at Staten Island in order to get rid of his affectionate attachment. For want of means the officers had been compelled to get what coal they could and from any source where credit could be had, and so after the scanty supply of bituminous coal was exhausted the fuel was limited to the stock of anthracite coal which some enterprising trader may have procured from Rhode Island. To the stokers, at least, it seemed to be absolutely incombustible and very safe as a place of refuge in the event of a general conflagration. There was not a stoker on board who had ever used anthracite coal or indeed had ever seen it. The Captain, Sir James Anderson, came to us and said, "We cannot get along. We have burned up all the coal, and that ———— (using a nautical phrase) that stuff we have down there won't burn. Can you tell me what to do?" So Mr. Stevens and I, old as he was and young as I was then, crawled down through many devious passages until we reached the boiler room and there found a very discouraged lot of people, who were trying to burn anthracite coal in the same manner as they would burn bituminous coal. Of course the fire went out, and you will be surprised to learn that he and I, and mostly he, spent nearly two days in the boiler room, teaching the stokers how to burn anthracite coal, which we succeeded in doing and were finally landed at Brest. This is a simple illustration of the character of this remarkable man. I might give you innumerable instances of the interest which he took in all practical matters, but I am afraid you will think me an old and garrulous man, so that I will bring these desultory remarks to a close with a single observation. The Stevens family of the last generation were creators as well as founders. You gentlemen who have profited by the beneficence and foresight of Edwin A. Stevens are reaping the fruits of the seed which they in their day and generation sowed so abundantly. They were men of not only great sagacity and untiring energy, but of a high order of courage and fortitude. When Robert L. Stevens found that Fulton had preceded him by a few weeks in placing the *Clermont* on the Hudson, thus securing the monopoly of the navigation of that river, he boldly took the *Phoenix* by sea from New York to Philadelphia, thus gaining the imperishable glory of having been the first man to traverse the ocean with a boat propelled by steam. The honor is increased by the fact that while Fulton had imported his engine from England, Stevens used one which he had constructed in America and which I believe in part to have been the identical one which I have referred to as used in the boat propelled from Belleville to New York in 1799.

> Illi robur et æs triplex circa pectus erat, qui fragilem truci
> Commisit pelago ratem primus.[1]

They were not only men bold in conception and courageous in action, but they were men of the highest order of integrity. There is no blot upon the record by which they achieved success and accumulated a great fortune. When at the beginning of the late Civil War the necessities of the country seemed to demand the legislation by which paper money was made a legal tender, Mr. Edwin A. Stevens, who was then the sole survivor of the family, insisted that the Camden & Amboy R. R. Co., which he controlled, should continue to pay the obligations which it had contracted before the war, principal and interest, in gold; when he might have availed himself, as many others did, of the privilege of paying in depreciated paper money. But it never formed any part of the code of morals or of honor of the Stevens family of that day to take advantage either of accident or of technicalities in the discharge of their obligations. Rough experiences they often encountered, but the star of personal honor was never dimmed.

[1] Oak and triple brass surrounded the breast of him who first trusted the frail raft to the cruel sea.

Papers on Iron and Steel

The Production of Iron and Steel in Its Economic and Social Relations

REPORT AS UNITED STATES COMMISSIONER TO THE
PARIS EXPOSITION, 1867

[Hewitt in 1867 was easily the foremost American ironmaster. During most of the preceding twenty years the Cooper, Hewitt works at Trenton had been the largest and best equipped in the country, and they had always been the most progressive. Hewitt was the first American ironmaster to experiment (unsuccessfully, his ores not being adapted to it) with the Bessemer process; he was the first to roll wrought-iron structural beams of large size; his works were known for the high quality of the rails they produced with ore taken from a deposit at Andover, N. J., and for their excellent wire and rods. It was therefore fitting that he should be sent by the American Government as a commissioner to Paris to report on the progress of the European industry. He had done great service to the Union cause in the Civil War, particularly in the production of the first good American gun metal. His keen mind was certain to pick out what was significant in European exhibits and mills. Though he knew that Europeans had outstripped the United States, he was staggered when he saw the tremendous strides that had been taken abroad. At every point—in size of product, in quality, in new inventions, in the production of cast iron, wrought iron, and steel alike—the British, French, and German mills were far superior to anything in the United States. The new rolling mills, he wrote Edward Cooper, "beat us to death"; and he might have said as much for other departments. He did his best to carry home some of the new European processes. He hired an expert Swedish metallurgist, one of the first technicians of the kind employed in America. He obtained the American rights to the Siemens-Martin or openhearth process, which has since outstripped the Bessemer process in America as in the rest of the world. And he laid before the American public, in the report here reprinted, an admirably clear and thorough exposition of the recent advances made in Europe. The document is one of the classics of the American iron industry, and to the historian is full of interest. It will be noted that Hewitt was interested not merely in technical progress but in the relations of *capital and labor, in living conditions, and in the contributions of large-scale industry to general human welfare. On these also his observations have historical value.*]

CONTENTS

IRON ORES, ROLLED GIRDERS, PLATES, AND RODS

In the general arrangement of the Universal Exposition of 1867, iron and steel, as products of industry, were placed in the fortieth class of the fifth group. In the distribution of the work of the commission of the United States, made in conformity with the directions of the Secretary of State, a committee was constituted on "Metallurgy and the Extractive Arts in General," and to this committee was subsequently assigned, by resolution of the commission, the duty of reporting on "Minerals as Raw Materials in the Economic Arts." The committee consisted of Commissioners Hewitt, D'Aligny, and J. P. Leslie. To Commissioner Leslie was assigned the task of reporting upon "Mining Machinery and Processes of Mining"; to Commissioner D'Aligny, on "Minerals, as Raw Materials in the Economic Arts, and on the Metallurgy of the Precious Metals"; and to Commissioner Hewitt "On the Production of Iron and Steel in Its Economic and Social Relations."

In the preparation of this report, in order to bring it within reasonable limits, the general principle has been adopted of attempting only to describe specimens of material, machinery, and processes of manufacture, which differ substantially from the experience of the United States; thus presenting, as far as practicable, a purely differential report upon the iron and steel of the exposition. The necessity for this course will be apparent from the mere statement that the catalogue of class forty includes 2,395 entries, of which the far larger portion are produced in the United States, of equal quality and by processes equally economical. The exhibition of the United States, however, was of so meager a character that foreigners, judging from the lessons of the exposition, would have come to the inevitable conclusion that the iron and steel industry of the United States is not entitled to the rank which it undoubtedly occupies in the metallic production of the world. The various ores mainly used in the manufacture of iron in the United States were indeed to be found among the minerals exhibited from the primitive regions of Lake Superior, New York, and New Jersey, while the brown hematites of Connecticut, Pennsylvania, and Alabama, together with the red fossiliferous ore of Tennessee and Alabama, and a brochure published by Mr. Haines, agent of the State of Alabama, were sufficient to call attention to the unequalled resources of the United States for the foundation of an iron industry which, under equal conditions as to the price of labor, would soon be in advance of that of any other nation whatsoever. A single piece of spathic ore from Connecticut, and a few pieces of franklinite from New Jersey, alone served to indicate the possession of the indispensable material upon which the production of Bessemer steel, as at present practiced, is based. A few pieces of pig iron from Lake Superior, from Wisconsin, Ohio, and Alabama, and some inconsiderable specimens of wrought iron, made from the Lake Superior and the Alabama pig, were the sole indications of an annual production of more than a million tons of iron. The only proof of the existence of any manufacture of steel in the United States was contained in a case of very beautiful specimens contributed by Park Brothers & Co., of Pittsburgh, for which they received a silver medal. There was no evidence in the Exposition of our large and increasing product of bar iron, of the rolled girders—in the manufacture of which we preceded the world—of the cut nails, of which we enjoy almost a monopoly, and of the infinite variety of wrought and cast iron, in the skilful production of which we are not surpassed by the most advanced nations of Europe. On the other hand, there was a marked superiority in the products of the European makers designed for uses requiring difficult shapes—a requirement met in our country either by welding or riveting pieces together, and which, in Europe, at the present time, seems to be almost universally supplied by material of such admirable quality as to admit of being forged or pressed into the most intricate and unusual forms. Such articles as deeply-dished boiler heads, steam domes, tube sheets, and even culinary vessels of every form and variety, and many other articles of fancy, designed merely as *tours de force*, such as cocked hats, and series of square domes raised from a flat plate, were exhibited, made from a single piece without weld or joint. Nor was this evidence of peculiar excellence confined to any one country. In France the works at Le Creusot, Chatillon, and Commentry, and those of Messrs. Petin, Gaudet & Co.; in England, the Bowling and Low Moor works, and those of the Earl of Dudley; in Prussia the works of A.

Borsig, near Berlin, and of Hoerde; and in Austria the imperial works at Neuberg, may be enumerated, among others, as having exhibited material of such remarkable quality as to open an entirely new field for the application of iron and steel.

Again, there was unmistakable evidence in the Exposition of the readiness of the European ironmasters to grapple with difficulties in the way of rolling shapes from which at present the American maker would shrink. For example, Messrs. Petin, Gaudet & Co. (France) exhibited a rolled beam of the depth of 1 meter (39⅜ inches), in length, 9.72 meters (over 32 feet), and weighing 2½ tons. They also exhibited another beam weighing 2.3 tons, 12 inches in height, and over 106 feet in length. The works of Chatillon and Commentry exhibited a beam 43½ inches in height, and with a 12-inch flange, but of very moderate length; but another beam was exhibited, about 100 feet in length, 9 inches high, weighing about fifteen hundredweight. The Burbach (Prussian) works exhibited a rolled beam 47 feet long and 15 inches in height. A careful observation, however, of the various structures in process of erection on the Continent, failed to show that these remarkable specimens of rolling had yet been brought within such limits of cost as to admit of their use in building. In the exposition building itself, no rolled beams were to be found of a greater depth than 9 inches, and in the innumerable buildings which are being erected in Paris, and in which iron beams are invariably employed to the exclusion of wood, 4 inches, 6 inches, and 7 inches are the dimensions most generally employed. Thus far the construction of a fire-proof building in the United States is accomplished with less pounds of iron for a given strain per square foot than in France, and we have nothing to learn from the exposition in this respect. But now that it has been found possible to produce beams of such large dimensions by the simple process of rolling, it is but reasonable to expect that the cost will be reduced as experience is gained, and that they will gradually replace the riveted girders, which even in the Palace of the Louvre are invariably employed for spans of any considerable extent. It is proper, however, to call the attention of our American makers of rolled beams to the extraordinary specimens which we have described, and which it is understood are produced by the aid of the "universal rolling mill." Of this two forms were on exhibition, one in the pavilion of Chatillon (France) and the other in the Austrian department. The latter consists of four rolls, in two pairs, working at right angles to each other.[1] Of the mill at Petin Gaudet & Co. no model was exhibited, and no description of it was given in the documents furnished to the commission.

By a personal visit to the works, however, the construction of the mill

[1] For a description, illustrated by engravings, see the engineering periodical, *Colburn's Journal*, May 24, 1867. [Hewitt's note.]

was seen to be very simple and not remarkable for novelty. For each size of beam there is a pair of rolls, each having a working face at the middle of its length equal in width to the depth of the beam. The diameter of the roll at this part is very large, say 3 feet, 6 inches, the body of the roll for the rest of its length being about 22 inches in diameter. This formation of the rolls leaves a considerable space between the two except where the working faces come together. In this open space is placed a pair of rollers, working on vertical axes fixed in stout movable frames, by which they can be brought into juxtaposition with that portion of the horizontal rolls which is of largest diameter. The pile used is somewhat thinner than the width of the flange to be produced, and of a width somewhat greater than the depth of the beam, and is so made up as to conform roughly to the final shape of the girder. As the main rolls are brought together and form the trough in the beam, the friction rollers at the sides are also pressed towards the center, and tend by the pressure which they exert to extend the flanges at the same time that the web is being drawn out by the main rolls. An offset is turned in the side of the large portion of the rolls to receive and form properly the flange as it is extended by the pressure of the friction rolls. The latter are worked each by a screw in a horizontal frame bolted to the side of the housing, the screw being provided with a ratchet lever to be worked by hand. This enables the thickness of the flanges to be adjusted with precision. With this mill they have rolled girders of 40 inches height, 33 feet long, and feel confident that they could make them 90 feet in length. The essential features of this mill were all to be found in the first train for rolling beams erected in 1853 at the Trenton Works, New Jersey, but in that case the axes of the driven rolls and of the friction rolls were at right angles to the mill of Petin, Gaudet & Co., which is probably a better working arrangement than the old train at Trenton. The Universal mill is not yet introduced into England, but forms the subject of an English patent now expired, and is undoubtedly destined to fill a very important place in the rolling of iron, and the American ironmaster cannot too soon avail [himself] of its advantages before impediments shall be put in its way by the issue of American patents.

Next to rolled girders, or perhaps even more remarkable than these, were the specimens of plate iron contributed from England, France, Germany, and Belgium. John Brown & Co., of Sheffield, exhibited a plate which, after being dressed up to square edges and ends, was 30 feet in length, 2 feet, 6 inches, in width, and 6 inches thick, weighing 11 tons, 5 hundredweight; and also a piece of a plate which in its original condition was 13 feet long, 6 feet wide, 13½ inches thick, and weighed 20 tons.

For the production of these enormous masses of iron the machinery is of the ordinary kind in construction, but of dimensions proportionate to the mass of iron to be handled. The size of the rolls is 3 feet, and the handling of the iron is accomplished with facility by the aid of steam cranes and of iron chains winding upon the rolls themselves, which are reversible by a clutch gearing, and make about twenty revolutions per minute.

Other plates of 6 inches in thickness and of various weights up to 5 tons were exhibited by the works of Chatillon, of Messrs. Petin, Gaudet & Co. (France), and of Hoerde (Prussia).

Generally there may be said to exist a prevailing willingness and practice in the European works to handle iron in larger masses for every purpose than we do in the United States. For example, Belgium exhibited band iron three-fourths inches wide by 230 feet in length; Prussia exhibited sheet iron of 21½ gauge, 48 by 108 inches, and wire rods are frequently to be found in all the departments ranging from 30 to 50 pounds in weight, rolled in trains of the ordinary dimensions, and running at speeds no greater than we employ in the United States for 15 pound billets. This is accomplished by keeping the billet in many more grooves at the same time than we are in the habit of doing, by an ingenious system of doubling the rods backward and forward. This same method is employed at Montataire, in France, and at other works for rolling braziers' rods, and even bar iron; and this not from the necessities of the order, but from choice, as a matter of economy. In this way one-inch bars of 100 feet in length are regularly produced, and this system, unknown in the United States, can doubtless be introduced with great advantage.

But the most remakable specimen of rolling was in the English department, exhibited by Richard Johnson & Nephew, of Manchester, in the shape of a coil of No. 3 wire rods, weighing 281 pounds, in length 530 yards, rolled from a single billet. Also a coil of No. 8 wire weighing 200 pounds, 900 yards in length, and a coil of No. 11 wire weighing 95 pounds, in length 790 yards. These wonderful specimens of wire were not, however, produced in an ordinary mill, but were rolled in a machine invented by George Bedson, the manager of the Bradford iron works, in Manchester. This machine consists of rolls in thirteen pairs, placed one behind the other, instead of side by side, as usual, with guides connecting the successive pairs of rolls and revolving at such relative rates of speed that the billet being rolled receives the compressing action of the rolls all at the same time. The billet is fed from a long feeding furnace at one end of the train of rolls, being charged at the end of the furnace furthest from the train. A Siemens's generator is used to supply the furnace with gas, so as to insure a uniform heat. The average product of the train is eleven tons per day, and the weight of the billets usually rolled is from 80 to 100 pounds. A comparison of the work for six months with two old-fashioned trains also running in the same works shows that the waste is reduced from 10½ percent to 6⁹⁄₁₀ percent and that the consumption of coal is reduced from 14¾ hundredweight, 25 pounds, to 8 hundredweight, and 18 pounds per ton, most of which saving is doubtless due to the use of Siemens's furnace, and not to the train; the advantages of the latter consisting in an increase of product of nearly one-half in the increased weight of the billets rolled and in the economy of the labor employed. A personal visit was made to the Bradford iron works, to see the operation of this ingenious and successful machine. It appears to be all that could be desired, and the action of the rolls upon the iron unquestionably produces a sounder and better rod than when worked by the old process, and this is due doubtless to the higher and more uniform heat at which the rod is finished.[1]

In the use of wire for telegraphic purposes, for wire suspension bridges, and for cables and ropes, the superior value of long lengths is undeniable. Bedson's machine has therefore the double merit of producing a better article at a lower cost than has hitherto been obtained; and it is a matter of regret to those who have become familiar with its novelty and its merits that it received only the recognition of a silver medal, when it so justly deserved the highest prize.

Borsig, of Berlin, exhibited remarkable specimens of gigantic puddle balls, a single one weighing 1,064 kilograms (more than a ton), and he also exhibited a wrought-iron piston without a weld, weighing 590 kilograms (nearly 12 hundredweight). These are not mere *tours de force,* as he is prepared to take orders at a price which renders it economical to employ his product.

In connection with the large masses of iron with which, as demonstrated in the exposition, modern industry so much occupies itself, it is proper to refer to the crank shafts exhibited by Messrs. Marrel frères, of Gier (France). Of these one has three cranks placed 120° apart and a length of nearly 40 feet, the weight being 30,180 kilograms, or about 30 tons. Another is a four-throw crank, say 27 feet in length and 12 inches in diameter.

Among the new applications of iron exhibited in the exposition are the weldless bands made at the Bowling and Low Moor works [2] (England), employed for uniting the cylindrical sections of steam boilers, covering the joints, and strongly riveted on each side thereof, so as not merely to make a firm union but greatly to stiffen the boiler when finished. The Bowling ring has a cross section like the letter U, with wide flanges, and seems better adapted to stiffen the boiler or flue and to allow of expansion and contraction than the flat ring made by the Low Moor works.

[1] The same principle has been since successfully applied to the rolling of bar iron.
[2] For a description of the process of making iron at Low Moor, Bowling, and Farnley, the reader is referred to Percy's *Metallurgy of Iron and Steel,* p. 732. [Hewitt's note.]

The one on exhibition is 7 inches in total width, ⅜ inch thick, the arch in the middle rises 2 inches, and the width of the flanges is 2½ inches. These bands would appear to be thoroughly well adapted to their purpose and worthy of immediate adoption in our country.

STEEL

In cast steel, by whatsoever process produced, the same tendency to large masses and difficult shapes was to be remarked. In advance of [the product of] all other makers, the specimens exhibited by Krupp, of Essen (Prussia), were worthy of the highest admiration. The largest single piece of cast steel was a cylindrical ingot forged at one end into an octagonal shape, 56 inches in diameter and weighing 40 tons. The grain of this ingot was exposed by the fracture of the forged end and was uncommonly uniform and free from air bubbles. A piece had also been cut from the portion not forged which showed at the place of fracture an equally uniform grain.

At the English exhibition of 1851 a cast-steel ingot exhibited by Krupp, weighing 2¼ tons, caused more astonishment than the ingot we have just described, because the world has become familiar with metallic masses of enormous size; but the progress made in sixteen years in the production of cast steel is none the less marvelous, especially if considered in connection with the machinery necessary to produce and work the ponderous ingots into shape and the organization of the labor and skill required for their formation.

The establishment of Krupp occupies about 450 acres, of which one-fourth are under roof. The number of men employed in the works is 8,000, besides which 2,000 more are employed in the coal mines, at the blast furnaces, and at the ore mines. The production of these works in 1866 was 61,000 tons, more than the entire production of cast steel in the world at the time of the first English exhibition. The value of this product was over $10,000,000 in currency. It was accomplished by means of 412 smelting, reverberatory, and cementing furnaces, 195 steam engines, ranging from 2 to 1,000 horsepower, 49 steam hammers, in the largest of which the hammer block weighs 50 tons, 110 smiths' forges, 318 lathes, 111 planing machines, 61 cutting and shaping machines, 75 grinding machines, 26 special tools. One thousand tons of coal are consumed daily in the manufacture of steel alone, and 120 steam boilers are in use evaporating 150,000 cubic feet of water daily. Fifteen miles of rails are laid in the works alone, and 6 locomotives and 150 cars are required for its use within the limits of the establishment.

In order to appreciate the eminent justice with which the grand prize of the exposition was bestowed upon Frederick Krupp, it is necessary not merely to study these marvelous figures but to consider that this establishment, by far the most extensive ever produced by the energy of

man, and these processes, the most difficult ever attempted by his ingenuity, are the offspring of a single life, begun almost by the side of his
father's humble forge and rising through the various stages of poverty,
trial, discouragement, and final success to the very front of the industrial
achievements of the world. Such an establishment, such results, and such
a man, have special interest for the United States, where the natural resources of the country, the rapid progress of population and civilization,
and the genius of our free institutions, all invite a generous emulation
in order to equal, and in the course of time even to surpass, these magnificent achievements, which if Krupp, the great captain of modern
industry, had not lived in our day and generation might well have been
deemed impossible.

Among the other remarkable specimens exhibited by Krupp is a cast-
steel tire, rolled without weld, 8 feet in diameter, a cast-steel axle of
crucible steel, with cast-steel disc wheels, neither forged nor rolled, but
cast directly into shape, weighing 1,623 pounds; a cast-steel locomotive
crank axle, with cast-steel wheels 6 feet in diameter, weighing 3 tons,
13 hundredweight; a cast-steel junction ring of angular section for uniting the courses of steam boilers, made without weld, 8 feet in diameter,
weighing 483 pounds; a cast-steel double crank shaft for a screw steamer,
25 feet long, 14 inches in diameter, weighing (finished) 9¼ tons; forged
under the 50-ton hammer from an ingot originally weighing 27 tons.
And this is a proper place to note that cast-steel crank shafts appear to
be coming into general use, not merely for locomotive and stationary
engines, but for the massive marine engines which are required for the
steamers devoted to the business of transatlantic navigation. The experience with these cast-steel crank shafts for marine engines does not appear
to be sufficiently extensive to warrant any positive opinion as to the
comparative value of cast steel and iron for the purpose, and it is possible that in cases where great resistance to torsion is required, iron will
maintain its place. In any event the attention of engineers has been so
called to this subject by the exposition that we may expect soon to have
all doubts on this important subject removed.

The most striking object, however, in Krupp's exhibition, was the
cast-steel thousand-pounder rifled breech-loading gun, resting on a cast-
steel carriage, intended for the arming of coast batteries for the destruction of iron-plated ships. It consists of an inner tube, upon which are
shrunk cast-steel rings. This tube was forged under the 50-ton hammer,
from an ingot weighing 40¼ tons, but reduced in the process of manufacture to 20 tons by the loss of the sinking head and by forging, turning,
and boring. The cast-steel rings are three in number at the powder
chamber and two in number towards the muzzle portion of the gun.
These rings weigh 30 tons in the aggregate, and were each manufactured
from an ingot without welding. The total weight of the gun is 50 tons,

the diameter of the bore is 14 inches, and the total length of the gun is 210 inches. It has 40 rifle grooves, in depth .15 inch, and the twist of the rifling diminishes from one turn in 980 inches to one turn in 1,014.4 inches; the weight of the solid shot is 1,212 pounds, and of the shell 1,080 pounds, and the weight of the latter is made up of the cast-steel shell, 834 pounds, the lead jacket, 220 pounds, and the bursting charge, 17 pounds; the charge of powder for the gun is from 110 to 130 pounds. The cannon reposes upon a steel carriage weighing 15 tons, and the two together work upon a turntable weighing 25 tons. The turntable was not exhibited for want of space, but it was stated that the gun-carriage slides smoothly upon the turntable to the cheeks at the backstays at each discharge of the gun, and that two men can quickly and easily elevate, depress, and turn the gun so as to follow and cover with speed and certainty any vessel in motion. The price of the gun, which is understood to have been made for the Russian government, is £15,750 sterling, and of the carriage and turntable £6,000, being about $150,000 in currency. Sixteen months of unremitted labor, by day and night, were expended upon its manufacture, and its transportation from the works to the exposition required a car made entirely of steel and iron weighing 24 tons, resting upon twelve wheels.

It forms no part of the purpose of this report to institute a comparison between different systems of ordnance, or even to undertake to decide the relative value of cast and wrought iron and steel for the manufacture of guns, but it has been deemed best to give a somewhat elaborate description of this monster engine of war, in order to indicate the possibilities of construction in its most difficult and expensive form, in case experience should show that such weapons will hereafter be required in our own country. In this connection a comparison with the largest guns produced in England will be of interest. Sir William Armstrong exhibits a 12½-ton, 9-inch muzzle-loading rifled gun, constructed on the coil principle and mounted on a wrought-iron carriage and slide; the weight of the projectile is 250 pounds and the charge of powder 43 pounds. This gun is beautifully made, and is noteworthy from the fact that the compression for checking the recoil is wholly of iron and is thrown in and out of action by a lever-handle which is self-acting if neglected. The gun is designed for use on shipboard. The largest Whitworth gun exhibited is a 150-pounder, and is constructed exclusively of mild steel, wrought into tubes which are forced into each other by hydraulic pressure. But to us the most interesting gun is the 9-inch Paliser gun, made by casting an exterior coating of iron around an interior barrel of wrought iron, constructed on the coil principle. This gun carries a projectile of 250 pounds, and if in practice it should be found to have substantial advantages over our cast-iron guns, it suggests a method by which we may apply the principle to the reconstruction of the large number of cast-iron guns which have been accumulated during the last few years. The gun now manufactured at Woolwich by the British war department consists of a cast-steel tube, upon which rings of fibrous wrought iron, made upon the coil principle, are built up, and the specimen exhibited was a 12-inch muzzle loader, weighing 470 hundredweight, length of bore 145 inches, having 9 grooves, each 1½ inch wide and .2 inch in depth, the spiral increasing from one turn in 1,200 to one turn in 600. The weight of the charge of powder is 70 pounds, and of the projectile 600 pounds.

The only other gun requiring notice was a coiled steel gun, made by Petin, Gaudet & Co., weighing 16 tons, and intended to throw a projectile of 300 pounds in weight; but it was quite evident that the manufacture of steel and wrought-iron guns in France is still in its infancy, and there would seem to be the same uncertainty in regard to their value as prevails in the United States. But there would seem to be no doubt that within certain limits of size, and perhaps for all sizes of field pieces, cast steel is regarded as the best material, and Krupp has already produced more than 3,500 cast-steel guns, mostly rifled breech-loaders, and at the present time has orders in hand for immediate delivery of 2,200 guns, ranging from four-pounders to three-hundred-pounders. Not much accurate information is to be procured in regard to the endurance of the larger-sized guns, but Krupp exhibited a cast-steel rifled four-pounder breech-loading gun, belonging to the Prussian war department, which had been fired several hundred times, with gradually increasing charges up to 3¾ pounds of powder and 122 pounds of shot, without the slightest appearance of injury.

Although no evidence was afforded by the exposition of the substitution of cast-steel for cast-iron shot in the French service, my visits to the French iron works seemed to show conclusively that such is the case, as all the large establishments were actively engaged in the manufacture of cast-steel missiles of all sizes, but more especially of the larger caliber; and whatever the fact may be, it is quite evident that cast steel is regarded by French military engineers as superior to all other materials, where penetration is required.

Krupp also exhibited a cast-steel rail 50 feet in length and bent double, cold, in the middle, without fracture. His engineer in the exposition stated that their annual product of rails was about 30,000 tons and that no Bessemer steel was employed in their construction. In the absence of a personal visit to the works, we are bound to accept this statement as true, although it is stated on good authority that as many as nine pairs of converters are constantly employed at the works in the production of Bessemer steel, and there seems to be an impression that the tires latterly produced at Essen are not quite equal in quality to the remarkable material which was at first employed for this purpose.

This may be only the result of rival representations, and it is undeniable that up to the present time Krupp maintains his preëminence in the manufacture of locomotive tires, and is probably justified in the claim which he makes that his crucible cast-steel coils are superior to those made from Bessemer metal. In the year 1865 the sale of cast-steel tires amounted to 11,396 sets, and the guarantee of their endurance given by Krupp is that they will run 400 kilometers for each kilogram of weight (equivalent to 125 miles per pound); that is to say, a tire weighing 600 pounds is guaranteed to run 75,000 miles, but their actual performance as a general rule shows a much higher endurance. The results with these tires and those of other makers—such as Naylor, Vickers & Co., Firth & Sons, the Bochum Company, Petin, Gaudet & Co., the Bowling Company, and the Monk Bridge Company, and other respectable makers, would seem to justify the broad statement that the day for iron locomotive tires has passed by and that it is far more economical, if not more safe, to substitute cast-steel tires in every case. The same conclusion cannot yet be affirmed of rails, because the interest account, of but little consequence in the case of the tire, becomes a very serious, and, indeed, controlling element in the case of rails. It may be stated, however, that in all cases where iron rails wear out in consequence of hard service within the limits of duration assigned to a steel tire, it is quite as economical to use steel rails in lieu of iron ones as it is to use steel in lieu of iron tires. But, assuming the cost of cast-steel rails to be double that of good iron rails, it is quite evident that there must be a limit in the duration of iron rails beyond which it will not pay to substitute cast steel. This calculation is one which must be made by each consumer for himself, with reference to the available capital at his disposal; but it is safe to declare that on all roads where the iron rail has an average life of ten years it would not be profitable to substitute cast-steel rails, and so long as the average rate of interest paid by railroad companies in the United States amounts to 8 percent per annum it would be found expedient considerably to reduce the limit of ten years above assumed for the duration of iron rails before the substitution of steel rails could be justified on grounds of economy. Even in England, where capital is superabundant and the rate of interest on long obligations not over 5 percent and the traffic per mile of very large dimensions, requiring, as a general rule, the renewal of iron rails in seven years, cast-steel rails have thus far not been very extensively introduced; and even on the London and Northwestern Railway, which owns a mill devoted expressly to their manufacture from Bessemer steel, and which, from its enormous traffic, has every inducement to make its road as permanent as possible, the money question seems to check the use of cast-steel rails upon any very extended scale. And yet the necessity of more durable rails than those generally in use is so apparent that any attempt to secure greater durability without much additional cost is regarded with great interest, and hence in the exposition there were many specimens, and from all the leading nations, of *iron* rails with *steel* heads. In some cases the material employed for the head was puddled steel, in others cast steel, and in others Bessemer steel. It seemed to be generally admitted that the durability of the steel in the head was in nowise impaired by its being placed upon a cushion or bed of wrought iron, but the great difficulty appeared to be in securing a thorough union or weld between the two kinds of metal. In the Austrian department, where some admirable specimens of steel-headed rails were exhibited from the Neuburg works, the engineer in charge stated that 9 percent of the heads failed in the weld during the first year but that subsequently no failures occurred, and that even with this amount of loss the rails were regarded as cheaper than either steel or iron. At Crewe, where the works of the London and Northwestern Company are situated and where a considerable quantity of Bessemer steel-headed rails have been made, it was stated that some difficulty had been found at first in making a reliable weld of the steel to the wrought iron, and that as many as 5 percent of the rails first made had failed in consequence of the loosening of the steel top; but as experience was acquired in the manufacture this difficulty had disappeared and the percentage of loss had been reduced materially. The practice at Crewe is to place a bar of soft puddled iron between the steel of the top and the old rails used in the lower part of the rail, and as a further protection the steel for the head is rolled in the form of a channel bar, with ribs in the recessed portion so as to fold around and embrace, as it were, the head of the rail. Considerable experience has already been acquired in the United States as to the feasibility of making a sufficiently good junction between the iron and the steel for a durable rail, and it may be confidently affirmed that there is no practical difficulty in the way of making an iron rail with a steel head, whether of puddled, Bessemer, or cast metal, that will meet all the reasonable requirements of the case and reduce the failures to less than one percent. The cost of steel-headed rails is, of course, intermediate between that of all-iron and that of all-steel rails, and the system possesses the great advantage of rendering all the old rails available for remanufacture and of thus renewing the tracks with a bearing surface of steel by gradual steps and with a very moderate increase of cost. On the London and Northwestern Railway, which has had the most experience in the use of Bessemer and steel-headed rails, experience seems to show that the steel-headed rails possess all the requirements in point of cost and durability for their general introduction on the line, and the conclusion is irresistible in my own mind, after a careful study of the specimens in the exposition, that the steel-headed rail will ultimately prevail over all other kinds of rails now known and that in the United States the facilities for their manufacture are unusually favorable. It is a question in what manner the steel shall be made for the heads, and this point will be discussed when we come to speak of processes; it is enough to state here that a good steel head can be made from any one of the kinds of steel above specified.

In closing this brief statement of the remarkable specimens of cast steel in the exposition, the products of the Bochum Company (Prussia) should not be overlooked. An enormous cast-steel bell, weighing 29,500 pounds, remarkable for the admirable proportion which existed between its size and its tone, was not, however, more wonderful than the cast-steel railway wheels made in sets of ten or a dozen, united by a thin shaft of metal running through the centers, thus enabling one sinking head to answer for the whole quantity and securing greater density and soundness in the metal. These wheels, when cut apart and turned up, were beautifully sound and clean and gave evidence of ability to cast steel with as much facility as ordinary cast iron. Another evidence of this was to be found in a locomotive cylinder, bored and of such finish and soundness as not merely to excite general admiration but to induce the belief that possibly it was cast iron which had been deprived of its carbon by being annealed in a bath of oxide of iron or some other decarbonizing material.

In the Swiss department, machine-cut steel files were exhibited fully equal to any cut by hand; and this result is said to be due to the grinding of the blanks across the face instead of lengthwise, a point which may have great value to our own makers of files.

QUALITY OF MATERIAL

A careful observer of the iron and steel specimens in the exposition could not fail to be struck with the varieties in the quality of the metal exhibited and the evident attention paid to the adaptation of special qualities to special uses. In some establishments only a particular quality would be produced, but, as a general rule, all the large works exhibited, and seemed prepared to produce, a quality proportioned to the price to be paid.

In the pavilion of Le Creusot, for example, seven different qualities of merchant iron were displayed as examples of the uses to which each quality would be applied, and a personal visit to the works satisfied me that there was nothing fanciful in these grades. In the Welsh iron works it is notorious that the quality of the article produced is directly proportioned to the price paid for it, and in my visits to those gigantic establishments which have grown up in the mountains of South Wales it was humiliating to find that the vilest trash which could be dignified by the name of iron went universally by the name of the American rail.

This is no fault of the Welsh ironmaster, but has arisen from the almost universal practice of late years on the part of American railroad companies and contractors of purchasing the lowest-priced article that could be produced. Of course no iron of this quality was to be found in the exposition; but if prizes were to be given for mere human ingenuity, I cannot conceive of anything more entitled to it than the production of a well-finished rail from puddled balls that will not hold together under the alligator squeezer.

There is, however, one thing more remarkable even than this low quality of iron; and that is, the stupidity and reckless extravagance of the customers who are found to buy it. To this cause more than any other is due the necessity of almost annual renewals of rails in the United States and of the financial troubles of so many of our leading lines of railway; nor is there the slightest excuse for this result, for the Welsh ironmasters, to their credit be it said, make no concealment either of the inferiority of the material or the poverty of the process by which it is treated, and greatly prefer to turn out work creditable to themselves and profitable to their customers. But the inexorable law of competition and the unremitted cry for cheap iron in America have left them no choice.

For their own country, for the continent of Europe, and for India, no such system is practiced. As a general rule, all rails made for home consumption are guaranteed for from five to seven years, according to the traffic; that is to say, every rail that fails in the slightest degree within the time specified is renewed at the expense of the maker. The extra price paid for a guaranteed rail on roads of moderate traffic is about 30 percent, but on roads having a heavy traffic at least 50 percent additional is paid. In case the guarantee cannot be procured in consequence of the heavy usage to which the line, or any portion of it, is subjected, the conclusion is inevitable that a steel rail should be used. And until a similar system of guarantee and adequate payment therefor is introduced into the United States, shareholders in railway companies can place no reliance on the security of their investment and the permanency of dividends.

It is this difference in the quality of iron, with its corresponding money value, which enables particular works and special regions to thrive under local disadvantages as to cost. To some extent the same rule applies in the United States, but it may be affirmed that there is no civilized country in which the discrimination is made to so small an extent and which loses so much by its indifference.

A very remarkable proof of the adaption of particular qualities to particular purposes is to be found in Sweden, which possesses inexhaustible stores of primitive ores, many of them adapted to the manufacture of steel and the very highest grades of bar iron, and yet, for some purposes, ores which contain phosphorus are absolutely preferred to the purer ores, even though procurable at the same price. For tools, such as spades, shovels, hoes, and other utensils, and for roofing-sheets, which are to be subjected to severe wear, at least one-tenth of one percent of phosphorus in the iron is considered desirable. Again, in France, in order to produce the better grades of iron, ores are brought in large quantities from Elba and Algiers, at a high cost, which is reimbursed by the purchaser.

If there was any lesson clearly taught in the exposition, it was the willingness of the public to pay an adequate price for skill and quality, and this willingness must spring from an enlightened self-interest.

There is no difficulty whatever in producing in the United States any quality of iron and steel that may be desired, for we have an exhaustless profusion of the very best kinds of ore and coal, and, at the present day, so open to communication as to render them available with as little expenditure of human labor as the most favored countries of Europe. But the problem presented for solution to the American iron-master has not merely been to procure this labor at as low a cost as it is obtained in Europe (a requirement utterly impossible to be met), but to produce the highest grade of material in competition with the price of the poorest foreign article. For the difference in the price of labor a remedy may be found in the tariff, but for the other exaction there is no remedy but greater intelligence on the part of the consumers, and in all cases where life or limb is at risk, the enforcement of the law as to the responsibility for the use of inferior material.

PROCESSES OF MANUFACTURE

Having completed a brief survey of the articles in the exposition which to the eye of an American would appear remarkable, we come next to the consideration of the processes employed in the manufacture of iron and steel, which have not yet been introduced, to any considerable extent, in the United States. And first, in the natural order, comes the production of wrought iron and steel by a direct process from the ore. To some extent this branch of industry still continues in the United States, especially in the northern part of the states of New York and New Jersey, where the process employed is usually but incorrectly known as the Catalan method of making wrought iron. But in Europe this mode of making iron may be said to have died out, although in the mountains of Spain and some portions of Italy, a few fires still maintain a feeble existence. The practical mind of Europe and America, however, has never ceased its efforts to produce wrought iron and steel directly from the ore by some convenient and economical process, and perhaps at no time has this subject received more attention than at the present. Of this interest, however, the exposition afforded but a single example, but that example in a quarter so distinguished both for scientific and mechanical knowledge and for success so eminent in another direction as to have merited the grand prize of the exposition that it seems reasonable to expect the solution of this difficult problem, if it be at all possible, at the hands of Charles William Siemens, whose regenerating heating furnace will be the subject of subsequent consideration. In the exhibition of Mr. Siemens were some small specimens of cast steel, which had been made direct from the ore, but which would scarcely have been remarked but for the eminence of the maker. They were made in conformity to a patent issued to Mr. Siemens on the 20th of September, 1866, in which he states that his invention has for its object the production of iron or steel directly from the ore and in a continuous manner, analogous in this respect to the continuous action of the blast furnace. It consists in exposing a mass of ore, which may or may not be mixed with reducing agents or fluxes, upon an inclined surface to the surface action of intense heat and in introducing at the same time a current or currents of combustible gases or petroleum oil in among the mass from below the inclined surface, so as to percolate through the mass of ore, affecting or aiding in its reduction and at the same time enveloping its surface where exposed to the flame in a deoxidizing, or reducing, atmosphere, tending to facilitate its fusion. The fused metal and cinders accumulating at the foot of the inclined surface are from time to time removed, while a mass of ore is maintained upon the inclined plane by its own gravitation, fresh ore being supplied from hoppers at the top of the incline in regular quantities. The intense heat spoken of in this description as necessary for the process is produced by Siemens's regenerative gas furnaces. Mr. Siemens has been conducting experiments upon the red hematite ores at Barrow in Furness with a view to demonstrate the practicability and economy of this process, but it is yet premature to estimate the measure of his success. If, however, he should succeed in practice, with the magnetic ores of the Atlantic highland range stretching from New York to Georgia and the primitive peroxides extending from the Great Lakes through Missouri and Arkansas, with the command of the fuel and the petroleum indispensable for its success, this process will be of incalculable value to the United States.

In the preparation of ore for the blast furnace Sweden exhibits the model of a roasting furnace invented by Mr. E. Westman, which was adopted in the first place at Dannemora works and since then generally introduced at the other iron works in Sweden. It consists of a vertical furnace which is heated by a portion of the gas drawn from the blast furnaces themselves and introduced at the bottom of the roasting furnace through suitable flues by the aid of natural draught. The temperature in the furnace is carried to such a degree as to soften the ore and drive off the sulphuric acid arising from the oxidation of a portion of the sulphur, disengaged by a distillation of a lower temperature from the pyrites, which may be mixed with the ore; a portion, moreover, of the sulphur is oxidized by the oxygen of the ore. Ore thus roasted, however dense when charged into the roasting furnace, is discharged at the bottom quite porous, like a sponge, and almost entirely free from sulphur if it does not contain more than 4 percent in its natural state. With ore so roasted, which presents an entirely different appearance from ore prepared in a common kiln, the statement is not surprising that the blast furnace runs with far greater regularity and with much less consumption of fuel. The introduction of this roasting furnace will be of great value when magnetic ores are smelted with charcoal. It is highly probable that even in furnaces fed by mineral coal, it will bring into economic use a great variety of ore now rejected on account of sulphur. So important did this furnace appear, that the undersigned at once engaged a Swedish engineer to proceed to America, where he is now erecting a furnace at Ringwood, in New Jersey, so that at an early date it may be examined by the public. Besides economizing coal, the Westman furnace, in connection with other improvements resulting from a more accurate knowledge of the theory of the blast furnace and a careful study of its operation, has greatly increased the weekly product of the charcoal furnaces in Sweden. The general dimensions of the blast furnaces are from 8 to 9 feet across the boshes, and from 40 to 50 feet in height. The average product of these furnaces driven with a blast heated to 150° to 200° centigrade is about 75 tons per week, which is nearly double the product made a few years since and now made in the United States from the same class of magnetic ores, which must be carefully distinguished from the brown hematites of Connecticut, and the peroxides of Lake Superior. The charging of the furnace, in particular, is most carefully attended to; absolute uniformity in the size of the pieces of ore is insisted upon, and the charge is distributed over the furnace by a shovel, in which it is first weighed and then run on a suspended railway to the tunnel head of the furnace, which is never closed. The most intelligent engineers expressed the opinion that the furnaces would give better results if made larger; but as they are, 100 pounds of cast iron are produced with 90 pounds of charcoal, which is as near as possible at the rate of 112 bushels to the ton. To supply this quantity of coal it is estimated that 5,000 square meters (about 6,000 square yards) of woodland are required, and the most vigorous care is practiced in order to insure a perpetual supply of wood to the works. This is not in consequence of any regulation of the government, as is generally supposed, but by a concurrence of action among the Swedish ironmasters, who have an association administered with great vigor and intelligence. For the production of 100 pounds of bar iron from the pig, 100 pounds of charcoal are required where the works are upon a scale sufficiently large to work to the best advantage. The English run-out or refinery fire is not in use in Sweden, but the refining is all accomplished in the ordinary forge fire generally in use in Pennsylvania. Various modes of treatment in this fire are employed, but the one most generally used is the Lancashire method, substantially the same as the Welsh process generally employed in the United States. At Dannemora the Walloon method is employed, and at Elfsborg the method of Franche Comté is in use. At Kihlafors a combination of the Walloon and Lancashire methods is adopted, which is said to produce a very superior quality of iron with a very small consumption of coal.[1] They all give good iron if they are properly followed. The special interest which these Swedish irons have for us consists in the fact that at this day, as for many years past, they are regarded as indispensable for the production of the best quality of cast steel by the crucible process. Hence the exhibition made by Sweden was among the most interesting in the exposition, and it is creditable to that country and its ironmasters that it was not only most complete in all its details but afforded an opportunity of studying its peculiar process of manufacture, from the ore to its final result in the highest grade of cast steel. The Swedish exhibition was in charge of a most intelligent engineer, Mr. L. Rinman, who took the greatest possible pains to furnish whatever information might be desired in regard to the manufacture of metals in Sweden.

The Dannemora irons have generally a fine grain, but unequal in size, composed apparently of hard and soft particles, but in ductility and tenacity the strength of this iron still maintains its superiority over all others; and it has the remarkable peculiarity that when heated it becomes very soft and full of fiber, and when cemented and cast into steel the inequalities of fracture entirely disappear. The irons made by the Lancashire fires are generally the most equal in grain, and this is supposed to be due not so much to the primary process of manufacture as to the peculiar mode of reheating and hammering to which they are subsequently subjected. For reheating, the gas welding furnace, as it is called, is usually employed, by which the bloom is subjected to so high a heat as to become incandescent, so that when subjected to the hammer all raw iron breaks in pieces and is thrown off in the forms of small bits and blue sparks. Loops which act in this way are absolutely rejected for commercial purposes and are used only for the local wants of the works themselves. There can be no doubt in my mind that to the use of the gas welding furnace and the high heat, coupled with care in the selection of ores, is due the superiority which must be accorded to Swedish over American iron made by the charcoal process. For steel, iron ore containing phosphorus is absolutely rejected, and it is a curious fact that Mr. Le Play, so long ago as 1846, prepared a table of Swedish

[1] A detailed description of these methods may be found in Percy's *Treatise on the Metallurgy of Iron and Steel*, pp. 591, 604. [Hewitt's note.]

irons, arranging their rank according to the price which they bore in the steel market of Sheffield, and the subsequent analysis of these irons shows that this value, determined by the practical experience of the manufacturers of steel, is directly determined by the quantity of phosphorus and sulphur contained in the pig iron from which the bars are made. Inasmuch as the consumption of Swedish iron, in the United States is very considerable, and the demand for that quality of metal is likely to increase, to be met either by importation or by domestic production, I have deemed it best to append to this report a copy of the table obligingly furnished by Mr. Rinman, giving the names and marks and kind of ore used in all the Swedish iron works; and also to append an analysis of the different kinds of pig iron from which they are made.[1] A careful study of these two tables will not only guide the consumer in the selection of the kind of iron which he may require for special purposes, but will enable the American ironmaster to select the kinds of ore with which he may hope to replace Swedish iron in our own markets. But let it not be supposed that this last result can be achieved by ore alone. The same care in the manufacture, and the same severe test which is applied to the loops, heated to the highest point, will be required to insure a uniform and satisfactory result. The best form of gas furnace is probably that of G. Ekman, models of which were exhibited in the exposition.[2]

It is well to note that in the forge, or sinking fires, two tuyeres are generally employed, placed opposite each other, by which the production is increased and the consumption of coal diminished, and the iron is generally regarded as more homogeneous. Puddling with wood is also practiced to a considerable extent in Sweden; and, in this connection, although somewhat out of its proper order, it is best to describe the furnace devised by F. Lundin, of Carlstadt Munkfors, designed for the consumption of turf and peat, without drying, and of wet sawdust or other moist fuel; an invention deemed so valuable that the association of Swedish ironmasters have rewarded Lundin by a gift of $10,000, which, in Sweden, is a very considerable sum. In this furnace the fuel is fed by a hopper into a reservoir resting upon an inclined grate and is supplied from below with air from a blower. The products of combustion thus produced pass through a condenser, where all the moisture in the gas is condensed. The gas then passes to the heating furnace, which is furnished with Siemens's regenerators. It is found easy to use fuel containing as much as 45 percent of water, and the resulting gas contains about 33 pounds of water to 100 pounds of dry gas, and the water, after condensation, contains about 2 percent of its weight in

---

[1] These tables are omitted in the present reprint, as being no longer of any interest.—Editor.

[2] A description of this can be found in Percy's *Metallurgy*, p. 716. [Hewitt's note.]

gas, or 3 percent of its volume. The condensing apparatus consists of 3,500 pounds of iron bars piled crosswise on each other and kept cold by a jet of water from a tuyere. The heat of the gas before condensation of the water always melts lead easily, and sometimes zinc. The expense of the construction of a full-sized furnace in Sweden is about $2,500 in currency, and it is estimated that such a furnace will utilize 1,700 tons of fuel in a year, at a saving proportioned to the cost of other fuel in the particular locality where it is employed. In Sweden it is estimated that the annual saving resulting not merely from the cost of the fuel but from the repairs of the furnace and the increased temperature, amounts to over $5,000 per annum on the product of each furnace. In the Ekman furnace dry wood containing 8 percent of water produces in the generators gas of a temperature of 1,394°, while in the Lundin furnace the temperature is 2,666°, the combustion in both cases being produced by cold air. The gas produced by seasoned wood contains more water than that which proceeds from the Lundin condenser. The duration of the furnace is simply surprising and is to be attributed probably to the fact that there is no cinder. In eight weeks the thickness of the roof, 4 inches, was only diminished from $\frac{1}{4}$ to $\frac{3}{8}$ inch, and the side walls were entirely uninjured. So wonderful is the success of this system of condensation, in connection with the Siemens's regenerators, that in Sweden, and in fact everywhere where moist fuel is employed, the Lundin furnace will supersede every other. Its great merit is, that it is available for any kind of fuel whatever. In the United States it is believed that this arrangement might be employed advantageously for washing the gas obtained from mineral coal; but its chief merit consists in the fact that in mineral regions, far removed from the coal fields, it is possible to establish iron works, using sawdust or peat with entire success and great economy. In the lumber regions of Lake Superior it will be found to have a special value, because there is an abundant supply of pig accessible to the sawmills on Green Bay and in Michigan, producing enormous quantities of sawdust, slabs, and waste timber. . . .

The exposition presented very complete specimens of pig iron from all parts of Europe, but the experience valuable to our American ironmasters could only be acquired by actual visits to the works where they were produced. In South Wales the most remarkable feature was the endurance of the furnaces, some of which had been in blast for more than twenty years, and no furnaces were expected to go out of blast under ten or twelve years. As the production of these furnaces varies from 200 to 300 tons per week, and the ores and coal are not less calculated to wear the lining than our own, it would be very desirable to determine the cause of this greater durability. In Wales the heat of the blast is usually about 600°, and its pressure from 3 to $3\frac{1}{2}$ pounds per square inch. As all these conditions are to be found at particular works in the United States where furnaces continue in blast only from three to four years, it would seem that the quality of the bricks might explain the difference. Another peculiarity of South Wales is the great difference in the product of furnaces having the same dimensions and shape and using the same materials, and for which the experience of the iron-masters offered no adequate explanation. Again, at Ebbw Vale, the Sirhowy furnace, 73 feet in height, 18 feet across the boshes, with the hearth 7 feet, 6 inches in diameter, and the tunnel head 10 feet in diameter, containing 11,900 cubic feet, did not produce as much iron as another furnace 17 feet, 6 inches across the boshes, 48 feet high, with the same sized hearth and top containing 6,590 cubic feet. This latter furnace averaged about 380 tons of iron per week, using about $1\frac{1}{2}$ tons of raw coal to the ton of iron. Its interior section was in the form of two cones meeting at the boshes.[1] The only mechanical arrangement of these furnaces worthy of special notice is the cup and cone device at the tunnel head which is described in Percy, page 470, perfected at the Ebbw Vale iron works, and now generally adopted at all the large iron works in Great Britain and on the continent, except in Scotland and in the Cumberland region, where it is supposed to have an unfavorable influence on the quality of the iron. The object of this arrangement is to throw the small ore and coal against the sides of the furnace, and the large pieces to the center, and it was stated to be essential that the cone when drawn up to its place should have a space of 18 inches between it and the lining of the furnace. From the space thus produced the gas is drawn off for the supply of the hot blast ovens and the boilers, which in the great majority of cases were placed upon the ground and not upon piers, and no difficulty is experienced in procuring an adequate supply of gas below by the draught of high chimneys. It was generally stated that the adoption of the cup and cone arrangement had improved the running of the furnaces and diminished the consumption of coal.

The Cumberland region has long been remarkable for the large product of iron from its blast furnaces. Even as early as 1862 a weekly product of over 600 tons had been achieved in one furnace, and although the business has greatly extended in that region and is still characterized by large weekly products, it does not appear that any improvements have been lately made either in construction or in yield. At Barrow-on-Furness there are 6 furnaces 15 feet across the boshes by 42 feet high; and 5 furnaces $17\frac{1}{2}$ feet across the boshes and $47\frac{1}{2}$ feet high. When working for pig iron designed for the Bessemer process, the smaller furnaces make 300 and the larger 400 tons per week of extra gray pig iron, but this product is very largely increased when the furnaces are running on forge iron, a single furnace having made as much as 700 tons in a

[1] A drawing of it will be found in Percy among the Ebbw Vale furnaces, marked E. V., No. 3, p. 559. [Hewitt's note.]

week. This remarkable product is due to the admirable character of the ore, which is a red hematite yielding 60 percent, on the average, and is smelted with a ton of coke per ton of iron, but when the grayest iron is made the consumption of fuel is undoubtedly greater. Admirable as these works are in construction, producing annually the enormous quantity of 200,000 tons, there was nothing in the process of manufacture calling for special notice.

But at no point in Europe was the lesson of the superior advantage of good quality more plainly inculcated, for here, on the west coast of England, gray hematite iron was selling for 90 shillings a ton, while on the east coast of England gray Cleveland iron could be purchased for 40 shillings per ton; the one finding a market in the Bessemer process, where only the very best iron can be used, while the other had to be sold in competition with the great mass of inferior pig. But though the iron of the Cleveland region be inferior, it is there that the American ironmaster has most to learn. The ore of the Cleveland region is of the fossiliferous variety, yielding 31 percent raw, and 42 to 43 percent when roasted. The coke is extremely tenacious, enduring a heavy pressure without being crushed. The first furnaces built were about 18 feet in diameter and 55 feet high, making a weekly product of about 230 tons, with a consumption of 1½ tons of coke to the ton of iron and a temperature of blast of from 600° to 700°. The excellent performance of the stock in the furnace soon led to an increase in its height, with a corresponding increase in the temperature of the blast, and now there are furnaces in operation in the Cleveland district 102 feet in height, 27 feet across the boshes, and driven with a blast of a temperature of from 1,000° to 1,100°, or at least sufficient to melt pure zinc, back of the tuyeres, in from four to five seconds. The consequence is that the consumption of fuel has been reduced to a ton of coke to the ton of iron, and there has been a gain of 2 percent in the yield of the ore, which latter phenomenon is attributed to the use of the Player stoves for heating the blast. In this arrangement the gas is burned in a separate chamber, and only the resulting heat reaches the pipes. Thus all flocculent matter is disposed of, the pipes require no cleaning, and their liability to injury is far less than when the flames come in contact with the pipes, subjecting them to the danger of being burned in spots. The pressure of blast is from 3½ to 4½ pounds to the inch, and six tuyeres of 3½ inches diameter usually serve to convey it to the furnace. At the Norton works, where there is a furnace 85 feet high by 25 feet boshes, there were four stoves, containing 60 pipes weighing 126 tons, which heated the blast from a blowing cylinder of 7 feet by 7 feet, making 13 revolutions per minute. The general rule for blast is that there shall be 1,200 square feet of heating surface for each 1,000 cubic feet per minute.

The effect of this change in the size of the furnace and the heat of the blast in the Norton furnace above referred to was to give a weekly product of 365 tons. All these furnaces have the cup and cone arrangement at the tunnel head, and the gas is drawn off into a great iron flue forming a kind of cornice or moulding around the top of the furnace, but covered with brick so as to avoid radiation. A proper outlet for the gas is indispensable for the larger product and economical results which have been described. The pipe for conducting the gas to the ground must not be less than 7 feet in diameter and is lined on the inside with brick.

All the ore of the Cleveland region is calcined in vertical kilns, varying from 24 to 35 feet in height and from 4,500 to 8,000 cubic feet capacity, charged with ore and fine coal in layers, and consuming about one ton of coal to 24 tons of ore. This calcining might be far better done by the Westman furnace, but unhappily the supply of gas from the blast furnace is not more than sufficient to heat the boiler and stoves. All the usual modes of elevating material to the top of the furnace are to be found in this region, but the pneumatic lift more recently introduced merits attention as working in a very satisfactory manner. It consists of a cast-iron cylinder of the height of the furnace, made in sections bored out and bolted together, so as to provide a chamber 36 inches in diameter, in which the piston fits loosely, and weighs about half a ton more than the platform and empty barrows. Leather packing is used to render it air tight. The platform surrounds the cylinder and is put in motion by the movement of the piston, with which it is connected by wire ropes passing over four eight-foot pulleys at the top of the cylinders. Four barrows of material are raised at a time, weighing from one to two tons, and the upward and downward motion is communicated by the alternate exhaustion and compression of air beneath the piston to the amount of from 1 to 3 pounds per square inch, according to the load. A pressure of one pound to the square inch is required to lower the empty barrows. For the calcining kilns, a similar arrangement, but of greater power, is employed.

The early introduction of the high furnaces into the United States would seem to be inevitable, provided the fuel is strong enough to resist the pressure which is involved. Our magnetic, carbonaceous, fossiliferous, and red hematite ores, except in a few instances, are remarkably well adapted to these furnaces, and if it should be found that our admirable anthracite will not decrepitate when subjected to the incidental pressure, it is not hazarding much to predict that the consumption of fuel can be readily reduced to a ton for each ton of iron made.

An analysis of the coke used is subjoined as a guide to those who employ that fuel:

Carbon 91.42
Volatile hydro-carbons 0.64
Sulphur 1.00
Ash 6.66
Moisture 0.28

Among the other curiosities connected with the Cleveland iron is an analysis of the dust which is deposited by the gas in its passage from the furnace through the stoves and under the boilers.

Protoxide of iron 14.22
Oxide of zinc.. 10.48
Sulphide of zinc 13.70
Alumina 8.20
Lime 12.32
Magnesia 5.03
Chloride of silicon 4.74
Ammonia 0.70
Thallium .... Trace
Sulphuric acid 3.18
Free sulphur 0.17
Silica 22.60
Carbonaceous matter 4.50
                                                               _____
        Total 99.84

So large a proportion of zinc from an ore which contains no zinc is a phenomenon not unobserved at other places, but it has as yet received no satisfactory explanation.

The Player stove was the subject of commendation in the Cleveland region, and it appeared to be as satisfactory a mode of heating the blast as any in use. But it is proper to say that an equally high temperature can be procured in other ways. Its introduction into the United States will certainly effect a large saving of fuel, but the effect upon the quality of the iron must in a great measure depend upon the character of the ores employed. Its combination, however, with the high furnaces certainly affords one of the most interesting and instructive lessons in recent metallurgic improvements.

In Scotland, where for so long a time the yield of blast furnaces was in advance of all other regions, no progress seems to have been made, the furnaces rarely exceeding 200 tons per week. An attempt has indeed been made at Gartsherrie to increase this amount by the erection of two furnaces 60 feet in height, but the consumption of fuel has not been reduced, and the yield of the furnace in iron [has] not [been] materially increased.

This is noted here in order to suggest caution in our own progress toward higher furnaces, because the increase in the height of the furnace at Gartsherrie appears to have increased the quantity of solid matter which falls down into the hearth, and very much adds to the labor of working the furnace. It has been suggested that a modification in the shape of the furnace might relieve this difficulty, and some new furnaces erected by Mr. D. Adamson in North Lincolnshire are cited as an example of the advantages of bringing down the lines of the furnace almost parallel to a very low point and then drawing them in quickly toward the hearth. But in the absence of a larger experience it would be unsafe to recommend any other course but extreme caution in departing from successful practice.

Passing from blast furnaces to rolling mills, the most striking change presented in the new works is the simplicity of the machinery, its large dimensions, and their arrangements for dispensing with labor in the handling of the material. Reversing mills are generally employed in Great Britain in preference to three-high rolls, but in France it is to be noted that at Anzin, in Isère, three-high trains have been in use for rolling girders since June, 1849. There is also a three-high plate mill at Le Creusot, and the principle of three-high mills appears to be perfectly well understood in Europe, but the reversing mill is generally preferred. Direct-acting engines, that is, engines without intermediate gearing, are generally preferred, but at Crewe, in the plate mill, the fly wheel was dispensed with; a pair of engines similar to a locomotive engine were used, running at a high speed and geared down so as to give the proper number of revolutions to the train. At Ebbw Vale there is an engine driving a small train running 250 revolutions per minute. In both these cases the result was entirely satisfactory to the managers. Another striking feature in the rolling mills and in some of the larger steel works was the adoption of the hydraulic crane for moving the masses of metal, and where the hydraulic crane was not used the steam crane often supplied its place. The ratio between human labor and the quantity of material handled has thus been greatly reduced and apparently brought to a minimum, and in the United States, where labor is so dear, the introduction of hydraulic machinery as a substitute for human muscles is an imperative necessity.

The arrangements necessary for this purpose are not complicated although somewhat expensive. Where an adequate pressure of water, say 300 pounds to the square inch, can be procured from an adjacent height, as at the admirable works of Naylor, Vickers & Co., in Sheffield, the expense is lessened, but in other places it is only necessary to erect an accumulator and supply the pressure by artificial means; and even the accumulator may be dispensed with by the use of the duplex steam pumps generally employed in America. The steel-rail mill of John Brown & Co., at Sheffield, and the new steel works of Naylor, Vickers & Co., at Sheffield, are admirable examples of the perfection to which this hydraulic system has been carried; and taken as a whole I regard the latter establishment as the best specimen of mechanical engineering at present in existence.

Attention should also be directed to a tool for slotting the ends of rails, so that they may be all of exact length, which is indispensable in order to secure a perfect railway joint. The cost of this operation is about two pence per rail, and the machine is not expensive. Another machine for cutting rails cold, at John Brown & Co's., was worthy of observation. It was a circular saw 16 inches in diameter and ¼ of an inch thick, making 20 revolutions per minute and cutting 6 steel rails per hour. Another feature admirable for the order and cleanliness of the mill was the cemetery for rolls not in use, which were all buried in special tombs prepared for their reception under the iron floor of the mill, whence they were easily removed by cranes.

Among the names of those who give dignity to the grand prize of the exposition stands that of C. W. Siemens for his gas regenerative heating furnace; and although this invention has been long enough in use thus to command the homage of the scientific world, it is only within a few months that it has been introduced for the first time into an iron works in the United States. Its practical success is, however, undeniable, and for the reheating of steel, whether made by the crucible or the Bessemer process, or for the heating of iron, where a clean incandescent heat is required, or for any of those operations in which wrought iron is required to be kept in a melted condition, its necessity is unquestionable. Its merits, however, are not limited by these results, for which it was originally designed, but enable hitherto useless or nearly worthless forms of fuel to be employed with entire success. At Crewe, where coal alone is used for reheating, 5 hundredweight suffices to do the work of a ton under the old plan, and at the time of my visit they were using half sawdust, saving thereby one-fifth of the coal, that is to say, 2½ hundredweight of sawdust was found to be equal to one hundredweight of coal. At the wire works of Richard Johnson & Nephew, as we have already seen, the consumption of coal was reduced from about 15 hundredweight to 8 hundredweight per ton of billets heated, and the waste from 10½ percent to 6.9 percent. At Bolton the manager assured me that the results were equally satisfactory, although he considered it an open question whether in cases where the waste heat was used for making steam there would be much economy of fuel by the use of the Siemens furnace, but he had no doubt whatever as to the saving in waste and the increase of product from the furnaces. Aside from the question of the quality of the iron produced, the Siemens furnace in the United States will be found of most value where coal is dear, and, above all, at works driven by water power where the surplus heat is now allowed to go to waste. The application of the Siemens furnace to puddling is quite recent. I saw it in operation at Le Creusot, in France, and at Bolton, in England.

At the former place the coal, which is an impure kind of anthracite, had required some modifications to be made in the generator, so that the advantages could not be estimated; but at Bolton the furnace worked so much more rapidly than the old furnace that it was necessary to put on three shifts of hands per day, and no difficulty of any kind was found in the operation of the furnace. I regard it, therefore, as one of the most important improvements to be introduced into American iron works at the earliest possible day.

The success of Siemens has given rise to many attempts to improve the ordinary puddling furnace, and at Bolton I found in operation the Wilson furnace, which differs from the common furnace in having the coal fed in from a hopper over the fuel chamber on to an inclined grate, and a bridge which causes all the smoke to be consumed before reaching the stack. Although this furnace has been tried previously at other places and abandoned, yet at Bolton it appears to be working well. The consumption of coal was less than a ton to the ton of iron, the number of heats in twelve hours was increased from six to seven, and the waste of the iron was stated to be decidedly less. In case subsequent experience should confirm the promise of the experiment as I saw it, it would seem that in works where the waste heat is required for raising steam, the Wilson furnace could be introduced with more advantage than the Siemens furnace for puddling.

In the exposition, among the articles exhibited by the Dowlais works was a puddle ball of unusual dimensions, made in the mechanical puddling machine constructed by Mr. Menelaus, the able and experienced manager of this extensive establishment. A visit to the works proved that no expense had been spared in order to substitute puddling by machinery for the work by hand. A building and engine had been put up expressly for the purpose, and four massive machines erected, each capable of heating a quantity of iron sufficient to produce a ball of 6 hundredweight. The puddling vessel is of a shape that would be produced by revolving the bottom of a puddling furnace and is caused to turn on a horizontal axis resting on firm bearings. The vessel is first charged with iron, either cold or melted, then lifted by a steam crane and placed on its proper bearings, and as soon as the metal is melted thrown into gear and caused to revolve. It was expected that the puddling operation would be accomplished by the simple revolution of this vessel, supplied with the products of combustion from a furnace placed at one end. When the heat was completed, the vessel was lifted from its bearings by the crane, the bridge end turned down, and the ball dropped out upon a carriage ready to be taken to the hammer. There were of course many other details which it is unnecessary here to describe, as the results achieved were not such as to encourage imitation. The first difficulty was found in procuring a lining material which would withstand the chemical action of the metal and cinder and the mechanical action of the iron from the time it came to nature until it was balled up. Ganister was tried, and [it] failed because the iron produced was invariably cold-short. Titanic ore from Norway was found to stand nearly as well as the ganister, and the iron produced was less cold-short, but with neither could a satisfactory iron be produced. Iron linings failed, because the iron under treatment adhered to the sides of the vessels; and Mr. Menelaus makes this important statement, that it is next to impossible to prevent puddled iron from adhering to the *clean* surface of an iron lining heated to the temperature necessary for puddling. It was also found that artificial blast was necessary, but notwithstanding over 600 tons of iron were made in these vessels and the highest order of mechanical talent brought to bear upon the process, neither could the lining be made to stand nor the iron be brought up to a merchantable quality. The problem of mechanical puddling, therefore, still remains unsolved, but the manual labor of the puddler can undoubtedly be considerably diminished by the use of puddling tools or rabbles, moved backward and forward around the furnace by a series of levers put in motion by steam or other power. At the Northfield iron works, near Sheffield, such machinery, invented by John Griffiths, was in operation on a single double puddling furnace, in which 10 hundredweight of pig was charged and six heats were made daily by one puddler, and two boys helping him. It was claimed that 2,400 pounds of puddled iron was being produced with 16½ hundredweight of coal, and there certainly was a saving of one skilled workman. And yet it was stated that where these machines had been put into the works and left to the option of the puddler to be used or not, and the same price per ton paid for the result, the puddlers had declined to use them. But whether because they were really found to be of no service or because they feared their use would bring down the rate of wages, it is impossible to say.

So far as my judgment goes, I think they could be introduced with great advantage to both masters and men.

At Le Creusot, in puddling white pig iron for rails, they make eleven heats per turn, or 2½ tons, in a furnace with one puddler and two helpers, which is a larger yield than I have any knowledge of elsewhere, but it is certainly not due to any peculiarity in the furnace.

Player, the inventor of the hot-air stove, has also taken out a patent for what he terms a blooming process, by which the entire heat is removed from the puddling furnace in one mass and carried to the hammer on a suitable carriage, thus saving the expense of separating the heat into small balls. Trials are now being made with this process, but it is yet too early to give any positive opinion as to the result.

Of the value of another improvement, however, made by John

Beard, there can be no doubt. This invention consists in placing the grate-bars of the puddling furnace upon two axles, at the front and back of the fire chamber. To these axles a vibrating or rocking motion is given by means of levers, the effect of which is to raise the grate-bars alternately at opposite ends so that each grate-bar vibrates up and down in an opposite direction to its adjacent grate-bar. The value of this improvement consists in the facility with which the grates are cleaned and freed from all clinker without breaking up the fire. It was already introduced into the Blaenavon works, in South Wales, and those of John Brown & Co., at Sheffield, where it was stated to give an additional heat from the furnace per turn and to make a considerable saving in coal.

The manufacture of puddled wire rods is a very extensive business in Great Britain, but no one has succeeded in naturalizing it upon American soil. With the best grades of charcoal iron it is indeed possible to make good puddled wire rods in the United States, but at a cost too high to compete with the foreign article, in the production of which no charcoal is employed. I visited the works of J. C. Hill & Co., near Newport, in South Wales, and those of Richard Johnson & Nephew, at Manchester. In both these works, a mixture of several brands of coke iron is employed, costing on the average about £4 per ton. Single puddling furnaces alone are used, the charge of iron is 4½ hundred-weight, and the yield from 3¼ to 3½ hundredweight, made up into five balls and showing a waste much larger than usual. These balls are hammered under a 5-ton helve, to a bloom 4 inches square, and this bloom is taken hot to a balling furnace, where it is heated and rolled down to the ordinary 1⅛-inch billet for wire. The greatest possible care is taken at all stages of the operation, but the result of my observation is that the puddling furnace is the stage in which the iron receives its proper preparation for a wire rod, and I think I may say that as a general rule, when high grades of iron were to be produced I remarked a higher standard for the puddled bar than I have been accustomed to see in the United States. The practice of puddling for grain instead of fiber is more general, and I think I cannot be mistaken in saying that the puddle balls are far more thoroughly cleaned of cinder when puddled for grain. At Blaenavon and at Le Creusot, at which works very superior iron is made, the grain of the puddled iron resembled puddled steel more than iron, and it seems probable that we shall hardly attain to the same regularity of product in America until the same careful attention is paid to the puddling process.

The propriety of rerolling old rails seems to be involved in as much doubt in England as in the United States. The general practice, however, is to sell the old rails and purchase new ones, but at Crewe the London and Northwestern Railroad Company, and at Swindon the

Great Western Railroad Company have mills for reworking their old rails. There was a concurrence of opinion in both establishments that new iron should be used in the head, and at both the steel-headed rail with old rails in the base was looked upon with favor. At Swindon I saw a beautiful steel-headed rail which had been made by balling up cast-steel turnings in a common balling furnace and placing the resulting bar on top of a rail pile. The fracture was admirable, and the weld appeared to be perfect. There seemed also to be a general agreement that the top slab of a rail pile should not be less than 1½ inch in thickness, and 2 inches is preferred. At Blaenavon puddled steel is used for heads with very satisfactory results, but care is taken that the layer of steel on the finished rail shall not be less than ⅝ inch thick.

PROCESSES FOR THE MANUFACTURE OF STEEL

By common consent it seems to be agreed that the most striking feature of the industry of the present day is the marked advance in the manufacture of steel and its progressive substitution for iron in all cases where strength must be combined with lightness. Notice has already been taken of the enormous masses of steel in the exposition, but it was only by observing the infinite variety of forms and purposes to which it was applied that the intelligent observer was compelled to admit the transition which is taking place from the age of iron to the age of steel. Another conclusion could not fail to be reached from a careful study of the products and processes represented in the exposition, namely, that good steel can only be made from good material no matter what process is employed. For the best steel the crucible process still maintains the first rank, and although the exposition contains some beautiful specimens of material made by other processes, yet it is quite evident that no plan has yet been made sufficiently practical to infringe upon the domain of crucible steel for the more difficult and higher uses for which this metal is required. The process of making crucible steel is too well known at this day to require description at my hands, but like all other branches of the metal business it has of late undergone an immense extension in the size of the works and of the products.

At the establishment of Thomas Firth & Sons, in Sheffield, the old system of making steel is maintained in its integrity and of a quality unsurpassed by any other maker. And yet here I saw a 12-ton ingot cast for the tube of a Woolwich gun, poured from crucibles containing each about 50 pounds. In order to make a solid ingot it is indispensable that the metal should be poured continuously into the mold at a high temperature, inasmuch as any delay in discharging the crucibles would be fatal to the quality. The difficulty of preparing this quantity of metal in such small instalments so as to reach the mold in due season and of organizing the gangs of men necessary for its transfer will easily be appreciated by those who are familiar with the magnitude of the task. The only evidence in these works, besides the masses of steel, of the new era upon which the business has entered was to be found in the enormous steam hammers, furnaces, and cranes which had been rendered necessary in order to fabricate ingots of such massive character. So admirable were these arrangements that there seemed to be no greater difficulty in dealing with these heavy masses of steel than with the smallest ingot on the premises. Here the fabrication of cast-steel locomotive tires had just been undertaken, with every possible facility for its successful operation. A cylindrical ingot is first made sufficiently large for six or eight tires; this ingot is then cut in a lathe into sections each of the shape of a cheese, sufficiently large for a single tire. The steel cheeses thus produced are heated and thoroughly hammered under an immense steam hammer and after being reduced in all directions by this process are again heated and punched with a conical-pointed punch under another steam hammer. The ring thus produced is enlarged by successive heatings and hammerings until it reaches the size suitable for the tire rolling mill, where after being again heated it is rapidly finished, producing a ring without weld or joint. Inasmuch as the relative value of tires made by the crucible process and the Bessemer process is still a subject of discussion, I took special pains to compare the toughness of the crucible steel, as shown in the clippings of the fin on the finished tire, with the same clippings from the Bessemer tires, and no doubt was left in my mind as to the superiority of the crucible material; but I do not wish to be understood as saying that the Bessemer material is not good enough for the purpose, and, in view of the relative price, more economical in use, Firth's tires being sold at £45 per ton, and the Bessemer as low as £28. The mode of making crucible tires at the works of Naylor, Vickers & Co. was somewhat different, and it appeared to be less expensive; and here one could not fail to be struck with the admirable adaptation of mechanical means to the objects in view and with the very complete arrangements for the production of large masses of crucible steel. Here again was presented the perpetually recurring question as to the relative value of Bessemer steel for special purposes, such as crank shafts and locomotive crank axles, which are produced at these works in large quantities and from crucible steel. Of the value of the latter no doubt seems to be entertained, and the makers of the former insist that their work is equally reliable at a far less cost; but I must again acknowledge that I saw no Bessemer steel in England of equal toughness with the product of the best makers of crucible steel. In the exposition, on the other hand, there were specimens of Bessemer steel from Sweden and from Austria which appeared to be fully equal in quality to any crucible steel, and these may be the precursors of the coming day when crucible steel will be a thing of the past, but that day has not yet arrived. The past year may be said also to have decided the substitution of cast steel for iron in guns of small calibers. The peculiar excellence of the Marshall iron is still admitted, but it cannot be denied that cast steel is freer from "greys," or specks, and in point of tenacity quite as reliable. When steel is employed for this purpose the barrel is not welded, but is generally bored after being forged to the proper length.

The Chassepot rifles are all being made in this way, but another method, known as that of Deakin & Johnson, is being introduced, with considerable probability of its general adoption. In this process the ingots, after being hammered to about five inches in diameter, are cut into pieces of suitable weight for a gun barrel and punched in the same manner as has been described for the punching of tires. The blanks so punched are heated and hammered and then rolled over a mandril into a cylindrical tube about a foot in length, which is again heated and rolled over a mandril into a gun barrel. This process forms the subject of a patent, although it is difficult to find anything in the process which is novel, except, possibly, in its limitation to gun barrels. It is applicable, however, either to cast steel or to Bessemer steel, the latter being generally employed.

The Bessemer process is, of course, the great feature of our day in this department; and in order that it might be treated in such detail as its importance demands, it was deemed by the committee best to make it the subject of a special report, and this duty was confided to Mr. Fred. J. Slade, an American mechanical engineer, who had already devoted several months to its careful study in the interest of the American patentee. His report is hereto annexed,[1] and will be found fully to justify the confidence of the committee in intrusting him with this important duty. I have verified the accuracy of his statements by extended personal examination, and it is only necessary for me to add one or two general conclusions at which I have arrived. The first is that the Bessemer process will not, as Mr. Bessemer originally supposed, supersede the puddling process, which appears to be, as yet, the only method applicable to the conversion of by far the larger portion of the pig iron made into wrought iron; because by far the larger portion of the pig iron made is of a quality not good enough for the Bessemer process, which, in the absence of sulphur and phosphorus, is absolutely exacting. It is true that an antidote may yet be found for these two poisons, in which case the area of the Bessemer process would be enormously extended. But even then there would be a limitation to its general use (and this is my second conclusion) arising from the uncertainty as to the quality of each particular cast, requiring a special test for each in every case where it is to be subjected to great strains. But even when this precau-

[1] Not here included.—Editor.

tion is taken, it is found that in the manufacture of tires and of gun barrels there is a very considerable percentage of failure from undiscovered flaws, which show themselves in the cracking of the ingot when subjected to the severe test of the steam punch. Hence, in my judgment, it is not safe to use Bessemer metal in any case involving the security of life or limb, unless in the process of manufacture it has been subjected to such tests as will certainly show all its defects.

I think it is safe to use it for tires and for gun barrels that have been made by the punching process, but I should think it unwise to employ it for solid railway axles made in the ordinary way. If punched and made hollow, this objection would not apply, and doubtless it would not be difficult to devise a method of making a solid axle from Bessemer steel that would be free from objection.

In view of the small amount of Bessemer steel as yet produced in the United States, we are struck in Europe with surprise at the enormous provision made for its supply; and it is quite evident that the business is overdone, and, contrary to all past experience, the inventor and the public at large seem to have profited by its introduction at the expense of the manufacturer.

As an adjunct to the Bessemer process, the Parry process must be mentioned, having for its object the conversion, in a cupola furnace, of wrought iron which had been freed from phosphorus and sulphur by the puddling process into pig iron adapted for the Bessemer process. For this method of operation extensive works were erected at Ebbw Vale, but they have been abandoned, and the patent has been purchased by Mr. Bessemer.

This process would have very considerable value if the metal could be tapped from the cupola in the form of steel instead of pig iron; but this does not appear to have been practicable, inasmuch as the product was a white pig iron, containing 2 percent of carbon. A charge of 22 hundredweight was worked at a time, and from 55 to 75 minutes [were required] for its treatment, which involved a waste of 12 percent. It might possibly be used advantageously for the conversion of the ends of Bessemer rails into pig, in case they should ever become so cheap as to warrant the operation. It might also be used for melting down the metallic sponge, which can be made by cementation from our rich ores in America, but certainly without advantage in point of cost unless the product should have qualities attainable in no other way. The production of steel from the cupola furnace is still a desideratum to be attained, but among the possibilities of the future.

A careful study of the exposition showed but two other processes for making steel worthy of notice, and both French: the one patented by A. Berard and tried at the forges of Montataire; the other that of Emile and Pierre E. Martin, in operation at Sireuil. In both these systems cast

steel is made in a reverberatory furnace. In Berard's process the conversion of the pig iron into steel is sought to be achieved by subjecting the
melted metal alternately to a decarbonizing and recarbonizing flame, for
which purpose it is necessary to employ blast. He uses a Siemens furnace
and avails himself of the changes of current required in working the
regenerators to effect the changes of flame. The furnace is divided by a
bridge into two halves, and he thus operates upon two masses of iron at
the same time, one of which is freshly charged, while the other contains
material which is nearly decarbonized. Some specimens of Berard's steel
were on exhibition, and although creditable in themselves, it was generally understood that he had not yet succeeded in making steel regularly
for market. The Messrs. Martin, on the contrary, were not only making
steel regularly at their own works at Sireuil, but the process is also in
operation at two of the largest works in France—Le Creusot and
Firminy, and is in process of erection at various other works in Europe,
and arrangements have been made for its immediate introduction into
the United States. In this process the pig iron is deprived of its carbon
by the addition of pieces of wrought iron or steel either in the form of
shingled puddle balls or of scrap. The quantity, however, of wrought
iron necessary to reduce the carbon to the required limits, is much less
than would be inferred, from the consideration of the quantity contained in the pig and does not in practice much exceed the quantity of
pig itself. A charge of gray pig or of *speigeleisen* is melted in a Siemens
furnace having a bed hollowed out to contain it, and it is allowed to
remain about half an hour after fusion to bring it to an intense white
heat; portions of malleable iron previously brought to a bright red heat
are then added in successive charges of about 200 pounds, at intervals of
20 minutes to a half hour, each charge being thoroughly melted before
the next is added. After two or three such additions ebullition com-
mences in the bath of metal and continues till the carbon is wholly
removed from the pig. The exact condition of the metal is ascertained
from small proofs taken from the charge after each addition of iron
toward the end of the operation. These are run into a small ingot mold
and when cooled to the proper heat hammered into a plate about $\frac{5}{16}$
of an inch thick by 5 inches in diameter. When the decarbonization is
completely effected these proofs will bend double cold and show a fracture quite fibrous. A quantity of pig, generally of the same kind as was
used for the preliminary charge, is then added in such proportion to
the amount of iron in the furnace as to give the desired hardness to the
steel, according to the use for which it is required. When this is melted
the bath is well stirred to insure homogeneity in its substance, and a
final proof [is] taken which is treated in the same manner as the others
and gives reliable evidence as to the state of the metal before pouring.
This enables the quality to be very exactly adjusted to the degree of

hardness required. Should it be too soft, more pig is added, while if it is too hard, the mere waiting from a quarter to half an hour will materially soften the metal. Arguing from this fact, Messrs. Martin claim that under the influence of such a high temperature, the carbon is to some extent spontaneously disassociated from the iron, and [they] attribute in a measure to this the fact that so small a proportion of wrought iron is required to effect the decarbonization of the pig. The coating of scale formed on the iron in the preliminary reheating which it undergoes before being charged into the furnace also assists in the removal of the carbon. When the metal has been brought to the desired condition, it is tapped off at the rear of the furnace into ingot molds placed on a railway car, and thus brought successively under the gutter.

A considerable number of specimens of steel made by this process were exhibited, ranging in hardness from a metal too hard to be touched by a tool to a true wrought iron, intended to be used in the manufacture of armor plates. At Messrs. Martin's works, at Sireuil, the process has been in regular operation during the past two years for the manufacture of gun barrels, and some remarkable specimens of these were exhibited. Thus there was one that had been tested with very large charges of powder and a heavyweight of shot, which by very palpable bulging just behind the balls testified as to the softness and toughness of the metal. In another, which had been burst by a similarly severe charge, the metal had merely torn open for a certain length of the barrel, and the lips so formed were simply folded back 180 degrees, without any sign of cracking. There were also shown specimens of tool steel, of excellent fracture, castings of pieces of machinery, such as gears and framing, and a large tube for a cannon of extremely soft metal, or "melted iron," as it is named.

The hardest variety of metal, called by the patentee "mixed metal," is considered suitable for castings which do not require to be worked by tools, but where great strength is required, such as hammer blocks and anvils, large gears, and so forth. By a subsequent process of annealing or decarbonization, carried on in a gas furnace under the influence of an oxidizing flame, these castings may be softened so as to be quite malleable and easily worked, and they then retain the advantage of being free from blow holes. This metal is produced by adding to a preliminary bath of say 1,600 pounds of pig 2,400 of wrought iron and adding at the end 1,200 pounds of pig. For tool steel, to a bath of 1,600 pounds of gray pig would be added 2,600 pounds of puddled steel from the same pig, and at the end of the operation 400 to 500 pounds of *speigeleisen*. For homogeneous metal, the preliminary bath at Sireuil is 1,200 pounds of *speigeleisen*, to which 2,000 pounds of soft iron, puddled to grain, from the same pig, is added, and at the end of the process 200 to 300 pounds of the same pig is charged, to give the requisite amount of carbon. The softest metal of all, which, however, has not as yet been made an article of regular manufacture is made in the same way with the exception that the final charge of manganiferous pig is but 5 percent of the contents of the furnace. With certain kinds of grey charcoal pig this proportion rises, however, to 20 percent, since under the influence of the high temperature they refine spontaneously with great rapidity.

Messrs. Martin's patents also cover the use of ore either with, or in place of, the wrought iron or steel used for removing the carbon from the pig, and when this is used the progress of the operation is much more rapid. It has the objection, however, that the slag formed attacks violently the bricks forming the sides of the furnace, and therefore requires frequent renewals.

This process has the great practical advantage that all the scrap arising in the manufacture of any product, such as the ends of bars, and so forth, is readily remitted in the furnace and immediately returned to the form of useful ingots.

The flame in the furnace is kept always slightly surcharged with gas; an effect which the use of the Siemens furnace renders easy and certain, and by this means the waste of the metal is always moderate.

For the production of soft steel suitable for gun barrels or for tires this metal already enjoys considerable reputation in Europe, and, indeed, were it not for its excellent quality it would be impossible to sustain the manufacture at Sireuil, where there is neither iron nor coal, the latter being brought from England and the former from various parts of France.

The results here stated were verified by a personal residence of Mr. Slade during several weeks at the works at Sireuil, and the regular and commercial success of the process was in that way seen to be fully achieved.

It is not asserted that cast steel can be made as cheaply by this process as by the Bessemer; but where a product of definite quality is to be produced day by day, without rejections to any considerable extent, the Martin process has a decided advantage over the Bessemer, and in comparison with the crucible steel it is decidedly less expensive. Its chief drawback would seem to lie in the difficulty of keeping the furnace in order, and only the most refractory materials will withstand the high heat required for its operation. As much as 5 tons of steel have been produced by this process at a single heat, and there is no difficulty in combining the product of several furnaces where larger masses are desired, inasmuch as the temper of the heat in each furnace can be brought and maintained to exactly the same standard. It would seem also to present the best solution yet devised for the difficulty experienced by the accumulation of the ends of Bessemer steel rails, inasmuch as these can be used in lieu of the puddled iron required by the process.

It is possible, also, to use old rails in the same manner, and, indeed, any old scrap, but the resulting quality of the steel will, to a great extent, depend upon the quality of the old iron so used.

A visit to the works of Messrs. F. F. Verdié & Co., at Firminy, showed, in confirmation of facts gathered from other sources, that the steel manufacture of France, instead of being in the advanced degree of perfection often supposed in our country, has been but very moderately successful. These works were established for the manufacture of crucible steel and forgings on a rather large scale, but today the production of steel by this process has been entirely abandoned, and with the exception of some puddling all the steel now made is by the Martin process, for which three furnaces are now in operation and others in course of erection. The same thing appears to be true at other works, and it is quite certain that no considerable amount of good cast steel is produced in France. . . .

WORKS FOR THE PRODUCTION OF IRON AND STEEL

The description of the large masses of steel and iron exhibited in the exposition has led, incidentally, to an account of the magnitude of the iron works of Krupp. But this report would fail to give an adequate idea of the magnificent scale upon which the metallurgic industry of Europe is conducted at the present day if reference should not be made to other establishments in other countries. In France the most extensive works are those of Le Creusot, near the center of the empire, which are especially commended in the report of the jury of recompense for organizations which best develop a good understanding between masters and workmen and secure the material, moral, and intellectual welfare of the operatives.

In 1845 the product of Le Creusot was about 60,000 tons of coal and 4,000 tons of iron. At the present time the production is 250,000 tons of coal, 130,000 tons of cast iron, and 110,000 tons of wrought iron. The works cover an area of 300 acres, of which more than 50 acres are buildings in which mechanical operations are carried on. The coal is mined in the immediate vicinity, and the quantity of ore which the region now furnishes is stated to be 300,000 tons per annum, but my impression is that this includes a large quantity brought from Algiers and Elba. There are 15 blast furnaces of large dimensions, fed by 160 coke ovens and using the blast of 7 blowing machines of 1,350 horsepower, and 10 other engines for other purposes. The forge contains 150 puddling furnaces, 85 heating furnaces, 41 separate trains of rolls, 30 hammers, 85 steam engines of 6,500 horsepower in the aggregate. This mill is all under one uniform roof, made of iron, is about 1,400 feet in length, and is altogether in appearance and construction the most complete rolling mill in existence. And it is a remarkable evidence of the intelligence and courage of Messrs. Schneider & Co., the proprietors, that within the last few years they have deliberately abandoned their old works and machinery and erected an entirely new establishment, in order to avail themselves of all the modern improvements in machinery and process. The machine shops require engines of 700 horsepower for their operation and contain 26 hammers and 650 working tools. The total number of workmen employed is 9,950, being by a remarkable coincidence the precise number of horsepower represented by the steam engines in the works; that is to say, each man employs a machine power of one horse in addition to his own labor, showing the wonderful extension of human power which in our day has been realized out of the steam engine. Forty-five miles of railway, 15 locomotives, and 500 cars are required for the local operation of the works, and the enormous quantity of 1,400,000 tons of traffic is annually moved at the central depot of Le Creusot. All parts of the works are in communication by telegraphic wire. The total value of the productions is now about $7,000,000 per annum in gold.

On the whole these works may be regarded as the best model offered by Europe for the study of the iron business as it is, and they are not only an honor to the proprietors but one of the chief glories of France.

The works of Petin, Gaudet & Co. are distributed among several establishments, which in the aggregate employ 5,200 men and a steam power of 6,000 horses. The annual production is about 50,000 tons of iron and steel, of the value of $7,000,000 in gold.

There are several other establishments in France which approach very nearly to these large proportions, and considering the disadvantages in point of fuel and ore under which the business is carried on, as compared with Belgium and England, the present development of the iron industry of France, amounting to an annual product of 1,200,000 tons of pig iron and about 800,000 tons of wrought iron, is one of the most striking features of the industrial progress of France during the present century.

In Belgium the iron industry has made remarkably rapid strides, the product of pig iron having advanced from 134,563 tons in 1845, to 449,875 tons in 1864, and there are many establishments in Belgium organized on a scale comparable to the best works in other countries. That of Cockerill at Seraing, in which the government is directly interested, produces 50,000 tons of pig iron, 26,000 tons of bars, and 5,000 tons of steel annually, consuming 80,000 tons of coke and 146,000 tons of ore, and mining 260,000 tons of coal.

In Prussia the works of Krupp have already been referred to, and there are many other extensive establishments organized upon the best principles of modern construction. The Phœnix works near Ruhrort, for example, produced during the last year over 50,000 tons of pig iron and 40,000 tons of wrought iron with 11 blast furnaces and the corresponding number of puddling furnaces. The total production of iron ore in Prussia for the year ending 1865 was over 1,700,000 tons, which represents a production of iron of about 770,000 tons: In England there are many works approaching in capacity to Le Creusot, among which may be enumerated the Dowlais and Ebbw Vale in South Wales, those of Bolckow, Vaughan & Co., in the Cleveland region, and of the Barrow Hematite Iron and Steel Company at Barrow-in-Furness, and of John Brown & Co., at Sheffield. A production of 2,000 tons per week is achieved in each of these vast establishments. Large towns are required to house the workmen and their families; hundreds of miles of rails and thousands of cars are appropriated to their special use. The human mind is lost in wonder at the combination of material and intellectual elements required for the organization and conduct of such gigantic operations, and standing in the presence of tools which seem formed to shape the universe and of an artificial power which in the aggregate is too vast for any other estimate than by comparison with the force which moves the earth in its orbit, the triumph of man over matter is realized to an extent making it possible to comprehend in some degree the omnipotence of Deity Himself.

One striking consequence of the vast size which has been given to particular works is their general transfer from individual ownership to that of stock companies; and although this transfer is not considered favorable to the economy of manufacture, the saving produced by production on so large a scale would seem to counterbalance the advantages in point of cost which are connected with individual ownership. Nor is this feature of association of ownership peculiar to any one country, but may be said to be the general rule in all. In England, owing probably to the business being overdone, none of these companies can be said to have achieved a pecuniary success, and the shares of all of them are at a considerable discount. This fact, producing profound dissatisfaction on the part of the owners, coupled with the feeling of restlessness and discontent with their wages among the workmen, has paved the way for the consideration and discussion of the problem whether in these large establishments the true relations between capital and labor have been established, and in what way they may be placed upon a sounder basis, avoiding the ever recurring contention between masters and men which culminates in strikes injurious alike to both classes. The question has already stepped beyond the limits of private discussion, and governmental commissions are now investigating both in France and in England the facts and the principles upon which the organization of labor rests at this day, the points in which there is a collision between it and capital, the wrongs, if any, upon either side; with a view to such legislation as may render the march of industry regular and profitable to all concerned. In some establishments engaged in the mining of coal and other branches of industry, outside of the iron business, the system of "co-operation," as it is termed, has been introduced, with manifest advantage. But in all these cases the business is a profitable one, and it has never yet been subjected to the strain which will attack the system when it is forced to deal with losses instead of profits. The general plan adopted in these co-operative establishments, such as Crossley's great carpet factory in England, is to reserve to the capital a fixed rate of interest, as high in some cases as 15 percent per annum; next to pay to the workmen, a fixed rate of wages, being usually those which were in force at the time of the introduction of co-operation into the works, and to divide the surplus, if any, between capital and labor, on such terms as may be agreed upon, but usually in proportion to the amount of each employed during the year. There is a wide difference of opinion as to the practicability of introducing this system into the iron business, and there is a fear that it would not stand the trial to which it would be subjected in the long periods of depression to which the iron trade has hitherto been invariably subjected, and from which the co-operative system would not relieve it, because there would still be the same competition between the several co-operative associations and the several nations as now exists. Under the present system the capital is the first to lose its profits, and then comes the reduction in the wages of labor. Under the new system the reduction would fall first upon labor, or in strict equity there would be the same percentage of reduction upon the earnings of capital and labor. It is feared that the laborer would not look with content upon any reward to capital under such circumstances, and that the old warfare between the two would thus be renewed.

On the other hand, it is believed that by the obvious harmony thus established between the interests of capital and labor, the latter would be led to see that the co-operation of the former is indispensable for the payment of wages at all, and that any attack upon capital or any diminution of its quantity would be a direct attack upon labor, by depriving it of the fund out of which it is paid, and that the conservation of capital would thus become so apparent as the highest interest of the laboring class that strikes would cease, and even in bad times from the steady employment thus insured the labor would be better paid than under the present intermittent system. It is urged, moreover, that the personal interest thus excited in the workman would lead to greater economy in the manufacture and [would] bring down all waste to the minimum, and that it would be possible to establish such intelligent relations among the owners and workmen of the several co-operative establishments that over-production would be checked by common consent in time to prevent the serious losses to which it now subjects the industry of the world. It is quite certain that this latter end is achieved in an imperfect degree even in present practice. In Scotland the number of furnaces in blast during the present year has been very considerably reduced, with a corresponding reduction in the enormous stock of iron which had weighed down the prices below the cost of production. In France, by a resolution of the Ironmasters' Association, a reduction of 6 percent was inaugurated in the early part of the present year, and there is a general recognition of the necessity and wisdom of this course in times of over-production among the ironmasters of Europe. And it is impossible to see that there would be less discretion exercised or a less prompt remedy applied, if the workmen had such a direct relation to the business as to enable them to feel that it would be better to work less days at the old rate of wages than more days at a reduced rate, producing precisely the same pecuniary result.

No intelligent observer can fail to remark the universal cry which comes up from the laboring classes in all parts of Europe for the reorganization of the relations of capital and labor. In England it has shown itself in strikes long continued and in all branches of business, reducing the workmen to beggary and destroying the profits of capital to such an extent that in a spirit of self-preservation it takes flight where it can from the walks of industry and remains unemployed rather than incur the risks and the anxiety of its uses in active business. In France, where, as will be hereafter seen, the organization of a strike is full of difficulties, the same longing manifests itself, not merely in the organization of minor co-operative associations for the supply of the necessaries of life, the erection of houses, and the production of goods, but in a literature which seeks to analyze the social phases of industrial life and develop some better system for its reorganization. In the course of this almost microscopic examination of the social relations, property has been pronounced to be robbery, communism has been advocated as the remedy for all the social evils, and the autonomy of the individual lost sight of in the attempt to promote the welfare of mankind.

In Germany, on the other hand, under the practical guidance of Schulze-Delitzsch, there have been established up to the year 1865 one hundred and eighty associations, with about ten thousand members, for the supply at wholesale prices of the raw material required by the members of the association in their several trades. These associations consist principally of shoemakers, carpenters, and tailors, and their business amounts to about two million *thalers*[1] annually. There were fifty "magazine" unions, comprising about one thousand members, and doing a business of about five hundred thousand *thalers* annually, having for their object the sale of goods produced by the members of the association in a common store. There were also twenty-six co-operative associations for the production and sale of finished wares on common

[1] Each about seventy-five cents in gold.

account, some of which appear to have been successful, while others have failed to realize the expectation of the members; and as this is the only feature of the Schulze-Delitzsch system which has not proved succesful, it is well to note that all the associations were organized independently of any existing business or capital employed in its conduct. They proceed upon the basis of disassociation from capital, as such, in the management of the business, and although the founder still expects to achieve successful results with associations formed on this basis, it would seem to be too wide a departure from the experience of mankind in all times to dispense with the watchfulness and patient scrutiny with which capital guards itself from destruction. Of co-operative stores there were, in 1865, one hundred and fifty-seven. These are said to have been of slow growth at first, but [they] are now rapidly extending. But the great success of Schulze-Delitzsch has been in the organization of his credit and loan associations, of which in 1865 there were thirteen hundred in existence, with more than three hundred thousand members. These "credit banks," as they are commonly called, are formed by the workmen themselves, who are supposed to be without any capital of their own. The capital of the bank is procured by the subscriptions of the members, payable in instalments, and by loans contracted on the credit of the association. Of course the share capital can only be slowly accumulated, but experience has shown that loans made to the association are quite safe, because each member is absolutely liable for all the debts, and the funds of the bank are loaned to its own members only within limits restricted by the nature of the business to be carried on by the borrower and after a rigid scrutiny of his character. The cardinal rule in the conduct of these banks is to take the minimum of risk and the maximum of responsibility. This report is not the proper place to enter into the history and details of management in these credit banks, but in order to show the progress of the co-operative movement in Europe I append a brief statement of the business of four hundred and ninety-eight of these banks, whose statistics happen to be accessible. These banks had 169,595 members, and the total amount of money advanced to them during the year 1865 was 67,569,903 *thalers*, or, in round numbers, $50,000,000 in gold. The total income of these banks, mostly, of course, in interest paid by borrowers, was 1,401,896 *thalers*, of which 699,558 *thalers* was paid for interest by the banks on money which they had borrowed, and 316,403 *thalers* was absorbed by the expenses of management. The total losses were 20,566 *thalers*, and the net profits were 371,735 *thalers*. The share capital accumulated by these banks amounted to 4,442,879 *thalers*, the borrowed capital amounted to 11,154,579 *thalers*, the savings deposits of the members amounted to 6,502,179 *thalers*, and a reserve fund of 409,679 *thalers* had been accumulated to meet losses. When it is remembered that these banks were started by workmen without any capital and it is observed that the accumulations of capital, deposits, and reserve funds exceed 11,000,000 *thalers,* or $8,000,000 in gold, the beneficent operation of the principle upon which they are founded will be appreciated and some conception may be formed of the wonderful economy which will be introduced into the industry of the world when it becomes the interest of each man not only to produce the best possible result from his own labor but to see that his fellow workman does the same thing. In such a reorganization of industry the eye of the owner will be literally everywhere, and the loss either of time or of material will become almost impossible. This topic of co-operation is introduced here because in the exposition there were constant evidences not merely of its importance, but of its becoming the leading social question of our day and generation. A special prize was constituted in favor "of persons, establishments, or localities which, by an organization of special institutions, have developed a spirit of good feeling between those who co-operate together in the same labors and have secured the material, moral, and intellectual welfare of the workmen." Although Schulze-Delitzsch was not an exhibitor, and no application for this prize was made on his behalf, and the special jury who had this order of recompense in charge lost the great opportunity of making themselves illustrious by voluntarily recognizing the greatest benefactor of the human race in our days, the labors of Schulze-Delitzsch and the success which has attended his system, based as it is upon a profound knowledge of human nature and the laws of social science, will survive the memory of the exposition and erect his monument in the reorganized structure of modern society.

In the United States, strange to say, we lack the legislation, either national or state, which makes it possible to introduce the co-operative system in any of the forms which the experience of Europe has shown to be practicable. In most of the States it is true that there are general laws of incorporation, but these do not meet the case in which a proprietor wishes to divide the profits with his workmen without making them partners, or to give them a voice in the management of the business. It is a subject which demands immediate attention if it is expected to prosecute the iron business, or any other branch of industry, without the perpetual recurrence of strikes. . . .

PRODUCTION OF IRON

Originally the geographical position of the ore and the natural avenues of transportation determined the establishment of iron works when the fuel employed was wood, which was to be found everywhere. But the demands of modern civilization soon outran the narrow bounds imposed by the supply of charcoal, and in our day the controlling element in the production of iron is the possession of mineral coal. And,

throwing out of consideration the moderate quantity of iron still produced by charcoal, the iron business in Europe is found to be developed
substantially in proportion to the quantity of coal possessed by the
respective countries. A glance at the geological map of the world shows
that within the limits of temperature favorable to active industry, the
deposits of coal are widely distributed throughout Great Britain and
the United States. In France there is but a limited area of irregular
formation. In Belgium there is a larger coal field, but in veins of very
moderate size. In Prussia, in the neighborhood of the Rhine, there is a
small but valuable deposit of coal, while in Russia there is a considerable carboniferous area, the ultimate value of which is not yet very well
determined. The productive powers of these several coal fields are now
pressed to limits approaching very nearly, if not quite, to their ultimate
capacity. In Great Britain the production in 1866 reached 101,630,500
tons; in France, between 11,000,000 and 12,000,000 tons; in Belgium
more than 12,000,000 tons; and in Prussia, in 1865, 18,000,000 tons were
produced. The statistics procured at the exposition have enabled me to
construct the following table of the production of iron in the world
in 1866, and there is every reason to believe that the figures given are
substantially correct, as estimates were resorted to in only one or two
cases, and those [were] based upon former official returns:

Countries	*Pig Iron*	*Wrought Iron*
England	4,530,051	3,500,000
France	1,200,320	844,734
Belgium	500,000	400,000
Prussia	800,000	400,000
Austria	312,000	200,000
Sweden	226,676	148,292
Russia	408,000	350,000
Spain	75,000	50,000
Italy	30,000	20,000
Switzerland	15,000	10,000
Zollverein	250,000	200,000
United States	1,175,000	882,000
	9,322,047	7,005,026

Allowing for the production in barbarous countries and something
for the use of scrap iron, it may be stated in round numbers that the
production, and consequently the consumption, of the world has reached
9,500,000 tons of 2,240 pounds each, or 21,280 millions of pounds; so
that if the population of the world has reached 1,000 millions, a consumption of a little over 20 pounds of iron per head. A careful calculation, after allowing for the iron exported, shows that the consumption
per head in England is 189 pounds of iron. The consumption in Belgium has reached about the same limits. The consumption in France is
69½ pounds per head, and in the United States not far from 100 pounds

per head. If the industry of the whole world were as thoroughly developed as it is in Great Britain, the consumption of iron would reach nearly 90,000,000 tons per annum. If brought to the standard of the United States, a little less than 50,000,000 tons per annum would answer; or if to that of France, a little over 30,000,000 tons would be required; figures to be increased further by the steady increase of population in the world.

It will be interesting, therefore, to inquire into the sources of future supply possessed by the nations upon whom this great demand must come.

Sweden possesses exhaustless supplies of the very richest and best kinds of primitive ore, but she has no coal, and a heavy expense for transportation must be incurred in bringing coal and ore together, and, as a general rule, it is found more economical to transport the ore to the coal than the coal to the ore. The limits of the manufacture of iron by wood have long since been reached, and hence Sweden can be looked to only as a source of supply of ore to other countries possessing mineral fuel when their iron mines are too heavily drawn upon.

In Russia, also abounding in immeasurable supplies of ore, there is a possibility, but not much probability, that mineral coal may be developed to an extent sufficient for its own supply of iron. The production of charcoal iron is also capable of some, but not indefinite, extension.

The same remark applies to Austria and the states of the Zollverein. In Italy there is no coal, and hence its rich ores are in the same category as those in Sweden, only far less abundant. Algiers abounds in ore, which has to be transported to the coal. Spain is rich in ore and has a carboniferous formation on its northern borders, but no attempts have been made to render it available for the production of iron. In France the present manufacture of iron is only maintained by the aid of the importation of coal to the extent of over 7,000,000 tons and of 495,000 tons of iron ore in 1867.

In Belgium the size of the coal field, the vertical character of the veins, and their small thickness render it impossible that there should be any very considerable extension of the business, at least if the supply is to endure for any protracted period. Already it is estimated that Belgium produces as much coal as France, two-thirds as much as Prussia, and one-eighth that of Great Britain, out of a coal field only 97 miles in length and 12 miles in breadth at its widest point, and in veins of from 30 inches to 3 feet thick. Belgium is already an importer of ore, and although it is quite evident that it will be the seat of a vigorous and possibly increasing metal industry for years to come, it has no resources adequate for serious competition in the supply of the greatly increased quantities which the world will yet require.

Prussia has a somewhat larger supply of coal than Belgium, and it is remarkably rich in quantity and quality of its iron ores, but it is scarcely possible that in the future she can do more than supply her own wants. Upon England, then, so far as Europe is concerned, still rests the great burden of supplying the world with iron, if the supply is to come from Europe at all. It has been seen that already nearly one-half the total consumption of the world comes from within her borders. In 1866 she was able to furnish 9,665,013 tons of iron ore, and [she] only imported 56,689 tons.

A careful survey of the sources from which her ore is derived leads to the conclusion that in Wales the local supply is not adequate to the present consumption, and large quantities are transported thither from other parts of the kingdom. The natural limits of production have therefore been reached in Wales, although there will probably be a still further extension of the business in that region either with domestic or foreign ores, in consequence of the possession of enormous supplies of admirable coal available for the furnace without coking. The Staffordshire region, by common consent, has reached its culminating point; and a careful consideration of the local supply of carbonaceous ore in Scotland would seem to indicate that not much extension of the business is possible in that region, except at much higher prices than now prevail. The main reliance in Scotland has heretofore been upon its blackband iron ore, "and the development of its iron trade has been co-extensive with the exploration of that famous mineral, furnaces following everywhere in the wake of its discovery. The clay bands are in such small seams, and of such irregular character, that the business would soon languish and be greatly reduced if dependent upon them alone. The thickest and best seam of blackband, commonly called the 'Airdrie,' is now substantially exhausted, and the reliance is on seams of no greater thickness than eight inches. Blackbands are notoriously irregular, and are not found uniform in thickness; for example, the Airdrie blackband occupies but a small portion of the space allotted to it in the Lanarkshire coal-field. A more notable example of caprice of blackband is to be found in the slaty band, which occurs occasionally in patches of irregular thickness, sometimes six inches and sometimes six feet in thickness; but there is always something to mark its position, either a coal or iron stone. Indeed, all the iron stones in all portions of the coal-field are erratic. They are persistent throughout in no field, yet it is a singular fact that we have in all the fields blackband iron stone." This extract from a paper of Ralph Moon, government mining inspector in Scotland, is made for the double purpose of showing how impossible it is that there should be any considerable increase in the annual product of Scotch iron unless foreign ores are brought to utilize the unlimited supplies of admirable coal which exist in that country; but with the further object of giving some information which may be of use in the development of the blackband iron ore which have been recently discovered in Schuylkill County, in Pennsylvania, the value of which to the country can hardly be exaggerated if it should prove to be in quantity and quality equal to its British prototype. An analysis of the best Scotch ore is here annexed—rather out of place, but too valuable as a guide to be dispensed with:

	Raw	*Roasted*
Protoxide of iron	49.82	27.1
Peroxide of iron	....	60.1
Lime	1.67	2.7
Magnesia	2.33	3.8
Alumina	1.52	2.4
Silica	2.40	3.9
Organic matter	7.60	
Moisture	0.32	
Carbonic acid	34.34	
	100.00	100.00
Iron, percentage	38.75	63.1
Specific gravity	2.857	

There still remains upon the east coast of England the great Cleveland region and upon its west coast the Cumberland or red hematite region. The latter is now yielding about 1,400,000 tons of ore per annum, taken from beds of irregular shape and formation, in, or adjacent to, the limestone. There are certainly no signs of exhaustion yet apparent in this wonderful district, but all analogy leads us to doubt the permanency of these irregular beds, formed in pockets in the rocks, without any regular walls to indicate their continuity. Besides, the extremely good quality of this ore and the value of the iron which it produces will always restrict its use to those better purposes for which a high price is paid and naturally withdraws those mines from any competition in the supply of the great mass of iron required by the world for ordinary purposes. Not so, however, with the Cleveland region, where the ores exist in beds of from 8 feet to 15 feet in thickness, in the lias or oolitic formation, extending over a tract of country 40 miles in length and 15 miles in width. This ore is lean and the quality of the iron inferior, but by the application of a high order of skill, a quality is produced sufficiently good for the ordinary purposes of commerce, and at a cost below that of any other locality in the world. The consequence has been that, since the erection of the first blast furnace in 1850, 125 furnaces have been erected and 14 more are now in process of erection; 27 rolling mills and a large number of foundries and iron ship-building yards are in operation, and cities have grown up with a rapidity and to a size that would strike even a western pioneer with surprise. The present production exceeds a million tons per annum, and it is difficult indeed to assign any limits to its future growth. But there is one limitation which applies to the whole question of the production of British iron, and that is, England's ability to supply coal on the scale of consumption already beyond 100,000,000 tons per annum. This question has received the serious attention of the British Association for the Advancement of Science, and Mr. Gladstone, by one of those happy ellipses characteristic of men of genius, has coupled the extinction of the national debt with the exhaustion of the supplies of fuel, evidently acting under the idea that an honest man ought to pay his debts while his capital lasts. It is presumed, however, that there is still margin enough for the addition of the "Alabama claims" to the sum total of indebtedness, without seriously interfering with the means of payment which the coal-fields afford.

So far as the production of iron is concerned, and so long, at least, as any human being now in existence may have an interest in the question, I see no good reason to doubt why England should not maintain her position as the source from which one-half the required amount will be obtained; but beyond this I do not think that she can or will go, from the intrinsic difficulties of producing the required supply of materials and labor, without an enormous increase of cost. There will, therefore, remain a very large deficiency which must be supplied from some other source, and that source can only be the United States of America, for in no other quarter of the globe are the supplies of ore and coal sufficiently large, or so related to each other geographically, as to admit of its production, not merely within reasonable limits of cost, but on any terms whatever.

The position of the coal measures of the United States suggests the idea of a gigantic bowl filled with treasure, the outer rim of which skirts along the Atlantic to the Gulf of Mexico, and thence returning by the plains which lie at the eastern base of the Rocky mountains, passes by the Great Lakes to the place of beginning on the borders of Pennsylvania and New York. The rim of this basin is filled with exhaustless stores of iron ore of every variety and of the best quality. In seeking the natural channels of water communication, whether on the north, east, south or west, the coal must cut this metalliferous rim, and, in its turn, the iron ores may be carried back to the coal, to be used in conjunction with the carboniferous ores, which are quite as abundant in the United States as they are in England, but [which] hitherto have been left unwrought in consequence of the cheaper rate of procuring the richer ores from the rim of the basin. Along the Atlantic slope, in the highland range from the borders of the Hudson River to the State of Georgia, a distance of one thousand miles, is found the great magnetic range, traversing seven entire States in its length and course. Parallel with this in the great limestone valley which lies along the margin of the coal field are the brown hematites, in such quantities at some points, especially in Virginia, Tennessee, and Alabama, as fairly to stagger the imagination. And, finally, in the coal basin is a stratum of red fossiliferous ore, beginning in comparatively thin seam in the state of New York and terminating in the state of Alabama, in a bed of 15 feet in thickness, over which the horseman may ride for more than one hundred miles. Beneath this bed, but still above water level, are to be found the coal seams, exposed upon mountain sides whose flanks are covered with magnificent timber, available either for mining purposes or the manufacture of charcoal iron. Passing westward, in Arkansas and Missouri, is reached that wonderful range of red oxide of iron, which, in mountains rising hundreds of feet above the surface or in beds beneath the soil, culminates at Lake Superior in deposits of ore which excite the wonder of all beholders; and returning thence to the Atlantic slope, in the Adirondacks of New York, is a vast undeveloped region, watered by rivers whose beds are of iron and traversed by mountains whose foundations are laid upon the same material; while in and among the coal beds themselves are found scattered deposits of hematite and fossiliferous ores, which, by their proximity to the coal, have inaugurated the iron industry of our day. Upon these vast treasures the world may draw its supply for centuries to come, and with these the inquirer may rest contented, without further question, for all the coal of the rest of the world might be deposited within this iron rim, and its square miles would not occupy one-quarter of the coal area of the United States.

With such vast possessions of raw material, we are naturally brought to the consideration of the elements which enter into the cost of producing iron in the United States as compared with the other iron-producing countries of the world. And first the distinction must be drawn between the cost determined by the quantity of labor expended in the production of a ton of iron and the cost in money as determined by the price paid for the labor. The former is the absolute and natural cost, and it is the only just standard of comparison between nations if national wealth is defined as the amount of capital in existence plus the amount of labor available for production. The other is the artificial or accidental cost, of which, indeed, we may take advantage in our buying or selling, but which forms no just standard of comparison in estimating the relative cost of production in different countries. There is a difference, familiar to all in the United States, between the cost of articles measured by gold or by currency, which makes it, for the time, easy to understand the difference in cost measured by money or by day's labor.

England, having the largest and most accessible stores of coal and iron ore, can produce a ton of iron with less labor than any other European nation; and hence it will be most profitable to institute the comparison of cost measured by labor, first, with Great Britain. In the

Cleveland region, which is most favorably situated for the cheap production of iron, the cost of producing a ton of pig iron is about forty shillings, which, at the average rate of wages paid around the blast furnace, is equivalent to eleven days' labor—that is to say, the labor of eleven men for one day. It is possible that in one or two works this may be reduced to ten days, but in others it rises to twelve or thirteen. In the United States the cheapest region for the manufacture of pig iron as yet extensively developed is on the Lehigh River, in the state of Pennsylvania, where, taking coal and ore at their actual cost of mining, pig iron is produced at an average cost of $24 per ton, which represents, at the present rate of wages, the labor of about thirteen days. But when the iron business is established along the great valley which extends from Virginia to Alabama, the labor of bringing the coal and ore together will be considerably less than on the Lehigh River, and it is safe to say that there iron can be made in any required quantity, [and] when the avenues of communication are sufficiently opened, with as little labor, to say the least, as it can be produced in the Cleveland region. In France, Belgium, and Prussia, each now requiring a larger expenditure of human labor to produce a ton of iron than is required in England, there are no such possibilities of reduction, because every year their ore is becoming more expensive, and the cost of mining coal will increase more rapidly than in England in consequence of the size and character of the veins. Hence follows the deduction that if France, Belgium, and Germany are to compete with England in the open markets of the world, the competition can only be maintained by the payment to labor of a lower rate of wages; or, to state it in another form, the greater the natural advantages possessed by a country for the production of iron, the larger will be the rate of wages paid to the workman; and this is found to be verified by existing facts.

From the statement published by Schneider & Co., at Le Creusot, it appears that the average rate of wages paid in 1866 was as follows:

	Francs
Ore miners	3.33
Coal miners	3.25
Blast furnaces	2.95
Rolling mill	3.83
Machine shops	3.40
Miscellaneous	3.03

And the average price paid for the whole of the ten thousand workmen employed at this great establishment was 3.45 francs per day.

Unfortunately the rates paid for the specific branches of work are not specified, but at the iron works at Sireuil this information has been procured in detail:

	Francs per day
Common laborers	2.50
Puddlers	8.00
Puddlers' helpers	2.50
Puddle rollers	5.00
Shinglers	5.00
Heaters	7.00
Heaters' helpers	2.50
Finishing rollers	6 to 7
Machinists	3 to 3.50
Blacksmiths	....
Masons	5.00

In South Staffordshire, in 1866, the following rates were paid, as shown by the official returns published by the government:

	Per day			
Common laborers	2s.	6d.	to 3s.	od.
Puddlers	7	6	to 7	10
Puddlers' helpers	2	6	to 2	11
Puddle rollers	9	0		
Heaters	7	0		
Heater helpers	3	6		
Finishing rollers	11	0		
Shinglers	9	0	to 15	0
Machinists	4	0	to 16	0
Blacksmiths	4	0	to 5	0
Masons	7	6	to 8	6

A comparison of these two tables will show that for every franc paid in France, there is more than a shilling paid in England, and this corresponds with the general statement made by M. Schneider to me at Le Creusot. Assuming a little more than a shilling to the franc, 3s. 6d. per day would appear to be the average rate of wages paid in England for labor in iron works of all kinds, skilled and unskilled, and in no part of England does it exceed 4s.

In Belgium, according to Creed & Williams, in the coal mines the following wages are paid:

	Per day			
Common laborers	1s.	6d.	to 2s.	6d.
Loaders of coal	2	6	to 2	11
Wood cutters	2	6	to 2	11
Wood or tree setters	3	1	to 5	0
Miners	2	11	to 4	2
Exceptional men	5	0	to 6	0

At the blast furnaces:

Fillers	1	1	to 2	1
Box fillers	1	4	to 1	8
Common laborers	1	5	to 1	8
Furnace keepers	2	1	to 2	11

In the rolling mill:

Puddlers	4	2	to 5	0
Helpers	2	3	to 3	1
Rollers	4	2	to 5	10
Helpers	3	4	to 4	2
Shearers	1	10	to 2	6
Common laborers	1	5	to 2	1

A comparison of these tables shows that the rate of wages is higher in Great Britain than in Belgium and France, being certainly in the order, and probably nearly in the ratio, of the natural advantages of these countries for the production of iron; and this view is confirmed by the selling price of iron in the respective countries, at the present time, when it is admitted on all hands that there is no profit to the maker.

The price of merchant bar iron at the works is:

	Price per ton	
England	£6 10	
France	8 0	(200 francs)
Belgium	7 0	(175 francs)

The difference between the cost of French iron and Belgian and English, aside from cost of transportation, which is very light, is compensated by the import duty, which, on iron from England and Belgium amounts to 60 francs per ton. Independently of this tariff, which admits of a considerable importation of iron into France, it would not be possible for the iron business to be continued on any considerable scale, for the reason, as will be seen, that the wages are already at the lowest possible point consistent with the maintenance of human life in a condition fit for labor; the average earnings of all the workmen, skilled and unskilled, employed in an iron work being at the rate of 3.45 francs per day, or about 66 cents per day in gold; the great mass, however, of common labor receiving less than 50 cents per day in gold. In order to estimate the purchasing power of this sum, it is necessary to give the prices of the principal articles required for the support of life, and for this purpose I have selected the department in which Le Creusot is situated as the proper locality for comparison, with the rate of wages there paid:

Wheat bread	0.25 francs per lb., equal to 5 cents in gold.
Rye bread	0.20 francs per lb., equal to 4 cents in gold.
Beef	0.65 francs per lb., equal to 13 cents in gold.
Mutton	0.75 francs per lb., equal to 15 cents in gold.
Veal	0.75 francs per lb., equal to 15 cents in gold.
Pork	0.75 francs per lb., equal to 15 cents in gold.
Chickens	1.00 to 2.50 francs, equal to 20 to 50 cents in gold.
Geese	3.00 francs, equal to 60 cents in gold.
Ducks	1.50 to 2.00 francs, equal to 30 to 40 cents in gold.

Butter	1.00 francs per lb., equal to 20 cents in gold.
Dozen eggs	0.50 to 1,00 francs, equal to 10 to 20 cents in gold.
Potatoes	0.50 francs per decalitre, equal to 40 cents per bu.
Ordinary wine	0.40 francs per litre, equal to 5 cents per pint.
Beer	0.25 francs per litre, equal to 3 cents per pint.

House rent is cheap; a small, ordinary, but comfortable house, with a garden, renting for $16 per year in gold. Clothes are also cheap, costing not more than half the price of similar articles in the United States; but fuel is rather dearer on the average. It does not require any very extensive observation in order to verify the obvious conclusion deducible from the above figures, that the general condition of the working classes in France, from a material point of view at least, is simply deplorable. It requires the utmost economy on the part of a laboring man and the united labor of his wife and his children to keep his family in existence; and it is the accepted rule and practice for such a family to have meat but once a week. Any change in this condition of affairs, involving a change in the remuneration paid to the common laborer would put it out of the power of the ironmasters of France to carry on their business in competition with Belgium and England, in the absence of a higher tariff on imports. The existence of the iron business in France, therefore, as a national branch of industry, may be said to rest upon the elementary condition of giving meat once a week only to the great mass of laborers who are engaged in iron production. In Belgium substantially the same state of affairs prevails. In the despatch of Lord Howard de Walden, the British minister at Brussels, to Lord Stanley, dated February 11, 1867, on the subject of Belgian industry, he says: "The characteristics of the Belgian workmen are steadiness and perseverance, combined with great intelligence in working after models; their habits are not so expensive as those of English artificers; their diet is more humble, they consume less meat, and their bread is seldom purely wheaten or white in quality; rye, and the cheaper quality of wheat called 'epeautre,' enter in great proportion into the composition of the loaf; beer and spirits are both lower in price than in England; they seldom use tea, and the chicory root constitutes a very economical and wholesome substitute for coffee. . . . The system of schools for infants from two to seven years, and from seven to twelve years, is very general, and affords great facilities—the children being cared for—to both their parents to occupy themselves in daily service, and by combined industry to ameliorate the condition of their family. In all these respects, therefore, the necessaries of life being the base of wages, the Belgian enjoys advantages over the British workman."

From our American point of view, these "advantages over the British workman" in dispensing with meat and tea and in substituting chicory for coffee and in appropriating the labor of both parents for a mere existence are not so apparent. But we are naturally brought by it to consider the condition of the British laborer.

It has been seen that the natural advantages of Great Britain in the possession of its vast stores of coal afford a fund for the payment of better wages to the laborer in England than on the continent, and the British workman has not been slow to assert his rights to all he can get, and his physical condition is undoubtedly superior to that of his French and Belgian neighbors. If he is not better lodged, he is at least better fed, and in the iron works it is probable that the workmen generally get meat once a day. But, as a general rule, the labor of the women and children is required in order to eke out the subsistence of the family. In Wales women are extensively employed in the works, doing the labor for which a man would be required in America and earning from ten pence to one shilling, three pence, per day, or rather less than half the wages that would be paid to a man for the same labor, which they perform equally well. In Staffordshire and in the north of England and in Scotland women and children are still extensively employed above ground about the mines and around the coal heaps at the mouth of the pits, the substantial result of which is that the labor of the whole family is procured for the sum which would be paid to its male head if he alone labored for the support of the family, of course at a far lower cost in the resulting production of iron than would otherwise be possible. Restraining laws have been enacted in England of late years in regard to women and children, limiting the number of hours during which they may be employed and also providing that they shall not be employed during the night, except in certain specified cases. But if the women and children were altogether withdrawn from those occupations, as they are in the United States, it would not be possible to produce iron except at a considerable advance on its present cost.

Passing from the material to the intellectual condition of the workmen in France and England, the provision for the education of the children is upon a very limited scale indeed, and although there are creditable exceptions in particular localities, mainly due to the enlightened conscience of the proprietors, the great mass of the working classes out of the large cities are deplorably illiterate. In the department of Saône et Loire, where the works of Le Creusot are situated and where the most commendable efforts are being made by Messrs. Schneider & Co. to educate the rising generation, it appears that 36.19 percent of those who were joined in marriage in 1866 could not write their names, and of the conscripts drawn for the army from the same department in the same year, 24.51 percent were unable to read. And the same statistics show that, taken as a whole, in nearly two-thirds of France the number of those who cannot write their names on marriage is between the limits of 30 and 75 percent of the total number. This deplorable state of affairs has, of late, led to the establishment of schools for the instruction of adults, mostly voluntary, upon which there were in attendance during the present year 829,555 adults, of whom 747,002 were men and 82,553 were women. Of 110,503 who could neither read nor write on entering the course in October, 1866, 87,211 had learned to read by the 1st of April, 1867; 12,632 instructors have given their services gratuitously, and the whole movement and the statistics above given prove both the depth of ignorance into which the working classes have been plunged and their earnest desire to emerge from it.

Surprise may be expressed that in view of the inadequate reward for labor in France, there has not been a larger emigration to our own country, where labor is so much better paid. The difficulties arising from the difference in language would of themselves be a great impediment to any extensive emigration movement; but there are impediments of another kind, not generally understood, which tend to prevent any relief to the laboring classes from this source. The law of *livret,* as it is called, is peculiar to France. By its terms every workman is compelled to obtain from the police a kind of passbook, or register, in which his name, age, and occupation are inserted, and which he must show to an employer before being taken into his service; and no employer is permitted to receive into his works any workman upon whose *livret* is not indorsed a full discharge from his previous employer. Provision is also made for the indorsement upon the *livret* of any indebtedness which may be due from the workman to the employer, and his debt therefore follows the workman as a mortgage upon his labor from place to place. Although in express terms there is nothing in the law which would warrant the employer in withholding an indorsement on the *livret,* yet in practice it is a restraint on his freedom of action to such an extent that workmen employed in the large works usually remain there permanently, so that there is but little change and no opportunity whatever for practical combination in strikes and turnouts. . . .

The moral condition of men is so dependent upon their physical and mental status that it is probably unnecessary for me to enlarge upon the obvious conclusions that might be inferred from the facts above recorded; but the conviction in my own mind was so profound, after a very careful survey of the whole field, that I deemed it my duty to accept an invitation to testify before the Trades Union Commission in England, in the hope that a full discussion of the physical and moral elements involved in the organization of industry would result in the ultimate elevation of the working classes of Europe to such a standard, at least, as would render the conditions of competition between our own country and Europe more just and equitable. It is quite evident that in the effort to produce cheap commodities and to undersell each other in the markets of the world, the rightful claims of humanity have been disregarded to such an extent that the reorganization of labor, in its relation to capital is felt by all thoughtful men to be an imperative necessity.

It cannot be that the aim of society is only to produce riches. There must be moral limits within which the production of wealth is to be carried on, and these limits have been and are being so obviously transgressed that a spirit of discontent pervades the entire industrial world; and in the very countries where this competition has been pressed to its utmost limits capital has ceased to become remunerative, although humanity itself has been sacrificed to its demands. The evidence which I gave before the Trades Union Commission was delivered in this spirit of deep concern for the welfare of the working classes; and inasmuch as a few incidental sentences repeating statements which had been made to me in regard to the Pittsburgh strike, but of no consequence in reference to the main question, were seized upon by the London *Times* as a groundwork for characteristic unfavorable comment on American institutions, and some feeling was excited among the working men in the United States in reference to these misrepresentations, against which, it will be seen, I took occasion to protest on my second hearing before the commissioners, long in advance of any knowledge on my part of the effect produced by them at home, it is deemed proper to state that the evidence so given, in Europe at least, was universally regarded as an appeal in behalf of the working classes, not in defense of any violation on their part of the fundamental principles of social science, but in assertion of their just rights to education, domestic happiness, and adequate remuneration for labor.

There are some statements made thereon of no great importance in themselves, based upon information derived from other parties on whom I had reason to rely, which may have been erroneous; but in all such cases, where I did not speak of my own knowledge I expressly so stated, and this was particularly the case in regard to the Pittsburgh strike, where the evidence shows that I expressly disclaimed personal knowledge of the facts; but I desire now to state that the information was derived from a resident of Pittsburgh in whom I had reason to feel entire confidence. In my second evidence before the commission, it will be seen that I took occasion to correct some errors of this kind, having in the meantime received more correct information. There are also some replies bearing on the nationality of workmen, elicited in answer to questions over which I had no control; but in so far as they may appear to be invidious to any one nation, there is no real cause for complaint when the answer is understood. For example, the statement that the Irish are rarely first-class puddlers was made as a matter of fact in nowise depending on the land of their birth, but because they do not begin to learn the business until they arrive in America, full grown adults, whereas in England the education of the puddler begins in boyhood and is pursued for many years before he takes a furnace. The same answer would, therefore, have been given to the same question, if asked with reference to the natives of any other country who had not learned the business from boyhood.

But if in comparison with the ample provision made in our country for the education of the masses the arrangements in France and England are upon a meager scale, the opportunities for scientific and technical instruction, in France especially, are of a far more complete and generous character. For the governing classes or for those who, rising out of the lower ranks, are educated to fill positions of trust and responsibility, there exist a series of educational establishments of so thorough a course in their respective departments as to exhaust all that experience and science can do for the preparation of engineers and conductors of industry. The Ecole Centrale des Arts et Manufactures, at Paris, the Conservatoire Impériale des Arts et Métiers, several large agricultural schools, L'Ecole Impériale des Ponts et Chausées, L'Ecole Impériale des Mines, L'Ecole Impériale de Commerce à Paris, the three schools des Arts et Métiers at Chalons, Aix, and Angiers, the School of Mines at St. Etienne, the School of Watchmaking at Cluses, of the Mining Classes at Alais, the Naval School at Marseilles, are all sustained by the government in the interests of industry and commerce and give to French industry that intelligence, science, and skill which, in the exposition, extorted universal admiration and the general confession that its products, even in machinery and metals, were up to the highest standard of excellence. Similar schools in the United States ought to be the fruit of the great endowment of lands given to the states by Congress for the establishment of institutions designed to teach mechanical and agricultural science and art; but it is to be regretted that, at the present time, the application of this grant has not been so directed as to secure such a result, and we must console ourselves with the reflection that if we are deficient in the higher education necessary for the best industrial development, we have in a measure supplied its place by a general diffusion of knowledge, which, evoking the ingenuity and individuality of each workman, has rendered it less necessary than in countries where the masses are in ignorance. But it cannot be disputed that this individuality and ingenuity in our American character will be more valuable and powerful when directed by the highest order of intelligence and thoroughly trained scientific leaders.

It is obvious that the abnormal rates for labor which we have been considering cannot prevail in any one branch of industry alone, but must extend to all, as labor, like water, must seek a general level in each community governed by the same laws and subjected to the same influences. All articles of commerce are, therefore, produced below their

normal cost—that is, the cost which would be possible if the fundamental laws of humanity were not violated in the employment of women
and children and the payment of a rate of wages to the common laborer
inadequate for the proper support and culture of the family. In those
commodities which require in the United States more human labor for
their production than is necessary in Europe, where labor is so inade-
quately paid, we have, perhaps, no other interest than a general concern
in the welfare of the human race; but so far as iron is concerned, from
the fact that we can produce it with as little consumption of human
labor as any other nation in the world, the case is different, because
there is no absolute loss of wealth and no misapplied power in its production; and the only question to be discussed is, whether it shall be
taken out of the general category of manufactures not so favorably
placed as to the cost of production and by positive legislation placed
in the same condition as it would have occupied with reference to
foreign competition if the rate of wages in other countries had never
been reduced below their normal standard. We have seen that the cost
of making iron in England, Belgium, and France, at the present time,
varies from £6 10s. to £8 per ton, and £1 additional suffices to pay its
cost of transportation to the seaboard of the United States. At these
ports American iron cannot possibly be delivered at a less cost than
$60 in gold, against $40 in gold for the foreign article, and the entire
difference consists in the higher wages and not in the larger quantity
of labor required for its production in the United States, where the
physical, mental, and moral condition of the working classes occupy a
totally different standard from their European confrères, and where the
wages cannot be reduced without violating our sense of the just demands
of human nature. At the same time it is to be observed that the business
is so far overdone in Europe that no profit can be realized by the
capitalist, except in special cases, for which adequate reasons can be
given. The actual remedy for this over-production would be to withdraw the women and children, as we do, from this class of industry,
whereby the production must be reduced, the rate of wages raised, the
cost and the selling price increased, capital become remunerative, and
the ability to procure iron, made cheap by its adulteration with the
violated laws of humanity, be forever extinguished. To what result the
general discussion which this subject is now receiving in Europe will
lead it is not easy to decide; but it is a curious phenomenon to listen
in France to the loud complaints which are made against the competition of Belgium in the manufacture of iron, and stranger still in England to the same complaint and the broad declaration that it will not
be possible to do anything for the education and elevation of the
working classes without exposing their manufacturers to ruin in consequence of the competition with the worse-paid and worse-fed labor of

Belgium. The truth is that the whole system is false, and now, when pressed by the energy, enterprise, and competition of the age to its legitimate results, humanity is in rebellion, and there is a general cry from all classes, laborers, employers, philanthropists, philosophers, and statesmen alike, for relief. The necessity for this relief becomes painfully apparent when the poor-law returns made in England are carefully examined, from which it is evident that there is an army of paupers pressing upon the occupations of the common laborer and striving to push him over the almost insensible line which divides these two classes from each other. It is not possible that the laborer should receive more than bare subsistence wages, and there can be no relief for his patient suffering so long as there are thousands who, unable to earn any wages at all, stand ready to fill up every gap in the ranks of industry; and to the honest laborer himself, standing on the edge of this line over which he is liable at any moment to be forced into the ranks of pauperism, the anxiety and miserable state of uncertainty for himself and his family must be fatal to all rational happiness and is well calculated to drive him into vicious indulgences and temporary excesses whenever a transient opportunity is afforded, as a momentary relief from a condition of hopeless misery.

From the returns made to the British Parliament as to pauperism in the month of September, A. D. 1867, it appears that out of a population of 19,886,104, dwelling in the area for which the returns are made, 872,620 persons were on the list of paupers supported by public charity, of which number 129,689 were in the workhouses and 738,726 were relieved in their own houses. This latter portion constitutes the army which substantially regulates the rate of wages for labor, as they are ready, to a greater or less extent, to take any vacant place which may offer itself. And this state of the case exists not in mid-winter, but just after the close of the harvest, and the returns show that the evil is an advancing one, as there is an increase of 27,521, or 3.3 percent, in 1867 over the corresponding week in 1866. . . .

By another parliamentary return it appears that the average number of scholars attendant upon the schools under government inspection in the year 1866 was 871,309 in England and Wales, showing this suggestive fact, that the paupers receiving public relief and the children receiving instruction in schools aided by the public funds were about equal in number. This statement alone, if other evidence were lacking, would serve to prove that the working classes of Great Britain have not yet achieved the position in point of education and social comfort to which humanity is entitled. Nor can it be alleged that this is due to any deficiency in the resources provided by nature for the reward of industry. The coal and iron-ore mines of England afford the most magnificent fund to be found on the face of the globe for the abundant remunera-

tion of the capital and labor engaged in their development, and every
class in the community, except the operatives themselves, have enjoyed
a bountiful return for their interest in this national endowment. The
landowner has been largely paid, not only by the royalties derived
from the minerals, but in the enormous increase in the value of the soil
by the rapid growth of population engaged directly and indirectly in
the manufactures based on their consumption. The capital invested in
manufactures in Great Britain has, in the main, reaped a most abundant
reward, and the general result has been an accumulation of capital in
the hands of the higher and middle classes unequalled in the history
of mankind.

That the working classes have not been equally well rewarded is
due simply to the improvident and even reckless manner in which these
great natural resources have been employed, giving rise to a competition
unlimited by any other consideration than the immediate profit to be
derived by the capital invested in the business. Of course, the less the
rate of wages, the longer the number of hours of work to be got from
the laborer, the greater the number of women and children that could
be employed, the lower will be the cost of the product, and the more
decided the ability to undersell all foreign competitors in the markets
of the world. Hence, in the absence of restraining laws and an enlightened conscience on the part of the operators and manufacturers, and in
the presence of a large population in a restricted area, governed in the
interests of special classes, it was inevitable that the superior natural
resources of Great Britain should be used, as they have been, rather to
crush out foreign competition than to elevate the working classes; and
this very attempt to undersell foreign nations in their own markets
necessarily involved the lowest possible rate of wages, in those countries,
consistent with mere existence; reacting, in turn, upon the English labor
market and compelling lower rates of wages than would otherwise have
been required, if the aim of the nation had been directed to the payment
of the largest possible compensation to its own working classes rather
than to the control of the markets of the world even at the expense of
humanity itself. The possession of these wonderful deposits of coal and
iron as a fund for the payment of adequate wages to labor in Great
Britain is equivalent to our virgin soil in the United States, enabling
both nations to pay the highest possible rate of wages consistent with
the conservation of capital; but this advantage in Great Britain has been
deliberately and recklessly thrown away by a competition between the
English manufacturers themselves, resulting in over-production and compelling a steady pressure upon the wages of labor in order to keep up
the production and secure larger consumption by lower prices for the
commodities. It is a mistake to suppose that this reduction in price has
been caused by the competition of foreign nations with Great Britain,

for we have seen that France cannot produce enough iron for its own consumption and that Belgium turns out only one-tenth as much iron as Great Britain, and is therefore governed as to price solely by the rate at which Great Britain is willing and able to furnish the remaining nine-tenths. If it were possible for Belgium to alter the ratio of production, she might in the long run make the price for the total product; but it is simply ridiculous to apprehend, in view of the natural resources of the two countries, that any such change can ever be effected.

The most interesting industrial and social question of the age is, therefore, the policy which will be pursued by Great Britain in the administration of its mines of coal and iron. And the royal commission, now making an official inquiry into the exhaustion of the coal fields, will stop far short of the real scope of the question if it fails to investigate whether by wise and suitable regulations the annual product of coal cannot be so regulated as to secure a far better remuneration to the labor engaged in its production than it has heretofore received. I am perfectly aware that such regulations must necessarily be restrictive in their character, and, at the first glance, will appear to be at war with the commercial policy of free trade advocated in Great Britain. Very little reflection, however, is required to show that by far the greater portion of the legislation of all enlightened nations is necessarily of a protective and restrictive character; and at this day no enlightened statesman would advocate the deliberate sacrifice of local advantages for the sake of any mere abstract theory, which might be ever so well founded in reason, but fails to be applicable in the presence of exceptionable facts and resources. The protection of life, liberty, property, and social order, the title to lands and personal property, rest entirely upon protective laws; and all provisions for the protection of capital and health and the establishment of police are so many restraints upon the natural freedom of the individual; and surely legislation looking to the wisest possible use of national resources and the prevention of the waste or misapplication of the raw material upon which the structure of the national industry and prosperity and the welfare of the working classes rest is not merely a natural but a necessary step in the progress of industry and the development of civilization.

In no country in the world are so many proofs of the wisdom of this course to be found as in the history of British legislation in reference to the working classes during the last thirty-five years. The repeal of the corn laws was a measure of eminent protection to the working classes, relieving them of the taxes imposed upon food for the benefit of the landowner, and of the landowner alone; because the condition of the agricultural laborer could not be made worse, but could only be improved by any change. The series of laws regulating the employment of women and children in factories and mines are not merely highly restrictive, but by common consent have produced the happiest results on the moral and physical condition of the working classes. The laws recognizing the legal existence of friendly societies; for the encouragement of building associations; [for] the conversion of the post offices into savings banks for the working classes; for the granting of annuities and life assurance guaranteed by the government to the working classes, on the payment of small periodical instalments; for the encouragement of co-operative stores and associations; for "partnerships of industry" in which the workman is allowed to have an interest in the profits of the business without becoming liable as a partner for the debts; the statutes authorizing the establishment of free reading rooms, libraries, and museums by a vote of the rate-payers in any borough, town, or city, constitute a course of wise legislation unmistakably protective, restrictive, and enabling; persistently advocated and successfully established by the most sagacious, liberal, and philanthropic statesmen of the present age and resulting in so marked an improvement in the condition of the working classes, accompanied with so decided an advance in the rate of wages that it is scarcely possible longer to deny that the first step toward securing to the working classes an adequate reward for their labor is such legislation as protects them from the evils which seem to be inseparable from the spirit of unrestrained competition between nations and between men, which experience has shown to result in the utter disregard of the moral and physical condition and social welfare of the working classes, unless regulated by positive legal enactment.[1]

This wise course of legislation may be said to be but fairly initiated in England, but the intelligent observer cannot fail to be convinced that it will be persisted in until all special privileges which interfere with the normal distribution of the proceeds of labor and capital will be removed. The effect will undoubtedly be a rise in wages, [which is] already apparent; and this result is unquestionably a matter of deep concern to the manufacturers and capitalists of Great Britain, who fear that it will deprive them of their ability to control the markets of the world, as they now do, with the products of their mills. But there is in reality no just ground for this apprehension. The distribution between capital and labor may, and must, undoubtedly, be changed, but the aggregate income will not on the average of years be reduced, because the control of the fuel of the world, that is to say, of the condensed power which has been stored up by Divine Providence for its use, is in the hands of the Anglo-Saxon race in Europe and America, who alone have reduced

[1] Readers desirous to investigate the effect of protective, restrictive and enabling legislation on the condition of the working classes, are referred to the very able treatise on "The Progress of the Working Classes, 1832-1867," by I. M. Ludlow and Lloyd Jones, published by Alexander Strahan, London, 1867. [Hewitt's note.]

prices by a competition with other nations, impossible but for the possession of the mineral fuel in such vast quantities and for the violation of the natural laws which should govern the employment and the compensation of labor. The transition to a more equitable basis of production will simply enable other countries, who, as we have seen, cannot do more than supply themselves with coal and iron, to raise their laboring classes out of a condition still more deplorable than exists in England, without by any possibility enabling them to keep up any effective competition in the markets of the world, for the supply of the iron required for the future progress, development and civilization of mankind. A rise in wages in England, therefore, will not only be a blessing to the workmen of that favored country, relieving it of pauperism, so far as it may be possible to extinguish poverty at all, but will be a harbinger of light to the unpaid, unfed, and unhappy operatives throughout all lands in which human industry is now weighed down by the effects of British competition, based upon superior natural resources. And to me it is a suggestive and for humanity an encouraging fact, that the agitation and restlessness which characterize the working classes of our age are mostly apparent in Great Britain and the United States, who are not only so far in advance of all other countries in the possession of natural industrial resources, but who from the habit of free discussion and prompt obedience to the popular voice (the result of constitutional government long in force), will be most ready to accept the conclusions deduced by the stern logic of experience and facts, and [to] modify their legislation so as to conform to the just demands of humanity whenever the proper course is discovered and made plain to the common sense of the people.

When by reason of such legislation the wages of labor in Great Britain have reached their normal condition there will no longer be any occasion for us to consider the question of protective or prohibitory tariffs; but in the meantime, to the people of the United States, who in consequence of the possession of a virgin soil have in comparison with their European neighbors suffered but little from violations of the fundamental principles of social science, two courses are open. We can either take advantage of the unnaturally cheap rate at which our wants can and will be supplied from abroad, while the present system lasts, and by throwing open our ports to foreign iron purchase foreign labor at a far lower rate than we are willing to sell our own, and thus abandon a business which so long as our present rates of wages are maintained cannot be conducted in the United States even without profit, or we can impose such a duty on foreign iron as will make up for the difference in the amount of wages paid for making a ton of iron in Europe or in this country, less the expense of transportation.

The decision of this question is mainly of interest to the working classes themselves and to the great body of the farmers, because if the iron business is abandoned for the present in the United States, the labor now employed in it must in the main take to the soil, and a larger yield of agricultural products [will] be insured. The surplus so produced must seek its market in the open marts of the world, and the mouths that would have been fed on this side of the Atlantic will simply be fed elsewhere, although not so abundantly and so generously. But it must be remembered that whatever may be the price of bread in Europe at the works where the iron will be made will be the price which the same operatives could afford to pay if the iron works had been placed where the grain is grown, and that the cost of transportation thence is just so much deducted from the price which the farmer would have received if the grain had been consumed at home.

The question is one, also, which more concerns the West than the East, because the loss caused by transportation from the West is greater; and the final decision of this great question should therefore be well considered, especially with reference to the point whether the saving produced by the purchase of cheap iron and other articles will compensate for the loss entailed by the transportation of the grain.

It forms no part of the purpose of this report to deduce any conclusion on this subject, but only to state the facts in such form as will enable intelligent legislation to be enacted, keeping in view the interests of all classes and above all the considerations of independence essential to the dignity of the American republic and the welfare of mankind. But in the discussion of this question, and in the legislation which may be proposed to meet the best interests of the nation in regard to a supply of iron and steel, the broad distinction which exists between the nature of the question in Europe and the United States must never be lost sight of. On the continent, protective duties on iron are imposed in order to counterbalance the superior natural resources and advantages of Great Britain for the production of iron, and not to secure higher wages to the laborer; whereas, in the United States, protective duties, if imposed at all, are not necessary because our natural advantages for making iron are inferior in any particular to those of Great Britain, but simply because the wages of labor are fixed upon a more just and liberal scale to the workmen in the first instance, and by the law of equivalents to the whole industrial force engaged in the great work of production, of whatever form and nature.

If the facts and suggestions contained in this report, the result of half a year of careful study of the exposition and the knowledge which it enabled me to acquire in reference to the social condition of the working classes in Europe shall in any way aid Congress in arriving at a judicious solution of these grave questions, involving so many and such varied interests, and if, as I hope, the terrible evils of pauperism shall be even for a time, and possibly forever, averted from our own country by legislation based upon sound, social, and economical principles, I shall cease to regret the strange and cruel misrepresentations to which I have been subjected among the working classes, in whose behalf mainly the duty confided to me was undertaken.

Whatever policy may be finally adopted with reference to American industry, it is a source of profound satisfaction, and should be a subject of general congratulation, that a careful survey of the natural resources of those nations who stand in the van of European progress and civilization justifies the declaration that the great problem of democratic institutions is being solved in a land having in addition to a fruitful soil the largest and best supplies of the fundamental elements upon which industry, progress, and civilization are based; and that there is good reason to hope that here it may be shown how wealth may be created without the degradation of any class which labors for its production, the only advantage (if advantage it may be termed) possessed by Europe over the United States for the cheap production of iron and steel being in the lower and inadequate rate of wages which there prevails, and not in any superior natural resources in ore, fuel, or geographical position.

A Century of American Mining and Metallurgy

PRESIDENTIAL ADDRESS BEFORE THE AMERICAN INSTITUTE OF
MINING ENGINEERS, PHILADELPHIA, JULY 20, 1876 [1]

[*The Centennial Exhibition in Philadelphia in 1876 brought many
foreign ironmasters, metallurgists, and mining engineers to the
United States. Desiring some man of public reputation to act in
receiving them, the American Institute of Mining Engineers elected
Hewitt—then a member of Congress and also Democratic National
Chairman—its president. He took unusual pains with his address.
In his report on the Paris Exposition he had given a thorough,
detailed, and somewhat technical account of the existing state of
the iron and steel industry where most advanced; now he supplemented it by an historical account of mining and metal working
in the United States since the days of the Red Men and the first
colonists. Much more thorough investigative work has since been
done on the subject. But Hewitt's rapid coup d'œil nevertheless
has interest for his appraisal of the most important steps in the
exploitation of American mineral resources. Once more he turned,
in closing, to the social problems connected with the rise of large-
scale industry. It was well known at the time that the great hard-coal
companies connected with the anthracite railroads had been making
exorbitant gains. They could well afford to distribute part of their
profits in social-welfare work; and Hewitt made the interesting
suggestion that they set industry an object lesson by establishing
departments to ameliorate the moral, social, and physical lot of
their employees. He was anxious to impress capital with a sense of
its responsibility for the steady betterment of the position of labor.
His thinking on this subject was shortly to find a more elaborate
exposition.*]

In the great charter of King James, by which, in 1606, the right
to explore and settle the North American continent from the thirty-
fourth to the forty-fifth parallel was granted to the London and Plym-
outh companies, it was provided that one-fifth of the gold and silver
and one-fifteenth of the copper which might be discovered should belong
to the crown. One of the earliest expeditions of Captain John Smith,

1 Published by the Institute in pamphlet form.

in Virginia, was the exploration of the Chickahominy River, in the hope that it might constitute a waterway to the Pacific Ocean; and one of the next events in the history of the same colony was a mining excitement, such as would be called in our California tongue a "stampede," caused by the supposed discovery of gold; in which, fortunately, John Smith did not avail himself of his official position to take "stock." It is a curious circumstance that gold really occurs in that region, though the glittering dust of which a shipload was sent by the deluded colonists to the jewelers of London proved to be but mica or iron pyrites; and it seems probable (albeit this suggestion is not based upon any explicit record known to me) that the presence of gold among the Indians and the discovery of specimens of the quartz or slates of Virginia containing visible particles of it, gave rise to the general excitement under the influence of which, without further tests of value, a large amount of worthless material was collected, to the neglect of necessary and profitable industry. From this point of view the Jamestown mining fever was the prototype of many that have since occurred—all of which may be summed up in the general expression, that the mine "did not pan out according to the samples."

A more promising industry was inaugurated at the same time by the sending of a quantity of iron ore from Jamestown to England in 1608. This ore, smelted in England, yielded 17 tons of metal, probably the first pig iron ever made from North American ore. In 1620 a hundred and fifty skilled workmen were sent to the colony to erect iron works; and it is said that a fund subscribed for the education of the colonists and Indians was invested in this enterprise as a safe and sure means of increase. But in 1622 an Indian massacre broke up the enterprise; and both the manufacture of iron and the education of citizens and Indians have been obliged, ever since, to rely upon other sources of support.

For an interesting collection of facts relative to the beginnings of the iron industry of the American colonies, I refer you to the forthcoming work on that subject, by our fellow-member, Mr. John B. Pearse, to whose courtesy I am indebted for the opportunity to consult the advance sheets of a portion of the book.[1]

According to the statement of Colonel Spotswood, quoted by Mr. Pearse, it appears that, previous to 1724 neither New England, Pennsylvania, nor Virginia possessed blast furnaces. Their product of iron was from bloomeries only. According to Professor Hodge, quoted by Professor Whitney, however, a furnace was built at Pembroke, Mass., in 1702; and another authority states that in 1721 New England possessed 6

---

[1] The reference is to *A Concise History of the Iron Manufacture of the American Colonies up to the Revolution, and of Pennsylvania till the Present Time*, published by the chemist John B. Pearse in 1876.

furnaces and 19 forges. In 1719 was passed the famous resolution of the British House of Commons, "that the erection of manufactories in the colonies tended to lessen their dependency on Great Britain." Only the earnest protest of the colonial agents prevented the prohibition at that time of the American iron manufacture. The next thirty years witnessed two instructive contests. The first was that of the colonial with the domestic pig iron manufacture—a competition in which America was favored by the abundance of her vegetable fuel (the employment of mineral coal in iron making not having yet found introduction) in comparison with the rapidly waning forests of Great Britain. The British manufacture being protected by heavy duties on colonial pig iron, the latter began to be more and more worked up into bar iron, nails, steel, and so forth, at home; and this brought on a new competition with the British manufacturers of these articles. In 1750 a further legislative attempt to regulate this trade was made by Parliament, which decreed the admission of colonial pig iron duty free, but prohibited the erection in America of slitting, rolling, or plating mills, or steel furnaces, ordering that all new ones thereafter built should be suppressed as "nuisances."

It will be recollected that arbitrary acts of this kind for the destruction of our infant manufactures were among the grievances cited in the Declaration of Independence. The extent of the American iron manufacture during the ante-Revolutionary period can be inferred only from scanty records of exports. These, beginning in 1717 with 3 tons, had increased, in 1750, to about 3,000 tons; in 1765 the total is reported at 4,342 tons; and in 1771 at 7,525 tons, the maximum annual export. The outbreak of the war of course put an end to exportation and caused a great demand for war material which occupied and rapidly extended the means of manufacture possessed by the country. The expanded iron industry suffered a severe collapse when at the close of the war not only this demand ceased but the reopened ports admitted large quantities of foreign iron—the successful employment of mineral coal, the steam engine and puddling having by that time laid the foundation of English supremacy in the iron manufacture.

The earliest copper-mining company of which we find any record—according to Professor Whitney in his excellent work on the metallic wealth of the United States [1] the earliest incorporated mining company of any kind—was chartered in 1709 to work the Simsbury mines at Granby, Conn. These mines were abandoned in the middle of the eighteenth century, afterward bought by the state of Connecticut and used as a prison for sixty years. Mining was resumed in them about 1830, and

---

[1] Hewitt refers to *The Metallic Wealth of the United States Described and Compared with that of Other Countries,* by the eminent geologist Josiah Dwight Whitney (1854).

after a few years they were again abandoned. The ores were mostly shipped to England and seem to have been lean. The deposit belongs to the class of irregular bunches, nodules, seams, or limited beds, in the New Red Sandstone, near its junction with trap. This formation was the scene in New Jersey, also, of early mining activity. The Schuyler mine, near Belleville, on the Passaic, was discovered about 1719 and proved more profitable to its owners before the Revolution than it ever has been since that time to any of the series of individuals and companies that have expended large sums in its development. In fact, the chief blessing conferred upon mankind by the Schuyler mine arises from the circumstance that the first steam engine ever built wholly in America was constructed in 1793–94 at the small machine shop attached to the smelting works at Belleville, my father being the pattern maker in the party of mechanics sent out by Boulton & Watt for the purpose of erecting an engine for the Philadelphia Water-Works in Centre Square. In 1751 a copper mine was opened near New Brunswick; and the Bridgewater mine, near Somerville, was operated previous to the Revolution, though even then, it is said, with much loss of capital. New Jersey's record in copper mining is not a cheerful one; but her unsurpassed ranges of iron ores may well console her. Betrayed by the treachery of Triassic and trap, she can flee to the shelter of the crystalline schists. Pennsylvania was not without her copper mining in the colonial period, the Gap mine, in Lancaster County, having been opened in 1732.

Already during the colonial period the first red gleams of the future glory of the Lake Superior mines had appeared. The intrepid Jesuit fathers, Marquette and others, who penetrated the wilderness from Acadia to the Gulf, to carry both the Cross of their religion and the Lilies of their Sovereign, had made extensive explorations on the Upper Peninsula and published glowing accounts of the abundance of copper, to which later travelers added legends of gold and precious stones. Before them, the Indian tribes, whose stone tools now furnish subjects of inquiry to the archeologist, had wrought rudely upon the deposits which nature had left in a condition so exceptionally pure as not to need, for the production of limited amounts of metal, the intervention of metallurgical processes. The first recorded mining operations on the part of white men were those of Alexander Henry, near the Forks of the Ontonagon, in 1771. As is well known, however, the active development of this region dates from the publication of Houghton's *Geological Report*, in 1841, and the extinguishment of the Chippewa title by the treaty of 1843.

Lead mining in this country may also claim an ancient origin— as we reckon antiquity. As early as 1651, Governor John Winthrop received his famous license to work any mines of "lead, copper, or tin, or any minerals as antimony, vitriol, black-lead, alum, salt, salt-springs, or any other the like," and "to enjoy forever said mines, with the lands, woods, timber, and water within two or three miles of said mines." As he received also a special grant of mines or minerals in the neighborhood of Middletown, Conn., it is not unlikely that the old Middletown silver-lead mine, the date of the discovery of which is not precisely known, was opened by him or his successors. The nickel and cobalt mines near Chester, in Connecticut, once held to be very promising deposits, are also believed to have been originally worked by Governor Winthrop; but nickel was not valuable in those days; and the lead and copper in these ores do not seem to have been abundant. Unfortunately, now that nickel and cobalt are so valuable as to repay amply the cost of extracting them when they are present in a small percentage only, these Connecticut ores no longer correspond (if indeed they ever did) to the analysis and accounts formerly given as to their niccoliferous character.

The old Southampton silver-lead mine, in Massachusetts, well known to mineralogists, was commenced in 1765, by Connecticut adventurers; but its operations were suspended by the Revolutionary War. Lead mines in Columbia and Dutchess Counties, N. Y., were also worked at an early period; and, no doubt, all over the country occupied or controlled during the war by the American forces, there were small and desultory surface operations furnishing lead for the use of the army.

The Indians inhabiting the Mississippi Valley before the advent of the whites probably did not understand the metallurgy of lead. Galena has been found in the Western mounds, but, it is said, no lead. In 1700 and 1701 Père Le Sueur made his famous voyage up the Mississippi, discovering, as he claimed, many lead mines. Lead mining was begun in Missouri in 1720, while that country belonged to France, and under the patent granted to Law's famous Mississippi Company. Mine la Motte, named after a mineralogist who came over with Renault, the superintendent, was one of the first discoveries. It has been in operation at intervals ever since and is now successfully managed by Mr. Cogswell, a member of our Institute, who may, I think, truthfully claim that he has charge of the oldest mining enterprise still active in the United States. The ores yield a small percentage of nickel and cobalt, as well as lead.

It was in 1788 that Dubuque obtained from the Indians the grant under which he mined until the year of his death, where the city now stands which bears his name. The land was subsequently ceded to the United States by the Indians, and the representatives of Dubuque were forcibly ejected.

Such, then, was the condition of our mining industry at the commencement of our national existence. We occupied but a strip of territory on the Atlantic; and even in that limited area we had scarcely learned the nature and extent of the mineral resources to be utilized.

Anthracite and petroleum, quicksilver and zinc, were unknown as treasures within our reach. The rapid extension of possession, government, population, and industry over plains and mountains to the Pacific which has been effected in a hundred years is but the type of a conquest and progress which has advanced with equal rapidity in every department of human labor, and nowhere more notably than in the departments of mining and metallurgy. The tables which Dr. Raymond has prepared and which will be printed to accompany these remarks [pages 110-11], show that this country has produced during the century ending with 1875, of gold, about 66,680,000 troy ounces, worth about $1,332,700,000; of silver, about 201,300,000 troy ounces, worth about $261,450,000; of quicksilver, 840,000 flasks, or 64,206,000 pounds avoirdupois; of copper, 200,000 tons; of lead, 855,000 tons; of pig iron, 40,000,000 tons; of anthracite coal, 351,521,423 tons (the ton in all these cases being 2,240 pounds avoirdupois); and of petroleum, 76,594,600 barrels. The product of these leading industries for the year 1875 were: gold, $33,400,000; silver, $41,400,000; quicksilver, 53,706 flasks; copper, 15,625 tons; lead, 53,000 tons; pig iron, 2,108,554 tons; zinc, about 15,000 tons; anthracite, 20,643,509 tons; bituminous coal, about 26,000 tons; petroleum, 8,787,506 barrels.

In order that a clear idea may be formed as to the relative position now held by the United States in the world of mining and metallurgy, I have selected the production of coal, which is the main reliance for power of all organized industry, and of iron, which is the chief agent of civilization, as the basis of comparison with other nations, using, so far as coal is concerned, the figures given in the 42d *Annual Report* of the Philadelphia Board of Trade, for the year 1873.

	Tons	Percent
Great Britain	127,016,747	46.4
United States	50,512,000	18.4
Germany	45,335,741	16.5
France	17,400,000	6.4
Belgium	17,000,000	6.2
Austria and Hungary	11,000,000	4.0
Russia	1,200,000	0.5
Spain	570,000	0.2
Portugal	18,000	...
Nova Scotia	1,051,567	0.4
Australia	1,000,000	0.4
India	500,000	0.2
Other countries	1,000,000	0.4
Total	273,604,055	100.0

The following estimate, in round numbers, of the world's present production of iron is taken from various sources and may be considered approximately correct. The figures for Great Britain and France are those of 1874, and the product of the United States for the same year has been taken. For other countries the estimates are principally for 1871 or 1872, except Austria and Hungary, for which the official returns for 1873 have been taken. The quantities are given in tons of 2,240 pounds.

	Tons	Percentage
Great Britain	5,991,000	45.2
United States	2,401,000	18.1
Germany	1,600,000	12.1
France	1,360,000	10.3
Belgium	570,000	4.3
Austria and Hungary	365,000	2.7
Russia	360,000	2.7
Sweden and Norway	306,000	2.3
Italy	73,000	0.5
Spain	73,000	0.5
Switzerland	7,000	...
Canada	20,000	0.2
South America	50,000	0.4
Japan	9,000	0.1
Asia	40,000	0.3
Africa	25,000	0.2
Australia	10,000	0.1
	13,260,000	100.0

An examination of these tables will serve to show that in the products which measure the manufacturing industry of nations, Great Britain stands first and the United States second on the roll, and that there is a clear and almost identical relation between the product of coal and the product of iron. The United States now produces as much coal and iron as Great Britain yielded in 1850. We are thus gaining steadily and surely upon our great progenitor and in the nature of things, as the population of this country grows, must before another century rolls around pass far beyond her possible limits of production and become the first on the International list, because we have the greatest geographical extent and our natural resources are upon so vast a scale that all the coal area of all the rest of the world would only occupy one-fourth of the space in which within our borders are stored up the reserves of future power.

In a hundred years we have thus reached a point at which for coal, iron, gold, silver, copper, lead, and zinc, we are independent of the world, with abundant capacity to supply as well our growing wants as to export these blessings of civilization to other and less favored lands, as soon as our labor and our legislation are adjusted to the conditions which will enable us to compete in foreign markets. One hundred years ago we proclaimed our political independence, and we maintained it by force of arms; we are now in a position to proclaim our industrial and commercial independence and maintain it by the force of peaceful agencies against friendly competition.

A striking view of this prosperous development is presented by the magnificent mineral collection under the charge of Professor Blake, in the Government building at the neighboring exposition [1]—a collection which constitutes the first worthy National Museum of Mining and Metallurgy.

Never was a century of free government celebrated under such favorable conditions, never was free government so justified by the material results it has produced. But let us not conceal from ourselves the fact that mere growth in wealth, mere development in industry, mere increase in population are not the best evidences of national greatness; and unless our progress in art, learning, morals, and religion keeps pace with our material growth we have cause rather for humiliation than for glorification.

"Whatsoever things are true, whatsoever things are honest, whatsoever things are just, whatsoever things are pure, whatsoever things are lovely, whatsoever things are of good report" constitute the real glory of a nation, without which the magnificent material structure which in a century we have reared will disappear "like the baseless fabric of a vision."

In a hundred years, as I have said, we have reached a point at which, for every one of the minerals and metals named, we are independent of the world, having the capacity to supply our own growing domestic demand and also to export to foreign lands.

It is not my purpose to trace in detail the steps by which this degree of progress has been achieved. The narration of successive events alone, without any discussion of underlying causes and accompanying effects, would consume far more time than I could command. So far as the leading epochs of the history are concerned, I think they may be fairly summed up in the following mere catalogue:

1. [*The steam engine*].—First of all must be named the erection in Philadelphia, in 1794, of the first steam engine in America. We celebrate this year the centennial anniversary of a greater power than the United States of America—a wider revolution than our War of Independence. It was in 1776 that James Watt presented to the world the perfected steam engine, all the improvements of which since his day are not to be compared with those which he devised upon the rude machines of his predecessors. In one hundred years the steam engine has transformed the face of the world and affected to its remotest corners the condition of the human race. Few changes have been so profound; not one in history has been so rapid and amazing. With reference to the

[1] That is, the Centennial Exposition in Philadelphia.

special subject now under consideration, if I were asked what elements had most to do with the swift progress of our country, I should answer, freedom and the steam engine. But deeper even than any organized declarations or outward forms of freedom lies the influence of the steam engine, which has been from the day of its birth, in spite of laws and dynasties and all accidents of history, the great emancipator of man.

2. *Gold mining in the South.*—Already Jefferson, in his *Notes on Virginia,* mentioned the finding of a lump of gold weighing seventeen pennyweights near the Rappahannock; and about the beginning of this century the famous Cabarrus nugget, weighing 28 pounds, was discovered at the Reed Mine, in North Carolina. But the great gold excitement in the South followed the discoveries in Georgia from 1828 to 1830. The maximum of production (probably never more than $600,000 in any one year) was from 1828 to 1845, since which time it has declined to insignificance, though a few enterprises, both in hydraulic and quartz mining, are now actively prosecuted.

3. *The opening of the anthracite coal fields and the use of anthracite in the blast furnace.*—The first of these events practically dates from the year 1820, although some anthracite found its way to market much earlier, and the second from the year 1839. The latter was followed by the development of the vast anthracite iron industry, which has contributed so much to the prosperity of Pennsylvania. The connection between anthracite and civilization was long ago pointed out by Sir Charles Lyell, in connection with his visit to this country, when he observed in this state, and in this very city where we now stand, the strange phenomenon of a vast manufacturing population, dwelling in neat houses and able to keep themselves and their houses clean. This smokeless fuel is a great moral and æsthetic benefactor. It has also proved specially useful in metallurgy—one process at least, the American zinc-oxide manufacture, being impracticable without it, and in war no one will deny its superiority who remembers how our cruisers burning anthracite, and hence not traceable at sea by their smoke, were able to spy and pursue the blockade runners, whose thick clouds of escaping bituminous smoke betrayed them. A table of the production of anthracite is given herewith; and some further observations concerning its control and management will be appropriate under another head of my remarks.

4. *The use of raw bituminous coal in the blast furnace.*—This was introduced in 1845.

5. *The development of the copper mines of Lake Superior,* beginning in 1845 and increasing slowly but steadily to 1862, when about 8,000 tons of ingot copper were produced, then declining for some years, to recover in 1868 and 1869 its lost ground, and since the latter year, by reason of the great production of the Calumet and Hecla Mine,

to attain an unprecedented yield. The tables of copper production for the United States, herewith given, show that our present product is not far from 16,000 tons, of which three-fourths must be credited to the Lake Superior mines.

6. *The discovery of gold in California,* in 1848, or rather its rediscovery, since it had previously been known to both the natives and the Jesuit missionaries and also to hunters and trappers. The wonderful direct and indirect results of this event have been too often the theme of orators, historians, and political economists to need a further description from me. Its direct result in the way of mining was the rapid exploration of the Western territories by eager prospectors, and the successive development of placer mines in nearly all of them. It is difficult to fix the dates of these beginnings; but we may assume with sufficient accuracy that gold mining practically began in Oregon in 1852, in Arizona in 1858, in Colorado in 1859, in Idaho and Montana in 1860. With the completer exploration of the country and the decline of the placer mines, stampedes have grown less frequent and extensive than in the earlier days. There is scarcely any corner of the country left, except the Black Hills of Dakota, which has not been ransacked sufficiently to show whether it contains extensive and valuable placer deposits; and those districts which present accumulations of gold in such a way as to offer returns immediately to labor without capital have been already overrun. The principal reliance of our gold-mining industry for the future must be quartz and hydraulic or deep gravel mines. These may be expected to maintain for years to come their present rate of production, if not to increase it. In the table of gold production, herewith given, there is, it is true, a falling off of late years; but this is to be attributed to the placer mines.

7. *The commencement, about 1851, of regular mining operations at the New Almaden Quicksilver Mine, in California.*—The production of this metal in the United States has been thus far confined to the state of California; and it will be seen from the table of the production of the New Almaden Mine, that it has always furnished a large, though of late a waning, proportion of the grand total for the country.

8. [*Miscellaneous events*].—The middle of the nineteenth century was crowded with important events in metallurgy and mining. It was in 1856 that Mr. Bessemer read his paper at the Cheltenham meeting of the British Association for the Advancement of Science which inaugurated for both continents the age of steel. Within sixty days after that event an experimental Bessemer Converter was in readiness at the furnaces of Cooper & Hewitt, at Phillipsburg, New Jersey. But the experiment was not carried far enough to demonstrate the value of the newly-proposed process, and it was left to the late John A. Griswold and his associates to introduce and perfect this wonderful method in

the United States. I speak more briefly on this point than its far-reaching importance deserves; but in the presence of one whose acquaintance with it is so profound and whose services in relation to it have been so brilliant as those of our honored president, Mr. Holley, and of so many gentlemen as I see before me who are worthily associated with him in its glorious history, I could afford to be silent altogether.

9. *The commencement of the hydraulic mining industry.*—The position of the auriferous slates and quartz veins on the west flank of the Sierra with the precipitous mountains behind them and the broad plain before, has favored exceptionally the formation of deep auriferous gravels in which California far exceeds any other known region. And the same topographical features furnish the two other prime requisites of hydraulic mining, namely, an abundant supply of water and a sufficient grade of descent to permit the use of flumes and the escape of tailings. These advantages the keen-witted miners of the Pacific coast were quick to make available; and I think we may set down the invention of hydraulic mining, which occurred, I believe, about 1853, as an epoch in the progress of American mining. It has given us an entirely new and original branch of the art, involving many ingenious hydrodynamic and hydrostatic contrivances; and it has certainly made possible the exploitation of thousands upon thousands of acres of auriferous gravel which could not have been profitably handled in any other way. The mountain torrents of the Sierra, caught on their way to the Pacific, have been forced to pause and do the work of man. The same agencies that buried the gold among the clay and pebbles of the river beds are now made to strip the covering from it and lay it bare again. The hydraulic mines produce, at present, not less than $10,000,000 or $12,000,000 annually; and many enterprises of this kind which have been prosecuted through years of expensive preparation, and are now just beginning to touch their harvests of profit, will add henceforward to the product. I may mention as an illustration the extensive operations of the North Bloomfield and its two allied companies in California, which have expended in works $3,500,000 and will have six deep tunnels, aggregating over 20,000 feet, and canals supplying 100,000,000 gallons of water daily.

10. [*Iron mining in the vicinity of Lake Superior*].—We must turn for a moment to the East again, to note the commencement of iron mining at Lake Superior, about the year 1856. The extraordinary pure and rich ores of the upper peninsula of Michigan now find their way, to the extent of a million of tons per annum, in fleets of vessels across the lakes to Cleveland, and are thence distributed to the furnaces of Ohio and Pennsylvania. The similarly pure Missouri ores have built up in like manner their own market. . . .

11. [*The Comstock lode*].—The next great event in the history of

American mining was the discovery in 1859 that the Comstock lode was rich in silver. This opened an era of activity and speculation which has scarcely ceased since that time. Single districts have been subjected to fluctuating experiences, passing from the first enthusiasm through all the stages of hope to reaction and despair; but though the fortunes of each have risen and fallen like the changing tide, it has nearly always been high water somewhere. Thus we have had a succession of favorites in the way of silver-mining districts, each one crowding its predecessor out of the public notice. Of these the following list includes the most permanently productive: In Nevada, the Unionville, Reese River, Belmont, White Pine, Eureka, Esmeralda, and Pioche districts; in California, the argentiferous district of Inyo County; in Idaho, the Owyhee district; in Utah, the Cottonwood and Bingham districts; in Colorado, the silver districts of Clear Creek, Boulder, and Summit Counties, to which the latest favorite, the San Juan region, may be added. I have named those localities in which mining industry is still active and flourishing. There is a longer and a sadder list, the funereal effect of which I will not intrude upon this festive occasion. But it ought to be remarked, that the apparent failure and abandonment of many districts heretofore does not argue their lack of prospective value. It is, on the contrary, amazing that under the adverse conditions surrounding the industry of mining in regions "remote, unfriended, solitary"—though not "slow"—so many communities should have succeeded in taking permanent root. Too much is expected of this industry when it is required to supply the lack of labor, food, transportation, government, and the organized support which in settled societies all the trades and occupations give to each other. Pioneer work is full of peril and of waste; and in view of the wonderful results achieved by our pioneers in mining, it ill becomes us to sneer at the losses and failures which constitute the inevitable cost of such conquests. When the battle has been gloriously won and the spoils of victory are ours, we do not greatly mourn over the number of bullets that may have been fired in vain.

But through all the vicissitudes of silver mining in other districts, the Comstock mines have maintained their place, an instance of rapid exploitation, and of aggregated wealth of production unexampled in history. Here, too, there have been intervals of failing hope; but a new *bonanza* has always made its appearance before the resources at hand were entirely exhausted; and we have seen extracted from the ores of this one vein, during the past fifteen years, the round sum of $200,000,000 in gold and silver. Dr. Raymond, in the table herewith given, assumes the product of gold to have been (on the authority of Mr. Hague) about 40 percent of the entire value. We have, therefore, from the Comstock mines during the period named, $80,000,000 gold and $120,000,000 silver.

The swift development of these mines, and the active commencement, about the same time, of deep quartz-mining operations in California led to a remarkable progress in mining machinery and to the perfection of two distinctively American processes. I refer to the California stamp mill and amalgamation process for gold and the Washoe pan process for silver. Neither of these is so novel in principle as the hydraulic process of gold mining already mentioned; but both of them have received the peculiar impress of an ingenuity and mechanical skill, partly innate in our national character and partly the product of the stern pressure of economic necessities. Into the fruitful field of further metallurgical improvements born of our Western mining industry—or adopted by it—such as the Blake rock breaker, the Stetefeldt roasting furnace, the Brückner cylinder, the Plattner chlorination, and many others less widely known, I cannot enter here. Our people have advanced in this line with headlong energy and accomplished great results—at great expense. Much, undoubtedly, remains to be done; and it may be hoped that future progress will be equally rapid, but less costly. The introduction three or four years ago of the smelting processes of Europe for the treatment of the silver ores of the West, is a striking and encouraging instance of the quickness of our mining communities to seize upon the advantages of experience elsewhere as soon as they are brought to notice. The ignorance which has led to many disasters in such enterprises was not voluntary or obstinate. Give our people light, and they do not keep their eyes shut. I am assured that already the smelting works of the West present many features of interest and suggestiveness even to the eyes of our skilful colleagues from abroad.

12. [*Improvements in the manufacture of iron*].—I may be permitted, in closing this imperfect review, to refer to the great improvements in mining machinery, in rock drilling, in explosives, in the use of gaseous fuel, in the construction and management of blast furnaces, puddling furnaces, rolling mills, and other branches of the iron manufacture, which have crowded upon us during the last ten years. It is impossible here to give even an enumeration of them which shall do them justice. They have been worthily commemorated in many papers before the Institute. With regard to one of them, the Martin process for the manufacture of open-hearth steel, I may speak with some personal satisfaction, since I had the privilege of introducing it into this country, after studying its merits in 1867 abroad. I am convinced that it has a great future, as the ally, if not the rival, of the Bessemer process.

Returning now to the contemplation of the general field over which we have passed, we may inquire what the Government of the United States has done with regard to the mining industry. Other nations have elaborate mining codes and bureaus of administration. In comparison with these, the meagerness of our governmental supervision of mining is remarkable; yet, in view of the progress I have sketched, may it not be possible that our system has been on the whole the best for us? Certainly a complicated mining code like that of Spain and Mexico, whatever it may have brought to the coffers of the State, seems to have conferred, in centuries of operation, little benefit upon the people.

The common law of England is the foundation of our jurisprudence in this as in so many other respects. According to that law, as laid down in a noted case in the reign of Elizabeth, all gold or silver ores belonged to the crown, whether in private or public lands; but any ores containing neither gold nor silver belonged to the proprietor of the soil. Apart from the claims of the crown, the property in minerals is, according to the common law, *prima facie* in the owner of the fee of the land, but the property in minerals, or the right to search for them, may be vested in other persons by alienation, prescription, or custom. Since the two latter rights require an origin beyond the time of legal memory, they are practically out of the question in this country. The crown right to the precious metals, as declared in the case referred to, was a survival or remainder of the royalty claimed in ancient times by the sovereign over all minerals. This sweeping claim, born of the despotisms of the Orient and made the subject of much conflict among emperors, feudal lords, and municipal authorities during the Middle Ages, dwindled at last till it covered only gold and silver. But it disappeared entirely from English America, for the simple reason that there was no private land ownership in this country, and the sovereign of England claimed, by right of discovery, soil and metals alike, barring only the Indian title, which it was his exclusive privilege (or that of his authorized representatives or grantees) to extinguish. After the Revolution, the United States succeeded to the rights of the British crown, and by the treaty of peace and the subsequent cessions by the different States of their colonial claims upon the public lands, the Federal Government became possessed of a vast domain over which, after extinguishing the Indian title, it had complete control. In the territories subsequently acquired from France and Spain, the United States assumed the rights and obligations of those sovereigns; and this circumstance, particularly in the adjustment of Spanish mineral and agricultural grants, has caused some apparent variations from the general policy. But it is sufficiently accurate to say that at the present time, throughout the country, the owner of the fee, or the party who has obtained from him by lease or purchase the mineral right, has supreme control. The mining legislation of the United States, therefore, is simply a part of the administration of the public lands; and for this reason it is executed by the Commissioner of the General Land Office.

In 1807 an act was passed relating primarily to the lead-bearing lands of Illinois. They were ordered to be reserved from sale and leased to miners by the War Department. The leases covered tracts at first three miles square (afterward reduced to one mile), and bound the lessee to work the mines with due diligence and return to the United States 6 percent of all the ores raised. "No leases were issued under this law," says Professor Whitney, "until 1822, and but a small quantity of lead was raised, previous to 1826, from which time the production began to increase rapidly. For a few years the rents were paid with tolerable regularity; but, after 1834, in consequence of the immense number of illegal entries of mineral land at the Wisconsin Land Office, the smelters and miners refused to make any further payments, and the government was entirely unable to collect them. After much trouble and expense, it was, in 1847, finally concluded that the only way was to sell the mineral land, and do away with all reserves of lead or any other metal, since they had only been a source of embarrassment to the department."

Meanwhile, by a forced construction (afterward declared invalid) of the same act, hundreds of leases were granted to speculators in the Lake Superior copper region, which was from 1843 to 1846 the scene of wild and baseless excitement. The bubble burst during the latter year; the issue of permits and leases was suspended as illegal, and the act of 1847, authorizing the sale of the mineral lands, and a geological survey of the district, laid the foundation of a more substantial prosperity.

This policy of selling the mineral lands has been that of the Government ever since. But it has necessarily been modified in the West by the peculiar circumstances under which that region has been settled. Before lands can be sold they must be surveyed; and before they can be sold as mineral lands, their mineral-bearing character must be ascertained. Our miners and explorers overran and occupied the Pacific slope in advance of the public surveys. They built cities that were not shown on any map; they cut timber, turned water courses, dug canals, tunneled mountains, bought and sold their rights to these improvements under laws established by themselves and enforced by public sentiment only. For nearly twenty years the government looked on without asserting its dominant ownership of the public lands; and when by the acts of 1866, 1870, and 1872 and other minor enactments, a general system was created, it was necessary to recognize as far as possible the rights which had grown up by general consent, and to seek only to give to them certainty, practical uniformity, and reasonable limitations. It is not my purpose to discuss in detail the mining laws of the United States, or to trace the curiously complicated origins of the local customs on which they are largely based. Suffice it to say that the system recognizes the English common law principle, that the mineral right passes with the fee to the lands; so that, in the words of the commissioner (July 10th, 1873) "all mineral deposits discovered upon land, after United States patent therefor has issued to a party claiming under the laws regulating the disposal of agricultural lands, pass with the patent, and the Land Office has no further jurisdiction in the premises."

But the principle is also recognized that the mineral right may be separated from the fee by the owner, whether he be an individual or the United States; and this principle is curiously applied in the form of patents for mining claims upon lodes, which, following the form of the possessory title, grant to the patentee the right to follow all veins, the top or apex of which lies within the exterior boundaries of his claim, downward to any depth, though they pass under the surface of the land adjoining.

As the size and the price per acre of the tracts sold under the agricultural laws are different from those to which the mining laws apply, and as under the homestead law a certain amount of agricultural land may be obtained without any payment, it is evident that no known mineral deposits can be acquired under the agricultural laws; and this reservation is enforced both in the preliminary proceedings and in the patents finally issued under those laws.

With regard to the mineral lands, however, it is certain that the patent for a claim carries with it both the fee of the land and also a mineral right, though not the same mineral right as is contemplated by the common law; since it is enlarged on the one hand by the permission to follow mineral deposits beneath the surface of adjoining land, and limited on the other hand by the operation of the same permission in favor of the adjoining owner. The latter limitation is incorporated in agricultural patents also, and may become operative whenever they adjoin mining patents.

Previous to the application for a patent, the law permits free exploration and mining upon the public lands to all citizens and those who have declared their intention to become such. The rights of this class of miners, under what is known as the possessory title, are regulated by local laws and customs, subject only to a few simple conditions, which the United States enforces upon all, and which chiefly concern the maximum size of individual claims, the definite character of their boundaries and landmarks, and a certain quantity of labor which must be bestowed upon them annually, in order to maintain possession. I will not pause to state the different features which these conditions present for lode and placer claims. It is sufficient to say that the miner conforming to them and thus maintaining his possessory title, may, after a certain expenditure and upon due application, survey, and advertisement, in the absence of any valid opposing claim, perfect his purchase from the Government, receive his patent, and be thereafter free from the necessity of performing any given annual amount of labor to hold his claim. There are features in the present law concerning the rights of prospecting tunnels which seem both obscure and unwise; and some serious questions remain to be settled as to the precise meaning of the law in these and other respects; but these we must pass by.

Looking at the legislation on this subject as a whole, we see that it is confined to one department—that of title. The whole system is devised to facilitate the purchase of the mines by citizens. They are freely permitted to work them experimentally, but it is made their interest to buy them. No inspection, no police regulation, no technical control, is exercised by the Government.

Turning to the state and territorial legislatures, we find that they have in some cases provided for inspecting mines, in the interest of the safety of workmen. Perhaps the best law of this kind is that of Pennsylvania, in which state the peculiar perils of coal-mining have forced the legislature to take measures of protection. But we find nowhere such a technical control of mining as is exhibited in many European States, where the government requires of the miner that he shall not waste wantonly or ignorantly the resources which, once exhausted, will never grow again. Our people waste as much as they like, and no one interferes. Admitting that this is an evil, it still remains a matter of doubt how far, under the circumstances of our particular case, the supervision of authority could remedy it. For my own part, though inclined to restrict as far as possible the functions of government, I am not disposed to say that for so great an end as the conservation of the mineral wealth of the country it may not properly enforce some measures of economy with as good right as it may forbid the reckless waste of timber or the slaughter of game out of season. But, in our nation, at least, governmental interference is the last resort and a poor substitute for other causes, which, in the atmosphere of freedom and intelligence, ought to be effective. We are, perhaps, in our material career as a nation, like the young man who has "sown his wild oats," and now, by mature reflection and the lessons of experience, is likely to be better restrained than by the hand of parental authority.

Permit me, in drawing my remarks to a close, to suggest two agencies which seem to me to be co-operating already and to open still wider future prospect for the steady social and economical improvement of our mining and metallurgical industry.

The first of these is the spread of knowledge on these subjects throughout the country. Under this head we must recognize the great importance of that series of explorations of our great Western domain, which was recommended by Mr. Lincoln, with sublime faith in the salvation of his country, in the midst of the Civil War, and which has been, by the liberality of the Government, prosecuted under various departments ever since. I need hardly make special mention, in addition, of the reports of the Commissioner of Mining Statistics, which have appeared annually since 1866 and have reflected upon our own community the light of the gathered technical knowledge of the world, while they have in turn exhibited to the world the resources and the progress of America. Such works as these, together with the technical periodicals and the occasional volumes, translated or original, which have come from the American press, have contributed already a great deal to the education of our mining communities. The Government has not done too much in this direction; but it seems to me that it should continue this most necessary and proper work in a more systematic and uniform way. There ought to be no conflict of authorities, no duplication of work, no unnecessary expenditure of labor and money in the face of a task so great.

Next in order, I may rank the influence of the technical schools. The number of these has rapidly increased during the past ten years; and I venture to say that many of them compare favorably, in theoretical instruction at least, and several of them in the apparatus of instruction, with the famous schools of the old world. The Massachusetts Institute of Technology, at Boston; the School of Mines of Columbia College, at New York; the Sheffield Scientific School of Yale College, at New Haven; the Stevens Institute of Technology, at Hoboken; the Pardee Scientific Department of Lafayette College, at Easton; the excellent school at Rutgers College, under the direction of Professor Cook; the new Scientific Department of the College of New Jersey; the School of Mining and Metallurgy of Lehigh University, at Bethlehem; the School of Mining and Practical Geology of Harvard University, at Cambridge; the Scientific Department of the University of Pennsylvania, in this city; the School of Mines of Michigan University, at Ann Arbor; the Missouri School of Mines and Metallurgy, at Rolla; the Polytechnic Department of Washington University, at St. Louis, and the similar department of the University of California, at Oakland; and perhaps some others which I have omitted to name—this is a list of schools for instruction in the sciences involved in mining and metallurgical practice of which we need not be ashamed. What our schools undoubtedly need is a more intimate relation with practice. But this theme I need not touch. It has been ably and amply discussed at the joint meeting last night of the two bodies most fully aware of all its bearings.

One more agency of the spread of technical knowledge deserves special mention. I refer to the influence of societies like the Institute of Mining Engineers. The five years' activity of this Institute has impressed upon the professions which it represents a spirit of union, an enthusiasm of progress, a mutual recognition of the claims of theory and practice, which cannot be too highly estimated. Perfect our schools as much as we may, the association of the young engineer with experienced engineers, the contact of his mind with mature minds, their recognition of his merit, their correction of his errors, constitute the necessary supplement to the school training. The average man, at least, should not be left to wrestle with his professional career alone. He will make better progress and take more pleasure in it if he calls to his aid the element of social sympathy and the intellectual reinforcement expressed in the proverb, "many heads are better than one."

One further consideration, and I have done. The effect of growing intelligence and knowledge in improving our methods of industry would come short of some great ends if it operated only through the self-interest of the individual. Many reforms are beyond the power of the individual; some are not even to his interest. Thus the miner under a possessory title on a gold-bearing quartz vein in Colorado may know that with a greater investment of capital he could manage to reduce his losses of gold in extraction; but the capital may be wanting; or, he may know that by robbing the mine of its richest ores only, and allowing it to cave, he is probably destroying more valuable resources than he utilizes; but the mine is only temporarily his, and he prefers quick gains to permanent ones. So long as the anthracite lands of Pennsylvania were leased to countless small operators, who paid royalty only on the coal which they sent to market, it was useless to explain to them that they wasted a third of the coal in the ground and another third in the breaker, or that they ruined thousands of acres of coal beds overlying those which they recklessly worked. If there were no natural remedy for this wicked waste of the reserved force upon which the future prosperity and comfort of mankind depend, it would be the highest duty of Government promptly to take into its own hands the direction and management of the mines of coal which society holds in trust for the future; but already it is easy to detect the operation of a new social law developed within the memory of man, but the fruit of the preparation of the ages during which society has been slowly built up and matured into its present form and conditions.

To the philosophic observer, the controlling law which runs through the whole history of man down to the present century is the law of dispersion, diffusion, distribution—the centrifugal social force, so to speak, which by its irresistible power has tended not merely to scatter mankind over the face of the habitable globe but through what are termed civilizing and Christianizing agencies to place communities and individuals upon the common plane of equal rights in the domain of nature and before the law.

From the time of the confusion of tongues at the Tower of Babel, through the long history of the early Oriental Empires, which reduced society to the rule of order and then broke up into fragmentary political organizations, retaining, nevertheless, the principles of cohesion acquired by bitter experience; through the Greek and Roman imperial political structures upon which were ingrafted the civilization and the religion which their downfall made the common heritage of the northern barbarians who came for destruction, but were themselves transformed into the apostles of a more liberal and enlightened social organization, this law of dispersion has never ceased to exercise its power and its supremacy. The very inventions of man are only so many proofs of the unceasing operation of this law. In warfare, gunpowder and firearms merely enlarged the area over which it was possible to carry on military operations; the magnetic compass only widened the field of commerce; the printing press and the telegraph are merely agencies for the diffusion of thought; the steam engine is but a means whereby it becomes possible to establish local industries in every part of the habitable globe; and the canal and the railway are essentially distributers of the products and the wealth of the human race.

Although there is an impression abroad that this age is one of growing concentration of property, no man can study the history and the facts of the development of society without coming to the conclusion that at no period has there been so general and equal a distribution of rights and property as in the present age. The destruction of the feudal system was, in reality, the establishment of a new and better theory in regard to the ownership of land, which has borne its legitimate fruits in the subdivision of estates in France through the convulsions of a revolution; in the more general distribution of landed property in Germany; and in that steady, remarkable, and successful agitation in England, which is now showing its results in the limitation of entail, the simplification of transfer, the enlargement of the suffrage, and the acquisition of small freeholds, whereby political power is being slowly but surely transferred from the great landholders to the middle classes of the most powerful and compact political organization which the world has ever seen.

While, then, there is thus an unmistakable progress in the world toward a juster and more general distribution of the control of the resources of nature and of the fruits of human industry, the present century has, undoubtedly, developed a new and remarkable centralizing tendency, which might be denominated the centripetal industrial force. I speak of the application of the corporate principle to the management of industrial enterprises, producing a concentration of property and management through the diffusion of ownership. Under the corporate system, the number of owners may be unlimited, but the management is necessarily confined to a few hands. It is the political idea of representation applied to industrial enterprises; it is the common wealth in its industrial, and not its political sense, which is concentrated for the material wants and progress of the human race. Now, this law of universal ownership under limited management, heretofore applied with marked success during the latter half of the present century to great manufacturing establishments in this country and of late in Europe and of necessity to railroads everywhere, has at length, by slow but irresistible steps, taken possession of the great mining enterprises of the United States, and today has its strongest and most interesting development in the anthracite coal region, which may be said to be monopolized by six great corporations, administered by a very small number of able officers representing a vast body of owners who rely upon steady but not excessive dividends for their support. It is the fashion to denounce these corporations as monopolizers, but it is only the thoughtless who do not investigate below the surface who take this view of what is really the most interesting and suggestive application in our day of a powerful and irresistible force originating in the very heart of the social fabric. The monopoly is not the monopoly of ownership, for everybody is free to buy and sell, and there is no day when a man with money may not, at its value, procure a share in these enterprises. And no one familiar with business will pretend that the profits have been out of proportion to the cost and the risk of the undertakings, and no more conclusive answer, to any complaint on the score of monopoly can be made than that today the shares in these corporations, in many cases, are selling below the original money cost. These corporations are, in fact, not the creators, but the outgrowth of a new and beneficent principle which has begun to assert itself in society and will continue to grow in power until the end of time. This principle is the practical association of diffused capital, through the agency of corporate organization, with labor, for the promotion of economy, for the improvement of processes, and for the general welfare of mankind.

The capital is derived from innumerable sources, just as the little rills finally through streams and rivers constitute the great ocean. The laborer himself may thus be the capitalist, and the capitalist may thus be the laborer, each taking his share of that portion of the fund which is appropriated to labor and to capital, and often in a double capacity taking a share from both.

In its perfect and ultimate development it embodies the Christian idea of "having all things in common," yet "rendering unto Cæsar the things that are Cæsar's."

The rate of profit which may be derived from these great enterprises, subject as they are to the scrutiny, criticism, and judgment of the public in an age when nothing escapes notice and all rights and property are virtually subordinated to the popular will, can never be excessive, for two reasons: on the one side the public will inevitably demand lower prices for an article of primary consequence in every household, and these corporations, creatures of the public will as they are, could not successfully resist such a demand, based upon excessive or unreasonable profits. On the other hand, whenever the dividends rise above a reasonable rate of compensation, the laborers engaged in the production of coal, from whom these profits cannot be concealed, will justly claim and rightfully secure a larger share of the fruits of their labor. The checks upon any unreasonable exercise of the power conferred by the ownership under limited management of the anthracite coal fields are in reality so powerful that the public have nothing to fear from this cause, but the corporations have reason rather to dread that they may not have justice at the hands of the public and the working classes. This justice they can only hope to secure by the wisest, best, and most economical management and administration of the property they control, and whatever profits they may hereafter derive and be allowed to divide among the owners will be rather due to the economies which they may be able to introduce, whereby the article is furnished at the lowest possible rate, than to any fancied monopoly which they may have in the coal itself or in its transportation to market.

Already, by the application of adequate capital, guided by the largest experience and the highest technical skill, the anthracite coal mines, from being worked in a wasteful and extravagant manner, are being rapidly put in the best possible shape for the economical delivery of coal at the surface and for the preservation of every portion of the store upon which the future value of the property must depend. But besides economy in mining and care in preserving, there must be regularity and stability in the operations of the mine. There can be no real profit where these operations are subject to constant interruption caused by strikes or other artificial impediments. The loss of interest on the plant at the mines and in the lines of transportation caused by any serious stoppage to the works, would, of itself, be sufficient to render investments of this kind unprofitable. Hence the output must be regulated and proportioned to the wants of the market. But this regulation must be continuous and not spasmodic. To enable this to be done, large stocks of coal must necessarily be kept on hand, in order that any sudden demand may be properly met without any serious increase in price; and in dull times the accumulation and restoration of the stocks will give steady employment to the miners, to whose families any cessation of work is a calamity of the most serious character, and to society an unmitigated evil. To insure continuous operations the best relations must exist between the corporate owners and the laborers in their employ. It is notorious that throughout the coal regions these relations have been of the most unsatisfactory character, resulting, at often-recurring intervals, in strikes and lockouts, which have no redeeming feature, but, on the contrary, have raised the price of coal to the consumer, have impaired the dividends of the owners, and have reduced the working men and their families to a condition of suffering and demoralization appalling to every well-wisher of his race. It is fortunate, therefore, that the interests of all classes concur in the prevention of these destructive and demoralizing collisions and that the owners of the property, for their own self-protection, will be driven to remove the causes which have produced them. It is idle for them to expend their capital for the best machinery, for the highest skill, for the most economical transportation, unless they can at the same time insure a continuous production from a contented laboring population.

This they have it in their power to do. If the same spirit of sacrifice which has sent out our missionaries into every heathen land had been shown in the coal regions, and the same efforts had been made to establish and maintain the schoolhouse, the church, and above all the Sunday school, which have borne such fruits elsewhere in this broad land; if the hospital for the sick and the comfortable refuge for the unfortunate had been carefully provided; if reading rooms and night schools and rational places of amusement had from the outset been maintained for a growing and restless population, the coal regions today might have been a paradise upon earth instead of a disgrace to civilization. And here it is that this new power of concentrated management can exert itself with sure and absolute success. The appropriation of a few cents per ton on the coal mined to the work of improving the moral and intellectual conditions of the miners and their families will, in a time incredibly short, change the whole face of society in the coal regions.

To be effective, however, this consecration of a fixed amount on each ton of coal sent to market must be as absolute and final as that portion of the proceeds which is devoted to pumping the mines or driving the gangways. It must come not from grace but from a sense of duty involved in the ownership of property and dictated by a wise regard for its preservation and permanent value. Even if this percentage were added to the price of the coal the addition would not be grudged by the public; but in fact no such addition could possibly occur, as there is no surer way of promoting economy in the cost of production than by improving the social condition, the self-respect, and the intelligence of those who are engaged in the work of production, which thus becomes continuous and systematic. Until the great companies thus recognize the duties, the responsibilities, and the opportunities for good which are offered by the new social development which has rendered their existence a necessity as well as a possibility, they must not complain that they are regarded with distrust and as enemies, both by the public which consumes their products and by the working classes who see in them only grasping employers without a conscience. What individual owners could not do, it is easy for these great companies to put in practice; but the effort must be as earnest and serious as is the business of producing the coal and getting it to market. The very best talent must be secured for the organization and management of the various agencies necessary for the moral, intellectual, and social improvement of the working classes, who must be themselves associated in the administration of the fund created and expended for their benefit. Five cents per ton would produce an annual revenue of over $1,000,000 applicable to this necessary and noble use, and five years of its intelligent and conscientious administration would convert what in some regions has been aptly termed a "hell upon earth" into a terrestrial paradise which would be the pride and the glory of the new world.

What more fitting celebration of the centennial year of American Independence could be possibly suggested or devised, or how could the advent of the incoming century be better signalized, than by the foundation on the part of the great anthracite coal companies of a new department in their administration for the moral, mental, social, and physical improvement of the workingmen and their families, and by the appropriation of a fixed charge on coal for this purpose. Let each of them select a well-paid and competent agent to devote himself to this work, let the various agencies be wisely organized and surely perfected, and there will be realized one of the greatest triumphs of that gospel which proclaimed , "Peace on earth, and good-will toward men." The example thus set will soon extend itself to other industries, and to every branch of business which can adapt the corporate principle of the concentration of management through diffusion of ownership; the result of which will be that the strange phenomenon now felt throughout the civilized world of a general glut of products in the face of general want of them will never again be witnessed; because, when the working classes, through the diviner agencies of Christian effort, shall have constant employment and adequate compensation, the sure results of general enlightenment and a cultivated conscience in the use of property, the power of consumption, now so far in arrear, will surely overtake the power of production and re-establish the equation which nature intended to subsist between them. Thus may be realized that Christian commonwealth which has been the dream of the patriot, the philanthropist, and the statesman in all ages, in which every man who is willing to work shall find employment, and in which the products of industry will be so distributed that every man shall feel that he has received his fair share of them; in which there will be neither abject and hopeless poverty on the one hand, nor superfluous riches on the other, because the problem of how to distribute capital through the concentration of management will have been fully solved and be thoroughly comprehended by all classes in the community; in which the quaint questions put by Sir Thomas More three hundred and sixty years ago will at length have been answered, and his suggestive commentary thereon have lost its significance.

TABLE OF PRODUCTION OF LEADING METALS AND MINERALS IN THE UNITED STATES DURING THE FIRST CENTURY OF NATIONAL INDEPENDENCE

PREPARED BY R. W. RAYMOND

	Anthracite, in tons of 2240 ℔s. avoir.	Pig-iron, in tons of 2240 ℔s. avoir.	Lead, in tons of 2240 ℔s. avoir.	Copper, in tons of 2240 ℔s. avoir.	Quicksilver, in flasks of 76½ ℔s. avoir.	Gold, in dollars, U. S. coin.	Silver, in dollars, U. S. coin.	Petroleum, in barrels of 42 gallons.
1819	18,000 [a]	...	...	...	...	...	...	...
1820	1,965	...	...	...	...	...	...	...
1821	3,273	...	...	...	...	...	...	...
1822	4,940	...	...	...	...	...	...	...
1823	9,023	...	...	...	...	...	...	...
1824	13,641	...	4,432 [a]	...	...	...	...	...
1825	38,499	...	1,281	...	...	...	...	...
1826	54,815	...	1,771	...	...	...	...	...
1827	71,167	2,178,239 [a]	3,927	...	...	...	...	...
1828	91,914	130,000	7,815	...	...	...	...	...
1829	133,203	142,000	7,824	...	...	...	...	...
1830	209,634	165,000	7,163	...	...	...	...	...
1831	230,320	191,000	6,646	...	...	...	...	...
1832	448,171	200,000	8,888	...	...	...	...	...
1833	592,210	218,000	9,767	...	...	...	...	...
1834	456,859	236,000	10,552	...	...	...	...	...
1835	678,517	254,000	11,696	...	...	...	...	...
1836	825,729	272,000	14,216	...	...	...	...	...
1837	1,039,241	200,000	11,994	...	...	...	...	...
1838	873,013	308,000	13,512	...	...	...	...	...
1839	957,436	326,000	15,539	...	...	...	...	...
1840	1,008,220	347,000	15,000	...	...	...	...	...
1841	1,115,045	290,000	18,171	...	...	...	...	...
1842	1,286,618	230,000	21,586	...	...	...	...	...
1843	1,478,926	312,000	21,000	...	...	...	...	...
1844	1,899,805	394,000	22,000	2,680 [a]	...	...	...	...
1845	2,352,984	486,000	26,500	100	...	...	...	...
1846	2,707,321	765,000	25,000	150	...	...	...	...

1847	3,327,155	800,000	25,000	300	...	20,000,000[a]	...	...
1848	3,572,695	800,000	22,500	500	...	10,000,000	...	...
1849	3,724,806	650,000	21,000	700	...	40,000,000	...	...
1850	3,863,365	563,755	19,500	600	25,424[a]	50,000,000	...	...
1851	5,190,690	413,000	16,500	800	24,000	55,000,000	...	...
1852	5,725,148	540,755	14,000	1,000	20,000	60,000,000	...	...
1853	5,940,905	723,214	15,000	1,850	19,000	65,000,000	...	...
1854	6,846,556	662,216	14,000	2,250	27,000	60,000,000	...	...
1855	7,684,542	700,159	14,000	3,000	33,000	55,000,000	...	...
1856	7,999,767	788,515	14,000	4,000	30,000	55,000,000	...	...
1857	7,694,842	712,640	14,000	4,800	28,000	55,000,000	...	...
1858	7,364,230	629,552	14,000	5,500	31,000	50,000,000	1,000,000[a]	...
1859	9,010,726	750,560	14,000	6,300	12,000	50,000,000	100,000	3,200
1860	9,807,118	821,223	14,000	7,200	10,000	46,000,000	150,000	650,000
1861	9,147,461	653,164	14,000	7,500	35,000	43,000,000	2,000,000	2,113,600
1862	9,026,211	702,912	14,000	9,000	42,000	39,200,000	4,500,000	3,056,606
1863	10,953,077	846,075	14,000	6,474	40,531	40,000,000	8,500,000	2,611,359
1864	11,631,400	1,013,837	14,000	6,518	47,489	46,100,000	11,000,000	2,116,182
1865	10,783,032	831,768	13,165	6,811	53,000	53,200,000	11,250,000	3,497,712
1866	14,233,919	1,200,199	14,342	6,978	46,550	53,500,000	10,000,000	3,597,527
1867	14,345,644	1,305,015	13,662	7,774	37,000	51,700,000	13,550,000	3,347,306
1868	15,810,466	1,431,250	14,636	9,467	37,000	48,000,000	12,000,000	3,715,741
1869	16,375,678	1,711,276	15,653	11,858	33,713	49,500,000	13,000,000	4,215,000
1870	17,819,700	1,696,429	15,922	12,650	29,546	50,000,000	16,000,000	5,659,000
1871	17,370,463	1,707,685	17,854	12,546	31,881	43,500,000	22,000,000	5,795,000
1872	22,032,265	2,539,783	23,106	11,948	30,306	36,000,000	25,750,000	6,539,103
1873	22,828,178	2,560,962	46,661	15,573	28,600	35,000,000	36,500,000	9,879,455
1874	21,667,386	2,401,261	53,219	17,548	34,254	39,600,000	32,800,000	10,910,303
1875	20,643,509	2,108,554	53,000	15,625	53,706	33,400,000	41,400,000	8,787,506
Total	341,521,423	40,000,000	855,000	200,000	840,000	1,332,700,000	261,450,000	76,594,600

[a] Including the whole previous period from 1776.

Is not that government both unjust and ungrateful, that is so prodigal of its favors to those that are called gentlemen or goldsmiths, or such others who are idle, or live either by flattery, or by contriving the arts of vain pleasure; and on the other hand takes no care of those of a meaner sort, such as ploughmen, colliers, and smiths, without whom it could not subsist?

But after the public has reaped all the advantages of their service, and they come to be oppressed with age, sickness, and want, all their labors, and the good they have done is forgotten, and all the recompense given them is, that they are left to die in great misery. The richer sort are often endeavoring to bring the hire of laborers lower, not only by their fraudulent practices, but by the laws which they procure to be made to this effect, so that though it is a thing most unjust in itself to give such small rewards to those who deserve so well of the public, yet they have given those hardships the name and color of justice, by procuring laws to be made for regulating them.

Although I quote from the *Utopia,* let it not be supposed that there is anything Utopian or impracticable in the proposition which I have advanced. It seems to me to be the next great step to be taken for the amelioration of the condition of mankind. The law of diffusion which thus far has governed the progress of the human race toward a higher and better plane of civilization, has at length made an effective lodgment in the domain of capital, whereby it is rendered capable of infinite division without impairing, but in effect improving, the economy and force of its administration. The reproach that "corporations have no souls," must, and will, next be removed so soon as the beneficent possibilities inherent in these agencies shall be generally recognized, and those who are called to the management shall see that because capital is aggregated, the primary law on which all property rests, that it is a trust to be administered for the public good, loses none of its force but can, in reality, only assert itself in all its vigor when concentrated management is brought to bear upon great aggregations of capital. Man did not become a "living soul" until God breathed into him the breath of life. So corporations are mere machines until they are inspired by the associated conscience of society, to which they can give ready and effective expression, and I look for this expression first from the great coal companies, because their property and their peculiar organizations make it easy as well as profitable for them to put in practice the fundamental idea, that a fixed portion of the proceeds of industry should be invariably devoted to the social improvement of those who labor directly for its development.

If the seed here dropped should take root, as I pray and believe it will, then indeed will the country and the world have reason to rejoice at the industrial development of the last hundred years and the celebration of this centennial be the dawn of a better day for the patient sons of toil, who, let it be confessed, with all frankness and humility, have not yet been endowed with their fair share of the good things of this goodly earth.

Iron and Labor

[*In 1890 the British Iron and Steel Institute held its annual meeting in
New York City; this being in part a courteous recognition of the
fact that the United States had now outdistanced Great Britain in
the production both of pig-iron and steel. The similar German
body, the Deutscher Eisenheuttenleute, also sent a large delegation
to New York. The American Institute of Mining Engineers, acting
as host to these visitors, again elected Hewitt its president in order
that a public man of distinction might welcome them. The occasion
was marked by the presentation of the Bessemer Gold Medal, the
great award of the British body, to him. In preparing his presidential address he took a bold course. Instead of dealing with the
achievements of the American industry, he dwelt upon its unfaced
responsibilities and unperformed duties. Speaking in Chickering
Hall on September 8, he pleaded with these rugged conservatives—
most of them hostile to labor unions, indifferent to the plain consumer, eager for such special privilege as the McKinley Tariff was
about to provide—to take a more liberal attitude toward labor.
The labor problem, he declared, was the most serious of the age.
A great readjustment, not unlike that which followed the abolition
of serfdom at the close of the Middle Ages, was taking place. It
was the duty of great employers to guide and hasten the process
of liberal change, not obstruct it. He laid down a series of axioms
which were advanced indeed for American ironmasters in 1890,
and which even yet are not all outdated. The paper is one of the
most important expositions of Hewitt's social and economic creed.*]

After an interval of fourteen years, saddened for all of us by the
death of David Thomas, the father of the anthracite iron trade, first
president of the Institute, and by the untimely loss of his successor,
Alexander L. Holley,[1] whose memory we are about to honor by loving

---

[1] Alexander Lyman Holley (1832-1882) combined the patent rights of Bessemer
and Wiliam Kelly, and in 1865 put in operation at Troy, N. Y., the first Bessemer
steel mill of commercial significance in the United States. His inventions contributed
much to the design of other steel plants.

services, the members of the American Institute of Mining Engineers have conferred upon me for the second time the office of president, under circumstances similar to those which led to the choice in 1876. Then the whole world was represented at the great exposition of industry which was held in Philadelphia to celebrate the one-hundredth anniversary of our declaration of political independence. In 1890 it is our privilege to receive as guests the members of the British Iron and Steel Institute, who, with singular and graceful felicity, have appointed a meeting in the United States in the year when we pass from the second to the first place in the international column of the production of iron, and thus celebrate our industrial independence. For the honor of being chosen to extend to our distinguished guests the right hand of fellowship and a hearty welcome I return to my associates the grateful acknowledgment of one whose chief claim to your favor is to be found in his love for the professional occupation in which we are all engaged and in his efforts, public and private, to promote its advancement into new fields of usefulness.

In order to indicate the full significance of the visit of our foreign guests at this time it will be proper to explain briefly the origin, aims, and work of the Iron and Steel Institute. It unquestionably owes its birth to the international expositions held in London in 1851 and '62 and in Paris in 1867. These expositions served to break down the jealousies of nationality and to diffuse a better knowledge of industrial processes. Trade secrets which had been carefully guarded became common property; manufacturers who had previously regarded themselves as rivals formed bonds of union and ties of friendship as the result of an intercourse which broke down all prejudices and led them to see that their highest interests would be promoted by the free interchange of experience and ideas. The progress of the world in the arts of civilization since 1851 has been phenomenal. In fact, the face of the industrial world may be said to have been entirely reconstructed since the time when the first international exposition was held. The figures which I shall adduce in regard to the development of the iron and steel industries during the last decade, will make it clear that new agencies have been at work for the amelioration of humanity and the progress of civilization. Among these agencies I can think of none more powerful than the influence exerted by the Iron and Steel Institute through its meetings, its discussions, and the publication of its transactions. The comprehensive nature of its work and the absolute honesty and frankness with which it has been carried on afford the best illustration of the catholicity of the age in which we are so fortunate as to live, and give promise of the good time when all barriers to the intercourse of men shall be broken down and it shall be demonstrated that the true interests of mankind are best promoted by the free play of the laws of nature.

So far as I know, this was the first considerable organization of a special industrial interest deliberately formed for the acquisition and diffusion of scientific and practical knowledge independently of the question of profit and commercial results. I venture to say that in the history of the human race there is nothing approaching the records of the Institute in the disclosure to the whole world of the most valuable and intricate processes, in previous times regarded as special secrets and carefully concealed as the property of private establishments.

Although British in origin, the Institute has invited and secured the co-operation of the ablest men, both practical and scientific, in all countries; and its membership is as widely diffused as are the materials of the great industry to which it is devoted. Its organization dates from 1869, when it was formed with 292 members; today it numbers over 1,600. In 1870 the world's product of pig-iron was 11,900,000 tons; in 1889 it amounted to 24,869,534 tons. Meanwhile the processes of manufacture have been revolutionized, and a large portion of the world's consumption has been changed from iron to steel in consequence of the improvements which have been either originated by members of the Institute, or made the common property of mankind by the complete disclosures of new discoveries and processes made in its *Journal*. It is not too much to say that the tone of the trade has been raised to a plane of intelligence and liberality which would have been absolutely incomprehensible to the past generation and which opens for those who are to come after us a new world of generous competition in promoting the welfare of the race. The history of the achievements of the Iron and Steel Institute thus forms a complete answer to those who are inclined to take a pessimistic view of humanity; for it has shown how all the members of the largest branch of industry, lying at the very foundation of civilization, can be brought to work together for the common good and for the more equitable distribution of the products of human effort.

It has been from time to time the wise practice of the Institute to hold meetings outside of Great Britain in countries where there is a considerable development of the iron and steel business. It has reserved, however, its meeting in this country until by the inevitable growth of population and the consequent development of our resources we have become the largest producers of pig iron and of steel among the nations of the world.

In recognition of this felicitous compliment we can assure our guests that the time has been accelerated by many years in consequence of the inventions of members of the Iron and Steel Institute, chief among whom, we are glad to say, still survives the conspicuous personality of

Sir Henry Bessemer, *clarum et venerabile nomen,* whose absence on this occasion, in consequence of his advanced years, causes a feeling of profound regret throughout the length and breadth of the land. They have come largely to see the fruits of their own good work, and it will be our fault if they do not receive a hospitality which will remove from their hearts anything of regret that the primacy in the production of iron and steel is passing from the parent to the child. If they have divided their inheritance with us, we at least are ready to acknowledge the obligation, and as hosts to tender them the first fruits of the magnificent resources with which we have been endowed and which we have been enabled to develop with the co-operation, counsel, and large experience of the mother country.

Our own Institute, now consisting of nearly 2,000 members and the Verein deutscher Eisenheuttenleute of over 1,000 members, represented here by a numerous delegation, both owe their existence to the example of the parent society, whose record they have striven to emulate, and whose pre-eminence is acknowledged with admiration and gratitude.

Having thus endeavored to express our profound appreciation of the honor of their visit to this country, I proceed now, in a general way, to indicate the subjects to which their attention will necessarily be directed in order to understand the condition of the iron and steel business in this country and its further prospects. I shall carefully abstain, however, from all description of the great establishments which have grown up in the last ten years, of the improved processes which they employ, and of the technical details which will be presented at the international meetings by representatives of both continents, fully qualified to deal with the scientific and practical phases of the business. I shall devote what I have to say to a consideration rather of the conditions under which the iron and steel business has grown to its present proportions and to the difficulties in the way of its development on the scale demanded by the growth of the world and the progress of civilization.

The possession of fuel determines the direction, growth, and remuneration of modern industry. The mineral fuel of the world is largely under the control of the Teutonic races, and hence the iron .and steel business has been most extensively developed in Great Britain, Germany, and the United States. Of these three countries, the latter has the largest and most cheaply worked deposits of fuel. Of the country lying east of the Mississippi River, the coal field occupies about 135,000 square miles, generally covered by a fertile soil, traversed by natural waterways, and tapped by railways aggregating over 100,000 miles in length. Around the edges of this vast coal field the older geological formations bring to the surface the deposits of iron ore belonging to the successive strata from the crystalline rocks to the recent tertiary deposits. The accumulation of ore is in some portions of the country upon a scale of grandeur which may well excite the wonder of the beholder. The connection between these vast deposits of ore and the fuel required for smelting them is, as a rule, remarkably convenient and easy. The magnetites of New York and New Jersey have been connected by rail with the anthracites of Pennsylvania, so that they may be brought together upon favorable conditions. The hematites and specular ores of Lake Superior reach the coals of Illinois and Ohio by a water communication which has been so perfected as to reduce the cost of transportation below one dollar per ton. The magnificent deposit at Cornwall, in Pennsylvania, which our guests will visit, is within 40 miles of anthracite coal and accessible to coke at rates which leave nothing to be desired. When we pass to the South, we find in Alabama that the coal and ore are usually within 25 miles of each other and sometimes to be found lying one over the other upon the same property. Between Pennsylvania and Alabama the ranges of ore extend in and along the Appalachian chain, in close proximity to admirable fuel, which, during the last few years has been made accessible by railways and canals.

When the Government of the United States was organized under the Constitution in 1789 the existence of these coal fields was unknown, and only a few deposits of iron ore skirting the coast had been opened for the use of charcoal as a fuel. The first census of the United States, made just a hundred years ago, disclosed a population of not quite 4,000,000 inhabitants residing near the coast, without capital and with no industries developed, except those of a domestic nature carried on according to the rude methods of a primitive civilization. No steam engine had as yet been erected within our borders, and no other means of transportation existed except the waterways which had been provided by nature or the rough roads over which communication was kept up with difficulty between sparse and distant settlements. Except in natural resources no civilized people was ever poorer than was this nation at the close of the Revolutionary war, but none was ever endowed with so much hope, courage, and intellectual activity or with so grand a field for the exercise of these good qualities. Moreover, our fathers were God-fearing men, who thoroughly believed that "the earth was the Lord's, and that they were His people." In 1776 they had proclaimed political independence, but it was not until 1789 that they became a nation. The same instrument which decreed the fusion of the states into one Union as the fundamental condition of nationality, to be subsequently maintained by a war which cost eight thousand millions of dollars and the sacrifice of more than a million of lives and is attested today by a pension roll of over one hundred millions of dollars per annum, laid the foundation of industrial progress and independence by declaring that "no State shall pass any law impairing the obligation of contracts," and that "no man shall be deprived of life, liberty or property without due process of law." With the assurance of protection thus afforded, the young nation started boldly out to conquer sea and land. The genius of Alexander Hamilton set in motion the wheels of progress by the honest funding of the public debt and by encouraging the energies of a race of men ready alike to vex the ocean with their sails and to drive back the Indian by their steady march beyond the Alleghenies, disclosing the mineral wealth that was stored within the mountain fastnesses. Roads were built, over which toiled the cumbrous Pennsylvania wagons; and the men who had marched with bleeding feet from New Jersey to Yorktown crossed the Allegheny Mountains and occupied the rich regions of Ohio, Tennessee, and Kentucky. Their toilsome paths were over the coal beds, and in their train followed the canals and railroads which have enabled us so to assemble the raw materials as to place ourselves within a century at the head of the nations in the production of iron and steel. In these early days there was no time for strikes and no provocation for boycotts. There were no capitalists; and the only walking-delegates to be found were those who traveled on foot to represent their communities either in the Legislature or in Congress. They were all Americans, made brothers by mutual trials and struggles, not a mongrel mass of foreign races ignorant of the true basis of personal liberty which our fathers had incorporated into the Constitution as the perpetual guaranty of freedom and progress. In vindication of these fundamental principles of our national existence we may yet have to make greater sacrifices of men and money than were required for the maintenance of the Union. For, let our visitors from abroad be assured, the people who have been able to conquer a continent in a hundred years will not allow themselves to be deprived of the right to life, liberty, and the pursuit of happiness at the dictation of any organization, either of capital or of labor, however powerful.

Until communications by canal or rail had been established between the coal fields and the ore beds, the progress of the iron business was

Year	Production of Pig-Iron (In gross tons)	Rate of Increase per Hundredweight	Population	Rate of Increase
1830	165,000	..	12,866,020	32.51
1840	315,000	91	17,069,453	33.52
1850	564,000	79	23,191,876	35.83
1860	821,223	46	31,443,321	35.11
1870	1,696,429	106	38,558,371	22.65
1880	3,835,191	126	50,155,783	30.08
1890	8,552,679 a	123	64,000,000	28.00

a This is the product for the year ending June 30, according to the census returns, whereas the preceding figures are for calendar years.

necessarily slow. Its subsequent story is told in the table given above, showing the comparative rate of increase in population and in the production of iron.

This table brings out the striking conclusion that the production of pig iron has always increased more rapidly than the population and that the ratio is an increasing one. Between 1830 and 1860 the production of iron increased twice as fast as the population. Between 1860 and 1890 it increased four times as rapidly, thus proving that the national wealth continues to grow from decade to decade at a rate of acceleration of which the world affords no previous example. Inasmuch as during all this time we have imported iron in addition to our production, it follows that the consumption per capita has also increased more rapidly than population. In 1855, according to careful calculations which I made at that time, we were consuming iron at the rate of 117 pounds per head; whereas in 1890 the consumption has increased to rather more than 300 pounds per head, the whole of which, for the first time in our history, we are producing within our own borders.

Great Britain, on the other hand, produces more iron than it consumes and is still the largest per capita producer in the world. In 1889, with a production of 9,321,563 tons of 2,000 pounds and with a population estimated at 38,000,000, the production reached the large figure of 495 pounds per head. Deducting the exports, Great Britain is now consuming 250 pounds per head against a consumption of 144 pounds in 1855. But the production of iron in Great Britain appears to be now very nearly stationary, as will appear from the following table, giving the quantity produced since 1880:

	Gross Tons
1880	7,749,233
1881	8,144,449
1882	8,586,680
1883	8,529,300
1884	7,811,727
1885	7,415,469
1886	7,009,754
1887	7,559,518
1888	7,998,969
1889	8,245,336

This table discloses the fact that in 1889 Great Britain, while making an increase over 1888, was not able to reach the product of the years 1882 or 1883. It may, therefore, be concluded that no considerable increase of production is to be expected, especially in view of the facts that the present production is only maintained by the importation of foreign iron ores to the extent of 20.4 percent of the total ore consumption and that the ratio of foreign ore consumed in Great Britain is a steadily increasing one.

In the United States the case is otherwise. We have been able to increase our total product year by year without increasing the importation of foreign ores, none of which are in fact necessary to the existence and growth of the business, although in some localities near the coast foreign ores are desirable for the production of Bessemer pig. Assuming, then, that the production of Great Britain is not likely to be increased and that the growth in the consumption of iron is to go on with the increase of population and the progress of industry in the future as in the past, we are in a position to estimate the demands which will be made upon the resources of the United States for the next ten years. The population in 1900, allowing the same rate of increase of 28 percent as in the last decade, will be 82,000,000. A consumption of 300 pounds per head will require 24,600,000,000 pounds of iron, equal to 12,300,000 tons of 2,000 pounds. If, in accordance with the accelerated ratio of consumption, which has trebled since 1855, the per capita demands shall rise to 400 pounds, the total tonnage required will be 16,400,000 tons of 2,000 pounds, equivalent to 14,800,000 gross tons. The consumption of the world in 1889 is estimated at 24,867,534 gross tons, of which we produced 30 percent and Great Britain 33 percent. The consumption of the world has increased in eleven years from 14,117,902 tons to 24,869,534 tons, or nearly 11,000,000 tons. Assuming that the coming ten years will require an equal increase (and it is likely to require more), the United States must supply 7,000,000 tons and the rest of the world 3,000,000 in order that the two continents may not be forced to draw supplies from each other. I think it is safe to estimate, therefore, that in 1900 the world will require 35,000,000 gross tons of iron, of which the United States must supply 45 percent and the other iron-producing countries the remainder, in the proportion of half to Great Britain and half to Germany, France, Belgium, and the other smaller producers.

The question presents itself, whether this vast demand can be met without such an increase in price as will tend to restrict the use of iron within narrower limits. The increased call upon the European countries is too small to make any embarrassment, except such as may arise from the fuel and food questions, both of which are serious problems in the European industrial world. The answer to the question must, therefore, come from the United States; and in view of the changed relations of the two continents in regard to the supply of iron, it will be seen that tariff legislation will henceforth play no part in the solution of the problem. According to the traditions of the Institute of Mining Engineers it is not permissible to discuss commercial questions; but there is no impropriety in calling attention to the fact that one of the perplexing elements in the consideration of the future of the iron business is removed from the problem when the conclusion is reached that henceforth it will task the ability of Europe to supply its own demand for crude iron and that the United States must look to its own resources for the supply of the great demands of the coming century. It is quite evident that the only effect of transferring any considerable portion of this demand from the United States to Europe will be to raise the price of iron so that thenceforth the competition in the open markets of the world will be more favorable to our manufacturers than it has been in the past.

So far as we are concerned, then, the question is substantially whether this country can nearly double its production in the next ten years without so seriously increasing the present cost of iron as to restrict the consumption and arrest the rate of progress at which the world is now moving forward.

The production of iron involves the five elements of fuel, ores, capital, labor, and skill.

Fuel.—Upon reference to the map of the United States [1] on which Mr. Kunhardt has outlined the coal fields, showing their relations to the deposits of iron ore, it becomes evident that there is practically no limit to the quantity of coal which can be supplied on demand. The growth of this product corresponds very closely with that of the production of pig iron:

	Coal Mined (In tons)
1870	28,312,581
1880	65,883,000
1889	137,455,172

More than doubling itself in each decade. The capacity for production is always so far in excess of demand that it is often necessary to limit the amount forwarded to market by the action of the great corporations engaged in the mining and transportation of coal. Doubtless there will be required to meet the demand in A.D. 1900 nearly or quite 300,000,000 tons of coal. This can readily be had from the fields which are now open and have direct communication with the deposits of iron ores.

Iron ores.—The map shows also the regions from which we now derive our present supplies. That these can be doubled in ten years does not admit a doubt. Probably the most remarkable points of interest to our guests will be the great deposits of Cornwall, in Pennsylvania, of the Marquette, Menominee, Gogebic, and Vermilion ranges, in the Lake Superior region, and the ores of Tennessee and Alabama, extending in an unbroken bed for hundreds of miles along the flanks of the great Appalachian coal field. The following statement of the growth

[1] This map was exhibited in Chickering Hall during the New York Meeting.

of the business in the Lake Superior region will serve to show the facility
with which the supply can be increased:

	Tons Mined
1885	2,466,372
1886	3,568,022
1887	4,730,577
1888	5,063,693
1889	7,292,754

Showing that in five years the quantity has increased threefold.

The South is practically a virgin country, in which the production
of ore is in its infancy; but the development is already phenomenal,
and even if the other regions ceased producing ore, the Southern states
could readily supply the deficiency. It is remarkable also that the vast
deposits of hematites and red fossiliferous ores with which the South
is endowed are adapted to the "basic" process, while the ores of Lake
Superior are suited to the "acid" process. Thus the two sections are
practically the complements of each other in the work of supplying the
needs of the country for steel. It will doubtless excite surprise in the
minds of our visitors to find that the basic process has made little
progress in this country. The delay has been due partly to the recent
development of the Southern ores and partly to the illiberal spirit in
which the basic patents have been managed. But it will not longer be
possible to arrest the manifest destiny of the South which is now erecting
a large number of furnaces, the product of which must find a market
through the basic process.

Capital.—The total wealth of the United States will be reported
in the census just completed, but the figures are not yet available.
In 1880 the amount was $43,642,000,000, which is equal to $870 per
head of population. The rate of increase of population for the previous
decade was 30.13 percent and of the per capita wealth 45.47 percent.
During the decade ending in 1890 the rate of increase of population
is 28 percent, and if the ratio of increase in wealth is only the same as
in the previous decade, it will amount to 42 percent, making the per
capita wealth $1,235. The actual figures will undoubtedly show a larger
amount for each inhabitant.

In Great Britain, according to Robert Giffen, the wealth per capita,
at present, is £270, equal to $1,300, so that the two countries are
probably on an equality of wealth as to each inhabitant; but the aggregate wealth of this country now, and for the first time, exceeds that of
Great Britain, although the amount of floating capital is larger there
than here. But it must be remembered that the floating capital of the
world is now practically mobilized, so that if a deficiency exists in the
United States it is promptly supplied from abroad.

Now, the wealth of Great Britain has been adequate for the annual production of 495 pounds of pig iron per head. It cannot, therefore, be doubted that with equivalent wealth we could meet a demand of the same extent. If such a result should be reached in 1900 we should produce 19,000,000 of gross tons of iron, which exceeds the estimate already made as to the probable requirements by more than 1,000,000 tons. The very large absorption of capital in the erection of new furnaces in the Southern states during the last two years, supplying a capacity of at least 1,000,000 tons per annum when the furnaces now under construction shall have been completed, has been readily met; and this goes to show that there is no practical difficulty in getting the means to supply any quantity of iron which the market will take.

Labor.—For the supply of the raw materials and the smelting of our present product of pig iron about 200,000 men are required. The labor of one man, therefore, now suffices to produce rather more than 40 tons of pig iron per annum. To produce in 1900 double the quantity now produced will require the labor of 200,000 additional men. This is not more than the number of male emigrants who come annually to our shores, and it is but a small percentage of the normal increase of our population, which between now and 1900 will reach at least 16,000,000 of persons. So far, therefore, as the supply of labor for the increased production is concerned, we need be under no apprehension.

Skill.—Our foreign visitors are about to make a critical survey of the iron and steel works of the country, and their judgment as to efficiency and management will be accepted as final. In 1876, when this country had not fully entered upon the manufacture of steel, in which it now leads the world, producing one-third of the whole supply, the foreign engineers bore testimony to the superiority of our appliances and to the greater yield per man. Our methods and labor-saving machines were at once copied by the best European establishments. I think I am safe in saying that we have not gone backward in the interval and that our guests will still find something of value to be given in exchange for the priceless contributions which since 1876 they have so generously made to the progress of metallurgy in this and other countries. At any rate, I think we have been quite ready to learn and to take advantage of every advance, at home and abroad, so that our technique will be found to be fully up to the highest known standard of excellence.

It seems to be clear, then, that in all the elements required to meet the increased demands of the world for iron and steel, the United States are abundantly equipped. But it is not enough to have adequate supplies of ore and fuel. They must be so situated as to be brought cheaply together at the place of production. This condition has recently formed the subject of an investigation by the Commissioner of Labor, the Hon. Carroll D. Wright, and his results, so far as published, serve to show that the assemblage of material required per ton of pig iron can be made with as little labor and expense, on the average, in this country as in any country of the world. Indeed, it may be asserted that in no other country can the quantity required for the production of 20,000,000 tons per annum be brought together so cheaply, if at all.

The most remarkable fact in this connection is the constant reduction in the cost of transportation, which has been mainly accomplished by the extension and improvement of the railroad system of the country. It appears by the table herewith appended that the average rate of freights on all classes of goods since 1882 has been reduced from 1.236 per ton per mile to 0.976 in 1889.

The following statement from *Poor's Manual* shows the volume of freight traffic on all the railroads of the United States during the eight years, 1882-89:

Years	Tons Freight Moved	Tons Freight Moved One Mile	Average Rate per Ton per Mile	Average Haul per Ton
	Tons	Miles	Cents	Miles
1882	360,490,375	39,302,209,249	1.236	109.02
1883	400,453,439	44,064,923,445	1.236	110.04
1884	399,074,749	44,725,207,677	1.124	112.07
1885	437,040,099	49,151,894,469	1.057	112.46
1886	482,245,254	52,802,070,529	1.042	109.49
1887	552,074,752	61,561,069,996	1.034	111.51
1888	590,857,353	65,423,005,988	0.977	110.72
1889	619,137,237	68,604,012,396	0.976	110.80

The rates on iron ore, coal, limestone, and pig iron are probably not more than one-half of the average rate, because they are raw materials of the lowest class. This showing, which compares most favorably with the rates on European railways, is the more remarkable because it is accomplished in the face of a higher rate of wages, thus indicating that other elements besides wages paid, enter into the determination of final cost and must be taken into account by economists and lawmakers when they deal with the subject. The principal factor, however, in producing this desirable result has undoubtedly been the use of steel rails, due to the genius of Bessemer. His contribution to American prosperity will form the subject of consideration in another place, but it would be less than justice if we failed to record here that among all the agencies which have produced the phenomenal development of the United States during the last ten years, there is none which approaches in importance or is so far reaching in its influence as the process which has enrolled the name of Sir Henry Bessemer among the great benefactors of mankind.

But when the materials, the men, the money, and the skill have been brought together, it still remains to secure such harmony of action between labor and capital as will insure steadiness of employment and continuity of operations. The final answer to our inquiry as to the ability of the United States to supply the iron required for the continued progress of the country and the march of civilization throughout the world depends therefore upon the establishment and maintenance of friendly relations between the employers and employed engaged in the work of production. Otherwise, it is quite conceivable that no considerable addition can be made to the present annual product. Indeed, this consideration throws much light upon the fact that Great Britain, with abundance of fuel and with access to adequate supplies of foreign ores, has not been able to maintain the product which was reached in 1882. We are thus brought face to face with the most serious problem of our age, because if we cannot increase our output, the growth of wealth, which now increases in a higher ratio than the increase of population and is necessary to the amelioration of social conditions, must become stationary.

It cannot be denied that throughout the world the relations between capital and labor are far from satisfactory. They are undoubtedly undergoing a process of readjustment not unlike that which followed the abolition of serfdom at the close of the Middle Ages. During the process of evolution leading to a new era there must necessarily be unrest, agitation, sometimes violence, and generally severe loss on both sides, to the great detriment of society at large. The solution, when it comes, must be based upon justice; and it cannot come until public opinion is definitely made up as to the rights and duties of the contending parties or until the contention shall cease to exist by the voluntary action of the combatants. Meanwhile, the severity of the struggle may be greatly mitigated and the final outcome accelerated if certain fundamental principles which have been established by the experience of mankind are kept steadily in view, and rigorously applied as each new complication shall arise. While the propositions which I shall state may be disputed by extremists, I think they will be generally regarded as axioms ingrained in the very constitution of human nature and therefore to be accepted as standards of right and wrong to which all contentions may be referred.

I. Individual liberty consists in the right of each person to control his own life and to use the products of his labor in his own way, so long as he does not interfere with the equal rights of any other person.

II. Individual liberty implies the right of two or more persons to combine together and to use their property and faculties as they may see fit, so long as they do not interfere with the equal right of other individuals or combinations of individuals.

III. As population grows, there will necessarily be interferences among individuals and combinations of individuals, which must be adjusted; and hence the necessity for government and for tribunals whose judgment must be final.

IV. In countries where law expresses the will of the majority and in which it can be amended as often as the majority may desire there is no justification for resort to private or personal force in order to rectify wrongs, correct abuses, and maintain the rights of men. If the courts of justice have not adequate jurisdiction, it is the duty of the Legislature which represents the public will to supply it, and all agitation should be directed to secure such legislation; and no man or set of men should be allowed to take the law into their own hands, to usurp the functions of the courts of justice, or to forestall the action of the Legislature.

Bearing these axioms in mind, the following conclusions may be submitted as incontrovertible:

I. It is the equal right of employers and employees to make combinations among themselves, respectively, or with each other to advance or reduce wages, or to establish or resist legislation which either or both may regard as essential, desirable, or objectionable.

II. Neither party has the right to coerce the other into submission, except through the action of the courts or tribunals duly constituted to hear and decide upon causes of action submitted to them by either or both parties.

III. The right of workmen to refrain from labor and the right of the employer to cease to employ are correlative rights; but no one has the right to compel any other workman to cease from labor, nor has the employer any right to lock out his workmen in order to compel submission to obnoxious rules.

IV. Strikes and lockouts are therefore equally indefensible on the ground of justice, and can only be tolerated in the absence of provisions for the submission of grievances to the adjudication of competent tribunals.

V. No man has the right to compel another man to combine with him in any organization, and when a man declines to combine it is a violation of right to refuse to work with him and to deny him the means of earning a living. It is equally wrong for employers to blacklist men so that others will not give them employment.

VI. A boycott cannot be defended under any circumstances whatever. It is in effect a declaration of private war, which is a crime of the Hatfield-McCoy class, to be stamped out by prompt and severe punishment.

VII. The claim of any body of men that under any circumstances they have the right to stop the operations of business by the issue of an order in the name of organized labor or associated capital cannot be tolerated. When such an order is given in regard to any railway or any other means of communication, it is a direct assault upon the common weal; and the failure to arrest and punish the offenders thus usurping the executive functions of the State and the judicial power of the courts is proof of cowardice on the part of the public officials and of degeneracy in public opinion, which excuses or permits the violation of the principle of the common law that "not even the king can obstruct the highway."

And yet we live in a country and under a government professedly of law founded upon public opinion in which all these abuses go unpunished. If they continue, disorders will increase and capital will retire from business subject to such outrage and disturbance.

The iron business, as now organized, is a field in which capital and labor are brought into direct and immediate contact. It requires the capital of at least one thousand dollars for each man employed. It has grown up under the wages system, in which one party hires the other at an agreed price and all the risks and profits of the business are assumed by the owners. Under the modern system of industry, its operations are conducted on a scale of such magnitude as to require the association of capital in corporate organizations which have almost entirely superseded private firms and ordinary partnerships.

As a rule the workmen have formed unions for the care of their interests and especially to secure a satisfactory rate of wages. The formation of such unions is alike a right and a duty; and so long as they confine themselves to the assertion of the rights and the protection of the interests of their members they are to be commended and encouraged. The employers, on the other hand, have also various associations for the promotion of their own commercial interests, but no general organization, so far as I am informed, for the regulation of wages. Both sides are thus prepared for argument; and in this fact is to be found the starting point from which may be readily reached the ground of conciliation and arbitration which ought to make strikes and lockouts a memory of the past, to be recalled as a warning and not as a menace. In England, which has taught us how to make iron and steel cheaply and well, the system of voluntary arbitration has been in operation since 1869 and has worked, in the main, in a manner satisfactory to both parties and with decided advantage to the public. Official arbitration under the law which was passed in 1872 has not been found to be acceptable to either workmen or employers, and no case has ever arisen under the provisions of the law, from which enthusiasts [at first] expected the most beneficent results. On the other hand, too much is not expected from or attempted in the voluntary arbitrations which have sufficed to settle most of the disputes of the last twenty years.

It is admitted that the question of wages is fundamental and that it can only be solved by the equal representation of both sides, with an umpire whose decision shall be final after the fullest submission and discussion of complete information as to costs, sales, and the condition of the trade. Attempts of either side to get the better of the other by tricks and misrepresentation have long since ceased, so that when a result is arrived at, the award of the arbitrator is accepted by both sides as a satisfactory solution. Here it is obvious that three fundamental elements of conciliation have been evolved from the contentions which formerly resulted in strikes and lockouts. The right of combination on both sides is admitted; the mutual equality of both parties is conceded; and the right of both to be informed as to the actual condition of the business is acknowledged.

In view of such an example and of the advantage of avoiding conflicts damaging alike to employers and employed, I am satisfied that we shall not be long in adopting a similar system of settling disputes by voluntary action and that there will not be any disturbances serious enough to interfere with the rapid increase of product, which, as we have seen, is required by the progress of our country.

It is manifest that this method of settlement involves publicity as to the profits of business. There is undoubtedly great reluctance and some ground of objection to the disclosure of cost and profit; but as a matter of fact, the transfer of business to large corporations has really made this information public property, and in the iron business there is no longer any pretense of concealment either from stockholders or competitors. Surely then, there remains no valid reason for denying to the workmen the information necessary to enable them to formulate reasonable demands; and it is to the interest of the owners to give this information, inasmuch as the margin of profit on manufacturing operations is now narrowed down to the smallest limits consistent with a moderate return on the capital employed. There is so much misapprehension on this point in the public mind that I am impelled to say that in the great staples of trade it is exceedingly difficult to get an adequate return for the capital employed, and the business is often conducted for long-continued periods on a basis which insures only wages for labor, without any return whatever for capital. Where large profits are realized, they are due either to the production of specialties covered by patents or to the possession of raw material under exceedingly favorable conditions of cost or locality.

There is no feature in the business more pronounced than the excessive competition which cuts down profits to a minimum, and hence attempts have been made to control product and prices through combinations looking to the maintenance of standard prices, and, in some cases, by the reduction of the output. In the public mind such arrangements are confounded with trusts, which have been the subject of so much recent criticism and denunciation. The objection to trusts is not to be found in the magnitude of their operations. This, in the modern development of industry, is unavoidable and constitutes, in fact, an advantage to society by insuring lower prices and better quality and to the workmen by providing the best appliances for labor and arrangements for the preservation of health and the increase of comfort. It is only when trusts attempt to create a monopoly and succeed in destroying competition that they become injurious to the public welfare. It is extremely doubtful whether it is possible to maintain in this country an effective monopoly of any staple product of industry, but whether possible or not in other branches, the iron business is too widely diffused and is too vast in extent to admit any monopoly not sanctioned by law. The concentration of business, however, in special localities and the consolidation of interests in order to secure efficiency of administration, are a public benefit. The greater the organization and the larger the capital employed, the more certain it becomes that the business will be steadily prosecuted, thus avoiding the greatest evil under which workmen suffer—lack of constant employment. The principle of association developed in great industrial corporations is therefore altogether beneficial and should have the hearty sympathy of the public and especially of the labor organizations.

In any previous period of history such vast establishments might have been converted into devices for oppressing the workman and for preying upon society by excessive prices; but in the presence of powerful labor organizations, whose right to demand information and whose power to obtain justice is now conceded, no oppression is possible, and no exaction can be continued under the scrutiny of an omnipresent and omniscient journalism. Society has therefore nothing to fear from the growing tendency of workmen to form unions, and of capital to centralize in great industrial corporations. But society has a duty to perform in the enactment of legislation which will regulate these organizations by a clear definition of their respective rights and duties.

Publicity, inspection, and discussion are the great safeguards which the public can apply, in order to correct abuses and avoid conflicts and disastrous losses. The discouraging feature of the time is that the legislative department has shown not merely indifference but abject cowardice in dealing with the questions which from time to time require the interpretation of the law. Some of the legislation which has been recently enacted is a positive violation of the fundamental axioms which I have ventured to lay down and of the provisions of the Constitution in reference to the liberties of the citizens, which are quoted in the outset of this address; but the greatest evil is the failure to legislate at all with reference to interferences which result in constant conflict, to the great injury of the public. What we need, therefore, is a recurrence to the well-settled principles of jurisprudence, a higher order of statesmanship, and the courage on the part of our public men to stand up for the right, though for the time it may involve the sacrifice of personal popularity.

The course of procedure is clear. All organizations which avail themselves of the provisions of the law for the creation of corporations, should be required to report the result of their business and be open to the inspection and scrutiny of public officers appointed for the purpose. This principle is already recognized and enforced with reference to savings and other banks, insurance and trust companies, and railway corporations. It has not yet been applied to industrial organizations; but these now exist on so large a scale and employ so many men, disputes with whom affect the public convenience and interests so seriously, that every safeguard should be applied to prevent the disturbance and dislocation of industry. Publicity as to profits and losses would at once remove the most serious cause of strikes, which often take place when it is impossible for the employer to concede the demands of his men, because his profits will not warrant the concession. With proper information the intelligence of the workmen may be relied upon not to make an issue which can only result in failure.

It will not be necessary to give any compulsory power of rectification to the officers charged with the duty of inspection. No real abuses can survive the criticism of the press when they have been fully investigated by an impartial tribunal. No strike can then succeed unless it is based upon an abuse recognized and reported as a positive grievance by competent authority. All trade regulations and the rate of wages can then be safely left to voluntary agreement between the representatives of masters and men, sitting as equals on a board of conciliation, and presided over by an arbitrator who has the confidence of both.

Violations of the fundamental principles of society should be made crimes to be promptly punished. The Legislature will readily respond to sound public sentiment in this respect; and a stern enforcement of the law is the best security for peace and order.

With industry under the control of great corporations endowed with adequate capital, with the workmen thoroughly organized to protect their rights and advance their interests, with proper public inspection and publicity as to the condition and results of the business, with legislation covering the grounds of conflict, and with the co-operation of the judicial arm clearly expounding and steadily enforcing the law, it does not seem difficult to forecast the outcome of the evolution which is going on in the industrial world, and which seems to be full of promise and encouragement under the beneficent law which Edward Atkinson discovered and which he and Robert Giffen have demonstrated, to wit: That labor is receiving a steadily-increasing share of a steadily-increasing product; and that capital is receiving a steadily-diminishing share of an increasing product still insuring for it an adequate remuneration.

More than fifty years ago John Stuart Mill laid down the proposition that when employers and employees had a common interest in the work, in the nature of a partnership, the means would exist of "healing the widening and imbittering feud between the class of employees and the class of capitalists." Since these words were written the feud has widened and the conflicts have become more frequent and more intense. On the other hand, the work of educating both employers and workmen has been going on in a bitter school of experience. Various attempts have been made to get the two classes together on some basis of organization which will make the remuneration of each directly and visibly dependent upon the profits of business. Under the existing system wages are necessarily paid out of profits in the last analysis, but the rate and amount are not determined by the actual results from day to day. On the other hand, they constitute a prior lien upon the business, as well from necessity as now by law, and are thus exempt and guaranteed against the losses of the business.

The workman, however, fails to perceive that he is thus dependent upon the profits in order to get wages and that he has the preference over all other claims upon the product of the business. Hence the sense of personal interest is lacking, and the success of the enterprise forms no part of the workman's current of thought. He has, in fact, no means of knowing the condition of the business, and his individuality is lost in the vast aggregation of energy which is combined in order to produce the results of modern industry. In England it is notorious that the action of the trade unions has been exerted in the direction of obliterating the individual to such an extent that special skill is rapidly declining, and in the finer grades of work it is almost impossible to find the experience required for the production of instruments of precision. This is a national evil of the first magnitude; and its disastrous consequences are becoming more apparent to the intelligent workman whose opportunities to rise in life are thus abridged and destroyed.

Slowly but surely, therefore, a new idea has been taking root in the industrial mind. Profit sharing is getting to be a familiar thought both with employers and workmen, and many promising experiments in this direction are now in progress in this and other countries. The practice is to pay the current rate of wages in the usual manner, then to allow a reasonable percentage on the capital employed, and, if there be any excess after these payments, to divide it equally or otherwise between the capital and the labor, estimated by the amount of wages paid. The success of this system depends obviously upon the ability of the business to earn the current rate of wages. As this is not possible at all times, the employer must have sufficient capital to carry on business at a loss for a season, with the expectation of recouping the loss out of the future profits. It is idle to expect that workmen will be able or willing to refund losses, the risk of which must remain therefore, as it now does, with the employer. Hence the necessity and usefulness of the great organizations under the control of which the iron business is passing by steady and irresistible progress. In such establishments the work of production will go on in bad as well as in good times, and the workman will be secured against the evils of intermittent employment.

But even this advantage is not sufficient for intelligent and ambitious men. Each man should be paid wages according to the value of his labor, and not on the mistaken basis of a dead level of mediocrity advocated and enforced by some trades organizations. Progress is only possible where the individual is encouraged to develop his skill and apply his labor, by a payment in proportion to the results achieved. But higher and beyond all this stands the stimulus of being engaged in a successful business and having a direct interest in its results. If the workman were a stockholder as well as a laborer working for wages, he would have such an interest; and this would tend to raise his self-respect as well as to develop his energies.

But profit sharing, as it is called, will never be popular with the workmen, because, on the face of it, it is an act of grace from the employer. A self-respecting workman is not willing to accept charity. What he wants is justice, and any concession from the employer which does not recognize the right of the workman will be, and ought to be, rejected by independent and self-respecting men. When a workman, however, becomes a shareholder, either by payment for stock or by an agreement to pay for it out of his earnings, he stands on a level with the capitalist, and in fact, as well as in theory, is in a position to feel that he is working for himself in doing his best to promote the success of the business in which he is engaged.

It should be a matter of congratulation, therefore, that the formation of trades unions contemporaneously with the rapid growth of large corporations whose stock is divided into such small shares as to admit of easy distribution clears the way for the new era when every intelligent workman will insist upon being an owner and every well-managed corporation will see that its workmen are directly interested in the results of the business. To effect this desirable end, no compulsory legislation and no addition to the powers of corporations are needed. The educational influence of the conflicts which have occurred has already done much, and the conferences which frequently take place as to wages and regulations are doing more to establish a better understanding, to create harmonious action, and to develop the idea that business cannot be carried on unless both the capital and the labor employed share directly in the proceeds. The two classes are organized, as it were, into armies of observation, and occasionally they come into conflict, but the chances of collision are becoming daily smaller and will disappear altogether when their differences are merged in a sense of common ownership through the agency of corporations, admitting and cultivating the direct participation of the workmen in the profits.

It is, however, by no means necessary that all workmen should thus become shareholders. There will always be a considerable element of an unstable and unintelligent character, whose participation in the ownership is neither desirable nor possible; but I think the time is near when it will be discreditable to a workman not to be also an owner in the establishment in which he works, and that all workmen of the better class will have such an interest. It is quite conceivable that the workmen may ultimately acquire the preponderating interest, in which case the best possible solution will have been reached, in which labor hires capital at the lowest possible rate and thus becomes the main factor in the conduct of industry. This process can only succeed in establishments which have all the elements of success in the way of location and the possession of raw materials and of appliances for work. But such corporations, in the iron business at least, are so numerous as to offer abundant opportunity for the inauguration and successful application of this beneficent policy. I am glad to say that one of the greatest of our organizations, recently formed by the consolidation of several large establishments most favorably situated in all respects, the Illinois Steel Company, has made a promising beginning in the direction of interesting its workmen in its business. The outcome of this experiment will be watched with very great interest; and it may be commended to the attention of our guests as the most important and encouraging feature of our wonderful development, because it shows how the concentration of force under one management in accordance with the modern tendency to centralization may be made to solve and must necessarily solve the problem of harmonizing capital and labor engaged in the work of production, without new legislation or the application of any other than familiar and well-recognized principles of social organization.

The points which I desire to enforce by these arguments are:

First, that the industrial world has been steadily moving during the present century in the right direction for the welfare of mankind, and that the disturbances which have occurred have been necessary incidents of a beneficent evolution in the steady advance in the wages of labor and in the distribution of the proceeds of industry upon the basis of equality and justice.

Second, that it is not necessary to invoke any new principles of government or to inaugurate any revolution in order that capital and labor may be associated together in peace and harmony. Progress is rather to be sought in diffusing a knowledge of the principles upon which government is founded and by appropriate legislation framed in accordance therewith to meet the necessities of the complex relations arising out of advancing civilization and the unprecedented increase of riches in our day. A rigid enforcement of the laws thus formed is the necessary and sole condition for the maintenance of progress, peace, and order.

Third, that the time is approaching when capitalists and laborers will more and more be joint owners in the instruments of production. That, while the wages system will necessarily survive, the workmen will to a large extent become their own employers and finally may hire capital as capital now hires labor. The facilities offered for the division of property through the distribution of corporate shares will lessen strife, develop skill, reduce cost, increase production, and promote the equitable distribution of wealth, which, it must never be forgotten, is the chief end of the social organization.

Fourth, that the invasion of government into the domain of industry must be met with uncompromising opposition. The proper function of government is supervision, regulation, and adjudication. The work of production and distribution belongs to the citizen. Any departure from this principle must result in the ruin of free government and in the substitution of despotism, the characteristics of which are communism, anarchism and nihilism.

Our contract-labor law is an example of the pernicious character of such interference. It affords probably the only instance in history since the expulsion of the Huguenots from France in which the government has deliberately decided to deprive itself of the highest order of skill, by refusing to admit trained workmen, although it is still willing to receive ignorant and incompetent immigrants. If this law had been enforced fifty years ago, David Thomas, the first president of this Institute, whose advent to the United States has added untold millions to its wealth, would never have seen our shores. . . .

But in condemning the interference of the Government in the actual work of production or distribution, let me guard against the inference that I am not in sympathy with the modern tendency of legislation to ameliorate the condition of the laboring class by suitable regulations of the hours of labor, by securing elementary and technical education, by improving the dwellings and providing for the general recreation of the masses. Neither do I object to the control by the Government of all functions which are of a general nature, such as the transmission of letters and the care of the public health. But even in these cases the general government should confine itself to administration and regulation, employing as far as possible the agencies provided by private enterprise.

The general tendency of the age is, however, in the right direction, and it cannot be arrested by a few temporary violations of sound states- manship. The remedy will speedily be found when the workmen generally shall acquire a direct interest in the great industrial organi- zations of our day; and it is to this result that all intelligent and patri- otic men should direct their efforts. The very simplicity of the plan may suggest doubts as to its efficacy, but all doubt will vanish, I am sure, if in our trade the proprietors and managers shall make an earnest effort to interest the workmen in the ownership of the property by making it easy for them to acquire shares upon the same terms as they can be purchased by capitalists. So certain am I of the disappearance of all strife when this diffusion of ownership shall become general, that I have been impelled to ask for this subject the thoughtful con- sideration of the representatives of the iron and steel industry of the world, now for the first time assembled in the country where the final development of this business must take place upon a scale of unprece- dented grandeur.

If I have ventured to give an exceptional and unusual direction to this address, it is because I am fully persuaded that the conflict between capital and labor cannot go on without impeding, and finally paralyzing, the operations of the industrial world, and interrupting the continued progress of society in wealth, comfort and civilization. The present century, now nearing its close, has been pre-eminently an era of inven- tion and of development in the forces of nature, enriching society and opening possibilities of general culture beyond the dreams of enthu- siasm. Industrial peace is, however, necessary to the fruition of the hopes of a better adjustment of social relations, and of progress which will remove all privilege and all artificial impediments to the final estab- lishment of equal rights. It is encouraging to think that this result can be reached without seeking for any new principles of government or introducing any new methods of legislation. *Natura viam monstrat.* We have no more reason to fear association than we have to dread competition, for they are the necessary and inseparable factors of prog- ress. They are the agencies which have transformed the face of society during the present century. They are only in the infancy of their power, and no man can measure their potency in overcoming the evils which survive or which have been incidentally occasioned in the application of the natural forces in new directions. If we are careful to secure the maintenance and the application of individual energy, we have nothing to fear from association and combination. Participation in the owner- ship of the instruments of production and the agencies of distribution, rendered possible through the subdivision of the shares of the great corporations which control the domain of industry, will give the work- men who are employed in their conduct full scope for individual energy and the development of special skill in every department. The general distribution of shares is, therefore, to be encouraged as the true solution of the conflict between capital and labor, and may be relied upon to bring peace out of contention without resorting to the exasperating fallacies of communism, or the dangerous tendencies of class legislation, or to governmental interference with industrial pursuits.

Sir Henry Bessemer

ADDRESS TO THE BRITISH IRON AND STEEL INSTITUTE,
OCTOBER 2, 1890

[*The British and German industrialists remained in the United States
some time inspecting mines, iron mills, and steel plants. Before they
left, the British Institute formally conferred the Bessemer medal on
Hewitt. He replied with a brief tribute to the great inventor who
had ushered in the age of steel. Written with zest and conviction,
it made a powerful impression upon his hearers.*]

No one can be more sensible than I am of the great honor conferred by the bestowal of the Bessemer medal, or more grateful for the
felicitous and generous words in which you have given expression to
the decision of the Council. Nevertheless, I am not able to accept this
distinction, the great object of ambition in our profession, without a
feeling of compunction which justifies me in referring to the fact that
when the decision was made known to me I asked the Council to re-
consider its determination and confer the honor upon someone who
had contributed directly to the improvement of the processes which
have brought the production of steel to its present state of perfection
in this country. My own connection with the business, although lifelong, has been rather in the direction of administration and of the study
of the economic conditions of the trade, and of legislation affecting its
interests, than with technical details. I can make no pretensions to either
the scientific or the practical knowledge which constituted the merit of
the eminent men whom you have heretofore decorated with the Bessemer medal. Nevertheless, I am somewhat reconciled to your decision
by the information that this particular medal is conferred out of the
ordinary course and has been provided by Sir Henry Bessemer in view
of your visit to this country, in order to enable you to make a recognition of the wonderful development of the steel industry which has
taken place during the last decade in the United States. Receiving it,
as I do, with a profound sense of the honor which its possession implies,
I feel that I hold it in trust, as it were, for the able engineers who have
had to deal with the new processes for the manufacture of steel and
of whom you have seen fit to select me as the representative.

In one respect, however, I may have been sufficiently in advance of my associates to attract your favorable consideration. Mr. Bessemer read his celebrated paper describing the process of producing steel without fuel at the Cheltenham meeting of the British Association for the Advancement of Science in the summer of 1856. An imperfect report of this paper was published in the journals of the day and attracted my notice. The theory announced seemed to be entirely sound, and the apparatus simple and effective. I gave orders at once, without further information than that derived from the published report, to erect an experimental vessel for the purpose of testing the possibility of producing steel direct from the pig iron. In the same year in which the paper was read the experiment was tried at the furnace of Cooper & Hewitt, at Phillipsburg, in New Jersey, and the result served to show beyond all doubt that the invention of Mr. Bessemer was one which could be successfully reduced to practice. The same difficulties, however, which confronted him showed themselves in this humble experiment, and the further prosecution of the matter was deferred to a more convenient season. We all know the obstacles which Mr. Bessemer succeeded in overcoming, and the marvelous ingenuity and wide range of knowledge which he brought to bear in perfecting his process. Today, not yet thirty-five years from the time the announcement was made, it may be said to have revolutionized the iron and steel trade of the world. The whole product of steel of all kinds made prior to his invention was insignificant. Today the production has reached 10,500,000 tons, being more than one-third of the whole consumption of iron in the world. It is still rapidly advancing upon the domain occupied by the ordinary iron of commerce, and it is quite evident that the time is not far distant when the use of that commodity will be restricted to special purposes, serving to remind us of processes which otherwise would have been consigned to history.

I do not propose to enlarge upon the practical application of the Bessemer process to the manufacture of steel; but, if you will bear with me, I think it would be well to direct attention to the effects of this invention upon the economic, social, and political condition of the world. A very few considerations will serve to show that the Bessemer invention takes its rank with the great events which have changed the face of society since the time of the Middle Ages. The invention of printing, the construction of the magnetic compass, the discovery of America, and the introduction of the steam engine are the only capital events in modern history which belong to the same category as the Bessemer process. They are all examples of the law of progress which evolves moral and social results from material development. The face of society has been transformed by these discoveries and inventions. It is inconceivable to us how the world even existed without these appliances of modern civilization, and it is quite certain that if we were deprived of the results of these inventions, the greater portion of the human race would perish by starvation and the remainder would relapse into barbarism. I know it is very high praise to class the invention of Bessemer with these great achievements, but I think a candid survey of the situation will lead us to the conclusion that no one of them has been more potent in preparing the way for the higher civilization which awaits the coming century than the pneumatic process for the manufacture of steel. Its influence can now be traced, although the future results are still beyond the reach of the imagination.

Its principal characteristic is to be found in its cheapness. Steel is now produced at a cost less than that of common iron. This has led to an enormous extension in its use and to a great reduction in the cost of the machinery which carries on the operations of society. The effect has been most marked in three particulars: 1. The cost of constructing railways has been so greatly lessened as to permit of their extension into sparsely inhabited regions and the consequent occupation of distant territory otherwise beyond the reach of settlement. 2. The cost of transportation has been reduced to so low a point as to bring into the markets of the world crude products which formerly would not bear removal and were thus excluded from the exchanges of commerce. The practical result of these two causes has been to reduce the value of food products throughout the civilized world; and inasmuch as cheap food is the basis of all industrial development and the necessary condition for the amelioration of humanity, the present generation has witnessed a general rise in the wages of labor, accompanied by a fall in the price of the food which it consumes. I think it would be a very modest estimate of the improvement in the condition of the working classes as a whole to say that in the essential elements of comfort the working classes of our day are enabled to earn and to expend at least double the amount which was at their command in any previous age of the world. This result appears to me to be due very largely, if not altogether, to the economy in the agencies of production made by the cheap steel of the Bessemer process and of the other inventions which have followed in its wake. These are material results, but they are accompanied with the slow but sure elevation of the great mass of society to a higher plane of intelligence and aspiration. No better evidence of this can be afforded than the association of workingmen together for the advancement of their mutual and social condition. Troublesome as the trade unions may have been, they indicate a step in advance which should be the subject of congratulation among all well wishers of the race. I see nothing but good to come out of the modern tendency to association, and I hold it to be one of the chief glories of Sir Henry Bessemer that he has contributed more than any other living man to that condition of industry which compels all who are engaged in its conduct to combine on a scale unknown before his time in the work of economic production and equitable distribution.

The first striking result in the cheapening in the cost of the production and transportation of food products was felt in Great Britain, which is now compelled to import at least two-thirds of its consumption. The competition of our western wheat regions with the products of India in the English market altered the whole condition of agriculture in the British Isles. The profitable raising of wheat practically became impossible, and the farmers who had depended upon it could no longer pay the rents stipulated in their leases. A general reduction of rent, therefore, became necessary, which of course reduced the income of the landlords. The aristocracy of Great Britain is a survival of previous conditions, depending for its existence upon the ownership of the land and the revenue derived from it. Hence a serious if not fatal blow at the domination of what may be termed the privileged class of Great Britain was struck, unintentionally, doubtless, by the invention of Bessemer. We have not yet seen the final result of the competition it has introduced, but enough is apparent to show that the structure of the British government will necessarily undergo very serious changes, all tending to the transfer of power from those who own the land to the commercial, manufacturing, and working classes of the people. I think it is doubtful whether any event in modern times, of equal significance, has occurred. Sir Henry Bessemer has certainly been the great apostle of democracy, and although he may be inclined to disavow the claim, history will record the fact that he has been the most potent factor in the reconstruction of the British Constitution upon the basis, ultimately to be reached, of universal suffrage.

Turning from Great Britain to this country, the effects of the Bessemer invention have been even more pronounced and striking. The cheapening of the cost of transportation enabled us to increase enormously the sales of food products in foreign markets. In accordance with the well-known law of commerce that a nation cannot sell without buying, our imports of foreign merchandise have been increased in a corresponding degree. Under our fiscal system, made necessary by the war for the Union, a revenue has been derived enabling us to reduce our national debt in twenty-five years from about four thousand millions of dollars to less than nine hundred millions of dollars at the present time, notwithstanding the payment of a pension roll which now amounts to fully one hundred and twenty millions of dollars per annum. We can trace, therefore, directly to the Bessemer invention the ability to reduce our national debt and finally to pay off the outstanding bonds at maturity. This proposition can easily be verified by examining the results of the operation of our railroads, by which it will appear that since 1870, when Bessemer rails began to be largely used, the rate of transportation has been reduced about two-thirds, and an eminent authority has recently stated that the difference in a single year would now amount to one thousand millions of dollars, a very large portion of which is directly traceable to the greater durability of the track, due to steel rails and the capacity to haul increased loads, not only in the cars, but in the train. I doubt whether it ever occurred to Sir Henry Bessemer to consider the effect of his invention in furnishing us the means of paying off our national debt, but it certainly ought to secure for him the gratitude of every American citizen; and I am glad to have the opportunity, on this occasion, to bring this obligation to the notice of my countrymen.

The third point to which I would call attention is the vast extension and new direction of commerce which has resulted from the construction of steel vessels. The size of these vessels has enormously increased, and the cost of operating them has been reduced in a corresponding degree, comparing very favorably with the reduction of cost upon land, which is about one-third of what it was ten years ago. The characteristic of modern commerce is in the rapidity with which exchanges are made and in the fact that all portions of the habitable globe are quickly reached. The commercial world has been converted into a vast clearing house for the exchange of products. One country may sell more than it buys or buy more than it sells to particular country, but the difference is counterbalanced by a corresponding sale and purchase from some other country. The balances are not paid in money, but are passed to the credit of each country in the general settlement which takes place in the banking centers of the commercial world. Thus the function of the precious metals is reduced simply to the payment of final balances which in the course of any one year are small in amount. The economy in exchange thus effected is largely due to the improvement in transportation, made possible by the general use of steel, aided by the telegraph and particularly by the submarine cables which now reach every part of the civilized world. The interdependence of the human race has thus been increased, and the possibilities of hostile action by war diminished in a corresponding degree. The name of Bessemer will, therefore, be added to the honorable roll of men who have succeeded in spreading the gospel of "Peace on earth and good will towards men," which our divine Master came on earth to teach and to encourage.

I have some hesitation, in conclusion, in referring to another point which seems to me to be required in order to complete this hasty reference to the claims of Sir Henry Bessemer to the admiration and gratitude of mankind. It is to be hoped that out of the stupendous results of his genius he has acquired for himself an ample fortune. How large the amount may be I have no means of knowing, but if he should be in the receipt of even a small percentage of the annual saving to society, he would have the largest income of all men in the world. It is the fashion of the day to rail at the possessors of large fortunes, and there are people who imagine that they have been wronged by the existence of such aggregations of wealth. It is doubtful whether, in proportion to the total wealth of mankind, the portion which may be controlled by the few who are recognized as great capitalists is as large in our time as in other ages of the world. But even if the case were otherwise, no man can allege that he is not a positive gainer by the results of the Bessemer invention or that he suffers loss or damage in any way from the fact that Bessemer has secured for himself a small portion of the benefits which his genius has conferred upon mankind. His example is of inestimable value, therefore, in showing that the existence of large fortunes, as a rule, is the evidence of benefactions vastly greater to the wealth of the world, by which all have gained and none have lost. Although there are undoubtedly striking exceptions to this general rule in the possession of fortunes due to accident or even to fraud, these exceptions only serve to call public attention to the real question which underlies the accumulation of wealth in private hands, namely, the mode in which it is used by the possessors. A great capital is a great blessing if it is employed in adding to the resources and advancing the civilization of the world. It is a curse only when it is used for demoralizing expenditures and vicious indulgence. The career of Bessemer, therefore, is admirable, not only in having added to the general wealth, but in the employment of his share of the proceeds of his invention for the spread of knowledge, the progress of industry, and the reward of efforts to promote the welfare of the race. He is now in the evening of his days, but he is also at the summit of his fame, for he has lived to see the marvelous fruits of his genius in the advancement of his fellow men to a higher plane of comfort and intelligence than has been possible in any previous age.

I think, therefore, Mr. President, that I am justified in asking you to carry back to Sir Henry Bessemer the grateful regards of his kin beyond the sea, whose homes he has multiplied, whose country he has developed, whose burdens of debt he has lightened, and whose progress in all the arts of civilization he has placed upon a basis as durable as the material with which his name will ever be associated.

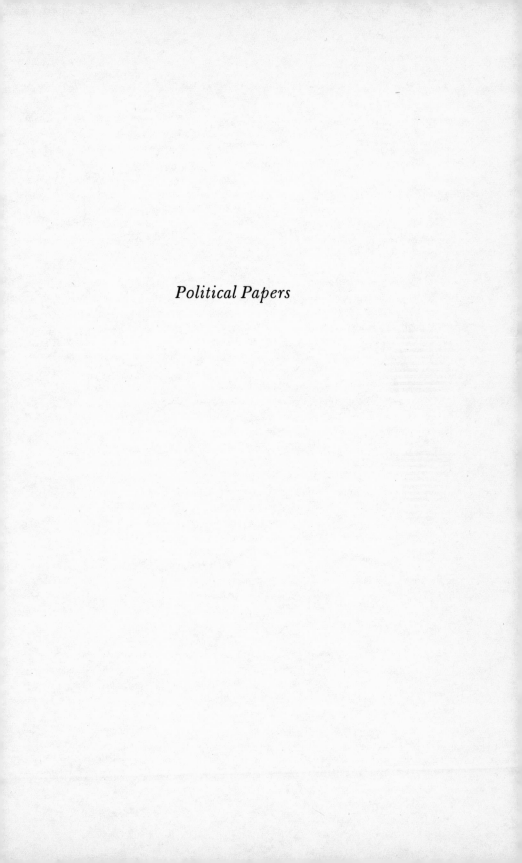

Political Papers

The Need for National Reform, 1876

SPEECH IN THE HOUSE OF REPRESENTATIVES, MAY 25, 1876

[Hewitt, elected to Congress in the autumn of 1874, entered that body as the Grant administration began to reap the harvest of its laxity and incompetence. He at once became one of the leaders in the fierce Democratic onslaught upon the record of the Republican Party since the Civil War, and in the demand for administrative and legislative reform. The country was in the grip of a fearful depression and filled with unemployment and misery. It had lost all faith in the President, if not all of its old admiration for him. One scandal after another in 1874-76—the Whiskey Ring scandal, the Belknap scandal, the Robeson scandal, the Interior Department scandals under Delano, the exposure of Orville E. Babcock's activities—filled the public with consternation and indignation. It was evident that the next Presidential campaign would bring an overwhelming demand for change. The Republican Party must disown the deplorable list of follies and failures under Grant and purge itself of its worst machine politicians; but even if it did so, it was not improbable that an aroused electorate would repudiate it. Hewitt expected to see the host of Democrats, Independents, and reformers led by his close friend Samuel J. Tilden. If the country could be sufficiently awakened to the corruption of the national administration; to the degree in which selfish plutocratic interests had fastened themselves upon the Republican organization; to the tragic and tyrannical blundering in Southern reconstruction—then it would place the government in new and competent hands. If Tilden became President, Hewitt would have an important place and a large influence in the new administration. Meanwhile, he took such a part in creating the demand for reform and in building up an efficient and militant Democratic organization, that later Don M. Dickinson and others testified that he, not Tilden, had been the true leader of the movement for regenerating the national government. One of Hewitt's activities in the Forty-fourth Congress was the investigation of the Emma Mine scandal; that is, the connection of the American Minister to England, Robert C. Schenck, with a Utah mining scheme which had cost British investors large sums of money. Hewitt brought in a moderately-phrased but extremely telling report, which left Schenck totally discredited. He laid it *before the House with the following speech on the need for a purification of the national administration; a vigorous appeal, not at all partisan in character, to the highest principles and instincts of the American people.*]

Such, Mr. Speaker, is the unanimous verdict of the Committee on Foreign Affairs in reference to the connection of General Schenck, late the American minister at the Court of St. James's, with the Emma Mine, and such, doubtless, will be the verdict of this House and the general judgment of the country. This verdict has been reached only after weeks of patient investigation, in which General Schenck has had every possible opportunity for his defense and for his vindication. The committee have performed their duty with a profound sense of the consequences to General Schenck, after a career of over forty years in the public service, and with a sincere desire, if possible, to shield him at the close of that career from the censure which they are now reluctantly constrained to inflict.

If his reputation had been alone concerned, the mantle of charity and silence might have been drawn over the facts of this unfortunate affair; but unhappily the honor and dignity of the people of the United States became necessarily involved in the affair, when, upon the receipt of a copy of General Schenck's letter of resignation, the administration failed to recall him at once from his mission for having deliberately violated, in this letter, after explicit notice from the Secretary of State, the well-settled principles which should govern the conduct of our representatives in foreign countries.

The committee would have failed in their duty if they had admitted by their silence the doctrine that an American minister may use his official station for the purpose of promoting private gain and be allowed to retain his high office. Of all the positions in public life, the ambassador occupies the most delicate, the most responsible, the most honorable. He represents abroad the majesty of the people; he carries with him into foreign lands an absolute immunity from arrest. The flag of his country makes his domicile sacred from intrusion. No matter what crimes he may commit, he is amenable only to the laws of his own country, upon the soil of which he is supposed to stand wherever his foot may rest.

But while no harm can come to him personally by any act of his, he can commit no act, whether noble or infamous, which does not directly affect the honor of the nation which he represents. Hence his guiding rule of action must necessarily be to subordinate all personal and private interest to the national honor; and his immunity from prosecution is the very reason why he should refrain from engaging in any operations by which others may sustain loss while he is protected from personal responsibility. Of all places in the public service, it is the one in which self-denial is the most necessary, the most conspicuous, and the most honorable. On the other hand, so delicate is his position that the slightest intimation from the power to which he is accredited that his presence is unacceptable is held to be the warrant for his recall without demurrer and without explanation.

It is true that foreign nations exercise a wise discretion on subjects of so much delicacy and generally forbear to intimate dissatisfaction even when there is good ground for it; but this is all the stronger reason why a proud and sensitive people should not be humiliated before the civilized world by the continuance in office of a representative who has fallen below that high standard of honor which we desire to maintain among the nations. "Cæsar's wife should be above suspicion." The honor of the ambassadors of the United States should not from their own acts become the subject of criticism in the newspapers, the clubs, and the social circles of the countries to which they are accredited; and above all, when admonished of a fault which would be venial if promptly and publicly confessed, they should not aggravate the offense by repeating it, as General Schenck did in his letter, of resignation, suffered to go upon the records of the State Department without prompt and just rebuke from the Government, which could only thus relieve itself from the responsibility of this flagrant violation of the well-settled usages of diplomatic intercourse and conduct, whereby he proved himself unequal to the trust reposed in him by his own Government and abused the confidence of that government to which he was accredited.

If this view of the subject be correct—and there would seem to be no possible escape from it—the responsibility for every hour of the disgrace which for more than four years has, out of this transaction, rested upon the American name and caused every right-minded lover of his country to blush for shame, is brought home to the administration, and there would be no occasion to make further comment on this unhappy business except for the purpose of showing the deplorable consequences which are sure to result from failure on the part of the Government to deal promptly and sternly with its servants for any serious violation of its own regulations, its instructions, or of the well-settled principles and long-established usages of diplomatic intercourse, to the end that the repetition of such offenses may hereafter become impossible, and the fair fame of the American people never again be tarnished by such disgraceful transactions. I do not forget the wise and witty French proverb, *Lavons notre linge sale en famille;* but this linen was soiled abroad, and has so long been worn in the face of the whole world that we have no choice but to make its purification as conspicuous and as public as was the transaction by which it was polluted.

For this dreary and unpalatable task, necessary and profitable, how-

ever, "for doctrine, for reproof, for correction, for instruction in right-
eousness," the materials furnished by the evidence submitted with the
report are ample.

They serve to show how an ambassador of the United States so far
forgot his high station that he not only consented to become a director
in a company proposing to sell its shares in the country to which he
was accredited, but allowed his name and the official title of "American
minister" to go forth in the prospectus as the voucher of its "exceptional
character"; how, by subscribing publicly, according to his own statement, for £10,000 of the stock, apparently upon the same terms as the
other subscribers, but in reality upon a private arrangement previously
made with the vendors, in which he put no money at risk and was absolutely guaranteed against loss, the envoy of the great republic placed
himself in the unconscious attitude of a "puffer" at an auction sale; how
he speculated in the stock of a corporation which he had thus helped to
create and direct; how he seemed to be incapable of drawing the distinction between investment and speculation; how he associated one of his
secretaries of legation in these speculative operations and availed of the
services of the other to watch the fluctuations of the stock market and
practically act as his broker for the sale of shares; how he records his
opinion that it is a proper thing, not merely for an ordinary man, but
for an American minister, "to sell stock short," that is, to sell what he
does not own, and expresses his regret that he did not do so and indem-
nify himself against loss by transferring it to someone else not in possession of the information which he had received through private sources;
how he so confuses his accounts of profit and loss that he cannot separate
the profits which he actually did [realize] or might have realized out of
his original transaction with Mr. Park with the losses which he made in
speculations in the stock having no relation to this transaction with
Park; how he accepts credits upon the note which he had given to Park,
the nature and origin of which he had no knowledge whatever, except
that they arose out of transactions wherein he was at no risk; how he
declines further credits of the same character, because he thinks that
the limit of favors has been reached; how he arrived at this conclusion
only after the public press had been filled with hostile criticism; how
his memory as to the mode of payment for the second allotment of
shares leads him in London to swear that Park did not provide the
means for the payment thereof, and how before the committee, when
it had been clearly shown that Park did provide these means, he re-
tracts the statement he made in London; how in the final settlement
with Park, he transfers to him, in payment of his indebtedness, stocks
upon which he continues to draw the dividends; how, on leaving London, he is forced to plead his diplomatic privilege as his defense against
the service of a writ in a civil action growing out of his unfortunate

connection with this disastrous undertaking; and how, finally, he reiterates his inability to comprehend the false and unfortunate position in which he is placed before the public, by a series of ill-advised transactions, in which it is charitable to regard his memory as at fault and to look upon him as the victim of designing and unscrupulous men leading and persuading him to an equal ruin of reputation and purse.

These materials serve to show how William M. Stewart, a Senator of the United States, while acting as counsel for a client, who had placed his interests unreservedly in his hands, with whom he had arranged for a contingent fee, which should have bound him all the more jealously to guard the interest of his client, became the purchaser of that interest, at a time and under circumstances when he could have computed its value with almost mathematical certainty, at a price which gave to the client $150,000, which was practically the contingent fee, and gave to the counsel the larger sum, $275,000, which should have gone to the client; how this magnificent sum, which was paid by Park to Stewart, not in pursuance of any express written agreement, such as usually regulates large money transactions even among the best of friends, but in accordance with an unwritten understanding apparently based upon a sentiment of honor, which has been formulated into the English language; how the legal redress wisely secured by the law to the client under such circumstances was cut off by a further payment at a later date, which Stewart stigmatizes as blackmail, and a release secured, which, as a summary of the whole transaction, as a legal curiosity, and a model form for lawyers who desire to secure protection from their clients, it is well to preserve:

Know all men by these presents that I, James Elias Lyon, of Racine, in the State of Wisconsin, in consideration of the sum of $50,000 to me in hand paid by William M. Stewart, of the State of Nevada, now of Washington, in the District of Columbia, the receipt whereof is hereby acknowledged, do hereby fully and forever release and discharge the said Stewart from all and every demand, claim, or right of action of every description that I have or may claim to have against him, whether legal or equitable, and especially from any and all claims, demands, or causes of action of every description growing out of his relation as attorney or counsel or agent for me in the litigation concerning the Emma Mine, so called, and the various proceedings, negotiations, contracts, and conveyances concerning or connected with said Emma Mine, and the property thereto belonging, and the conduct, management, and disposition thereof by him, the said Stewart, in every and all respects and particulars.

In witness whereof I have hereunto set my name, and seal, at the city of London, this eighteenth day of May, 1872.

JAMES E. LYON. [SEAL.]

In presence of—
OLIVER GAGER,
    45 *Albemarle Street, London.*
T. H. WRIGHT,
    Consul-General Clerk, U. S. A., London.

How thus was secured immunity from the claims of his client, but not from the impartial judgment of the legal profession and of the world.

These materials serve to show finally how Trenor W. Park, "a member of the American bar, the president of the National Bank at North Bennington, Vermont," and well known to the American public for his connection with the Mariposa Company, whose disastrous failure some years ago will not soon be forgotten by those who suffered, the great author of all this mischief, with a skill which has never been surpassed, going to London an entire stranger, but having carefully prepared the way by large shipments of ore and glowing accounts of the production of the mine, within one short month secured the services of Albert Grant, the greatest manipulator of speculative shares of modern times, agreeing to pay therefor a rate of compensation which may be small for him, but which in this country of primitive notions would be deemed decidedly magnificent; how he provided in the contract for sustaining the market pending the allotment, by purchases of the shares at fictitious premiums, so as to gather in the money of *bona-fide* investors, a process said to be usual in England, but which here would be regarded as little short of robbery; how widows and clergymen and half-pay officers and others living upon annuities were thus induced to invest their scanty capital in the hope of securing permanent dividends at a high rate out of an enterprise said to be "exceptional" by the American minister (let us be thankful that such *exceptional* cases are rare); how he ingratiated himself into the confidence of the American representative at the Court of St. James's so that within two short weeks he felt an irresistible desire to shower benefits upon him and to relieve him from the embarrassments arising from large expenditures out of a narrow official income; how he inspired the minister with that charming confidence which accepts favors without suspicion that they are to be requited; how he issues a prospectus containing statements calculated to persuade the most wary, but which turn out to be in mournful contrast with the actual issue of the enterprise; how, when he was about to lose, by the resignation of the American minister, the main stay upon which he relied for the sale of the remaining half of the shares of the company which had been tied up for a time, he procures a letter, which was declared to be in effect better than to have the minister remain as a director, wherein his own character is reindorsed and the great value of the property reaffirmed; how everybody who could assist or injure the successful perpetration of the sale was conciliated by "pulls," as the Senator from Nevada sarcastically describes them, upon the funds collected from a confiding public, so that "by a long pull, a strong pull, and a pull altogether," about a million of dollars was expended in preliminary expenses, of which the great American banking house of Jay

Cooke, McCulloch & Co. got "a pull" of $125,000; how, when doubts had begun to arise as to the continued productiveness of the property before the reserve shares had been sold, he procured the services of the vice-chairman of the company, Brydges-Williams, esq., M. P., to make a personal examination of the mine by the payment of £5,000, and a call for or right to take two thousand shares of stock at a price at which the call could only be profitable to the examiner as the result of a favorable report; how the favorable report was made and the reserved shares were sold at a premium of £3 per share; how when the public supposed these were still tied up for months to come they were all sold within two weeks of the receipt by telegraph of the report; how even the astute and accomplished Albert Grant was induced, by a process which no man can find out, to abate his claims for one-half the profits and accept £1 per share in lieu thereof; how he was induced to give up his just claim for £2,000 commission on the stock which had been allotted to General Schenck, and how the same was credited on Schenck's note to Park, falling like manna from heaven; how Park bought and sold the shares through dark and devious courses, coming out at the end with a profit even on these transactions; how, when the shares were selling at over £20 apiece in London, he bought out his partners in New York at less than half that price; how at the shareholders' meetings in London, which he attended, everything was made lovely for everybody, so that no one appears to have any legal ground against him for indemnity, although dividends ceased after thirteen months, and the shares are now selling at twenty-five shillings apiece; how the whole business is now involved in litigation on both sides of the Atlantic, so that Park declined, for fear of the consequences, to put his accounts upon the record, or to testify as to the amount of profit which he realized for the sale of the shares; how libel-suits are pending against newspapers who have ventured to express unfavorable opinions in regard to an operation which has caused a greater scandal in the business and diplomatic world than any transaction of modern times, to the specter of which the author of its being, Trenor W. Park, triumphantly exclaims:

> Shake not thy gory locks at me;
> Thou can'st not say I did it.

All this and much more of the same unsavory sort can be learned from a perusal of the evidence herewith submitted; but these are matters which only concern the American people because they serve to show the injurious consequences to the fair fame of the United States arising out of the failure of the Government to deal promptly and firmly with its minister, when, by his becoming a director and by his letter of resignation, he made the grave and irreparable mistake of indorsing and reindorsing the enterprise and the men who have caused this great disaster and this greater reproach.

What the Government failed to do the American people demand of their representatives, the stern condemnation of this departure from the traditions of the fathers and the accepted usages of diplomatic life, especially because, to its credit be it said, it is the first symptom in the foreign department of the Government of that general demoralization which seems to have crept into every other branch of the public service.

The Republic can now only be saved by the exercise of stern, relentless, uncompromising virtue, refusing to surrender any question of principle, and swiftly and surely destroying in their very birth the germs of corruption, which if allowed to live will surely sap the foundations of free government, our great inheritance, and the chief hope of our posterity.

The people are therefore in no temper to allow sympathy with any man, however eminent his services and long his tenure of public office and however much he may be entitled, by reason of his advanced years or his impaired fortune, to the tender consideration of this House, to interfere with the vindication of the name, honor, and majesty of the American people, from the criticism of the civilized world arising out of the errors of judgment of its public servants or of the administration. The time has come when the public sentiment demands more than economy, more than honesty; it demands purity and self-denial from its officials. The old generation of public men is passing away with the first century of the Republic. Few men are left alive who can date back to the time when this Government was founded by the virtue and the sacrifice of the patriots who achieved our independence; but the sentiment of honor and the spirit of self-denial which led them to stake "their lives, their fortunes, and their sacred honor" for the establishment of a government in which principle and purity should be the conditions of its existence, still survive, and it is a mistake to suppose that because they have grown rich and powerful the people of this country have become enervated, shameless, or corrupt.

The spirit abroad is the spirit of reformation. The people are determined to bring back that better era of the Republic in which when men consecrated themselves to the public service they utterly abnegated all selfish purposes; when public officers rejected gifts as dishonoring alike to the giver and the taker; when Presidents and great officers of state as a rule retired to honorable poverty; when Franklin with his modest income and his uncourtly costume, even though he had a thrifty mind, rejecting all thought of gain while employed in the public service, was held in more honor than the proudest ambassador of the proudest empire; when John Quincy Adams sold his bank shares before he would take his seat in Congress, lest his vote might be called in question;

when members of Congress knew not the mysteries of Crédit Mobilier; when members of the Cabinet were selected because they were statesmen, "honest, capable, faithful," and not because of their skill in managing party politics; when to be summoned into the public service was a priceless honor and not an opportunity for private gain; when a civil-service system practically existed in the Government, because it had not yet been formulated into the perfunctory platforms of party; when a change of administration did not inaugurate a disgraceful scramble for place and the fatal doctrine "to the victors belong the spoils" had not yet been invented; when the idea 'of a trust was the subordination of the trustee and all his personal interests to the rightful claims of those for whom he acted; when lawyers were not accustomed to speculate upon the rights of their clients; when vendors were not suffered to profit by false representations; when the honor and fame of the nation were dearer and greater than the reputation or the fortune of any citizen; when degenerate men who were willing to barter away the national honor in foreign lands in exchange for private gains, however great, would have been gibbeted for the general execration.

It is for this reason that the present investigation is of the gravest importance, and it indicates a more healthy state of public opinion, and it should be a matter of general congratulation that the committee have been able by the exercise of mutual forbearance and patience to come to a unanimous conclusion. No public money has been misappropriated; but the national honor, which is above all money, has been tarnished, thoughtlessly, if you will, but if so, by the mistake and unconscious ignorance of a great public officer, who has not yet, after the lapse of four years, been properly rebuked by his own Government.

There are positions and circumstances in which ignorance is as mischievous as crime; and I feel constrained and grieved to say that the connection of the American minister at the Court of St. James's with the Emma Mine belongs to that category. We may pity, we may sympathize, but we must condemn, in order that the condemnation which belongs to him and the administration should no longer rest upon the consciences and the name of the American people, and that it shall forever be impossible for this humiliating offense to be repeated by an ambassador of the United States or fail to be punished by his Government.

Much of what I have said, Mr. Speaker, might with more force and, it seems to me, with equal propriety have been included in the report. But the majority of the committee have deemed it better to yield somewhat of their convictions and make the report, as nearly as may be, a colorless statement of the facts developed by the testimony, in order to secure what they regard as of inestimable value to the rising generation of the country, the example of a unanimous report, made without regard to party affiliations and prejudices, upon a subject which concerns the reputation and dignity of the nation before the civilized world. Any other report would be open to the criticism that it was dictated by partisan feeling, and the condemnation of conduct which has brought disgrace upon the nation and might otherwise come to be regarded as a precedent would necessarily lose much of its value to the country, the honor and welfare of which should be regarded by every well-wisher of his race as infinitely beyond and above all party considerations. Parties are but temporary and will surely perish with the changing conditions of the times; but the nation will as surely survive forever if we can preserve the spirit of virtue and patriotism by which it was created, and which should make us all willing to sacrifice party and prejudice upon the common altar of the country and join in the universal Centennial prayer, "God save the Republic."

Secret History of the Disputed Election, 1876-77 [1]

[At the opening of the Presidential campaign of 1876 between Rutherford B. Hayes and Samuel J. Tilden, Hewitt was chosen chairman
of the Democratic National Committee. Contrary to statements
later made by John Bigelow and others, he, not Tilden, was the
active head of the party canvass; one of the most energetic, judicious, and efficient canvasses ever made by the Democrats. It resulted in a popular plurality of more than a quarter of a million
votes for Tilden; but the Republican control of three Southern
states, South Carolina, Florida, and Louisiana, where the contest
was close and was marked by fraud on both sides, enabled them to
claim the election. The moment the dispute over the result began,
Hewitt favored an energetic course. He wrote an emphatic address
to the people which he asked Tilden to sign—an address calling
for great mass meetings on Jackson Day to assert Democratic rights.
But Tilden, who was "deep in lawbooks" on the constitutional
niceties of the dispute, vetoed this appeal. Indeed, Tilden exhibited
marked indecision and timidity throughout the controversy. It was
immediately taken up in Congress, and this gave Hewitt a double
rôle. He was not merely Democratic national chairman, but the
ablest Democratic leader on the floor of the House. In the tense
weeks between December 4, 1876, and March 4, 1877, he labored
to prostration trying to maintain the Democratic rights, to meet
the wishes of the wavering and enigmatic Tilden, and to help find
a peaceful solution for a quarrel which threatened civil war.

The course which Hewitt followed is vividly outlined in the following pages. He was an American before he was a Democrat; he
regarded his duty as a member of Congress as higher than his duty
as national chairman. He therefore, like Senators Bayard and Thurman, supported the plan for an adjudication of the dispute. A stub-
born insistence by both parties on their "rights" would merely
mean deadlock and disorder; arbitration was imperative. But he
did insist upon a plan of arbitration which would be agreeable to
Tilden, and no final sanction was given to the Electoral Commission until Tilden had assented to it. He insisted also upon a plan
so molded as to be fair to the Democratic Party. But for two un-
foreseen circumstances—the abrupt resignation of David Davis from
the Supreme Court and his refusal to serve on the Commission, and

[1] Dictated in Bath, England, June 1-June 10, 1895; never before published in full.

*the failure of Judge Bradley of the Supreme Court to play the part
of non-partisan arbiter which it was his plain duty to take, Tilden
would have been seated as President. When he was defeated, Democratic chagrin ran high. Hewitt, Bayard, Thurman, and other Democratic leaders in Congress were viciously assailed by some of Tilden's friends. These attacks were redoubled after the disclosures by
the Potter Committee threw suspicion of improper conduct on
Tilden; for it was important to make him still appear a martyr.
Public statements by Henry Watterson led Hewitt in 1878 to write
out an exact account of his rôle in the dramatic contest. But he
did not publish it; and when in 1895 John Bigelow's inaccurate
life of Tilden repeated the charges, Hewitt merely amplified his
narrative and laid it among his papers for posthumous publication.
It is here presented in full for the first time. The second version
(1895) differs from the first (1878) in little except fullness of detail.
Both are in manuscript among the Cooper-Hewitt Papers.]*

The recent publication of the life of Samuel J. Tilden by John
Bigelow,[1] reopens the discussion which immediately followed upon the
result of the Presidential canvass of 1876 and the creation by Congress
of the Electoral Commission. My connection with these events was so
intimate and has to some extent been so much misrepresented, that it
becomes necessary to make a record of the actual occurrences of this
memorable era so far as I had personal knowledge of the events which
preceded and occurred during the Presidential campaign and of the
proceedings of Congress resulting in the final counting of the votes and
the inauguration of Rutherford B. Hayes as President of the United
States.

It is proper to premise that I did not enter public life until I had
reached my 54th year. I had, however, always taken a deep interest in
public affairs, and for many years had been a close student of politics.
In the various political campaigns from 1848 to 1874 I had taken an
active part in the conventions and in the consultations of leading Democrats as to the policy and platforms of the party. I had often prepared
resolutions for the approval of the Democratic Party and had occasionally, but not often, discussed important questions before popular
audiences.

[1] Published in two volumes by Harper & Brothers, 1895. The *Nation* declared
(May 16, 1895) that "Mr. Bigelow has conceived his office as biographer to be that of
an advocate for Mr. Tilden and the Democratic Party," and that his treatment of the
events of 1876 was "a one-sided statement that does not rise to the plane of history."
Unfair in some ways to the Republican opponents of Tilden, it was also, and with less
excuse, unfair to Hewitt, Allen G. Thurman, Thomas F. Bayard, and other Democratic
leaders.

The iron business in which I was engaged made it convenient for me to live in New Jersey, although I was born and brought up in New York and had intimate associations with the leading politicians of the latter state.

The Republican Party had been in the possession of the Government uninterruptedly from 1860 until 1874, a period of fourteen years during which the Civil War had been fought out and the preservation of the Union had been assured. So long a tenure of power during a period of vast public expenditure necessarily led to extravagance, abuse of power, and actual fraud on the part of many officials entrusted with the patronage of office and the disposal of contracts. The public mind therefore was ripe for a change of administration. It seemed evident that the election of 1874 would result in a political revolution and in the election of a majority of Democratic members in the 44th Congress.

It was intimated to me that the Democratic Convention of the 5th Congressional District of New Jersey would certainly nominate me for Congress. I was not ambitious of political preferment. The Republican representative of the district, William Walter Phelps, was my personal friend; he had already served two terms in Congress with great ability, independence, and general acceptance.[1] I thought that he deserved re-election and was unwilling to be his competitor for a position which I did not desire. I decided therefore to change my legal residence from New Jersey to New York, where I had a house and lived for one-half of the year. I therefore resigned various official positions of an honorary nature which I held in New Jersey, and in a letter to the Governor announced my change of residence to the City of New York. This event occurred in the month of October, 1874.

Greatly to my surprise I was nominated for Congress by the Democratic Convention for the 10th Congressional District of the State of New York in which Mr. Tilden, who had already been nominated for Governor, as well as myself resided. I have good reason to believe that the suggestion for my nomination came from Mr. Tilden, with whom I had long been associated in various public affairs and private business and more particularly in the friendly intercourse of domestic life;[2] in fact for more than twenty years I had been on terms of the closest intimacy with him and was often made the recipient of his opinions

[1] Phelps was a New York banker who resided in Englewood, N. J. He had, as a matter of fact, served only one term in Congress, 1873-75, being defeated for re-election in 1874 because he had broken from his party on the Civil Rights Bill. He entered Congress again in the eighties, and was Minister to Germany under Harrison.

[2] Hewitt in his year as a law-student had known Tilden, and the friendship had gradually ripened. After marriage, Hewitt made his winter home with Peter Cooper on lower Lexington Avenue, a few doors from Gramercy Park; Tilden lived on the southern side of the Park. They were thus close neighbors and saw much of each other. Hewitt and Tilden also had important iron interests in common.

on important questions before. they were made known to the public.

The campaign which followed resulted in the election of Mr. Tilden as Governor by a very large majority; I was returned to Congress after an exciting contest against what was then regarded as the disreputable section of the Democratic Party in the City of New York.[1] For the first time in my life I was compelled to discuss public and personal issues before the people; their approval gave me courage to undertake the onerous duties which fell to my lot in the 44th Congress which met for organization in December, 1875.

The position assigned to me by Speaker Kerr on the Committee of Public Buildings and Grounds was not such as my friends expected and was not agreeable to me because it placed me in an attitude where I was compelled to pass upon expenditures which would affect my private business. I therefore declined the assignment and was told afterward that it was due to the suggestion made by Mr. Manton Marble,[2] who thus early, for some unexplained reason, manifested his personal hostility.

Subsequently my colleague, Smith Ely, Jr., who felt that I had not been properly recognized, arranged a transfer with the Speaker by which I took his place on the Committee of Foreign Affairs. For this exchange I was, and still am, grateful to Mr. Ely, mainly because in the progress of the session I was able thus to put my knowledge of business and particularly of mining to what proved to be an important purpose.

It will be remembered that the House of Representatives in the 44th Congress had a large Democratic majority, composed chiefly of members from the South, with a small addition of Democratic members from the North. As the Senate and the President were still Republican, the House was powerless to enact legislation except by their consent. It had power, however, to institute and conduct investigations into the operations of the Government and the expenditure of the public money. Hence it was decided to undertake these investigations and each committee proceeded to such an inquiry in its proper sphere of action. The results were astounding; corruption was found to permeate every branch of the National Government. So far as foreign affairs were concerned, the most important subject of investigation was known as "The Emma Mine Scandal" with which was connected the name of the Minister of the United States to Great Britain.[3] This inquiry was conducted by a subcommittee of which I was the chairman. I drew the report,[4] presented

[1] That is, the remnants of the old Tweed Democracy.

[2] At this time editor of the New York *World*, the principal Democratic organ of the metropolis.

[3] Robert C. Schenck of Ohio.

[4] House Report No. 579, 44th Congress, 1st Sess.; a very severe document, written throughout by Hewitt.

it to the House, and made the explanatory speech which resulted in the passage of a resolution without division, recommending the recall of the Minister, who had allowed his name to be associated with a disreputable transaction in the country to which he was accredited. The adoption of this resolution was the beginning of a series of reports by the several committees, proving that every department of the Government had become demoralized and was open to just criticism. These reports paved the way and indeed formed the foundation for the political revolution which followed in the Presidential campaign of 1876, when for the first time since the Civil War a Democratic President was elected, and both House and Senate came under Democratic control.

Governor Tilden was regarded by thoughtful politicians to be the logical candidate of the Democratic Party for President. His efforts in overthrowing the Tweed Ring in the City of New York had made him Governor, and his corresponding success in unearthing the Canal frauds had given him a commanding position before the country as a proper representative of the Reform Movement which had driven the Republicans from power in many of their strongholds.

To make his nomination possible, however, required earnest and active preliminary work in the several states and especially in the South where he was not as well known as statesmen like Thurman and Bayard, who had seen long service in the Senate of the United States and were idols of the Democratic Party.

It was necessary, therefore, to organize a propaganda in behalf of Mr. Tilden and to send out publications and missionaries in order to make his character and career known to the Democratic masses in the South, whose votes would necessarily be controlling in the coming Presidential convention. This movement was the origin of what came to be known as the "Literary Bureau," afterwards so efficient in the Presidential campaign of 1876. Whether the suggestion for the formation of this agency came originally from Mr. Tilden or not, I do not know; but I do know that the cost of the enterprise was defrayed by Mr. Edward Cooper, who was my partner in business and whose sister I had married. The outlay was about 20,000 dollars.

When the convention met at St. Louis the results of this preliminary work became apparent. Mr. Tilden was in the lead from the outset and on the second ballot was found to have more than two-thirds of all the votes, which finally were made unanimous.

I was a member of this convention and, doubtless by the wish of Mr. Tilden, was made the representative from the state of New York on the National Democratic Committee, to whose management the coming campaign was entrusted. On this committee I was at once made the chairman. It was understood that in taking this place I became the personal representative of Governor Tilden, as I was his intimate personal friend.

The committee proceeded at once to provide headquarters in the City of New York of which Col. William T. Pelton, the nephew of Governor Tilden, was placed in charge. I returned to Washington and remained there until the close of the session in August, 1876. In the interval, however, I directed operations in New York by letter and proceeded to prepare in Washington the *Campaign Textbook,* which for the first time in the history of Presidential campaigns became an arsenal from which ammunition was supplied for assault upon the enemy and for defense against his attacks. This book contained a summary of the results of the investigations instituted by the various Congressional committees. It was generally regarded at the time as the most effective instrument which had ever been devised for supplying facts and arguments upon which the campaign might be successfully conducted; as a matter of fact, I believe that the preparation and publication of this book determined the result of the struggle.

In the preparation of the *Campaign Textbook* Mr. Tilden had no part. He was not even consulted, but it was in accordance with the general policy which he had announced that the campaign must be one of education. The responsibility of deciding upon the documents which should be included in the work devolved upon me alone. I was fortunate, however, in securing the assistance of Mr. A. M. Gibson, who at that time was the Washington correspondent of the New York *Sun* and who had commended himself to my confidence by his energy and the ability to prepare clear and convincing statements.

On my return to New York about the middle of August I was able to place the manuscript in the hands of the printer, and to have a large edition ready for circulation before the first day of September.

With the publication of this book the campaign began in earnest; public meetings were arranged in every state in the Union, and a corps of able speakers [was] organized whose services were at the command of the committee wherever they might be required. In the meantime the "Literary Bureau" which had been so efficient in promoting the nomination of Mr. Tilden was reorganized upon a larger basis for the preparation of editorial articles for the country newspapers and the circulation of such speeches made by leading Democrats in and out of Congress as appeared to be desirable campaign documents. Every day circulars were issued by the Democratic newspapers outside of New York City, containing carefully prepared leaders or suggestions for articles calculated to convince the public that the Government could no longer safely be left under the control of the Republican Party. The speeches, on the other hand, were published in the form of leaflets, resembling railway time tables so that they might be carried in the pocket and circulated from hand to hand with facility. These leaflets became very popular and produced great results. It is estimated that at least one copy was published for every inhabitant of the United States which would amount to about five for each voter. The effect was magical, and the result upon the election was controlling.

At the time there seemed to be a general impression that the Campaign Committee was supplied with unlimited resources in the way of money. Such, however, was not the fact. Mr. Edward Cooper [1] was the treasurer of the committee, and the total amount received and disbursed by him did not exceed $150,000. The money was raised with great difficulty, so that Mr. Cooper and I, in addition to our personal subscriptions which were the largest ones made to the committee, were often in advance to a very considerable amount. It is proper to add, however, that considerable sums of money were handed directly to Mr. Tilden and by him were not handed over to the treasurer. Out of the funds thus placed under his personal control the expenses of the "Literary Bureau" were defrayed, and in the final settlement of the accounts, more than two years after the election, Mr. Tilden finally reimbursed Mr. Cooper and myself for the excess of our disbursements beyond the subscriptions which we had made. This statement is made in order to correct the impression that Mr. Tilden used a large private fortune in order to secure his election. From facts which are within my knowledge, I think the money received by him directly was nearly, if not quite, equal to the total amount of his expenditure, including the balance finally paid to Cooper and Hewitt.

I do not think it is necessary to enter upon the particulars of the campaign, which, as everyone knows, was of a very exciting nature. In its conduct it was impossible to have much consultation with Mr. Tilden. He was necessarily absent in Albany in the performance of his duty as Governor. During a considerable portion of the time when in New York he was beset with visitors, who occupied his time and diverted his attention from the work of the campaign. None of the manifestos of the committee were prepared by him, although when opportunity offered they were submitted for his approval, which was never withheld. In fact the committee seemed to possess his confidence to such an extent that its members at times felt disposed to complain of Mr. Tilden's indifference. If he interfered at all, it was usually to counsel economy in the expenditures. As a matter of fact not much money was disbursed through the local committees of the several states, and none was used for methods which might be regarded as unlawful or immoral. The chief outlay was for the expenses of the speakers and the diffusion of political information. Compared therefore with more

[1] Son of Peter Cooper, and brother-in-law and business partner of Hewitt; later mayor of New York.

recent Presidential elections, that of 1876 was a model of economy, although it struck out a new line of effort and inaugurated the "campaign of education" which has been followed in every succeeding election.

The struggle resulted in the triumphant election of Mr. Tilden, not merely by a majority of all the votes cast, but by a majority of all the states in the Union. It was not until two days after the election that any doubt was expressed as to the result. The country, however, was then astounded by the claim of the Republican National Committee that Hayes had secured 185 electoral votes and would therefore be declared President by a majority of one vote. As soon as this claim was made, based upon the votes of South Carolina, Florida, and Louisiana, I caused letters to be sent to the leading men of the North—Democrats and Republicans alike—inviting them to proceed to South Carolina, Florida, and Louisiana for the purpose of seeing that a fair count was made and the returns honestly canvassed. The next day President Grant, who was in Philadelphia, issued a similar request to leading Republicans only, and thus it happened that two sets of "visiting statesmen" repaired to the several states in doubt, one selected by General Grant acting as partisans and the other selected by me for their standing and character without reference to their political affiliation.

The result is known to all men. The returning boards of the several states referred to gave the votes of these states to Hayes, although it was then known and is now universally admitted that the states of Florida and Louisiana were carried for Tilden. In this emergency the state of Oregon seemed to offer an antidote to the fraud thus perpetrated. Oregon had been carried by the Republicans, but one of the electors was disqualified from acting by a Constitutional provision forbidding Federal office holders to act as electors. One of the Republican electors was a postmaster, and hence the Governor, who was a Democrat, refused his certificate and gave it to the highest candidate on the Democratic ticket. Thus one vote was secured for Tilden giving him 185 votes against 184 votes for Hayes, including all the votes from the three Southern states fradulently secured through corrupt returning boards.

Feeling, however, that the vote secured in Oregon was not in accordance with the popular will and ought only to be counted for Mr. Tilden in order to offset the palpable frauds in Florida and Louisiana, I prepared an address to the people of the United States setting forth the facts as they then appeared and have since been demonstrated to have been true, and calling upon the people to assemble in their several places of meeting throughout the country to protest against the frauds which had been committed and to express their determination that the people should not be robbed of their choice for President. This address as originally drafted is herewith inserted as the evidence that I did not fall short in my duty as the chairman of the committee either in promptitude of action or in suggesting to my countrymen a plan of action for the prevention of the greatest wrong in the history of the Union. This address was submitted to Mr. Tilden on the 9th November, 1876.[1] He made a few verbal alterations and struck out the passage inviting public meetings on the ground that in the excited state of public feeling there would be violence. Moreover, he added that it would be safe to trust to the sense of justice which sooner or later would show itself in the public mind and make the consummation of the fraud impossible. The address as thus amended was then copied in a fair hand and is attached to this statement. Before, however, it could be given to the newspapers Mr. Tilden informed me that he preferred to delay action, and hence the address was never issued, and the committee was left in the position of apparently acquiescing in the policy of inaction from which I absolutely dissented.

The remainder of the month of November was occupied in preparing the cases as far as possible for the consideration of Congress which was to meet on the first Monday of December. In the meantime leading Democrats from all parts of the country were called into consultation, and at length a very brief address [2] was issued to the people practically referring the final decision to the two Houses of Congress under the provisions of the Constitution.

In the Senate sat two Democrats who enjoyed the confidence of the Democratic Party to an extraordinary degree. They were Thomas F. Bayard, of Delaware, and Allen G. Thurman, of Ohio. Both had been candidates for the nomination of President before the St. Louis Convention and had only been put aside because of the superior availability of Mr. Tilden. Nevertheless their position in the party was one of controlling influence—hence it was decided to request Judge Thurman on his way to Washington to pass through New York in order to consult with Mr. Tilden as to the course of action to be taken in the unprecedented controversy which was about to occupy the attention of Congress. Judge Thurman arrived in New York on Saturday prior to the meeting of Congress, and on Sunday at the house of Governor Tilden the conference took place, at which I alone was present with them.[3]

The ground was carefully gone over and the policy to be pursued was for several hours thoroughly discussed. The conclusion was thus

[1] A slip of the pen; Hewitt meant December 9, 1876. The work of the dishonest Returning Boards in Louisiana and Florida was completed on December 2 and December 5, respectively; Hewitt received a report from his representatives in Louisiana on the 6th; and on the 7th and 8th he wrote the document here described.

[2] Given in Nevins, *Abram S. Hewitt, with Some Account of Peter Cooper*, 330-32.

[3] Thomas F. Bayard also conferred with Tilden; Edward Spencer, *Life of Thomas F. Bayard*, p. 261.

briefly summed up by Judge Thurman, who stated the alternatives which presented themselves to his mind as follows:

"We can fight; we can back down; or we can arbitrate." To which propositions Mr. Tilden replied, "It will not do to fight. We have just emerged from one Civil War, and it will never do to engage in another Civil War; it would end in the destruction of free government. We cannot back down. We can, therefore, only arbitrate." And thus the conference was brought to an end. Judge Thurman is still alive and can confirm this statement. He left for Washington with the determination to arbitrate, and I certainly understood that this was the determination of Judge Thurman and of Governor Tilden; and this conclusion governed me in the course which I subsequently pursued in Washington as a member of the House of Representatives. Whatever may have been my preference as chairman of the National Committee, I felt as a member of the House that my superior duty was to my country, and I was greatly relieved that my sense of duty was not at war with the wishes of Mr. Tilden, who declared himself as desirous of a peaceful settlement of the controversy.

THE MEETING OF CONGRESS

Congress met upon the first Monday in December. It was felt by Democrats and Republicans alike to be necessary to make provision for counting the electoral votes for President and Vice-President. Lincoln and Grant had both been inaugurated by virtue of what was known as the 22nd Joint Rule, which was adopted by the Republicans in 1865, and by virtue of which no electoral vote objected to by either House of Congress could be counted except by the concurrent vote of both Houses. Under this rule the three successive electoral counts of 1865, 1869, and 1873 had been completed. At the previous session of Congress, however, in December, 1875,[1] the Senate readopted the joint rules of the two Houses except the 22nd Joint Rule heretofore in use. At first the House of Representatives was disposed to insist that the 22nd Joint Rule remained in force until it was repealed by the action of both Houses. Mature reflection, however, led to the conclusion that the joint rules only continued from Congress to Congress, and that in the absence of the specific action of both Houses renewed by each Congress no Joint Rules existed for the government of their action. The House, therefore, concurred in the adoption of the joint rules governing the proceedings of Congress, except the 22nd Joint Rule. If this rule had been readopted it would have been competent for either House to have objected to the counting of the votes of South Carolina, Florida, Louisiana, and Oregon, by which Hayes secured his election as President by a majority of one vote. If the

[1] Actually in January, 1876.

vote of either of these States had been objected to by the House, Tilden would have been inaugurated as President of the United States. The restoration of the 22nd Joint Rule therefore was proposed by the Democrats and rejected by the Republicans. Some criticism has been indulged in as to the action of the House of Representatives in assenting to any joint rules which did not include the 22nd, but such criticism is based upon the erroneous idea that the House, which was Democratic, could have coerced the Senate, which was Republican, into the adoption of any joint rule not acceptable to either House.

The question of counting the votes was therefore relegated to the provision of the Constitution that "The President of the Senate shall in the presence of the Senate and the House of Representatives open all the certificates, and the votes shall then be counted."

In view of the claim made by leading Republicans that the President of the Senate under this clause was invested with authority not only to open the certificates but to count the votes, it was evident that there would be a conflict of authority between the Senate and the House unless some mode of procedure as to the counting of the votes and the declaration of the result should be reached by the two Houses in advance of the date prescribed by the Constitution for the opening of the certificates and the counting of the votes.

Hence, after much consultation and the consideration of the question by a joint caucus of the Democratic members of the Senate and House, the House of Representatives on the 14th December, 1876, appointed a committee of seven to act in conjunction with any similar committee of the Senate [1] "To prepare and report without delay a measure for the removal of difference of opinion as to the proper mode of counting the electoral votes for President and Vice-President which might arise as to the legality and validity of the returns of such votes made by the several states *to the end that the votes should be counted and the result declared by a tribunal whose authority none can question and whose decision all will accept.*"

The words in italics were framed by me for the purpose of calling public attention to the fact that the House of Representatives controlled by Democrats, largely from the South, desired to secure a peaceful result if possible to the controversy and were so inserted in order to give effect to the conclusion to arbitrate, arrived at in the conference between Judge Thurman and Mr. Tilden. Let it be observed that this resolution was adopted more than one month before the passage of the bill creating the Electoral Commission and called forth no criticism or sermon eloquence from Mr. Tilden.

[1] The resolution for this committee was introduced in the House on December 7 by George W. McCrary of Iowa, a Republican, and amended. Tilden indicated no hostility to it.

On the 18th December the Senate resolved to create a special committee of seven Senators "with power to prepare and report without unnecessary delay such a measure either of a legislative or other character as may in their judgment be best calculated to accomplish the counting of the Electoral votes and best disposition of all questions connected therewith and the true declaration of the result." And this committee was instructed to confer and act with the committee of the House of Representatives.

The committee of the Senate consisted of George F. Edmunds, Frederick T. Frelinghuysen, Roscoe Conkling, Oliver P. Morton, Allen G. Thurman, Thomas F. Bayard, Matthew W. Ransom. The members of the House were Henry B. Payne, Eppa Hunton, Abram S. Hewitt, William M. Springer, George W. McCrary, George F. Hoar, and George Willard.

The House committee lost no time in holding a meeting at which Mr. Springer was appointed a committee to collate the proceedings for counting the electoral votes in all the preceding elections of President and Vice-President of the United States. Singularly enough this action was taken in ignorance of the fact that Mr. Tilden had already undertaken to prepare a similar compilation.[1] The two documents appeared almost simultaneously; but in the meantime the House committee proceeded to discuss the questions submitted to it at the very first meeting on the 23d day of December, 1876. Mr. McCrary produced a printed draft of a bill providing for the constitution of an Electoral Commission showing that thus early the matter had been under consideration by the Republican managers and leaders. The origin of this bill has been attributed to various persons. It seems, however, to be probable that the suggestion came from President Grant and that the draft of the bill was prepared at his request by Senator Conkling. Certain provisions of the bill were at once rejected, and a second reprint was ordered. At the next meeting this amended draft was considered and further amended; another reprint was ordered, making the third amended draft. Without approving the third draft the committee concluded that it was in a position to discuss the subject with the Senate committee, which thereupon was requested to appoint a time for joint conference, which was accordingly held, all the members of both committees being present. The discussion was long, patient, and thorough; upon one point all the members of the Joint Committee seemed to be agreed and that was that a commission should be appointed which should and would be invested with power to go behind the returns so

[1] Tilden was aided in this work by John Bigelow and Manton Marble; they devoted about a month to it and published the result in January, 1877, under the title *Presidential Counts.* Tilden also wrote a long argument which was inserted in the inaugural address of Governor Lucius Robinson, of New York.

as to arrive at the true result of the election in the disputed states. Judge Edmunds [1] alone declined to commit himself as to the meaning of the words "if any," by virtue of which the other members of the committee seemed to think that the action of the returning boards must be inquired into and should be reversed, if substantial justice should seem to demand such action. Subsequent events gave particular emphasis to this reservation on the part of Judge Edmunds, whose action on the Electoral Commission of which he was a member was not open to the criticism which attached to other members who had expressed a definite opinion as to the powers and duties of the Electoral Commission.

The Joint Committee adjourned without final action, in order to enable the two committees to consider the position in which after the consultation they found themselves to be placed. A resolution, however, was adopted imposing secrecy upon the members of the committees as to the nature of the bill and the discussions which had taken place.

This obligation of secrecy led me to consult with the Democratic members of the House committee as to whether it applied to Mr. Tilden. It was unanimously concluded that we had a superior duty both to the Democratic Party and to him, who was its leader and its elected candidate for President, and that he should be consulted and his approval secured before the House Committee would commit itself to any action whatever. In accordance with this decision I mailed to Mr. Tilden on Friday, 12th January, 1877, a copy of the bill with the proposed amendments, and informed him that on the next day I would report at his house on Gramercy Park for the purpose of getting his counsel and decision thereon.

On Sunday morning, therefore, January 14th, I saw Mr. Tilden and went over with him word by word the provisions of the bill as amended. Various persons came and went during the day, but so far as the consultation was concerned it was personal between Mr. Tilden and myself. The only person to whom the bill was submitted, so far as I remember, was the late Clarkson N. Potter, who was the next-door neighbor of Mr. Tilden and possessed his confidence so far as any person might be said to have had it. The injunction of secrecy was violated in his case alone, but it is certain that the bill was not during any conference with Mr. Tilden shown to any other person whatever.

Mr. Tilden complained that action was premature and of the secrecy which had attended the preparation of the bill. I explained to him that the work was preliminary and that the Democratic members of the House committee had authorized and directed me to say to him that they would not agree to have it reported to the House in case he should disapprove of its provisions or desire it to be amended. I stated,

[1] That is, Senator George F. Edmunds of Vermont, always a sharp Republican partisan.

however, that if the House committee should not report the bill I was sure that the Senate Committee would do so, because the Democratic members of that committee had already agreed to the provisions of the bill. Mr. Tilden thereupon asked whether it was not rather late to ask his counsel, to which I replied, "The Senate Committee have not sent me to consult with you as the Democratic members are acting upon their own responsibility in the performance of their duty. I am directed, however, by the Democrats of the House Committee to consult with you, and you may be sure that against your objection no bill will ever be reported to the House or can pass that body."

The question of approval or disapproval was thus distinctly presented to Mr. Tilden. On this point I did not get from him any definite opinion whatever. He objected to special features of the bill and declared against choosing any one of the Judges by lot, saying that he might lose the Presidency but he would never raffle for it. He asked for time to consider the matter, and finally before I left about 9 o'clock on Saturday night to catch the train he said he would communicate further with me through Mr. E. Cooper, who had a cipher which might be safely used. I remember perfectly well the remark with which I quitted his presence: "Now, Governor, understand that if you disapprove the bill it will be defeated, if you do not disapprove it it will be reported by the House Committee with such amendments as you may desire. I do not expect you to approve the bill as it stands, but we must take action of some sort, and I understand that if you do not disapprove, we are to make a report to the House with such amendments as you may desire to have inserted." We parted, therefore, without any distinct approval or disapproval on the part of Mr. Tilden, but with the distinct understanding that I was to secure if possible the modification of the Six Judge Plan which provided for the elimination of one of the judges by lot and for the substitution of some other mode of selecting the judges which might be satisfactory to Mr. Tilden.

That I was to make and did make this effort is proven by the very first telegram sent by me to Mr. Cooper in cipher on the day after my interview with Mr. Tilden—"Washington, January 15th, 1877. To E. C. The Senate committee will probably reject Five and report Six Judge Plan immediately. Our Senators feel committed to concur. House committee will not concur and for the present will probably not report."

To this telegram Mr. Tilden sent the following reply:

"New York, January 15th, 1877, to A. S. H.—Procrastinate to give days for information and consultation. The Six Judge proposition inadmissible. E. C."

It appears from this reply that Mr. Tilden did not utter a word against the principle of an Electoral Commission or against the Five

Judge Plan, but rejected the Six Judge Plan, leading me to infer as I had done in New York that the Five Judge Plan would be satisfactory.[1]

The next day I sent the following telegram: "Washington, January 16th, 1877. To E. C.—After protracted negotiations Senate 'committee' receded from Six Judge Plan, declined Five Judge and offered four Senior Associate Justices, who are to choose the fifth judge excluding Chief Justice. Our Senate friends earnestly favor acceptance because they did not believe it possible to pass over Field. The Democrats on House committee believe this iš last chance of agreement. We cannot postpone beyond eleven tomorrow, and if we decline Senate committee will report their original plan to which our friends are committed."

This telegram makes it clear that I did not understand Mr. Tilden to have been opposed to the principle and policy of a commission but only to certain details which were embodied in the Senate bill.

To this telegram I received from Mr. Tilden through Mr. Cooper the following answer—"New York. January 16th. Be firm and cool, Four Judge Plan will not do perhaps worse than Six—complaints likely to arise of haste and want of consultation with members and embarrassment in exercise of their judgment after plan is disclosed by premature committal of their representatives. There should be more opportunity for deliberation and consultation. Secrecy dangerous, probably a mistake in itself, and if it results in disaster would involve great blame and infinite mischief."

This telegram was the last one which I received from Mr. Tilden through Mr. Cooper or otherwise. It did not reach me until after the Advisory Committee of leading Democrats meeting in the Speakers' room on the evening of Tuesday, January 16th, had approved of the Four Judge Plan which Mr. Tilden thus disapproved. This disapproval gave me great concern and led me to decide at all hazards to get such a modification of the plan as would secure the substance of the Five Judge Plan, which I had originally suggested to Mr. Tilden, and which he had never disapproved either verbally or in any telegram sent to me. On the morning of the 17th of January, therefore, I recommended to the House committee to reject the original Four Senior Justice Plan—Clifford, Swayne, Davis, and Miller—which had been approved at the consultation in the Speakers' room the night before, and to insist upon the plan finally adopted, by which Clifford and Field, Miller and Strong,

[1] F. F. Marbury later testified that Tilden, discussing the Electoral Commission with him, said: "Why, if I were so disposed, I could kill this bill by a mere wave of my fingers"—snapping them in illustration. But he did not give the signal. Both Hayes and Tilden disliked the Electoral Commission. But moderate leaders of both parties agreed that it offered the only way out of the deadlock; moderate opinion was for it; and neither candidate dared to interpose an explicit veto of so statesmanlike a plan. Tilden, in fact, clearly accepted when he thought that it offered him—as it did—a probability of success.

two Democrats and two Republicans, were named by their districts with
the power to choose the fifth judge—it being generally conceded that
Davis must be selected, thus securing the original Five Judge Plan
except that Strong was substituted for Swayne, to whom Mr. Tilden had
expressed to me some personal objection. This suggestion met with the
approval of the Democrats on the House committee and was particularly acceptable to the especial friends of Mr. Tilden who were on the
spot, as being far more favorable to Mr. Tilden's interests than the
Four Judge Plan.

It was accordingly proposed to the Senate committee as an ultima-
tum, and after some hours of discussion it was adopted on the 17th
January against the vigorous opposition and protesting vote of Senator
Morton, who said to me that it was equivalent to the abandonment of
the contest on the Republican side.

On the Democrats' side, however, General Hunton of the House
committee reserved his decision for twenty-four hours longer, so that
the report of the committee was necessarily deferred until January
18th in order to give him time to make up his mind whether he would
concur in the report or not.

The Democratic Committee of Eleven took advantage of this delay
in order to communicate the result to Mr. Tilden, and for this purpose
his nephew, who was understood to be his personal representative in
Washington, was dispatched to New York with a copy of the bill as
finally amended to be submitted to Mr. Tilden for his approval or his
rejection. Colonel Pelton returned to Washington on the morning of
the 18th inst. and had a meeting of the Advisory Committee of eleven
Democrats, held in the Speakers' room before the meeting of the House.
He reported that he had consulted with Mr. Tilden, who regarded the
measure as a great improvement upon any previous proposition and
advised its adoption by the House Committee. Thereupon General
Hunton, who was present, and who is still living to confirm this statement, signed the report although with evident reluctance.

The general feeling, however, was that the victory was won, because
no one doubted for a moment that Judge Davis would be selected as
the fifth member of the commission.

The report was made both to the Senate and the House at the
regular session on the 18th January, and the debate thereon continued
for several days in the Senate, where it was adopted on the 25th January
by a vote of 47 yeas to 17 nays, the Republicans voting 24 yeas to
16 nays, and the Democrats voting 23 yeas to 1 nay. Absent who were
not voting, 9 Republicans and 1 Democrat.

In the House of Representatives the bill was passed on the 26th
January after a discussion which lasted for two days, by a vote of 191
yeas to 86 nays, the Democrats giving 158 yeas to 18 nays, and the

Republicans 33 yeas to 68 nays; absent or not voting, 7 Republicans and 7 Democrats.

An analysis of the vote proves that the Bill was regarded as a Democratic measure and that a large majority of the Republicans in Congress were opposed to its passage.

I thought at the time, and I still think, that the division of parties on this measure was largely controlled by the conviction that Judge Davis would have the casting vote, and that he could be relied upon to see that the will of the people as expressed in the election of Mr. Tilden should not be thwarted.

The surprise and disappointment, therefore, of the Democrats may be imagined when immediately after the passage of the bill the Democratic members of the legislature of the state of Illinois, reinforced by 7 Republican votes,[1] at once elected Judge Davis to the Senate of the United States without consultation with the National Democratic Committee.

This surprise and disappointment was intensified by the immediate refusal of Judge Davis to be a nominee for the vacant position on the Commission, although his election as Senator in no respect disqualified him for the performance of the duty which he was expected to discharge.

Whether rightly or wrongly, the conviction was general that a bargain had been made by the Republicans by which Judge Davis in consideration of his being made Senator should decline a position upon the Electoral Commission. Certainly if such an arrangement were made it was the last move by which in the long game which had been played between the two parties the final triumph was probably assured to the Republican Party. I can only say that Senator Morton, who had regarded the game as lost, showed as much surprise at this achievement as I felt and could not restrain the expression of his satisfaction.

It now only remained to arrange for the choice of the fifth judge, which was limited to Hunt and Bradley because, as stated above, Mr. Tilden advised against the selection of Swayne. On consultation with Senator Conkling, I was advised not to press the choice of Judge Hunt because, as Mr. Conkling believed that Mr. Tilden had been elected and as he was the personal friend of Judge Hunt, he feared that in his desire to prove his freedom from personal influence he might lean backward and thus unconsciously be unjust to Mr. Tilden.

Practically, therefore, the choice was limited to Justice Bradley, whom I had personally known for many years in New Jersey as a very able lawyer and a man of the highest integrity.[2] The confidence which I felt

[1] The balance of power in the Illinois Legislature was held by five Independents or Greenbackers. John A. Logan, Republican, and John M. Palmer, Democrat, had run neck and neck for more than thirty ballots when David Davis, whose party affiliations were uncertain, suddenly forged from behind.

[2] Joseph P. Bradley, after a distinguished career at the New Jersey bar, had been appointed to the Supreme Court in 1870 by President Grant.

in him was shared by Mr. Tilden, but in order to make assurance doubly sure I requested a mutual friend of Judge Bradley and myself, the late John G. Stevens,[1] of Trenton, N. J., to confer with Judge Bradley and to ascertain whether he felt that he could decide the questions which would come before the commission without prejudice or party feeling. The report of Mr. Stevens was entirely satisfactory. Judge Bradley was therefore selected with the distinct approval of the Democratic representatives, reinforced by the favorable judgment of Judge Clifford and Judge Field, who assured me that absolute reliance could be placed upon the judicial fairness of Judge Bradley. In fact they both stated that it was absurd to fear that any Justice of the Supreme Court would be governed by partisan feeling or influence, and this was in accordance with the general feeling in Congress and throughout the country.

The other members of the commission under the provisions of the Act consisted of three Republicans and two Democrats from the Senate and three Democrats and two Republicans from the House. The commission, therefore, was composed so far as political preference was concerned of eight Republicans and seven Democrats, practically giving the casting vote to Judge Bradley, in whose freedom from partisan influence absolute confidence was reposed.

The omission of Senator Conkling, whose preferences were supposed to be for Mr. Tilden and who was the putative author of the bill creating the commission, was remarked as tending to show the Republican animus in reference to the commission. The choice by the House of General Garfield who had opposed the bill was also regarded as significant, but the feeling was general that substantial justice would be done by the commission, as declared by Judge Abbott in the address prepared by him for the Democratic members of the commission after its work had been done, "The conscience of this whole people approved the law establishing the Commission, nay, hailed it with joy, because it established as all believed, a fair tribunal, to examine, to inquire into, and determine the charges of fraud and corruption in three States."

This illusion was, however, rudely dispelled when Judge Bradley pronounced his decision in the Florida case by which the vote of this state was unjustly counted for Hayes. The history of this opinion forms an important feature in the final outcome of the electoral count. As stated above, Mr. Stevens was the intimate friend of Judge Bradley. He passed the night previous to the rendition of the judgment in the Florida case at my house. About midnight he returned from a visit to Judge Bradley and reported to General Richard Taylor,[2] who was also staying with me, and to Senator Gibson who was awaiting his return, that he had

[1] While Hewitt writes John G. Stevens, he may mean John C. Stevens, son of the eminent engineer John Stevens, and brother of Robert L. Stevens.
[2] Of the Confederate Army; son of President Zachary Taylor.

just left Judge Bradley after reading his opinion in favor of counting the vote of the Democratic electors of the state of Florida. Such a judgment insured the election of Tilden to the Presidency with three votes to spare above the necessary majority. We parted, therefore, with the assurance that all further doubt as to the Presidency was at rest. I attended the delivery of the judgment the next day without the slightest intimation from any quarter that Judge Bradley had changed his mind. In fact, the reading of the opinion, until the few concluding paragraphs were reached, was strictly in accordance with the report of Mr. Stevens. The change was made between midnight and sunrise. Mr. Stevens afterward informed me that it was due to a visit to Judge Bradley by Senator Frelinghuysen and Secretary Robeson, made after his departure. Their appeals to Judge Bradley were said to have been reinforced by the persuasion of Mrs. Bradley. Whatever the fact may have been, Judge Bradley himself in a subsequent letter addressed to the Newark *Daily Advertiser* [1] admitted that he had written a favorable opinion which on subsequent reflection he saw fit to modify.

The decision in the Florida case produced a feeling of profound disappointment among the Democrats, but not of dismay. It was evident that the principle laid down in this case would necessarily secure one vote from Oregon, enough to ensure the election of Mr. Tilden even if the votes of Louisiana and South Carolina should be awarded to Hayes. Besides these states, there were cases of disqualified electors in other states and particularly one in Illinois cast by a Republican elector who, under the provisions of the Constitution, was disqualified in consequence of holding the office of postmaster. It was decided in view of the decision in the Florida case to object to the counting of this vote, although both sides conceded that Illinois had given a large majority for the Republican candidates. Before the two Houses met, however, on the morning of the next day after the Florida decision was rendered; Senator Conkling with whom I had had very intimate and confidential relations, leading me to suppose that as he had already taken ground against the claim of the President of the Senate to count the votes and declare the result and had practically demolished this pretense in a speech of remarkable range and power, he would also when a contested case was reached in which the vote clearly belonged to Tilden, not hesitate to take the responsibility of defeating the plans of the Republican leaders to count in Hayes at all hazards.[2]

Senator Conkling asked me whether it was the intention of the Democrats to object to the vote of the Illinois postmaster; on receiv-

---

[1] In the Newark *Daily Advertiser*, September 5, 1877.

[2] Various newspaper correspondents were aware of this intention on the part of Roscoe Conkling; see Nevins, *Abram S. Hewitt, with Some Account of Peter Cooper*, 374-77.

ing my reply in the affirmative, he said that he would advise us to refrain from this action, because it would be construed into a disposition on the part of the Democrats to claim a vote to which in justice they were not entitled, and that this would be quoted against us when the Oregon case should come up for decision. He added that there was a much stronger reason why we could make no claim in Illinois. He said that the Louisiana case, in which there could be no doubt as to the election having been in favor of Tilden by a large majority, would come up after the Illinois case, and that he would be met in the contention that Tilden was entitled to the electoral votes of Louisiana by the statement that the Democrats had not hesitated to claim a vote in Illinois to which they were not in justice entitled.

I replied that I would submit his views to the committee in charge of the objections and accordingly proceeded at once to confer with J. Randolph Tucker, of Virginia, who had the matter in charge. On full consideration by the committee Mr. Tucker informed me that in view of Mr. Conkling's position they had decided to pass over the state of Illinois without objection. It is proper here to state that no one on our side entertained a doubt of the Constitutional disqualification of this elector, but we all felt that our case would be weakened by the claim and that the Electoral Commission would find some way to defeat it on account of its admitted want of equity.

The Louisiana case was reached on the same day, and the returns were duly opened in the presence of both Houses; one return gave the vote of the state to Hayes, another return gave the vote to Tilden. To the surprise of everybody a third return was presented giving the vote of the state to Peter Cooper. This last return was supposed to be the work of a crank and was after some discussion omitted from the proceedings as having no validity whatever. Mr. Conkling was present at the joint meeting but took no part in the discussions. It was expected, however, that at the meeting of the Senate on the next morning Mr. Conkling would take ground against counting the certificate of the returning board of Louisiana in favor of the Hayes electors. My conference with him in the Illinois case led me to this conclusion, and in the evening Senator Barnum, who was in constant intercourse with Mr. Conkling, assured me that the latter would on the following morning denounce the action of the returning board and show that the vote of Louisiana belonged to Tilden.

But when the session of the Senate was opened on the next morning, Senator Conkling was not in his seat. On inquiry it was stated that he had been seen earlier in the day making his way to the railway station and had said that he was going to Baltimore. It is certain that he did not return until the next day, and in the interval the Louisiana case was, under the provisions of the law, sent to the Electoral Commission for decision, because the two Houses had disagreed as to the counting of the vote.

I do not propose to give any account of the proceedings before the commission in this case, but it is proper to state that the return actually approved by the commission appears to have been a forged return,[1] and that this fact was known not only to the President of the Senate, but to General Garfield, who was sitting as a member of the Electoral Commission. At this date I can now understand why the Peter Cooper return was interjected when the certificates were opened. Attention was thus distracted from the discrepancy which undoubtedly existed between the two sets of the Republican returns opened and submitted by the president of the Senate.

The votes of Louisiana were thus counted for Hayes, and those of South Carolina were also, under the decision of the commission, counted for him and probably justly so in view of the facts afterward developed by the inquiries of the Thompson Committee.

Previously, however, to the South Carolina decision the returns from the state of Oregon had, by the failure of the two Houses to agree, been referred to the commission. No doubt was entertained that the rule in the Florida case required the counting of one vote for Tilden. The commission, however, did not hesitate, but by the invariable vote of eight to seven reversed the precedents created by the commission in the Florida case and counted the three votes of Oregon for Hayes, on the ground that Oregon had undoubtedly given a majority for the Republican ticket. In the Florida case they had refused to go behind the returns and thus gave the four votes of that state to Hayes. In the Oregon case they decided to ge behind the returns and thus also gave the three votes of that state to the Republican candidate. This secured the election of Hayes by one majority, and the greatest fraud in the history of the country was thus practically consummated.

The count, however, was not yet completed, and it was possible by filibustering in the House to defeat its completion. The indignation and excitement were unbounded. Many Democrats declared their intention by dilatory proceedings to prevent further action; in this view many moderate members concurred, because the states of South Carolina and Louisiana were in the hands of carpet-bag governments, although at the late election the Democratic local ticket had been successful in both states. Personally I was anxious to have the count completed even though it should result, as it must do, in the declaration on the part of the two Houses of the election of Hayes and

[1] The names of two of the Louisiana electors had been forged on the return by the Republican leaders of that state; this being done to save time when a defect appeared in the original certificate of the returns. Had the irregularity been discovered, the Democrats might have made it embarrassing to the Republicans.

Wheeler. Finding, however, that it would not be possible to complete the count before the 4th March in view of this opposition, I addressed myself to President Grant in reference to the condition of affairs in South Carolina and succeeded in arranging with him a course of action by which the election of Wade Hampton was conceded as governor and the Democrats were recognized as having a majority of the legislature.

Thus the case of Louisiana only remained to be considered and arranged. As before stated, General Richard Taylor, the only son of ex-President Taylor, and a resident of Louisiana, had been a guest at my house from the beginning of the session of Congress and had been the means of communication between me and the representatives of the South, in and out of Congress. A committee had come to Washington from Louisiana, at the head of which was one Burke, afterward the state treasurer, but at that time the proprietor of the New Orleans *Times-Democrat*. He bore full credentials from General Nichols, who had received the majority as a Democratic candidate for governor.

A conference was therefore arranged between the Louisiana members and the personal representatives of Mr. Hayes, and thus came into existence what was known as the Wormley Conference. Mr. Hayes was represented by General Garfield and Mr. Charles Foster, both members of the House from the state of Ohio. The communications and telegrams were all conveyed to Mr. Hayes through Lieut. Governor Young at Columbus, Ohio. This conference occupied the better part of two days, during which it was necessary to occupy the attention of the House so as to avoid the completion of the count until an agreement had been reached between the Wormley Conference as to the recognition of the Democratic administration in Louisiana.

I had received a formal return from the state of Vermont, declaring that John Smith had received the seven electoral votes of that state. I had been informed that a similar return had been sent to the president of the Senate. When the returns from Vermont were opened, this return was not presented by the president of the Senate, although he had not hesitated to present the Peter Cooper return from Louisiana. The object of the Democrats was to gain time; on conference, therefore, with the legal advisers who had come to Washington on behalf of Mr. Tilden, I was uged to put in the return which I had received from the state of Vermont. This was done and resulted in the breaking up of the joint meeting without action and the disappearance of the document after it had been presented to the presiding officer. Subsequently a resolution was adopted by the House requesting that this return should be sent back to the House for further consideration. To this resolution it was replied that the return had disappeared and could not be found. Thereupon much debate and a wrangle followed between the two Houses, when unexpectedly a Senate page placed the return upon my desk and upon inquiry declined to state where he got it. The House thereupon adjourned, thus securing one more night for the Wormley Conference and the attainment of an agreement as to the Louisiana state government.

I have made this explanation as to the Vermont return because at the time my motives were misunderstood and misrepresented. Up to this time my action had received very warm commendation from all parts of the country, but when the Vermont return was introduced it was charged in some quarters that I had determined to defeat the count, the fact being that it was introduced in order to secure the completion of the count. In this transaction I had the full approval and co-operation of Speaker Randall, who had agreed with me that in the last event filibustering should be suppressed and the count completed even though no understanding was reached in regard to the Louisiana case.

On the following morning, however, Representative Levy appeared upon the floor of the House and announced publicly that an arrangement had been made which was entirely satisfactory to the representatives of the state of Louisiana. It was evident that a bargain had been made between the Louisiana representatives and the friends of Mr. Hayes by which the Nichols government should be recognized if the electoral count should be completed. It is proper to add [that] every telegram sent to and from the representatives of Mr. Hayes was promptly shown to me and that I was familiar with the negotiation at every stage. How this information was secured I do not feel at liberty to mention, but it is certain that Mr. Hayes when he became President kept his side of the bargain and that the Democratic Party in the state of Louisiana had no reason to complain of bad faith on his part, and so far as I know, no such complaint ever was made.

It is not necessary to go into any further details as to the completion of the electoral count. There was much excitement and doubtless scenes of violence would have been witnessed but for the firmness of Speaker Randall, to whose patriotic action the country owes a debt of gratitude for the peaceful issue of this long, exciting, and humiliating contro-versy, upon which the attention of the country had been concentrated for many months with painful anxiety. In fact, on this late day, eighteen years after these occurrences, it is almost impossible to form any adequate idea of the excitement and the apprehension which prevailed throughout the country. Business was arrested, the wheels of industry ceased to move, and it seemed as if the terrors of civil war were again to be renewed. Petitions from chambers of commerce and from all the centers of trade had deluged Congress in favor of a peaceful settlement of the controversy. Personally, I was satisfied that it would be better for the country to have four years of Republican administration based upon fraudulent returns, than to have four years of civil war. In this view

I had the hearty concurrence of Speaker Randall,[1] who was recognized as the firm friend of Mr. Tilden and the unyielding upholder of his rights under the law. To his action in concurrence with my advice as chairman of the National Democratic Committee was due in my opinion the escape from civil war. To this dread issue we were much nearer than was even at that time supposed. The Democratic forces had been organized in fifteen states and were composed chiefly of the veterans of the war who were quite ready once more to take up arms and move on Washington in defense of what they regarded as the rightful claims of Governor Tilden to the Presidency. In this communication I do not wish to use names, but even the commander-in-chief had been selected, and the governors of many states had declared their willingness to act, in case an emergency should arise demanding the inauguration of Tilden, by military force. These facts were as well known to Mr. Randall as to me. Pending the count I had no communication either by telegram or by letter from Mr. Tilden, but I was in daily conference with his nephew, William T. Pelton, who at that time was supposed to reflect his views, and with the lawyers who had come to Washington to present and argue the Democratic case before the Electoral Commission. Mr. Randall, however, was himself in communication with Mr. Tilden during this period; if his papers should have been preserved and shall be searched, telegrams will be found addressed to him by Mr. Tilden, in no one of which, I venture to say, as they were shown to me, will be found a single expression of dissent from the action of Congress. On the other hand, I do not think that one word of approval on Mr. Tilden's part will ever be found in any communication addressed to Speaker Randall or to anyone else. The habit of Mr. Tilden's mind was to criticize and postpone, not to decide or approve, but that he accepted the result as the only possible solution of the controversy, other than by the dread arbitrament of arms cannot be doubted. When the latter alternative was presented he did not hesitate to declare to Mr. Randall, as he had previously declared to Judge Thurman and myself, that nothing could justify the resort to physical force. Upon this conclusion both Mr. Randall and I acted. The result was the completion of the count, the inauguration of President Hayes, and the salvation of the country from the perils of civil war.

I did not witness the completion of the count. After the last state had been called, my nervous system yielded to the strain of many days and nights of excessive anxiety passed without sleep. I was taken from the House by my friends in a state of collapse on the night of the third

[1] Samuel J. Randall of Philadelphia, long noted as leader of the high-tariff wing of the Democratic Party in the House of Representatives; his firmness in insisting upon a peaceful solution of the disputed election is one of his best titles to fame.

of March, from which I did not recover until after Hayes had taken the oath of office.

I have stated above that the pledges given in behalf of President Hayes as to the recognition of the Democratic government in Louisiana and South Carolina were fully kept. He also kept other pledges which must have been made by the Republican visiting statesmen to the three contested states, because in all of them, the active participants in the frauds were promptly rewarded with public office, although in Florida, McLin, feeling aggrieved by the amount of recognition which he received subsequently, made disclosures which were not very agreeable to the Republican managers.

It has also been stated that the vote of Louisiana prior to the final count of the Returning Board was offered for sale. The price named to me was $200,000, and it was stated that the larger portion of the money would go to Wells and Anderson and a lesser amount to their colleagues on the Returning Board. I declined to make the purchase and notified Mr. Tilden personally of the fact on the Sabbath day when the offer was made. Long after the completion of the count I was informed that other Democrats less scrupulous than I was actually completed the arrangements for the purchase and provided the amount of money required to be paid in New Orleans. This transaction fortunately came to the knowledge of Governor Tilden before the money had been paid over and was arrested by his prompt intervention. As in the first instance he was not willing to raffle for the Presidency, so in the last event he showed that he was equally unwilling to purchase an office to which he was justly entitled. I record this fact because the country ought to know that Governor Tilden at no time ever descended to the low plane of corrupting the electoral functions even for the purpose of defeating a fraud.

Subsequent events, however, made it clear to me that the Republican managers were not governed by the same standard of rectitude. I had it from the mouth of Governor Wells himself that the offer rejected by the Democrats had been accepted by the Republican managers, and that they had agreed after the inauguration of President Hayes to raise the money and pay the amount in cash. In consequence of the failure to redeem this promise Governor Wells subsequently came to Washington and threatened to expose the whole transaction. Whereupon, as I was informed upon good authority, a considerable portion of the money was raised and paid over to Wells in Washington in order to quiet the immediate clamor, with the promise that the remainder should be paid in time. Whether it was paid or not I do not know. Possibly Wells was quieted by his appointment to the office of Collector of the Customs for the Port of New Orleans; his confederates were also provided for, some by offices and some by money.

With President Hayes I refused to have any intercourse, and although upon the floor of the House of Representatives I took occasion to declare that he held office by his sacred title, for which I was much criticized, I felt that he knew, as I knew, that it had been secured by frauds which ought to have led him to resign his high place and to appeal to the people in a new election for such decision as the sense of public justice might require.

Mr. Conkling never made any public declaration upon the subject, but he never concealed in private his opinion as to the iniquity of these transactions and habitually referred to the President as Ruther-*fraud* B. Hayes.[1] In the House, on the contrary, President Seelye, of Amherst College,[2] and Henry L. Pierce, both representatives for the state of Massachusetts, refused to approve of the Louisiana fraud and finally recorded themselves against counting the vote of that state for Hayes. With these honorable exceptions the Republican Party approved the result, and the country, anxious for peace and repose, cheerfully acquiesced in the decision.

As soon as I was sufficiently recovered I returned to New York and resumed my old relations of friendly intercourse with Mr. Tilden. He never made any complaint to me either in regard to my own action or that of my associates. If he felt any dissatisfaction with our course he never expressed it, and there was nothing either in his manner or in his conversation to indicate that my presence was less agreeable to him than it had been during the many years of our close and intimate friendship. My conclusion was that while he felt that the country had been defrauded of its rightful choice for President he experienced a sense of relief, in view of the state of his health, from the burdens which the Presidency would have imposed. He seemed to think that his place in history was secure, and in the immediate circle of his friends, as well as from the public at large, he was treated with as much respect as if he had actually been inaugurated into the great office to which he had unquestionably been chosen by the people.

It came to pass that both he and I as well as Governor Hendricks[3] had all decided to pass the summer of 1877 in Europe. I therefore met Governor Hendricks in London, to which city he had preceded me, and subsequently was joined there by Governor Tilden in company with Mr. Bigelow, his friend and his biographer. Our intercourse still remained as cordial as ever, and we subsequently met in Paris, where by request of Mr. Bigelow I had secured desirable apartments in the Westminster Hotel. We met daily as usual and saw many interesting

---

[1] As did also Charles A. Dana of the New York *Sun.*

[2] Julius H. Seelye, member of Congress from the Amherst district 1875-77.

[3] Thomas A. Hendricks of Indiana, ex-Senator and ex-Governor, and candidate for the Vice-Presidency on the ticket with Tilden in 1876.

men and places in common. We decided to return home together and
did so, crossing the channel in the stormy passage to which Mr. Bigelow
refers so graphically; and finally together sailed upon the steamship
"Scythia" for New York, where we arrived after a very stormy voyage.
I make this statement in view of events which followed in 1878 in
order to show that if Mr. Tilden felt any grievance against me or my
action it was most carefully concealed during many months of intercourse of the most intimate and friendly character. It is simply inconceivable that he had any such feeling, and I think I am justified in
assuming that, while the issue of the great struggle in which we had
been engaged was disastrous to his personal ambition, he felt that no
proper effort and precaution had been omitted either by me or those
who co-operated with me in the establishment of the Electoral Commission and in the subsequent proceedings of that unprecedented
tribunal.

The 45th Congress, to which I had been elected, began its Session
in December, 1887. Randall was re-elected Speaker. He offered to appoint me to the chairmanship of any committee which I might select
other than the Appropriations and the Ways and Means in reference
to which he felt himself committed to my colleague Fernando Wood.
I declined any important chairmanship, preferring the second place
upon the Committee on Appropriations, then the most important
committee of the House to which General Atkins with my concurrence
was named as the chairman. I refer to this matter only for the purpose
of showing that although after the 4th March, for reasons which will
hereafter be explained, I had resigned the position of chairman of the
National Democratic Committee, I still possessed the absolute confidence of Mr. Randall, who was then and always afterward regarded
as the special friend of Mr. Tilden.

During this session the frauds perpetrated in Louisiana became the
subject of investigation of a special committee of which Clarkson N.
Potter, who had been re-elected to Congress after an interval of some
years, was made the chairman. The report of this committee developed
and proved the frauds in Louisiana and particularly exposed the forgery
which had been perpetrated with the full knowledge of Republican
leaders in the electoral returns of that state. The duty of closing the
discussion in the House upon this report was assigned to me, and I
believe that the speech I made on the occasion satisfied the expectations
and the demands of the Democratic Party. At any rate, I received from
Mr. Bigelow a letter, written as he states by request of Mr. Tilden,
conveying to me his grateful acknowledgments for the manner in which
I had performed my duty and vindicated his position before the country. Up to this time, therefore, no adverse criticism of anything which

I had done had appeared from Mr. Tilden or from any of his personal friends who might be supposed to be familiar with his opinions.

Moreover the special work which I proposed for myself in the 45th Congress brought me into a very close contact with David Dudley Field, who in the 44th Congress had been specially selected by Mr. Tilden to fill the vacancy caused by the resignation of Smith Ely in consequence of his election as Mayor of the City of New York.[1] Mr. Field was not only an eminent lawyer, but a man of such aggressive and combative qualities as to give him peculiar fitness for the struggle which was before us in the determination of the Presidential vote. On all legal questions, therefore, Mr. Field was supposed to express the views held by Governor Tilden. He took an active part in the discussions of the House, and he was the chairman of the subcommittee which exposed the forgeries in the election returns made by the Louisiana precincts to the Returning Board of that state. The action of Mr. Field, therefore, was regarded as significant of the views entertained by Mr. Tilden; he supported the Electoral Commission Bill and made a legal argument in its favor, and no one doubted that this was done with the approbation of Mr. Tilden. I was subsequently assured by Mr. Field that during the week which elapsed between the report of the measure to the House and its adoption, after full discussion in the Senate and in the House, he had no communication of any kind from Mr. Tilden and never doubted that the measure had his approbation. If the fact had been otherwise the cordial relations which subsisted between Mr. Field and myself at that time and which continued until the day of his death could never have lasted. I call attention to this fact because the work which I proposed to myself in the 45th Congress and which induced me to prefer the Committee on Appropriations was largely due to the advice and the assistance of Mr. Field. It was apparent from the investigations carried on by the investigating committees of the House that the Republican Party had secured its majorities in several states, especially in South Carolina, by the unscrupulous use of the military power of the government, under the provisions of statutes which had been adopted during the stress of the Civil War. It seemed, therefore, to Mr. Field and to myself that the first and most important duty of the 45th Congress was to secure the repeal of these statutes, under which the Republican Administration had been able to ensure its continuance in power, and from which it could never be dislodged so long as it could control the suffrage by the use of the troops at the polls. Mr. Field was not a member of the 45th Congress, but at my request he prepared

---

[1] Representative Smith Ely resigned with two months of his term unexpired. At Tilden's suggestion, Field was chosen to fill his place. Field also served with high ability as Tilden's counsel, in opposition to William M. Evarts, before the Electoral Commission.

and published in the *Albany Law Journal* two articles giving an exhaustive account of the stages by which England had emancipated herself from a similar abuse of the military power of the state. These articles were as exhaustive as they were conclusive. On my part I accepted the chairmanship of the subcommittee in charge of the Army Appropriation Bill for the purpose of inserting in this bill the repealing clause necessary to protect the right of suffrage from the invasion and force under the control of Government officials.

The struggle was long and bitter. The bill passed the House containing these repealing clauses, but they were rejected in the Senate. Finally in consequence of the failure of the Conference Committee to agree the bill was lost, and no provision was made for the support of the Army. In a closing speech on the last night of the session I explained the issue to the House and the country, and retiring as I did from Congress at the close of this session, as I supposed for ever, I made my last speech in the House in defense of the right of the people to free elections absolutely divorced from the presence or the interference of the troops at the polls. The repeal of these obnoxious clauses was finally secured by general consent in the 46th Congress, of which I was not a member.

During this struggle I was in constant consultation not only with Mr. Field, but with Mr. Tilden, who both regarded this issue as the most important which could be presented by the Democratic Party in the next Presidential election. During all this time, which occupied the greater part of two years, not the slightest evidence was given to Mr. Field or to myself that Governor Tilden in any way had, or felt any grievances against me for the occurrences in connection with the creation of the Electoral Commission and the decision at which it had arrived. Mr. Field repeatedly expressed to me his surprise and indignation at the events to which I am now about to refer.

In the month of April of 1878 there appeared in the New York *Sun* a letter from Henry Watterson, then, as now, the editor of the Louisville *Courier-Journal*, in which my motives and conduct during the electoral controversy were attacked in terms of severe condemnation. He accused me of having misrepresented Mr. Tilden's views in regard to the Electoral Bill, of having suppressed an important telegram with deliberate treachery, not only to Mr. Tilden, but to the Democratic Party.

Mr. Watterson was a member of the 44th Congress and also acted as a member of the Advisory Committee of Eleven—to which reference has heretofore been made.[1] The charges, therefore, came from a source

---

[1] Watterson had opposed the creation of any Electoral Commission whatever; but he admits in his article, "The Hayes-Tilden Contest for the Presidency," *Century Magazine*, May, 1913, that at the critical meeting of the Democratic advisory committee and others in Washington, January 16, 1877, "there was no other protestant."

which demanded attention and reply. I lost no time in denouncing the accusations as false, and I set them down to inebriated malice on the part of Mr. Watterson. I was able to assert and prove that I had never represented to the committee or to my associates in Congress that Mr. Tilden had expressed any approval of the Electoral Bill. I declared that he had not in his conversation with me disapproved of the bill, but had suggested various amendments which would improve its details and make it more acceptable. Finally I pointed out that he had not produced a particle of evidence to sustain the charges of bad faith, and I suggested that all controversy on the subject would be ended by a reference to Mr. Tilden himself, who was the only authority to which both Mr. Watterson and I had the right to appeal, and I demanded that Mr. Watterson should secure from Mr. Tilden a distinct affirmance of the charges which he had made, and which I denounced as absolutely false.

In his reply Mr. Watterson declined the challenge to appeal to Mr. Tilden, but he called upon Mr. Manton Marble as the one personal witness who could show what Mr. Tilden's views really were, and would therefore demonstrate that I had been guilty of bad faith, in not having made them known to my Democratic associates in Washington.

At the time I confess that I did not understand the significance of Mr. Watterson's attack, and the reason why he appealed to Mr. Marble. I was surprised, however, and for the moment indignant that Mr. Tilden did not promptly contradict the statements of Mr. Watterson so far as my action and good faith were concerned. His silence, however, was explained when Mr. Marble on the 5th of August following, in response, as he states, to the call of Mr. Watterson, addressed a letter dated August 5th, 1878, to the New York *Sun,* in which is given what professes to be a complete statement of the views of Mr. Tilden and of the events which transpired in connection with my interview with him on Sunday, the 14th day of January, 1877, referred to in the letter of Mr. Watterson. It was understood at the time that the Marble letter was revised, if not inspired by Mr. Tilden himself. In his reference to this letter, which Mr. Bigelow uses as the basis and substance of his history of the Electoral Commission, he says,[1] "The tenor of this communication as well as the circumstances under which it appeared, leave little doubt that before it was given to the public it passed under Mr. Tilden's eyes." This fact, therefore, gives particular significance to the first footnote appended to the Marble statement which Mr. Bigelow, unfortunately, as it seems to me, does not reproduce and which is in the following words. "Please state that I have never questioned the good faith and patriotic purpose of Mr. Hewitt, or any whose counsels and guidance he thought it his duty to follow."

With this conclusive answer made by Mr. Tilden to Watterson's

[1] See Bigelow's *Tilden,* II, 75.

charges of bad faith, he can be dismissed from further consideration, but it is proper for me to add that at a dinner given two years afterward at the Union Club in the City of New York by Mr. Dorsheimer [1] at which both Mr. Watterson and myself were present, he publicly expressed the regret which he felt at having done me a great injury for which then and there he asked forgiveness. He has never, however, so far as I know, made the proper reparation through the public press in which his unfounded and unjust allegations appeared.

It is now necessary to consider in detail the contents of Mr. Marble's letter of August 5th, 1878, which Mr. Bigelow has adopted as the authority for his statements in regard to the attitude of Mr. Tilden toward the bill creating the Electoral Commission. It is proper to state at the outset that this letter contains material errors of fact, is remarkable for erroneous inferences rather by implication than by direct assertion, and is misleading in its conclusions.

Mr. Marble seeks to convey the impression that he was present at the interviews between Mr. Tilden and myself on the 14th of January, and he produces certain memoranda of the conversation which appear to have been made at the time by Mr. Marble. It is therefore necessary to state at the outset that Mr. Marble was not an auditor of what passed between Mr. Tilden and myself, and any report of the conversation must have been made to him second hand and, if made, must have been communicated by Mr. Tilden himself. Mr. Marble may have been present in Mr. Tilden's house on that date, but it is a remarkable fact that neither Mr. Cooper, who was present, nor I can recall any recollection of his presence on that occasion. We do remember that many persons passed in and out of the house on that day and particularly that Clarkson N. Potter was the only person who overheard any portion of the conversation between Mr. Tilden and myself. The details of that conversation have been heretofore stated and need not be repeated. There were two sessions, one in the morning and the other in the evening. In the afternoon I had a consultation with my lifelong friend, Chief Justice Charles P. Daly, to whom I stated fully the object of my mission and the nature of the conversation which I had had with Mr. Tilden at the conference in the morning. I told him that Mr. Tilden was not prepared to approve the bill but asked for further time for consideration; I explained to him that the Democratic Senators on the committee felt that it would be dangerous any longer to postpone some plan for the solution of the serious questions involved in the count, and that if the House Committee should disagree with the Senate committee, the latter would report the measure of their own

---

[1] William E. Dorsheimer of Buffalo, Lieutenant-Governor of New York under Governor Tilden and head of the platform committee at the Democratic National Convention in 1876; later member of Congress from the Buffalo district.

motion as necessary for the preservation of the peace of the country. Judge Daly after much consideration said that he thought the Senate committee would be justified in taking this course. As to the House committee, he would recommend concurrence unless Mr. Tilden should distinctly express his disapproval of the measure. This statement is important in this place because Judge Daly was so profoundly impressed with the gravity of the situation, that he took occasion on Sunday night after I had left for Washington to see Mr. Tilden on the subject and ascertain his decision. Judge Daly fortunately is still living and has authorized me to say that Mr. Tilden, after expressing grave doubts as to the course which ought to be pursued in the emergency, told him that he was not willing to take the responsibility of disapproving the plan proposed for arbitration, although he thought that it should be modified as to the selection of judges. He did not express any disapproval either of the principle or the policy of the bill but confined his criticisms to the details of the constitution and the tribunal. This statement of Judge Daly's is in exact accordance with the telegrams which were sent to me by Mr. Tilden through Mr. Cooper and which have heretofore been quoted.

The inference drawn, therefore, by Mr. Marble that Mr. Tilden expressed his disapproval of the bill is plainly erroneous and not in accordance with my understanding, the recollection of Judge Daly, and with the contents of the telegrams, which all look to the amendment of the bill and not to its defeat.

In his report of the conversation between Mr. Tilden and myself Mr. Marble quotes various remarks of Mr. Tilden's as having been made to him in answer to certain representations which Mr. Marble puts in my mouth. I can only say that these quotations from Mr. Tilden's conversation all bear the mark of deliberate preparation and are quite consistent with such account as Mr. Tilden might have seen fit to repeat to Mr. Marble as expressive of his opinions. This is particularly true of the following passage in Mr. Marble's report of the interview.

Mr. Tilden's criticisms of the details of the Bill of which in no shape could he approve, either the policy or the substance, exemplified the political sagacity of the veteran statesman.

If the arbitration is to be adopted the tribune ought to be fixed in the Bill itself, and not left to chance or intrigue.

If the arbitration is to be adopted the duty of the arbitrators to investigate and decide the case on its merits should be mandatory and not left a question of construction.

With both the vital points left at loose ends you cannot succeed, you cannot afford to concede and you can exact: 1st. The selection of good men to compose the tribune which is the controlling point and 2nd. The nature of the function to be performed by the tribune which is next in importance.

Fixed these two points—good men, explicit powers—and you might possibly get through—leave them doubtful and it's happy go lucky—the shake of a dice box.

Now I distinctly assert that no such remarks were addressed to me. They bear the internal evidence of having been carefully prepared afterwards, but whether they were dictated to Mr. Marble immediately after the conference or, much later when he was preparing his letter, I do not know, but I do know that they were never expressed to me or in my presence or hearing. Mr. Tilden did indeed object to the provision in the draft of the bill providing for the elimination of one of the six judges by lot, and in his subsequent telegrams he expressed opinions as to the constitution of the commission, which were acted upon by the committee as will appear from my telegram through Mr. Cooper on the 16th of January.

I have heretofore explained the changes which were made in the plan after the receipt of the telegram of Mr. Tilden bearing date January 16th, by which Mr. Tilden's objections were fully made and the commission constituted upon a basis which in the unanimous judgment of the managing Committee of Eleven ensured a favorable result to the Democratic claims.

And here Mr. Marble falls into an extraordinary error, he states that the final completion of the Joint Committee of the Senate and House was reached on the 16th and finally voted on the morning of the 17th. He seems to have been ignorant of the fact that after the receipt of Mr. Tilden's telegram of the 16th January and after General Hunton had refused to sign the joint report, a meeting of the Joint Committee was held at which, after many hours of discussion, the plan was modified so as to secure two Democratic judges and two Republican judges who were to choose the fifth judge; nobody doubting that the choice would fall to Judge Davis.

While these proceedings were taking place in Washington Mr. Marble says that on the night of the 16th January he

had called upon Mr. Tilden and found him in his library with several other gentlemen. The telegraphic correspondence given above was read and the situation freely canvassed; in their presence Mr. Tilden dictated and sent the following telegram in cipher to Washington through the National Committee rooms. Not having been sent to or seen by Mr. Hewitt it is not pertinent to any controversy concerning him; and indeed by the time it had arrived and been deciphered *the business was done,* but its value now and fuller written record of the same points gathered more briefly in the telegrams to Mr. Hewitt, which had followed a full conversation.

New York January 16th. No need of hot haste but much danger in it. Some days interval should be taken the risk to publicity (is) harmless.

No information here nor any opportunity to get information which could justify abstinence from condemning such abandonment of the Constitution and of the Government and of the rights of the two Houses and of the people.

Nothing but great and certain public danger not to be escaped in any other way could excuse such a measure. We are overpressed by exaggerated fears and forget that the other side will have greater troubles than we, unless relieved by some agreement.

They have no way out but by usurpation; (they) are bullying us with what they dare not do, or will break down in attempting.

So long as we stand on the Constitution and settled practice we know where we are. Consequence of new expedient not enough considered.

Only way of getting accessions in the Senate is by House standing firm. And judicious friends believe in that case we will go safely through. Opportunity to consult such friends should be given before even tacit acquiescence (by House Committee) if that is contemplated. Though details may be probably discussed, final committal by House Committee should be firmly withheld.

It is distinctly stated by Mr. Marble that this telegram was not sent to or seen by me, and as a matter of fact I never saw or heard of it until it was published in his letter. If it had been intended for me it would, like the previous telegrams, have been sent through Mr. Cooper in his cipher. It is stated that it was sent through the National Committee rooms in their cipher. It is not stated to whom in Washington it was sent, but inasmuch as the only person in Washington who had possession of the cipher of the National Committee was William T. Pelton, the nephew and personal representative in Washington of Mr. Tilden, it must have been sent to him. The suppression, therefore, of this telegram charged upon me by Mr. Watterson was due to another person, who appears not to have communicated it either to me or to Mr. Randall or to Mr. Field or even to Mr. Watterson who was a member of the Committee of Eleven and who seemed to regard himself as the special champion of Mr. Tilden's rights.

This telegram must have reached Washington not later than the morning of the 17th of January, and it is certain that if it had been communicated to the Committee of Eleven, General Hunton would not have signed the report and the House Committee would have repudiated it; for notwithstanding Mr. Marble's assertion that the business "was already done," as a matter of fact nothing final had been done nor was done until a direct communication had been received from Mr. Tilden through Colonel Pelton, recommending acquiescence in the report under the following extraordinary circumstances now made known for the first time.

After the modification secured on the night of the 16th and the morning of the 17th of the plan adopted by the Joint Committee, General Hunton, as heretofore stated, still refused to sign the report until Mr. Tilden should have distinctly given his approval. Colonel Pelton was therefore sent to New York by the earliest train, leaving on the morning of the 17th with a copy of the final report to be placed in Mr. Tilden's hands for approval or disapproval. He returned to Washington by the night train on the 17th and on the morning of the 18th reported to the Committee of Eleven in the Speaker's room that he had shown the report to Mr. Tilden and that it met with his approval. General Hunton thereupon signed the report, which was made to the House on the 18th, not on the 17th as Mr. Marble's letter would seem to indicate. The delay was made for the express purpose of communicating with Mr. Tilden, and this purpose was carried into effect. Although it is still conceivable that Mr. Pelton may not have correctly reported the views of Mr. Tilden, but if this were the fact it is not consistent with the suppression of the telegram of Mr. Tilden through the National Committee, which must have been in the possession of Colonel Pelton at the time when he reported Mr. Tilden's approval of the bill. If, therefore, the telegram were not suppressed with Mr. Tilden's concurrence, it might and would have been made public by him or his friends who had been assembled at his house as stated by Mr. Marble during the nine subsequent days of the debate which took place in the Senate and in the House.

During these nine days no syllable of dissent came from Mr. Tilden or his confidential friends either to me or Speaker Randall or Mr. Field or Mr. Watterson, all of whom except the Speaker made speeches in favor of the passage of the Electoral Commission Bill.

It thus appears that Mr. Marble's attempt to use the suppressed telegram as the evidence of Mr. Tilden's disapproval of the bill as finally reported, utterly fails, for the simple reason that the telegram referred to different arrangements, not to the bill as finally agreed to by the House Committee and reported on the 12th January. It is in fact a boomerang, clearly showing that the new arrangement must have been satisfactory to Mr. Tilden, or else the telegram would not have been suppressed, for its publication in accordance with Mr. Tilden's demand for publicity would undoubtedly have prevented the committee from reporting the bill, and if it had been reported before the publication of the telegram, there was abundant time during the nine days of debate which ensued in the Senate and in the House for Mr. Tilden to have made his objections known, if he felt any, and for Colonel Pelton to have made known to the committee any change of mind on the part of Mr. Tilden of which he had notice, either by telegram or otherwise. As a matter of fact not the slightest intimation was given by Mr. Tilden or by Colonel Pelton to any Democratic members of the House that the bill as reported was not regarded as satisfactory; on the contrary, Pelton was indefatigable in his efforts to secure votes for the bill.

Moreover, Mr. Marble attempts to give credit to Mr. Tilden for magnanimity in forbearing to communicate his opposition to the measure as reported, and yet with singular inconsistency he produces a telegram written originally in reference to another form of the measure as the evidence that Mr. Tilden desired the defeat of the bill as finally reported to the Senate and the House. If Mr. Tilden really desired the defeat of the measure and did not assent to the suppression of the telegram, the claim for magnanimity might be justly made, but in fact for nine days after his approval had been expressly reported by Colonel Pelton, it seems clear that not only was there no magnanimity but there was a distinct acquiescence in the general desire on the Democratic side for the passage of the bill. The use of the suppressed telegram, therefore, was an afterthought, the explanation of which is now to be given.

In the spring of 1878 the question of the next Presidency began to be emergent. On the Democratic side the opinion was universal that Mr. Tilden was the only logical candidate. In no other way except by his re-election to the Presidency could the popular indignation against the great wrong which had been committed find expression. To some of his personal friends, however, it seemed desirable that Mr. Tilden's opposition to the Electoral Commission which had perpetrated the great fraud should, if possible, be demonstrated. Tentatively Mr. Watterson was put forward to accuse me of having misrepresented Mr. Tilden and to make me the scapegoat of the Democratic Party, by whose representatives the Electoral Bill had been passed. Perhaps *my* magnanimity was counted upon not to interpose any contradiction; and certainly I should have refrained from the indignant denial which I was compelled to make if my personal honor had not been brought into question; because I regarded the re-nomination of Mr. Tilden as absolutely essential for the success of the party and the vindication of the national honor. I had never ceased to urge upon Mr. Tilden the duty which he owed in this emergency to his country, and I used to say to him when he spoke of his failing health that even if he had to be carried into the White House in his coffin he owed it to himself and to the country to face even death rather than the great fraud should be condoned.

When the tentative effort of Mr. Watterson had thus failed, Mr. Marble was called upon to make the vindication which the super-serviceable friends of Mr. Tilden seemed to regard as necessary, but as this latter involved the personal co-operation of Mr. Tilden, who knew that any imputation upon my good faith would be met by conclusive refutation, he required Mr. Marble to make a distinct declaration that he, Mr. Tilden, never doubted the good faith and loyalty with which I had acted.

In view of the facts which have been above stated, it may be properly asked why the answer to Mr. Marble's letter was not made at the time of its publication. As a matter of fact the answer was prepared within one week thereafter and would have been published then and there but for the advice of discreet friends whom I had called in consultation. They were of opinion that as my honor was no longer involved, owing to the express disclaimers of Mr. Tilden, there was no necessity for me to make any vindication and that any errors in history could be corrected after the next Presidential election if it were then thought advisable to make the correction. It was urged that the publication at that time would necessarily have the effect of damaging the popularity of Mr. Tilden if he should be nominated at the ensuing National Convention. These arguments prevailed with me because, as I have before stated, I was most earnest and pronounced in the conviction that Mr. Tilden alone could carry the Democratic Party to victory.

The question may now be asked why, having refrained from making any reply at that time and for all the years which have since elapsed, I now put in shape for publication a narrative of the facts and a demonstration of the errors contained in the letter of Mr. Marble.

The reason is to be found in the publication of Mr. Bigelow's life of Tilden, in which not only is the Marble letter used as the foundation for his account of the Electoral Commission and the footnote which expressly declared Mr. Tilden's confidence in my loyalty and good faith omitted, but an attack is made upon my Democratic associates, and particularly upon Messrs. Thurman and Bayard, with whom I had heartily co-operated in the whole business. Hence I am forced to reply to any censure which may be expressed against their action during the long and anxious controversy which supervened after the meeting of Congress in December, 1876. If they were guilty of bad faith, I also was guilty. We all had reason to believe that we were acting in the final outcome of the deliberation of the Joint Committee of the Senate and House in accordance with the views of Mr. Tilden. As has been shown, the original movement toward arbitration was the result of the conference in New York between Mr. Tilden and Judge Thurman. It is true, however, that Messrs. Thurman and Bayard declared that even if the House Committee should refuse to concur in the Electoral Bill, they would feel constrained as Senators and patriots to join in its report to the Senate as an independent measure. Nevertheless, in the efforts to secure the amendments finally made in the bill, by which Democratic success seemed to be assured, they were most loyal and earnest. This testimony is due to them and is given without their knowledge or request.

The most remarkable feature of the action of the Electoral Commission was the audacity with which the majority shifted their position in order to secure the votes necessary to elect the Republican candidates. They have never attempted to make any defense of their conduct. An explanation is to be found, first in the general desire felt throughout the country for the peaceful settlement of the controversy; and to some extent the Republican majority banked upon this overwhelming consideration. But this feeling alone would never have justified the commission in the contradiction involved in the Florida, Louisiana, and Oregon decisions, but for certain disclosures in reference to the latter case which came to light before it was decided. It has already been stated that the one vote in Oregon was only claimed by the Democrats in order to compel the commission to go behind the returns in the other disputed cases, and to apply the same principle in all the cases which might be submitted to the commission. In case this had been done there would have been no occasion to count the Oregon vote for Tilden, but if Hayes were to be counted in, he required all the disputed votes including the one from Oregon, involving a contradiction so glaring that it was not believed that any tribunal, especially one in which the final decision rested with the Judges of the Supreme Court, could possibly do otherwise than decide at least one of the cases in favor of Tilden. But accident came to the relief of the Republican majority in the embarrassment in which they were placed. During the count it was disclosed that in procuring the Oregon vote a considerable amount of money had been sent by the Democratic managers to that state and had actually passed through the hands of the governor, who had given the certificate of election to Cronin, the one Democratic elector. It was openly charged that the vote had been purchased, and it was proven beyond all doubt that money had been used. To me these disclosures were a great surprise. As chairman of the National Committee I had pointed out to the governor the importance of this one vote to be used as a lever to secure justice in the other disputed states. The demand for money was never made to me, and I had no knowledge of its transmission, although for necessary legal expenses it would have been proper to supply it. It is scarcely necessary for me to add that I do not believe that Mr. Tilden had any such knowledge. Nevertheless, the money was raised and transmitted by his nephew, Colonel Pelton, with the approval and co-operation of Senator Barnum who was a member of the National Committee. Subsequently it became apparent that the money was used for the payment of legitimate expenses, and not for bribery or the purchase of votes. But it was boldly charged at the time and apparently believed by the Republican members of the Electoral Board that the vote had been procured by corruption and hence they did not hesitate to reverse in the Florida case the rulings and to reject the Cronin vote, whereby they were enabled to give to Hayes the one vote required with those of the disputed states to secure his election.

I have reason to think that although this result was a great disappointment to Mr. Tilden, he nevertheless felt a profound sense of relief from the dangers of the situation. If the count had not been completed and Hayes had been declared President by the unconstitutional action of the Senate or by the equally unconstitutional recognition of President Grant or by the action of General Sherman in command of the military forces of the country, the position of Mr. Tilden would have been most embarrassing. He would either have been forced to take the oath of office under the constitutional choice of the House of Representatives which would undoubtedly have been made, or he would have been compelled to submit to the usurpation of the office to which he was legally entitled. No one doubted then, and no one can doubt now, that in the former event civil war would have resulted. To violence of any kind Mr. Tilden was by nature strongly opposed. He believed in peaceful methods, but he also believed in giving effect to the will of the people. For such a conflict the state of his health entirely unfitted him and, moreover, his intimate connection with many great industrial and corporate enterprises would naturally lead him to a conservative course of action. It is enough to say that the emergency did not arise, but Mr. Bigelow seems to think that if it had arisen Mr. Tilden would have taken the oath of office and insisted upon his right of Presidency.

At best it is a matter of speculation, which I do not care to pursue further; but I believe that on the whole Mr. Tilden was satisfied by the result and consoled by the conviction that at the next Presidential election justice would be done by his triumphant re-election to the great office of which he had been defrauded.

Mr. Bigelow admits that Mr. Tilden desired the nomination in 1880, but thinks that on the score of his health he would have declined it. I can only say that I used every effort to secure the nomination of Mr. Tilden at that time, and I went so far as to advise Mr. Manning not to deliver the letter of declination to the convention, until after the nomination had been made. Finally, when in compliance to Mr. Tilden's telegram Mr. Manning felt constrained to present the letter to the convention, I still insisted that Mr. Tilden ought to be nominated, and for that reason I declined overtures which were made to me to allow my name to be presented to the convention as a candidate for the nomination.

Finally when it was seen that the convention was ready to take Mr. Tilden at his word (a most grievous and irreparable mistake) I urged that the vote of New York should be given to Mr. Randall, and it was so given. This statement is made only for the purpose of eradicating any lingering doubt which may remain in the mind of any Democrat that I was the firm friend and advocate of Mr. Tilden when everyone else had acquiesced in his retirement from public life.

So in 1884, when Mr. Tilden's health was still more precarious and his voice had become almost inaudible, I still urged his nomination, and I think it should have been made and that Mr. Tilden should have been elected, even though his death had followed immediately upon his assumption of his duties as President.

Thus, and thus only, could the blot upon the National escutcheon have been wiped out and the sense of justice which should animate a great people have been vindicated.

In declining, therefore, to be a candidate in 1880 and again in 1884, Mr. Tilden made a regrettable and irreparable mistake, because he deprived the people of the great Republic of the opportunity to do justice to him and to themselves.

But great as was this error of judgment, it is not more regrettable than the effort now made by his over-zealous friends to deprive him of the credit of having approved of the Electoral Commission and of the settlement of the Presidential contest, which gave peace, order, and prosperity to the country. To me his bearing in the trying emergency in which he was placed was marked by modest self-control and noble dignity. His patriotism rose superior to partisan impulse and all personal considerations.

> More true joy Marcellus exiled feels,
> Than Cæsar with a Senate at his heels.

To attempt to rob Mr. Tilden of one ray of the great glory of self-sacrifice and of love of country superior to the lust of power is a crime in which I will have no part or lot. But if his professed friends shall thus succeed in dimming the luster of Tilden's fame as a statesman and a patriot, I will not permit them to rob me of the satisfaction of having borne a conspicuous part in the settlement of the great controversy in the crisis of the fate of the Republic; and I repeat now, as I once declared upon the floor of the House of Representatives, the hope that if ever a stone should be erected over my grave it shall record the fact that I was the firm friend and persistent advocate of the principle and policy of referring the disputed succession to arbitration and of thus securing a President whose legal title to the office could not be called in question, although it was based upon a violation of the spirit of the Act which created the Electoral Commission and is branded with "the undying penalty that History inflicts on wrong." [1]

[1] An accurate reappraisal of Tilden's rôle in the disputed election, correcting the various errors and injustices of John Bigelow's book, is shortly to appear in Alexander C. Flick's *Samuel J. Tilden.*

The True Road to Prosperity

SPEECH IN THE HOUSE OF REPRESENTATIVES ON BLAND-ALLISON
SILVER-COINAGE BILL, FEBRUARY 21, 1878

[*Hewitt, belonging to the conservative financial school of Horatio
Seymour and Tilden, consistently opposed inflationary measures.
From 1878 to 1897 he repeatedly warned the nation that proposals
for diluting the currency by large emissions of paper money or
silver coin presented the gravest possible threat to the welfare of
all groups; that under existing conditions, the gold standard offered
the only safe basis for national enterprise. Early in 1878 the House
responded to the great depression then just ending (which had
certainly been deflationary in effect) by passing the Bland Bill for
the free and unlimited coinage of silver at the ratio of 16 to 1.
The Senate, led by William B. Allison, amended this by dropping
the "unlimited" feature of the bill and fixing the coinage at not
less than 2,000,000 and not more than 4,000,000 silver dollars a
month. Even with this restriction the bill presented a threat to the
permanence of the gold standard. Hewitt made the speech here
reprinted on the Senate amendment. The bill passed, was vetoed
by President Hayes on February 28, and was repassed over his veto.
But Hewitt had placed on record his conviction that free raw
materials and freer commerce offered the best hope of wider employment and prosperity.*]

MR. SPEAKER: This bill is introduced as a measure of relief. I wish
to put it upon record that it will intensify and aggravate the prevalent
distress. I go further and say that recovery from distress will be impossible until this bill is swept from the statute book, as it will be within
one year by an indignant, deceived, and outraged people.

When the bill for the issue of subsidiary coin was introduced into
the Forty-fourth Congress I opposed it, and, standing almost alone
among the advocates for a specie currency, I made the following prediction:

There is still one other explanation of this bold attempt to secure the approval of
a Democratic House to this sham resumption in depreciated silver coins. It is perhaps
intended to follow up this movement with an effort to secure legislation making
silver a legal tender for the payment of debts larger than $5, possibly of all debts.
It may well be argued that if it be resumption to pay debts under $5 in silver, it is

equally specie resumption to pay larger debts in the silver, for they are only aggregates of five-dollar debts. The argument is so sound that it shows the hollow nature of the whole pretense that there is any specie resumption in the substitution for paper of silver worth less than the paper it replaces, when the paper itself is at a discount of one-eighth as compared with gold. Throughout the commercial world there is but one standard of value, and that is gold, measuring all commodities, silver included, and any attempt to substitute anything for gold, even though it be metallic, whether silver, copper, or iron, at a higher rate than its true value in gold, is to rob somebody of some portion of his existing property.

What was then prophecy is now reality, and we are brought face to face with a proposition which drives gold out of the country and places us in the same category with semi-barbarous countries, in which silver is the sole standard of value. Before the Constitution was made, gold and silver were the money of the country. The Constitution intended that they should continue to be the money of the country because it prohibited the states from making anything but gold and silver a legal tender. But the Constitution anticipates that the ratio of gold and silver will fluctuate, as all other ratios of value fluctuate, and therefore the Constitution provides that Congress "shall regulate the value thereof." Now experience has shown that the ratio of value between gold and silver is liable to periodic if not daily fluctuations. All attempts to establish a permanent ratio have been in vain. In practice one or the other is undervalued and leaves the country. In France, for example, prior to 1848, the currency was practically monometallic, that is, of silver. The gold discoveries of California and Australia lowered the relative value of gold. Silver in France was undervalued and left the country. Gold took its place, except for subsidiary uses. It was regarded at the time with serious alarm, and Chevalier proposed to put the coinage of France upon a monometallic silver basis in order to retain the silver, which had been the ancient money of France. Fortunately for France, his views did not prevail, and hence when silver fell it found France with a large stock of gold which would have left the country if the Bank of France had not been in a state of suspension. What seemed therefore to be the wise finance of France was really a piece of good luck arising from the misfortunes of the Franco-German War.

France has therefore now for commercial purposes a stock of gold, and her commerce foreign and domestic is carried on on a gold basis. Her domestic traffic settles itself in silver, which today in France, as in Germany and in England, is serving its only legitimate use as subsidiary coin. But it will be said that the bullion stock of the Bank of France is largely in silver. It is true that out of the $400,000,000 of bullion in the Bank of France about $170,000,000 is in silver and is in reality surplus stock, because with the present paper currency in circulation there is no room for it and it remains idle in the bank. It not merely loses interest but it cannot be exported and sold except at a loss of ten percent. How is the Bank of France dealing with this problem? It is transferring the loss from the stockholders of the bank to the public. It is calling in its one-hundred franc notes and paying out silver five-franc pieces for them, as it has a right to do under the law. The silver, therefore, is being transferred from the vaults of the bank to the pockets of the people.

The French people will not keep more silver than they can use. The surplus will leave the country and be sold for what it will fetch as bullion. They want a market for it. The Orient will take it, but at reduced rates. Hence if we remonetize silver and make it a full legal tender it will be sold to us at higher rates, and the result will be that we shall have transferred the loss due to this surplus stock of silver in the Bank of France from the French people to ourselves. Whether silver shall hereafter appreciate or not makes no difference; the present loss will be ours, deliberately assumed at a time when there is no earthly reason for it, because we can only become the owners of the silver by purchasing it with our bonds or our products, which can just as well be applied to the purchase of gold, on which there can be no loss, for under all circumstances it will pay balances among all of our foreign transactions, which are alone and always solvable in gold, or in its equivalent at gold values. By remonetizing silver, therefore, at a time when we are free from the embarrassments due to its fluctuating in value, we adopt a course directly the reverse of the policy adopted by the Bank of France when it was in a state of suspension and therefore able to keep its gold.

It thus appears that in the progress of modern development among commercial nations, in spite of all efforts to the contrary, gold and silver have by reason of their relative material qualities and cost of production forced themselves into their inevitable and natural relation, gold as a standard of value for foreign and large commercial transactions and silver as the money for small domestic traffic.

Gold and silver thus remain the money of the nation as they were before the Constitution and as they were intended by the Constitution to remain, so regulated in value as to keep both in circulation and each in its appropriate sphere. But they can no more be made permanently interchangeable upon a fixed ratio of value than can cotton and wool, or iron and pork, or flour and tobacco, or any other commodities the value of which fluctuates from day to day according to times and seasons and the law of demand and supply.

While, therefore, legislation is powerless to accomplish the good results which the friends of the unlimited tender of the silver dollar hope to produce by its remonetization, legislation can produce a vast amount of evil and retard the progress of the country in the development of its foreign commerce, to which alone we can look for relief from the stagnation which paralyzes the industry of the country.

The great mass of the people of this country are workers that depend for their livelihood upon their daily labor, whether it be in the walks of professional life, in the domain of trade, in the mechanic arts, in agriculture, or in what is known as common labor, where physical force is of more consequence than mental power. Of the class who live without labor, upon realized capital, we have but few. The capitalists of this country are in reality its workers. The great mass of loanable capital belongs to them. It is aggregated in banks of issue and deposit, in savings banks, in insurance companies, in joint-stock corporations for production and distribution, such as manufacturing and railway companies. The legislation of the country, therefore, if it is to look to the greatest good of the greatest number, must ever be directed toward the interests of the working classes, who are in reality the owners of the larger portion of the national bonds.

Unhappily a large number of our able-bodied workingmen are unable to find employment. So far as this state of affairs is due to legislation no time is to be lost in correcting it. That the evils complained of are due to some causes besides natural ones is self-evident. We have a fruitful soil, which has produced abundant harvests, so that of our surplus we are able to supply the wants of the world; we have unnumbered acres of unoccupied lands, which will give a generous return to the hand of toil; we have mineral resources unequaled on the face of the globe in variety, extent, and ease of exploitation; we have the skill to turn these resources to account, and by means of our natural and artificial avenues of communication we have every possible facility for their use and development. Why, then, do we stand idle? Why do we suffer? Why do willing hands and anxious hearts wait for the command which summons them to useful and to grateful labor?

We are told by some that it is due to overproduction; we are told by others that it is due to the contraction of the currency; we are told by others that it is due to the demonetization of silver; we are told by others that it is due to the act providing for the resumption of specie payments. But I tell you it is due first to overexpenditure and second to the fact that we have no access to the markets of the world for anything but our raw products. I insist that there is no such thing as overproduction in the presence of empty stomachs and naked bodies, and there is no road out of this condition of affairs but—first, in national and individual economy; and second, in removing the obstructions which by legislation we have put in the way of the sale of our manufactured products in foreign markets.

I insist that the passage of the silver bill and the postponement of the resumption of specie payments, which will be its inevitable consequence, can only result in the continuance and aggravation of the existing depression, and while it must tend to drive our people back to the soil, to keep themselves from starvation, the unavoidable results will be to reduce still further the narrow profits of agriculture, by producing a commercial glut of cereal and other agricultural products which the world cannot take and consume.

Our relief then must come from the outside, and not the inside. It must come from securing foreign markets for our merchandise. Does the House, does the country, realize the nature and extent of the relief which can thus be secured? Take one example: We purchased last year from the Spanish American states and Mexico to the amount of $149,719,995; we sold them to the amount of $51,664,693. The difference, $98,053,302, we paid in money. This money they sent to Europe to purchase manufactured articles which we can produce with as little human labor as the people from whom they were bought. Why, under the absurd doctrine that you cannot sell unless you buy, why did we not sell these goods to our neighbors who would naturally prefer to buy from us because we buy from them? Simply because our tariff laws do not permit us to compete with England and Germany and France. There the raw materials of manufacture are free. Here they pay heavy duties. We deliberately shut ourselves out from the natural and open markets at our door, and yet we complain that our people are idle and our mills are closed.

The demonetization of silver did not produce these results, and the progress toward specie payments has not contributed to them. We never had these markets when we had silver dollars and when we had the excessive issues of paper money which are now so loudly demanded. But we had then our own markets. We did not then produce enough for our own consumption. But at length, after a century of development, we are able to supply all that we need of every staple article for our own wants, and we have a surplus which we must sell elsewhere. It is because we cannot sell this surplus at prices which will compete with Europe that our mills now stand idle and our people seek work and wages in vain.

The remonetization of silver and further issues of irredeemable paper money will not relieve but will only add to our embarrassments.

Let me explain how and why. The object to be aimed at is to secure and control the foreign markets, to take that place in the foreign commerce of the world which is now filled by Great Britain. Let us first consider what it has done for her and how it has made her the richest nation and the greatest power that has ever existed since the world began.

The destiny of nations is pointed out by nature. The climate and the natural resources of every country determine its career; modified only by the physical, mental, and moral vigor of the people who inhabit it.

Nature has clearly indicated that the commerce of the world will be as largely controlled in the future by the United States as now it is by Great Britain. The capacity for production is the fundamental basis upon which the structure of commerce must be reared. The possession of raw materials of the varied kinds required for all the branches of staple industry will surely secure the establishment and success of manufactures, provided the climate is favorable and the soil is occupied by an honest, intelligent, and energetic race of people. In some respects Great Britain has enjoyed unusual advantages for the development of her industry, the extension of her commerce, and for acquiring the control of the markets of the world. In the first place she possesses a climate singularly favorable to physical development and active labor. How far the climate and her insular position have affected her national character let philosophers decide; but it is certain that, from some cause or causes, the English people during the last five hundred years have developed qualities of personal independence, of mental vigor, of untiring activity, of limitless acquisitiveness, which have no counterpart in any nation, ancient or modern. Hence today her rule extends over more than one-fifth of the surface and includes more than one-fifth of the entire population of the globe. And yet this enormous growth of political power has all occurred within two hundred years, and that vast accumulation of wealth which excites the wonder and the envy of the world has been built up to its great proportions within the last century. Its magnitude is simply stupendous and passes the comprehension of ordinary rules of estimate. In 1801 the amount of national wealth was believed to be eighteen hundred millions of pounds sterling, equal to £112 per head of population. In 1841 it had risen to four thousand millions of pounds sterling, equal to £150 per head. In 1858 it was six thousand millions of pounds sterling, equal to £206 per head of population, while in 1877 it has reached eight thousand five hundred millions of pounds sterling, equal to £260 per head of population. The best authorities reckon the annual accumulations during the last ten years to have been at the rate of £235,000,000 per annum, of which £65,000,000 are derived from investments of British capital in foreign countries. In other words, if this sum were equally distributed among the inhabitants of Great Britain, the rest of the world is paying about $10 per head annually to each man, woman, and child in the United Kingdom. Great Britain is therefore not only overflowing with riches at home but she has secured a mortgage-lien upon the industry of the rest of the world which practically absorbs a large portion of the profits of human industry.

That this statement is true is proven by the fact that for a long period of years the imports of merchandise and bullion into Great Britain have largely exceeded the value of the exports. . . . During the last nineteen years the aggregate of balances of excess of imports over exports amounts to the enormous sum of £1,193,608,433.

The percentage of this excess steadily increased on the average, and in the year 1876 it amounted to £125,968,263. That no portion of this vast value represented debts incurred abroad is proven by the fact that besides all the merchandise which she imported there was a balance received in bullion amounting to £7,590,000, and in two years of £13,230,000. Doubtless some part of this large excess was due to the collection of a portion of the indebtedness of foreign countries to Great Britain. And as confidence is restored it is possible that some portion of this fund may be again invested in foreign securities. But the broad fact remains that Great Britain every year draws from other countries in merchandise and in money a sum which is now sufficient to defray the annual expenses of her entire administration, including the interest on the national debt. It is not surprising, therefore, that the people of Great Britain have more of the comforts of life and suffer less from poverty than any other nation in the world. The present is an era of distress. Throughout the civilized globe the depression in business is universal, and the cry of suffering comes up from every land. How is it in England?

My own personal observation during the summer of 1877 in France, Germany, and England satisfied me that the condition of the working classes in England was less grievous and more comfortable than in either of the other countries or in the United States. Except in one branch of business, the manufacture of iron and steel, there was sufficient employment for the operatives; and although wages had been reduced they were still sufficient to maintain the working population in better case than here or elsewhere abroad. That this statement is true is clearly proven by the returns of the Poor-Law Board as to the relief extended to paupers. The number relieved in 1875 was 30,000 less than in 1874; and in 1876, 56,000 less than in 1875. The cost of pauperism per head of population in 1868 was 6s. 11½d. per head of population, while in 1876 it was reduced to 6s. 3/4d. per head. Moreover for the first time in the present century the immigration into Great Britain was equal to the emigration from its shores, proving its ability to employ its population at a better rate of compensation than could be had in foreign countries. The explanation of this unexpected and almost incredible state of affairs is to be found in the fact that while her exports had steadily diminished in money value from 1872 to 1876, they had increased in actual quantity in every staple industry except in that of iron and steel. This is not only proved by the official returns but by the unmistakable evidence in the fact that the coal raised increased from 127,016,747 tons in 1873, which was the largest quantity up to that period, to 133,344,766 tons in 1876.

In other words, more power had been employed in human industry than in any previous period of English history. As the result, therefore, of the British commercial system we have in an era of universal depression increase of employment, increase of income, increase of accumulated wealth, and increase of population. Here, then, is presented a situation worthy of the study of statesmen. How and by what means has Great Britain placed herself in this enviable position at the head of the nations in industry, commerce, prosperity, wealth, and empire? Are the elements of her prosperity peculiar to herself? Has she any monopoly of the sources of power and of growth? Have we, members of the Congress of the United States, representatives of the people, who are suffering from falling values, from the stoppage of the wheels of industry, from the want of employment of its working population, amid the wreck of parties and the confusion of ancient issues—have we sufficiently studied the causes of British growth? Have we inquired into the secrets of her policy? Have we taken the proper steps to follow her example, to appropriate her experience, and to secure to our suffering country that portion of her sources of wealth which are within our grasp and laid the foundations for the acquisition of that larger portion which nature has plainly indicated to be our right provided we act with intelligence, energy, and integrity, which is at the foundation of all permanent success?

Two hundred years ago the commercial superiority now enjoyed by Great Britain was possessed by Holland. How did Great Britain secure its transfer to her control? Doubtless navigation laws, protective legislation, and warlike operations had more or less influence upon the result, but the rivalry continued without material advantage to either side, until the discovery of the steam engine. England had coal, while Holland had none. Moreover the coal fields were near to navigation. A slight expenditure for canals made it accessible to every portion of the kingdom. The steam engine multiplied the productive power of man twenty-five-fold. Previous to its introduction exchanges were made practically on the basis of one day of human labor for another day of human labor. The steam engine enabled England to purchase with one day's labor the produce of twenty-five days. Of course the competition of other countries not having access to coal became impossible, and the profits of her exchanges in foreign trade were enormously enhanced. This new source of wealth enabled Great Britain to maintain the wars with Napoleon and resist for awhile the introduction of new political ideas which have since regenerated the face of the world. Out of these wars she learned one lesson, however, which has governed her policy from that day to this, to expend her power and her influence for the extension of her trade and commerce and not for the propagation of political ideas.

The Crimean War, although on its face produced by political considerations, was in reality undertaken by Great Britain for the protection of her Indian empire against Russian aggression and for the preservation of a vast trade amounting to a hundred million pounds sterling per annum which she carries on with her eastern dependency. The commercial element has become dominant in Great Britain. A great deal is said of honor, justice, and religion; but when her policy is analyzed there will always be found behind these noble sentiments inscribed upon her banners and written all over her foreign policy the words, "Pounds, shillings, and pence." De Tocqueville long ago pointed out this peculiarity, when he said: "Whatever makes for English interests is justice; whatever makes against them is fraud."

British commerce being thus founded on her possession of exhaustless stores of power in her coal beds, could not be disturbed or dislodged until other nations could secure equal access to stores of cheap fuel; and practically England secured the monopoly of the trade of the world long before other nations could make any progress toward substantial competition. The introduction of railways, however, was their release from bondage. It enabled them to get access to the sources of power; but England had got fifty years the start and during that fifty years had gathered unto herself the bulk of the accumulated floating capital of mankind, and now that other nations are in a position to compete, having got access to fuel, having acquired skill, having perfected and established the best machinery for production, they find that the profits of trade are reduced to that narrow margin which is due to the superior natural advantages of one country over another for special classes of products.

Let us consider for a moment the elements that enter into the successful production of manufactured goods. They are: first, capital; second, skill; third, raw materials; fourth, labor; fifth, money (for let it be noted that money is not capital); sixth, arrangements for intercourse, diplomatic and otherwise, between countries so as to keep open the channels of trade.

In regard to capital, as we have seen, Great Britain has in ownership a vast advantage over our country, but the inventions of exchange, of the telegraph and of the clearing-house system have practically made a common stock of the capital of the world. The security being equal, it goes where it will pay best and a difference of 1 percent in the rate of interest between New York and London suffices to transfer capital until there is an equation in the rates. Moreover, the outlets for the profitable use of capital in Great Britain are so narrowed up that it is forced to seek channels in foreign lands for its productive employment, and of all the countries in the world the United States is the most attractive to the Englishman because we speak a common language, have a common ancestry and a community of political ideas. Hence British capital, in the absence of disturbing causes, gravitates to this country and is available for the development of our resources and the growth of our industry as if its owners resided among us. I said "in the absence of disturbing causes." What are they? Sometimes, but rarely, of a political nature. Hence it is essential to maintain with England the closest diplomatic relations, for diplomacy deals primarily with politics and only secondarily with commerce.

Political relations being in a satisfactory condition English capital would flow naturally into this country whenever there is a vacuum, provided confidence in its security is not disturbed. Now, confidence is the offspring of honesty and judgment. Given a state of things wherein the basis for productive industry is sound, the judgment will be readily satisfied. It is not too much to say that unbounded confidence exists abroad in the productive capacities of the United States. Foreign capitalists appreciate our sources of wealth better than we do ourselves, because they have less than we possess. No other evidence is required of this fact than the vast sums, amounting to many hundreds of millions of dollars, which, in the period between 1865 and 1873, were sent from abroad to be invested in American enterprises, and it is largely to such investments that we have been enabled to establish throughout the length and breadth of the land convenient and economical communications between our coal fields and the sources of our food and raw materials, so that we may now compete upon equal terms with Great Britain for the commerce of the world.

For this purpose, therefore—that is, the development of communications—no more capital is at present needed; but capital is still required for working up our raw material into manufactured products and for establishing lines of steam transportation between our ports and the natural market for these products on the Gulf of Mexico, in South America, and the regions of the Orient.

Why does this capital withhold itself in alarm? For more than three years it has been so abundant in the great financial centers of the world that it has been difficult to make it earn even the lowest rate of interest ever known in financial history. The truth must be told. Foreign capitalists have lost confidence in our honesty. I shall not undertake to discuss whether there is good reason or not for this loss of confidence. I only deal with the fact, its causes, and its consequences. We are a debtor nation. It has been held out that our obligations will be paid in gold. This proposition was not disputed so long as capital was flowing into the country from abroad; but when speculative enterprises collapsed in 1873 and values began to shrink, suggestions were made and parties organized for paying off the bonds in paper money and latterly in silver, which had in the meantime depreciated about 10 per-cent in value. Capital prefers to·remain idle in security rather than to be employed where there is risk of loss. Hence the recovery which in the ordinary course of nature would have been produced by the transfer of floating capital into fixed investments has been retarded, and if such legislation as is proposed in the Bland Silver Bill and the repeal of the Resumption Act should be carried into effect, the time of recovery will be indefinitely postponed.

Money, in the sense of currency, can be created by legislation, but capital can be created only by labor profitably employed. It is the fruit of labor. It is the result of saving. It must have a substantial pre-existence. It can be transferred by money, but money cannot be substi-tuted for it. Capital is the freight; money is the vehicle on which it is carried. Therefore the creation of unlimited amounts of money will not secure the presence of capital any more than the building of thousands of railway cars will produce the freight which they are designed to move. What we want, therefore, is more capital, and not more money. Confi-dence alone will bring capital; legislation cannot. In this question the West and the South have an interest vastly greater than any other section of the country. The West and South produce the food and raw materials—cotton and wool—upon which our future development of industry must rest. This food and these raw materials are now carried to Great Britain, are there manufactured, and are thence transported to every portion of the habitable globe. There is no longer any good reason why the cotton should not be manufactured where it is grown, and the food transported from the West into the regions of the South, and the cotton of the South in like manner returned to the West, giving life to an industry so vast that we can only form a proper idea of its proportions by considering that it has enabled England to sustain a population of two hundred and sixty-five persons to the square mile, while in this country of superabundant food we maintain in the states of the Union, excluding the territories, a population of only twenty to the square mile. If our population were of the same density as Great Britain it would amount to over two thousand millions.

And there is no reason in nature why the same results will not follow the application of the same laws. Let one example show the results of English policy: Great Britain took from the United States in 1876 8,328,000 hundredweight of raw cotton out of a total import of 13,284,000 hundredweight. For the whole of this cotton she paid £40,181,000, and of it she retained about five-sixths for her own con-sumption and exported to the rest of the world manufactures of cotton to the value of £67,641,268. In other words, after supplying her own wants she drew from the rest of the world £27,500,000 more than the entire cost of the raw material. Of course she had to buy the food required to feed the labor employed in the production of these cotton goods, amounting to 479,515 persons. Her total imports of food amounted to £83,589,000, which enabled her to maintain a population of 33,000,000 of people upon an area not capable itself of supporting more than 10,000,000 of people.

What a contrast does this present to our condition! With a surplus of food, with a surplus of raw material, we have somewhere from 500,000 to 1,000,000 of able-bodied persons who seek employment in vain. We are of the same race and possess as much physical vigor and certainly equal intelligence with the English operatives.

It is an admitted fact that a day's labor produces a larger result, on an average, in this country than in England. And yet out of the very cotton which we sent them, manufactured by labor fed with the very food that we sent them, they actually sent back to this country, in payment for this cotton and food, cotton goods to the value of £2,451,751, and to other nations, just as accessible to us as to them, cotton goods to the value of nearly $300,000,000, an amount sufficient to have given employment directly and indirectly to at least one million of persons, more than all our idle population put together. So far as this state of things is due to the lack of capital the remedy is plain. Inspire confidence by strict adherence to the highest rules of honor and honesty, and capital will flow in abundant streams where it can be used to such evident profit. The rule should be where there is any doubt or question as to the medium of payment to decide in favor of the creditor and thus plant ourselves on the highest plane of honor. For one, I am at an utter loss to comprehend how the petty savings which any community can make by repudiating any portion of its debt in whole or in part, or by substituting in the payment of interest silver for gold because it is a little cheaper at the moment, can weigh in the popular judgment against the enormous profits and the vast volume of business which would accrue from investments of capital in the development of our unrivaled natural resources and the certain establishment of the means of transportation to the great markets of the world which we can supply upon better terms than any other nation.

Every interest in the country will then be invigorated with new life, and labor will find abundant and remunerative employment, whereas now there is complaint of depression and stagnation from every quarter. Progress and growth alone can give prosperity and increasing values. To stand still is to perish; to go forward is to prosper. And yet those portions of the country which have the most interest in development and growth are the very ones that are turning back the hands on the dial of time and postponing the industrial triumphs of the future.

Raw materials, then, we have. Capital we can have on the simple condition of stern, unbending honesty. What else do we need so as to carry no dead weight into the race? We must have the kind of money which the world uses in making its exchanges. Money is merely a tool of commerce. A workman with bad tools cannot compete with a workman of equal skill who has good tools. Commerce is only a barter of commodities; but in order that this barter may go on without friction the mode of estimating values must not only be simple but sure and permanent, because time is required for reaching the markets where the bartered goods are to be sold.

Gold and silver are the most unchangeable values and hence have been made the standards of value throughout the commercial world. Of late, silver has been subject to violent perturbations, and hence countries using the gold standard have had great advantages in the operations of commerce. They buy more cheaply and make closer estimates of results. Hence, today goods cannot be bought in South America or the Asiatic markets except for bills payable in London. No matter what kind of currency may be used for local purposes, all foreign commerce reduces itself to gold values, and countries using a currency not convertible into gold are subjected to deductions, commissions, and allowances due to the uncertainties caused by these fluctuations.

Therefore, gold being the best tool or instrument of exchange, whatever nation will enter the list for the control of the commerce of the world must adopt a gold standard as the basis of its money system. Hence Germany, intending to enroll herself among the great commercial nations, has adopted the gold standard as the preliminary step to the absorption of Belgium and Holland, which will give her coal and colonies.

So long as silver can be converted into gold at a fixed ratio it is equally available, except for its bulk, and it may possibly be restored to its old place by general agreement among the great commercial nations. But as the case now stands it is simply to retire from the race, if it is to be undertaken upon the basis of currency which is unstable, fluctuating, and not in any respect as good as the best in use among our competitors. In other words, I do not hesitate to lay it down as a fundamental principle that it is not possible to get the control of the foreign commerce of the world except upon the condition of a single gold standard of value.

By refusing to resume specie payments on a gold basis and by offering to pay national obligations in silver, we simply postpone the day when we can enter successfully upon the struggle with England for the commercial supremacy of the world.

But besides money and capital and raw materials, our commercial relations with the rest of the world must be of the most liberal and perfect character; we must not put any impediment in the way of getting such raw materials as we may lack at the lowest possible cost; we must take off duties which increase the cost of raw materials; we must lower taxes which add to the expense of transportation; and while we must at the outset protect our markets as far as possible from the influx of foreign manufactures when they are sacrificed below cost in order to get rid of a surplus, we must do nothing to add to the normal and regular cost of his supplies to the consumer: *Sic itur ad astra.*

In order to estimate the importance of foreign commerce to the United States let us compare its present dimensions with the volume of commerce carried on by Great Britain. In 1877 the total imports and exports of Great Britain amounted to £631,931,305, which was at the rate of £19 1s. 11d., or nearly $100 per head. The total imports and exports of the United States for the year ending June 30, 1877, amounted to $1,150,734,997; equal to $25.50 per head. If, therefore, the volume of our foreign commerce could be enlarged to that of Great Britain it would amount to about $4,500,000,000, or four times its present dimensions.

To those who want work for idle hands, here is the solution and remedy. To those who are in debt for property purchased when prices were high, and who are still clinging to it as shipwrecked mariners hug the spars, here is relief, for with abundant employment will come increased population, renewed demand, and a rising market for real estate. For those who complain of low prices for agricultural products, here is a home market which will not only increase demand but will save the loss now incurred for transportation to distant markets. For those who desire to develop the mineral and manufacturing resources of the South, here is the attraction for capital to transfer itself from the interior of England.

Consolidating the Western Surveys

SPEECH IN THE HOUSE OF REPRESENTATIVES ON THE GENERAL
APPROPRIATION BILL, FEBRUARY 11, 1879

[*The Federal Government had shown more enterprise than system in
the work of exploring, surveying, and mapping the trans-Missouri
West. Between 1867 and 1876 four great undertakings had been
set on foot. They were Clarence King's geological survey along the
fortieth parallel, George M. Wheeler's geographical survey of territories west of the 100th meridian, Dr. F. V. Hayden's work, and
Major J. W. Powell's work. The King and Wheeler surveys were
controlled by the War Department; the Hayden and Powell surveys
by the Interior Department. A consolidation of effort was much
needed. The National Academy of Sciences pointed out that geographical and topographical work ought to be directed by the Coast
and Geodetic Survey and that all geological and economic exploration should be consolidated under a single Geological Survey.
Hewitt went into the subject thoroughly with Clarence King. As
a result he wrote the legislation needed, and against much opposition from the War Department and Western interests, carried
it through the House. In this speech he also pointed out the enormous values locked up in the West.*]

MR. HEWITT, of New York, said:

MR. CHAIRMAN: I had prepared some notes with reference to the
land question which has been discussed so thoroughly by the gentlemen
who have preceded me. I will not therefore take up the time of the
Committee of the Whole with discussing that question, except to say
to my friend from Montana [MR. MAGINNIS] that it is because we wish
to preserve the public domain for settlement, to give the opportunity for
suffering labor to find a home in the unoccupied land, that we have
been moved to propose this new legislation.

I think it is the judgment of every man who has taken the trouble
to get at the facts of the case that the beneficent land-parceling system
which has sufficed for a hundred years of emigration and western settlement has reached the practical limits of its usefulness. In order that
the area which is beyond may be so utilized as to give homes to the
poor and employment to the laborer, it is necessary that a wise and

comprehensive system of administration should be digested, adopted, and put into operation.

Mr. Maginnis.[1] I hope the gentleman from New York [Mr. Hewitt] did not for one minute understand that I attributed to the Committee on Appropriations any purpose of this kind, because I have talked to the committee individually and I know they are as strongly in favor of keeping the public lands for the settlers as I am myself. I merely give it as my idea of the effect of the change here proposed, of the manner in which the new system will work. I hope the gentleman did not understand for one moment that I thought the committee even leaned in that way.

Mr. Hewitt, of New York. I did not so understand the gentleman. On the contrary, I had the honor and the pleasure of a personal conversation with him on this subject during a half-hour's walk, in which I was profoundly impressed by the earnest feeling which he showed that no step should be taken by which this great heritage of the future should be mortgaged to grasping corporations or to overpowering capitalists. I fully sympathize with him.

But I think, by the provision which we have incorporated in the bill for a new consideration and codification of the land laws under a commission to be carefully and I trust wisely selected, instead of narrowing the field for the energies of capital and labor, it will be widened so that there will be a growth of wealth, of prosperity, and civilization in the now barren regions of the West to which the world has heretofore been a stranger.

Mr. Patterson,[2] of Colorado. If it is necessary to codify all the laws of the land system and to suggest new methods, why is there any greater necessity for calling in a crowd of strangers to do this work than for seeking the aid of outsiders upon a thousand and one other matters of legislation that constantly arise here?

Mr. Hewitt, of New York. Practical legislation consists, first, in arriving at facts, and, secondly, in submitting the facts to the consideration of experts. Now, what the result of that consideration will be I know not; but I do anticipate from it a report which will lay the foundations of a system upon which for a hundred years to come the progress of this country in the settlement of that great region may be as rapid, as continuous, and as prosperous as it has been in the last century in the intervening region which is adapted to arable purposes. I want to get at the knowledge, and I want the knowledge to be arrived at before we legislate. That is my answer to the gentleman from Colorado.

[1] Martin Maginnis (1841-1919), delegate from the Territory of Montana 1873-85.
[2] Thomas MacDonald Patterson (1839-1916), successively a Democratic Delegate, Representative, and Senator from Colorado.

Now, a single remark upon one other point, suggested by what has been said here. We do not claim that this is a perfect system. It is the best measure we could devise under the circumstances. It is probable that this bill can be amended with advantage; and for one I wish to say to the gentleman from California [Mr. Page[1]] and to every other gentleman in this House that they will find in me, so far as I have anything to do with the Committee on Appropriations or its action, a ready co-operation in adopting any amendment which they may suggest in order to make this measure more acceptable and more useful to the public interest.

Having thus disposed of one or two preliminary considerations, let me say that those gentlemen who desire to arrive at a knowledge of the advantages which this legislation will present ought to read carefully an admirable exposition which is contained in the letter of Major Powell attached to House Document No. 5, the report of the National Academy of Sciences. Gentlemen will find in that document a comprehensive treatment of the whole subject. It is so much better treated than any gentleman on this floor can hope to do, that for my own part I shall not occupy any time in that direction. But I do entreat members to read that able document with care.

My own treatment of this subject will spring from the peculiar experience which I happen to have had with reference to the growth of industry in this country and with reference to the economical questions which are involved in this measure.

Nations may spring into being generated by the force of ideas alone, but the vigorous manhood, the mature growth of a state, can only be nurtured and built up upon the abundant and manifold productions of the earth. The very existence and advance of civilization are firmly grounded on material resources. Nations become great and independent as they develop a genius for grasping the forces and materials of nature within their reach and converting them into a steady flowing stream of wealth and comfort.

Without a sound knowledge of the facts of nature it is not possible to develop a healthy material growth. It was this conviction which gave birth to the national surveys, and disjoined as they have been, no man can estimate the value, scientific and material, of the results already achieved.

What is there in this richly endowed land of ours which may be dug or gathered or harvested and made a part of the wealth of America and of the world, and how and where does it lie? These are the questions which the enterprise, the capital, and the labor of the United States are engaged in working out with such signal energy, and it is to the solution of these questions, the greatest of all national prob-

1 Horace F. Page (1883-90), a Republican Representative from California 1873-83.

lems, that the scientific surveys of the public domain should be directed. For the manifold wants, for the daily and hourly need of the Government and the people, a comprehensive and accurate survey is now deemed to be a necessity. The need of a thorough survey for the wise organization and distribution of American industry is in the future as imperative as a constitution on which to found our laws.

In the comprehension of this need we are in no wise behind the older nations, and considering the youth of the Republic and the extent of its territory, we have made a beginning of which we have no reason to be ashamed. But the time has come when the character, organization, and scope of the surveys, their place under the care of Congress, and under the executive departments, their administration, and their results, can no longer be left to accident, and when their future value must depend largely upon a system wisely devised and resolutely carried into effect under the rigid sanction of law. When we bring to bear a careful scrutiny and unprejudiced criticism upon the results and modes of the scientific surveys now existing, fruitful as they have been, the real authoritative opinion of the best judges is that our present system, or rather the want of it, is defective in administration, contradictory and discordant in results, and devoid of that unity which can alone insure general excellence. So patent had these defects arising out of a want of system become, that I was induced to move to insert a clause in the last sundry civil appropriation bill referring the whole question as to the conduct of these surveys to the National Academy of Sciences as the only body who could form a proper judgment and render a wise decision upon a question which seemed to me to involve more momentous consequences than any problem of an industrial nature which has presented itself in my time.

The National Academy of Sciences was selected because it is a body expressly incorporated by Congress in order to maintain a lofty standard of scientific authority. By the very terms of its charter any branch of the Government has a right to ask for its advice and assistance, and the results of its researches have fully justified the theory of its formation. Among its members, Bache, Agassiz, and Henry have left their renown to us as a national heritage, and their fellows who still remain with us and guide its deliberations have made the National Academy what the country expected of it, a body whose ability and learning are so marked as to place it beyond the reach of ordinary prejudice.

In the compact, lucid, simple, but far-reaching report which the Academy has made to us concerning the national surveys it has vindicated its high reputation for scientific authority and given us a document of sound practical sense. Its propositions are of extreme simplicity. It proposes to group all surveys of mensuration, that is to say, the Coast and Geodetic Survey, all topographical and geographical reconnaissances, and the parceling or land surveys into one strong organization, centering around the public-land interest an organization which shall be charged with the whole business of measuring and mapping the national domain. It proposes also to consolidate all the geological and economic surveys under one United States geological survey, charged with the magnificent task of studying the structure and natural resources of the public domain.

During the last ten years the scientific surveys of the national domain have embraced five distinct organizations, no one of which has by law any harmonious relation with either of the others. They are the Coast and Geodetic Survey; the United States geological exploration of the fortieth parallel, under Clarence King; the United States geological and geographical survey of the territories, of which the first division is under Professor F. V. Hayden and the second division under Major J. W. Powell, and the geographical survey of the territories west of the one-hundredth meridian, under Lieutenant George M. Wheeler, Corps of Engineers.

In these several surveys have ordinarily been engaged over one hundred civilians, men of science, many of them of world-wide reputation as geodesists, mathematicians, astronomers, geologists, and experts in the various departments of science. The number of army officers so engaged has been comparatively small; nevertheless, in view of the fact that they belong to an arm of the military service whose special duty it is to make such reconnaissances and final surveys as may be useful upon the frontier and elsewhere in case of war, the public mind has very naturally concluded that the general surveys of the country would be wisely confided to their care and administration. I entertained this opinion myself at the time when the clause was inserted in the appropriation bill; but here let me say, in order to correct an erroneous impression, that the suggestion originated with myself and did not come from the engineers or from any outside quarter. It was the legitimate fruit of a discussion which occurred in the committee room, and the clause as it stands in the bill was written down at the close of this discussion.

When the report of the academy was rendered I was surprised to learn that it recommended the transfer of all these surveys, as well as of the Coast Survey, to the Interior Department. I was naturally led to a careful consideration of the reasons for this recommendation, and I confess that they appeared to me to be unanswerable and absolutely conclusive.

The work of the Land Office must necessarily be under the direction of the Department of the Interior. So far as the Coast and Geodetic

Survey is concerned, it is a matter of no consequence whether heretofore it was attached to the Treasury or Interior Department, but now that its operations are being extended across the continent and its system of triangulation enables it to fix points with absolute certainty, it becomes a matter of the greatest possible consequence that the parceling of the public lands should be made with reference to these fixed points. The early transfer of the Coast Survey to the Interior Department, therefore, would be a measure of wise legislation, if not of absolute necessity, under any circumstances. The geographical surveys under Hayden and Powell are already in the control of the Interior Department, and the only question left to be decided is, therefore, whether the whole system should be transferred to the War Department, or whether the single geographical survey carried on by the engineers should also be incorporated with the other surveys in the care of the Interior Department.

To this there can be but one answer. It is not to be expected that the large body of scientific men required to make these surveys a success will consent, willingly, to place themselves under the control of the younger officers of the Engineer Corps. Whatever may be their devotion to science, they are men of such eminence in their respective walks that they cannot and ought not to be reduced to the ranks. The fact is that the subject has assumed a magnitude which calls for the best talent of the most accomplished civilians in the country, and the special talent of the engineer, accomplished as he may be, is of comparatively insignificant importance in the sum total of the interests involved. These great national surveys must draw into their service the very brightest and strongest scientific intellects of the age; men powerful to investigate and free to press their honorable professional ambitions to the full limit of their strength. Such men are not going to enlist in a service in which at the end of years of devoted labor the reflected rays of the glory of their achievements shall be permitted to reach the public eye only through the medium of a military organization not popularly associated with scientific pursuits.

It is true that in Europe geographical surveys have been generally conducted under military supervision, but there is a radical difference between the history, traditions, and actual condition of European nations and our own position. Europe is a battlefield, and through the long ages, unhappily, war has largely filled the measure of its experience; but with us, more fortunately placed, the warfare has been directed against the obstacles of nature. The subjugation which we seek to accomplish is of her potent forces to the uses of men, the conversion of her vast resources into agencies of civilization. Our army is the great industrial organization of labor, devoted not to the work of destruction, but to that of construction and development and to the founding of prosperous and peaceful communities. In the case of European nations military knowledge is the main object in view. In our case it is but the incident. With them the military engineer is the central figure. With us the scientist is the leader advancing to new triumphs of knowledge and to new acquisitions which may be made to subserve the progress of the human race. *Cedent arma togæ* is the inscription on the banner under which we march, and the military engineer must not complain that he is not placed in the van of the advancing battalions of progress, for with us he occupies rather his true place as the protector of the peaceful ranks of industry in their onward march to a higher civilization.

Moreover, in the improbable but ever possible event of war, if these surveys were in the hands of the engineers they would instantly fall to the ground, for every engineer officer would at once hasten to his natural and legitimate duty of military defense, and hereafter as heretofore cover himself with the glory which they have won in many a well-fought field. They can well afford to leave the triumphs of civil life to men whose special business it is to study the forces of nature and develop its useful energies.

I take no part in and attach no consequence to the controversies which have arisen between the Engineer Department and the civilians who are in charge of the Coast Survey or other portions of the civil service connected with the Interior surveys. Questions have arisen as to the relative economy with which the work may be done by the military or the civil service. It is obvious to every reflecting mind that the cost of the surveys will be in proportion to the amount of detail which they involve, and with equal skill and diligence it is quite certain that no great differences could exist whether the surveys are executed under civil or military supervision. If there be differences of statement they must arise from estimating upon results of a different character. And I think it may be affirmed with absolute safety that neither side can reasonably claim any advantage over the other on the question of economy.

Again, all surveys of a purely military character, and others not strictly so, such as the survey of the northern lakes and Mississippi River, are left under the control of the engineer force, and it is well known that the requirements of these surveys will task their numbers and their energies to the utmost, and that they will be compelled in the execution of this work to employ a large number of civilians. . . .

The work confided to the Engineer Bureau is of such an extensive nature that it is now compelled to go outside and employ a very large number of civilians. There is all the work relating to the improvement of the rivers and harbors; there is a large amount of work still to be done in the Southern states in the opening of interior channels of navigation, the whole of which as it forms part of the future military possibilities of the country has been and always will be continued in charge of the engineers. So impressed with this fact have been the committees who have had charge of the reorganization of the army that they have never undertaken to reduce the Engineer Bureau; they have never undertaken to reduce the number of officers in that organization. And it is my own judgment, after most careful examination of the subject, that the Engineer Bureau might today be doubled with advantage to the interests of this country, and still there would be no occasion to detail a man for any work of a purely civil nature. The whole force is wanted for work of a character which, from the foundation of the Government, has been confided to them. . . .

The system of land surveys and land subdivision in operation since 1796 has proved to be one of the greatest blessings of the many wise American institutions. Under its beneficent operation millions have been able to secure for themselves homes and say of the fertile acres about them, "This is mine," the proudest privilege next to the birthright of freedom. But this system so wise and so peculiar to our country, no longer meets the wants of advancing and changing conditions. The public domain contained 1,814,769,920 acres. Of this enormous area 713,572,737 acres have been surveyed, and the larger portion thus surveyed is tillable land, upon which field crops can be grown without artificial irrigation. It lies within the area where the annual rainfall and its distribution through the year gives the necessary moisture for the growth of crops, and the farmer is not driven to artificial methods for watering the earth. Of the 1,101,197,183 acres which still remain to be surveyed, the character of the soils, the topography of the country, the climate, and the agricultural industries are governed by totally different conditions.

With the exception of less than 6 percent of the whole remaining public land, the great region west of the one-hundredth meridian and to the west of Kansas is made up of lands as barren and inhospitable as the Sahara; of immense plains stretching from Texas northward to the British borders, suitable for flocks and herds; of lofty mountains where agriculture is only possible in scattered, isolated valleys; and of broad areas of forest lands. Here, as a rule, agriculture is only possible with irrigation, and irrigation is only practicable where fertile lands lie contiguous to the few rivers and streams of the region.

There are millions of acres where a church mouse would starve on a homestead tract. To follow the old plan of sectionizing these pastoral, timber, and desert lands is wantonly to squander the public money and to destroy the only possible value of this territory. The old method of survey is too cumbersome, too costly, and does not meet the conditions of irregular topography. The running of baselines, meridians, and standards over the rugged heights of the Rocky Mountains and crossing the cañons and chasms of the great western system of mountain chains is to the last degree absurd, when a network of triangulations can be far more accurately made at a far less cost.

Wherever long lines of land surveys through mountain systems have been subjected to geodetic tests, they are found to be grossly inaccurate and their points literally miles out of the way. It is said that the surveys are good enough to part titles to settlers. In the first instance this is true, but when the perishable stakes and monuments which represent the boundaries of subdivisions are obliterated, as they frequently are within a few years, it is beyond the skill of surveying to relocate with any accuracy a given tract, for no second survey could by any possibility repeat the errors of the first and arrive at the same boundaries. The time-honored rectangular system, instead of hinging on a system of mountains and bases which are both perishable and grossly inaccurate, should be preserved but be connected with the imperishable and rigidly accurate monuments of that system of geodetic triangulation which is now well advanced, and today in progress under the management of the Coast Survey, between the two belts of coast states on the Atlantic and Pacific—in Tennessee, Kentucky, Ohio, Missouri, Wisconsin, Colorado, and Utah. A definite and secure connection of that system of triangulation with the land surveys is necessary to give any permanent value to the latter and prevent an endless entanglement of litigation. And this is true of almost all the lands west of the ninety-eighth meridian. The sectionizing is a useless expense, while the geodetic method furnishes a cheap and the only solution of the problem.

We have spent thus far over $23,000,000 in surveying the public lands, and of that sum a large portion has been literally thrown away. There are now surveyed, in advance of the demands of settlers, one hundred and twenty million acres of land. About one hundred million acres are desert lands, which can never be reclaimed by irrigation, and are positively worthless; $7,000,000 spent in sectionizing these lands are irretrievably lost, and this large sum has been squandered in the attempt to apply the present system of surveying to a portion of the country to which it is altogether unsuitable. While this vast body of one hundred and twenty million acres lies barren and arid, shunned by the emigrant and the settler and necessarily given over to driving sand and sagebrush, the great plains, the grandest pastoral region of the world, are unsurveyed, because the existing land system is utterly inapplicable to the wants of the settlers; the law providing no method of making that vast region available for the uses to which nature intended it.

The great basin of the Mississippi is our grain region, and under the old land system its tillable lands wisely distributed have given us our daily bread. Beyond lies a vast tract where grain culture is impossible from climatic causes, but where cattle are grown with uniform success. This is our great beef region, and its five hundred million acres are for the most part unoccupied, because our existing laws and our methods of survey are not adapted to the wants of the industry. We must modify the laws relating to the disposition of these pastoral lands and make the modes of survey inexpensive, and in ten years there will be one magnificent belt of cattle ranches from Texas to British America, and from the one-hundredth meridian westward throughout the Rocky Mountains.

Under the system of surveyors-general now in force we have one hundred million acres surveyed that never should have been sectionized, and five hundred million acres which ought to be surveyed lying vacant. This is no fault of the Commissioner of the General Land Office, who in his report for 1877, on page 9, uses the following language, by which it will be seen that officer may be fairly credited with having originated the proposition of merging the land-parceling system into a more comprehensive scheme, such as we now propose in the bill under consideration:

The practical result of the legislation increasing the number of surveyors-general has not been such as to commend it to the country, and I am clearly of the opinion that the whole system should now be changed. I suggest and urge this on the ground of economy and the belief that the work of public surveys would be more faithfully and permanently executed under the direction of one officer. There are now sixteen surveyors-general, the maintenance of whose offices will cost during the present fiscal year $128,609.27, while expending in public surveys only the small sum of $300,000, being at the rate of about forty-three cents for superintending the expenditure of each dollar.

One surveyor-general, employing not to exceed forty clerks, and at a cost not exceeding $50,000, could under the present contract system, if that were to continue, perform all the work in a more satisfactory manner than it is now done at a much greater cost. The reasons why this could be done are obvious to those who will investigate the subject. The salaries of sixteen surveyor-generals, the rent of sixteen offices, the fuel and lights for the same, the employment of sixteen chief clerks, each at a salary, in most instances, as great, if not greater, than that received by the principal clerk of surveys of the whole United States under whose direction and supervision all surveys are made, and by whom the accuracy of all the work is tested, could be dispensed with, and in lieu thereof substitute one surveyor-general, one chief clerk, and the necessary number of clerks, as before stated.

The contract system for public surveys should be at once annulled and set aside. All surveys should be made by a regular staff or corps of officers selected by the surveyor-general as his assistants on account of their fitness for the service. It should be the duty of such assistants to go into the field and make the surveys in person. If this system were adopted, it would certainly insure better work at less cost than by the present mode. The assistants, working at a fixed salary, would have no motive for doing the work imperfectly, as they might have if under contract, which, in my opinion, is a sufficient reason for saying that the surveys would be made in a more satisfactory manner. There can be no reasonable doubt that surveys made in this manner would cost less than by the present contract method.

It is true that the prices now allowed by law are too small to admit of large profits being made in the survey of mountainous or densely timbered lands, if the work be properly done. One reason why this is true is found in the fact that many of the persons surveying under contract are not well skilled in their work and have not the means of procuring the necessary equipment for camp and field to enable them to do the work in the most economical manner. Most contractors in the Western States and Territories have to pay ruinous rates of interest for money to enable them to go into the field at all, and yet, with all these adverse circumstances to contend against, they make good profits on surveys of arable or level lands.

During the fiscal year ending June 30, 1877, there were expended in the surveys of public lands the sum of $215,942.42, for which there were surveyed 10,847,082 acres. Add to this the further sum of $146,933.58, which it cost to maintain the surveyor-generals' offices in the sixteen districts where the surveys were made, and it is found that the total cost amounts to $362,876.

I hazard nothing in saying that under the system of having but one surveyor-general and assistants, as proposed, a much larger area could have been surveyed and in a better manner. In many of the surveying districts lines and corners, established only a few years since under the contract system, are entirely obliterated.

It may be urged against this system that it would not be convenient for settlers and others interested in any district where there are unsurveyed public lands to procure such surveys as might be desired if the surveyor-general's office in the district were abolished or removed. No such argument can be successfully maintained. The rule is now for the surveyors-general to make surveys in such parts of their several districts as they deem best, and all contracts for surveys before they become binding are sent to this office for approval. An order to survey any particular township in any district can be sent to an assistant in less time than a contract could be prepared, sent here, approved, and returned to the surveyor-general, all of which must be done before the work can be commenced. I therefore recommend—

First. The consolidation of all the offices of surveyors-general into one, which shall be located in Washington.

Second. The abolition of the contract system.

Third. The appointment of a surveyor-general of the United States, who shall be authorized to appoint as many assistants as may be required to personally make the surveys as fast as may be deemed necessary or provided for by law.

The Commissioner of the Land Office is today the most important law officer of the Government if measured by the money involved in his decisions. When he is relieved, as this bill proposes, of the responsibility of the land surveys, he will still be a most overburdened official; but if the new system of survey meets the expectation of its advocates, then he will be relieved of those intricate and troublesome questions which result from fraudulent, imperfect, or obliterated surveys.

This bill also provides for a codification and revision of the land laws, the necessity of which is made clear by the arguments of the Commissioner, in the same report for 1877, on page 3, and which are here inserted, as conclusive upon that subject:

JUDICIAL TRIBUNAL—CODIFICATION AND REVISION OF LAND LAWS

The subject of revising and codifying the entire land laws of this country, and the establishment of a proper judicial tribunal for the determination of questions arising before this office, is one of such pre-eminent importance that it seems a little remarkable that it has not been made the subject of legislation.

When we consider the vast number of decisions which in the courts and this department have been made, and acts of Congress, involving questions of land titles, and the number of cases daily arising in this bureau, to which all of this great amount of precedent and authority is more or less applicable, it becomes evident that there should be a careful codification and revision of the law upon this subject, and some tribunal established whose especial duty it should be to determine the questions here arising, and in accordance with the nicest distinctions of the law, and with a view, also, to the establishment of a consistent line of precedent which should not only be a guide to the department, but an aid and authority to the courts.

Perhaps there is no one who has had occasion to be brought into familiar contact with the decisions and rulings of this branch of the Government who has not remarked the conflicting expression of opinion and want of any clearly defined exposition of the law with reference to the important questions continually arising before it. I do not say this in disparagement of my predecessors or any one connected with the business of the office. This state of things results naturally and necessarily. It is impossible that any Commissioner of the Land Office, however eminent a lawyer he may be, should give the personal, patient, and thorough consideration to the many important and complicated questions of law and fact continually arising before him that should be given to them. He must almost entirely rely upon his heads of divisions, who in turn must largely rely upon their subordinates; neither of the latter can always be selected with a view to their legal attainments.

It may be safely premised that no court in the land decides a larger number of difficult and important cases each year than does this bureau. A court especially appointed for that purpose, who should hold daily sessions, would not be more than equal to the task of disposing of the vast amount of business that would properly come before it. Indeed, it has become a necessity that the heads of bureaus should be relieved of the burden of this great labor.

Not only should this be done on account of the impracticability of the labor being properly done by them, considering the great amount of other business daily brought before them, but because of the impolicy of allowing them to do it. The questions arising before this bureau are such that should have the most impartial decision.

The heads of bureaus are the officers of the Government who feel, and as a matter of fact too often act upon the supposition, that they are only the guardians of the public interest. Besides this, they may not always be uninfluenced by a question of responsibility, which has the effect to delay if not defeat the justice due the citizen. The judicial power should be vested in an impartial tribunal, and the Government, like the individual, only be represented before it by an attorney or solicitor.

I can only use space here to suggest the subject and some of the reasons of its notice. This mere suggestion, however, it seems to me, will be sufficient to induce favorable action upon it.

Lest the reforms proposed by the academy plan should startle timid legislators, let it be remembered that it does not propose to do away with the rectangular system of land parceling, nor even to modify the present method of parceling surveys for arable land. It simply infuses that elasticity into the system which is necessary for its application to the remaining portions of the public domain. It will sooner or later abolish sixteen needless offices held by men lacking the technical knowledge to adopt engineering knowledge to varying geographical conditions, and place the work under the control of the most competent, scientific, and economical surveying organization in the world, directing it to do this work in accordance with the existing land laws and such modifications thereof as may from time to time be adopted. To do at once and forever by the cheapest method is the only plan that has any permanent value. This national work is intrusted to a trained corps of competent engineers, whose tenure of employment depends on their activity and economy, and is taken out of the hands of a class of contract surveyors whose pecuniary interest is promoted by slighting their work and making as much out of the contract as the frontier standard of conscience will permit.

GEOLOGICAL SURVEY

For the institution and continuance of an effective geological survey there are abundant reasons. Works of this character since the dawn of modern science and the development of modern industry have been part of the life of every civilized country. Geology deals with the structure and mineral productions of the earth. Its most abstract inquiries, such as those which relate to the age and genesis of the rocks, to the deep underlying energies which have lifted the continents up out of the primeval oceans, are indissolubly connected with the origin, distribution, and availability of the various soils, coals, metals, clays, mineral fertilizers, and building materials.

Thus the science of geology and the science of wealth are indissolubly linked together. Over the great continents of Asia and Africa past and present civilizations have mostly permitted their mineral resources to lie dormant. China has indeed lately called to her aid an accomplished member of King's Fortieth Parallel Survey (Arnold Hague) to examine her virgin fields of coal and iron. Every country in Europe has its geological corps, and a single instance will show what magnificent results have rewarded the insignificant cost involved; when France instituted her geological survey she had not a single coal mine within her territory and no suspicion that a ton of coal could ever be mined there. Among the early labors of the geological survey was an examination of the coal fields of Belgium, which resulted in a calculation that the same great and valuable coal formation passed into France, but hundreds of feet beneath the surface. Out of that single theoretical conclusion has been developed the entire coal industry of France, yielding as much as one million and a half tons per annum.

Within the United States, owing to the vast area, geological surveys have until lately been mostly occupied in the work of general reconnaissance. Some admirable economic work, however, has been accomplished, such as King's *Mining Industry of the Fortieth Parallel,* Brooke and Pumpelly's *Iron and Copper of the Lake Superior Region,* the *Mineral Statistics* of Brown 'and Raymond, Whitney's *Lead Region of the Upper Mississippi,* and the *Land Classification* of Powell in Utah. But the time has now come for something far more systematic and comprehensive, if we desire to develop in our day the measureless possibilities of the industrial destiny which awaits us.

I never contemplate the great maps of the United States which hang in this hall or consider the natural resources of this broad continent without a deep feeling of wonder, love, and praise. The soils, their character, chemistry, origin, and value, form a vast theme of themselves, of which time will only permit me to give a single illustration. In Europe, in the fertile valley of the Rhine, and in China, in the great Yellow River Valley, and again in our own Mississippi Basin there is a geological formation called the loess, which is as wonderful as it is almost entirely unknown, even to the intelligent members of this House. This formation has the marvelous property of fertilizing itself forever, by drawing upward from the deeper sources of fertility all the elements which are required for the perennial nourishment of the cereal crops. In China, an area of about two hundred and fifty thousand square miles of this loess formation has for the last three hundred years supported a population of not less than one hundred and fifty million human beings, which is about one person to the acre, and this is the explanation of the amazing capacity of China to support the dense population which she is known to possess.

The area, depth, and nature of our own vast loess field, which covers a considerable part of the grain region of the West, are perhaps the most important factors in the prosperous growth of America for centuries to come. How extensive, how deep may be our American loess formation and where are its boundaries can only be determined by a thorough geological survey. That it is in Louisiana and Dakota gives some idea of the extent of the problem and opens up visions of the vast population which will at some future day exist upon our soil, and shows how transitory and how needless are the troubles which now embarrass the condition of the laboring population of this country.

We need to know all about the mineral fertilizers of the country, the green sand, and those singular deposits of phosphates in the South which seem to have been placed there by Divine Providence to balance the active drain which the cotton culture makes upon that soil.

As the soils are the very foundation of our animal life, so coal and iron are the necessary food of our national industry. Thus the industry of Great Britain has been developed to its vast proportions, but when we come to compare the resources in coal and iron in which she is so rich with our own stores of fuel and ores we can begin to realize the magnificence of the industrial future which awaits us, before which all that England has ever done or can ever do sinks into utter insignificance; nor is this future confined to any one section of the United States. More wonderful even than the vast area of our mineral riches is the peculiar and felicitous manner in which they are distributed and related to each other.

Three vast coal fields are traced from south to north across the area of the United States. The first to be developed, the greatest in its geographical connection with the center of population now and for all time to come, the greatest from its remarkably intimate and happy association with the natural avenues of transportation, is that vast bowl of the Mississippi basin, along whose eastern margin, turned up and brought to the light of day throughout the whole length of the great Appalachian Mountain system from New York and Ohio to Alabama, are the varied series of coal beds upon which is and ever will be founded the industry of more than half the states of this Union, opening a field for capital and labor which can never be exhausted and can only be limited by the capacity of the vast granary of food with which it is associated to support a free people in comfort and civilization.

The all but exhaustless beds of anthracite which lie like the leaves of a crumpled book under the broken hill slopes of Pennsylvania, and the rich bituminous coal of Virginia, West Virginia, Kentucky, Tennessee, and Alabama are produced westward in the coal strata of Ohio, Indiana, Illinois, Iowa, and Kansas. Of this prodigal abundance we know but the rude outlines, but we know enough to awaken the most profound interest, especially in the minds of those who are anxious to repair the ravages of the Civil War and rebuild the waste places of the South. When the time comes in which the commerce of Mexico and of Central and South America shall be tributary to our enterprise, as it now lies suppliant at our gates, the coal and iron of North Carolina, Tennessee, Georgia, and Alabama will pass on downward grade to the Gulf ports, and thence find its way to the markets which in exchange will send back their varied cargoes, and thus, as ever is the case, commerce will be the handmaid of industry, and the wealth of the great tropical regions of the western continent be drawn from its European drift into the natural channels of the Southern states of the Union. We look now with wonder upon the growth of the iron and coal business of England during the present century; but a century hence this will be far outdone by the development which must follow the vast beds of iron ore and fuel characterizing the Appalachian chain in its majestic elevations in the Southern states.

Throughout the great Rocky Mountain system from New Mexico to Manitoba and far on to the icy threshold of the Arctic Zone is a second broad belt of coal area, rivaling in extent and value the eastern field. Touched and discovered by the early explorers, Lewis and Clark, Frémont, and others, it has of late been vigorously attacked by the geological surveys of Hayden, King, and Powell, and speedily utilized by the Pacific railroads and the young but powerful industries of Colorado, Wyoming, Utah, and Nevada. Lying as it does in a region whose limited forests cling to the steep crags of the Rocky Mountains, it is the very foundation and key to the industrial problems with which the vigorous young communities of the heart of the continent have to deal.

And still farther west, where our continent like a tired giant bathes itself in the waters of the broad Pacific; where, as the fabled wonder of some glowing oriental myth, cities and states spring in a day from a golden soil, even there nature, as if to crown her prodigality with a treasure more priceless than the precious metals, has not forgotten to thread the mountain chains which stretch along the coast from Mexico to Alaska with a superb system of formations black with countless beds of coal. These three great zones of fuel, exhaustless reservoirs of force, one on either boundary of the continent, and the remaining one in its heart, secure for us not merely the first place in the commerce of the world, but what is of even greater consequence, the diffusion of a healthy and life-giving industry from shore to shore.

With iron, which is the inseparable and the indispensable ally of coal in the triumphs of man over nature, we are no less signally endowed. Along the rim of the Appalachian coal fields, just where they should be, are exhaustless stores of every form and variety of iron ores, in fruitful proximity to the coal which is required for their reduction. Close to the easy navigation of the great lakes are the deposits of Lake Superior, as pure as they are abundant. The rich magnetites of North Carolina, the marvelous mountains of ore in Missouri, the deposits of Arkansas, Arizona, and Texas, the hematites and ochres of Wyoming, and those vast bosses of magnetic ore which lift their black domes among the snows of the Sierra Nevada, leave us only to exclaim with Macbeth:

> What! will the line stretch out to the crack of doom?
> * * * I'll see no more.

And of all the other metals which play their parts in the useful and the decorative art the store is ample. When the prehistoric miners, of whatever race they were, with their rude stone hammers, laboriously gathered the fragments of pure copper which they patiently wrought into the first specimens of American art, the beads and knives which are now dug from the burial mounds of the vanished race, they little dreamed of the wealth which in mines like Calumet and Hecla lies hidden beneath their feet, awaiting the skill, energy, and enterprise of the nineteenth century for its extraction. Ores of lead and zinc, of cobalt and nickel, of antimony and tin we have dispersed over the continent. And lastly, the countless mountain ridges which go to make up the great western system of chains are actually riven and threaded with veins of silver and gold. In all that great mountain belt there is not a solitary range which has not yielded in greater or less abundance to the prospector's pick its sands of gold or lodes of gold and silver.

When the visitor stands in the busy streets of Virginia City and realizes that from under his very feet over $300,000,000 in silver has been taken in the short space of twenty years, and reflects that this is but one of thousands upon thousands of veins whose depths are still virgin ground, words and ideas alike lose their significance; "speech is silver and silence is golden."

In that broad expanse of mountain and of plain, wherein even the old river beds of vanished streams are filled with golden sands, centuries of toil will fail to exhaust the stores of the precious metals, all of which will be needed for the honest money of commerce, destined to grow with the march of civilization, until all trade shall be free and all men shall be brothers.

When we come to contemplate the whole field of these natural resources available for food, for industry, and for commerce; when we attempt to grasp in one act of thought the length and breadth and depth of the riches with which the Maker of the universe has loaded this continent on which happily our lot is cast; when we try to realize how every possible want, every material aspiration of man is bounteously provided for; when we consider how measureless are the values which spring into being at the touch of modern industry, and how these values when once created are solid and real and become incorporated into the enduring structure of human society, we may begin to estimate properly the measure of responsibility which rests upon this nation and its chosen rulers, not merely to preserve unharmed the priceless boon of civil liberty which leaves the individual citizen free to do his share in work of development, but to adopt such measures as will prevent the waste of natural resources, clear the way of progress, and promote the triumphs of civilization.

It is to these immeasurable elements of national wealth that we wish to direct the new surveys. It is to a rigid, profound study of these great fundamental problems of national progress that we mean to turn the new organizations. Is there any member of this House, is there any man living within our borders, who can suggest an undertaking more deeply fraught with all the elements of national prosperity? Has there ever been submitted to Congress a proposition more worthy of the support of patriots and statesmen?

I have attempted to draw the rough outlines of this great national picture, in order not merely to show the magnitude of the interests involved and the necessity of a comprehensive and intelligent system of administration, but to make it apparent how trivial are the objections which have been presented to this House, all looking to minor details and overlooking the great salient features, the superabounding merits of this beneficent scheme. How unworthy of the vast interests involved is the petty dispute between different branches of the public service as to the peculiar qualifications of one or the other for this great work. Let us brush them all aside as belittling the real question involved in this magnificent conception. It comes to us from the highest scientific authority in the land. It commends itself to the judgment of the men who have been most energetic and successful in the development of our resources, the "captains of industry" of our time.

If we can but rise "to the height of this great argument" we shall place the work of national development and the elements of future prosperity upon the firm and enduring basis, of truth and knowledge, from which they cannot be moved so long as the Republic shall endure. *Esto perpetua.*

The American Worker under High Tariffs [1]

SPEECH IN THE HOUSE OF REPRESENTATIVES ON THE MORRISON TARIFF BILL,
APRIL 30, 1884

[Few political slogans after the Civil War were more specious or more effective than the cry, "The tariff protects American workmen against the pauper labor of Europe." Not until after the Homestead Riot did many workingmen realize that tariff benefits were not passed on to them but were pocketed by capital. The injustice of high protection to labor was frequently pointed out by such economists as William Graham Sumner, such journalists as E. L. Godkin. In the political sphere nobody did more to demonstrate it than Hewitt. By 1884 the need for tariff reduction had become exigent. Though a Republican Tariff Commission had pointed it out in 1883, Congress had then actually raised the tariff again. Many rates were extortionate; while the high duties were piling up a dangerous surplus in the treasury. William H. Morrison, a Democratic Representative from Illinois, urged in 1884 a bill to reduce duties, which had no chance whatever of passage—the Senate being strongly Republican. Frank H. Hurd, of Toledo, Ohio, and Hewitt made the two ablest speeches in its favor. That of Hewitt was especially notable for the force with which he pointed out that free trade strengthens labor unions, while high protection cripples them.]

MR. HEWITT, of New York, said:

MR. CHAIRMAN: Though one should rise from the dead to convey to us a message on the tariff, I doubt whether he would change a single vote in this House upon this or any other tariff bill; and though an angel should come down from Heaven, he could not give us any message in favor of that liberty wherewith the founder of our religion has made us free, which could convey to us more forcible reasons in support of this measure than we had on yesterday in the eloquent argument of the gentleman from Ohio [MR. HURD], my colleague on the Committee on Ways and Means. And after hearing that magnificent speech, Mr. Chairman, I doubted whether it were worth while for me to take up the thread of this great argument; and it is mostly by his request that I

[1] Frank H. Hurd (1840-96), a Democratic Representative from Ohio 1875-77, 1879-81, and 1883-85; prominent in the movement for lower tariffs.

have concluded today to gather together some few sheaves of wheat from the great field over which passed his devouring sickle.

But there is an audience outside of this House; an audience of men who work with tools and who govern this House by the ballot. To them, constituting as they do, I am glad to say, the great majority of the people of this country, it is worth while to address an argument which will appeal to their judgment and their permanent interests. That audience I will acknowledge is probably against me. I fear that perhaps a majority of the great army of workers in this country stand where I stood in 1872 when I wrote the letter which the gentleman from Maine [MR. DINGLEY [1]] has just quoted. They are still in the bonds of prejudice, of false training, and of ignorance, where I was then myself. I have no apologies to make for having progressed out of the night of darkness into the open sunshine of truth. But I should have apologies to make if, having reached conclusions which contradict those that I held years ago, I should fail in this House and everywhere to announce them with that frankness which belongs to an honest man and a faithful Representative.

Now, though that army of workers may be against me on the question of protection for the sake of protection, there is one thing in which they are with me. There is an old instinct ingrained in the Anglo-Saxon race which tells us that surplus revenues are the result of unnecessary taxation and that unnecessary taxation is unjust exaction from the fruits of human labor. For that cause Charles the First lost his head. For that cause the last of the Stuarts was driven into exile. For that cause we fought the War of Independence and established this Government upon the eternal doctrine that taxation and representation should go together, in order that representation might correct unjust taxation. Upon that issue this great army of workmen are sound; and they were sound on it in the last election, when they turned the members of that side of the House out of their seats, because in the presence of a surplus of more than a hundred millions of dollars they did not attack the problem seriously, but undertook to hoodwink the people of this country as to the effect of their legislation. Upon that issue they placed here this great majority of Democrats; and if we are false to the duty thus imposed, if by reason of difference of opinion among ourselves we fail to deal with that question and to reduce taxation to the point adequate to the economical administration of this Government and the discharge of its just obligations, then this majority will be swept from their places; not upon the ground of free trade or protection, but upon the ground that to take $150,000,000 annually out of the hard earnings of the producing classes of this country, for upon them falls the burden,

[1] Nelson Dingley, Jr. (1832-99), Republican Representative from Maine from 1881 to his death.

is an act of tyranny not to be endured by a free people. It is a sure evidence of the decay of public spirit when excessive taxation is tolerated, and it is only among free peoples that the remission of taxation is ever accomplished; for it is only in constitutional governments that taxation is self-imposed.

But, Mr. Chairman, the gentlemen on the other side will tell us that they are just as anxious to get rid of this surplus as we are, and they point out the road to us by the abolition of the internal-revenue duties. But they tell us that we must not attack the sacred temple of protection which they have reared and which they think is essential to the safety, comfort, and happiness of the workingmen of this country. If that statement so often reiterated on this floor be true, then it would be an act of the grossest folly on the part of the majority of this House to interfere with these protective duties. If, on the other hand, it be false, then it is the duty of this side of the House to proceed fearlessly with the work of removing the unjust discriminations, the excessive duties, the obstructions to the healthy growth of business and the enlargement of the commerce of the country, by the natural process of the exchange of commodities which we produce in excess, for articles which we can not produce as cheaply as other nations.

The allegation is that the workingmen of this country in consequence of the existence of the protective system are contented and have happy homes; that their families are in comfort, and that all we have to do is to let them alone, and that all that they ask is to be let alone. I am amazed at the declarations which I have heard on this floor on that subject. It can only be due to the fact that the men who have made them are blind to what is going on around them. Why, sir, we have had hearings before the Ways and Means Committee of the representatives of every branch of protected industry in this country, and there was not one of them that did not tell us that his business was depressed, that his mills were being either closed up or working upon short time, that wages had been reduced, and that further reductions of wages were impending. No one who goes to and fro in this land will controvert the truth of these statements. There is stagnation everywhere in the protected industries, and where they are not protected, there is no stagnation other than that which is consequential upon stagnation in the protected industries.

Mr. Kelley.[1] Will the gentleman permit me to ask him a question?

Mr. Hewitt, of New York. Yes, sir.

Mr. Kelley. I wish to ask the gentleman whether there ever was such stagnation, industrial stagnation, in free-trade England as there is

[1] William Darrah Kelley (1814-90), Republican Representative from Pennsylvania from 1861 to his death, and a staunch leader of the protectionist forces; nicknamed "Pig-Iron" Kelley.

today; whether there ever was in England such a measure of starvation, amounting almost to famine, as there is under free trade today?

Mr. Hewitt, of New York. Now, if the gentleman has completed his little speech——

Mr. Kelley. It is not so long a one as you put into mine.

Mr. Hewitt, of New York. Excuse me. The gentleman from Pennsylvania appealed to me and I gave him an answer. That was all. Now that he has made his little speech let me say this: I am going to deal with that very question exhaustively if I am able to keep the floor for my hour. Therefore I will not be diverted at the present moment from the order in which I am trying to present this question.

The best testimony, Mr. Chairman, as to the condition of the workmen is the testimony of the workmen themselves. If the protective system can give them happiness and good wages and comfort, they certainly ought to have it today; for we have had nearly twenty-five years of uninterrupted protection under a higher tariff than ever existed in any civilized country on the globe. Now, what is the story told by the workingmen? The Senate Committee on Labor and Education have recently taken exhaustive testimony on this subject from the workingmen themselves.

That testimony is to be found in a volume which has not yet been laid on our desks, but which is in print and of which I trust this House will order a very large edition. The testimony of workingmen was for the first time in the history of this or any other country presented in methodical order and represented every branch of business in this country. That testimony is absolutely unanimous; first, that the wages and earnings of workingmen in this country are not sufficient to give them comforts or even a decent support for their families; and secondly, the testimony is equally conclusive as to the fact that there has been a steady degradation in the condition of the laboring classes of this country during the last twenty years, and that it is an increasing deterioration to be measured year by year. This testimony was given during the last year, before we had reached the present state of depression and stagnation under which we are suffering.

Aside from this testimony, there is much personal knowledge which every gentleman here can bring to bear upon this subject. I dislike to speak of the hardships and sufferings of men in this country who are ready to earn an honest living, but who are unable to do so. To use a plain phrase, one feels as if it would be "fouling one's own nest." Yet I have been in the coal regions of this country within the last six months and have seen with my own eyes a condition of things which made my heart sad, which made me hope that this Congress might be wise enough to remove some of the causes of the wretchedness and the misery which I saw there. When I saw that men who worked a whole day away from the light of heaven, and who took their lives in their hands every time they entered the pit, are housed in hovels such as the lordly owners of the mines would refuse to stable their cattle in, then I felt that something was wrong in the condition of the American laborer.

When I learn that there are miners of iron ore working in the state of Pennsylvania for 75 cents a day, then I know that there is something wrong in the legislation of this country, for the duty upon iron ore was put up by the last tariff act on an average from 40 or 45 cents a ton to 75 cents a ton in order to protect these very miners and to give them high wages. When that act was passed they were in receipt of $1.25 a day; today they are in receipt of 75 cents a day. Surely, if there be virtue in legislation these men, hard-working, industrious, independent voters, if you will give them the means of living, ought not to have been reduced to this wretched state of misery.

But the end is not yet. The owners of these great coal mines have recently met in conference in the city of Philadelphia, which my friend so ably represents, and which I trust he may continue to represent for many years to come—they lately met and solemnly came to the conclusion to suspend work for three days in the week, and after this month they concluded that possibly they might keep up the price of coal by suspending work only nine days in the month. Keep up the price of coal! Ay, to the workman, to the farmer, to everybody who earns his living by his daily labor, and put down the wages of the man who digs it from the earth, and then tell him that he is protected by the tariff. Can there be a more stupendous specimen of audacious assertion than we have heard upon this floor, that the workmen of this country are well rewarded and made happy by the operation of the tariff?

Now, to come to the iron works; my friend from Pennsylvania ought to know all about them. Last year more than half of the furnaces of this country were in blast. That was a great decrease from the year before. This year, after the passage of a bill arranged, constructed, and adopted by the friends of protection, what has happened? Two-thirds of the furnaces of this country—or nearly two-thirds, for I suppose I shall be held to a most strict account for every word I use on this floor—to be exact, four hundred and thirty-two furnaces are out of blast while only two hundred and sixty-nine furnaces are in operation, and the wages of the great army of protected workmen whom they employ have been largely reduced. I am among the unfortunate manufacturers who have been forced to reduce wages or stop work. I am compelled to offer to the workmen whom I employ the choice between no work or work at less wages than they ought to have. Yet I am protected by the magnificent and unnecessary duty of $6 per ton—or to be more accurate, $6.72 per ton. I do not mind the odd cents; no doubt the gentleman himself does.

Mr. KELLEY rose.

Mr. HEWITT, of New York. I would prefer that my friend would allow me to go on and finish this statement.

Mr. KELLEY. I only wanted to thank the gentleman——

Mr. HEWITT, of New York. Well, then, I will yield to the gentleman.

Mr. KELLEY. I simply rose, as the gentleman referred to me, to thank him most profoundly, most heartily, for enforcing my doctrine that production has so far outrun consumption the world over that a readjustment of the proportions in which the joint production of labor and capital shall be distributed must be made.

Mr. HEWITT, of New York. "And the Lord hath delivered mine adversary into my hands." The gentleman says that protection has been unable to prevent overproduction. That is the point of his remark. I go further. I say that protection creates overproduction; that overproduction is the logical end and unavoidable conclusion of protection.

Then, when you have overproduction what is the consequence? You have a limited market; it is walled in by the tariff; there is no access to the outside world. What can you do with the surplus? Nothing but pile it up as long as your money lasts, and then stop. And then these protected workmen are left to starve, so that starvation is thus the literal and logical sequence of protection.

Overproduction is not a cause; it is a result. It is the result of causes that are vicious, for if artificial obstructions and interferences had not been created, will any man in this world tell me that there would be overproduction? Why, sir, the gentleman's long appeal to this House was based on sympathy for the people who are starving for the very things which are superabundant but which they could not buy. Overproduction means that there is inability on the part of some one in some part of the world to procure and consume the things which are elsewhere in superabundance.

Under the beneficent laws of God production is a blessing. Good harvests mean comfort and happiness to the people. A large crop of pig iron, if I may use the phrase, means the progress of great industrial enterprises. God has not cursed His people with the great contradictory law, contradictory to His omniscience, to His omnipotence, to His universal Fatherhood, that the labor of man shall destroy his happiness and close up the gates of joy for him and his offspring. It is the laws of man that have done this thing. The laws of man have erected artificial impediments; for when in any country or in the world you come to the condition when people say, "There is overproduction," it means only this: that the machinery of distribution is not equal to the machinery of production; that mankind in the eager pursuit of wealth have pressed one side of the economical machine to its full power, and neglected to see that the other side of the machine, which discharges and distributes the product, is equally developed and improved.

Now, then, if lack of proper distribution be the real key to the situation, as it is, then what is the logical conclusion? Remove the impediments to distribution which you have artificially created; remove them here, remove them everywhere, and let the world taste for once the beneficence of an Almighty Father, who intended that His children should be happy.

The law by which value is created, Mr. Chairman, is simple, but it is not often considered. What we call industry is the conversion of natural energy, of physical force stored up in nature, into useful forms by the skill and labor of man. The cost is measured by the difficulty of reaching these natural stores, in other words, of extracting the crude material from the earth, and by the labor which is put upon it afterward giving it form and value.

Now the greater the benefaction of nature, the greater the stores of this force, the more accessible these treasures, the less human labor is required for their development and for their conversion into what we call property. Measured by that standard there are two countries that Providence has endowed with great resources, more accessible and in larger quantity than in any other countries in the world, and they are Great Britain and the United States. Hence wages in Great Britain, under a natural order of things, will be higher than in any other European country. Hence, under a natural order of things, wages in this country will be greater than they are or can be in Great Britain; for a less amount of labor will produce on the average in this country a greater amount of value than it will in Great Britain. What deductions are to be made from these results to labor? If there were no intervention of any other elements the answer would be simple. The laborer's wages would be what is left after paying for the raw material and selling his product in the open market of the world.

But there is another deduction. Capital is necessary for the exploitation of human industry, of these natural resources. It may be paid for in one of two ways, or in both of them—by profits or by interest, or partly by profits and partly by interest. The lower the rate of interest, the more cheaply the final value can be produced, and hence the lowering of the rate of interest all over the world, due to great accumulations of capital which have come from the inventions and progress of the age, is the greatest benefaction that the human race has yet seen. It is as the dew of Heaven; it "falls upon the just and the unjust."

But where the operations of industry are under the control of owners who have capital, the owner takes both interest and profits, and interest and profits are both deducted from the wages of labor. Is there any remedy, has any remedy been found to prevent the owner from appropriating to himself all the earnings of industry, except that which is required to give a bare subsistence of the lowest order to the workmen who perform the labor? Wherever and so long as protection prevails there is no remedy. Where there is free trade the power ultimately passes from the owner into the hands of the workmen. In this country we have tried to apply the great remedy which has been applied in Great Britain with such remarkable results and which is only at the beginning of its triumph. I mean the organization of labor into trades-unions, whereby labor is pooled for its own protection. Trades-unions are the weapons of attack and defense which free trade has created for the protection of the workingmen; and they are all the protection that the workingman needs.

But in this country trades-unions are paralyzed by protection. The two principles are at war with each other. As long as we have a protective system trades-unions must be feeble and finally die. Let us prove this conclusion by tracing the effect of the protective system to its necessary conclusion in overproduction and stagnation.

Protective duties stimulate industry, we are told; and they do so until the market is fully supplied. Business rapidly increases where there is a monopoly of the market. Where profits are large, capital rushes in. It is not the capital of the workman, it is the capital of the owner. He takes not merely the profits of the normal business, but he adds to it in times of good demand the entire duty which is imposed by the tariff. And this he did and was doing when I spoke in this House two years ago, in one great department of our industry, the manufacture of steel rails, which were then subject to a duty of $28 a ton. The price of the foreign rails had advanced to a point where it would have paid him to make rails without any duty; but of the duty of $28 a ton he added $27 to his price and transferred from the great mass of this people $50,000,000 in two years into the pockets of a few owners, who thus indemnified themselves, in that short time, nearly twice over for the total outlay which they had made in the establishment of the business. They had a right to it; the law gave it to them; it was the "pound of flesh." Did they divide any portion of that magnificent bounty with the men they employed? Were not those men subjected to the rigorous law of supply and demand? And how inexorable that law is, when applied to labor, can not be understood until you recollect those vast regions of the world which the gentleman from Pennsylvania tells us is filled with pauper labor, open to be brought here in competition with our American labor.

Wages were advanced a trifle, and something was doled out from the great mass of this legislated wealth to the workmen; but any attempts of the trades-unions to get a fair share of this great profit would have been met, as it is met today, by the importation of foreign labor. Aye, in the state of Pennsylvania today the Hungarian and Polish immigrants are fighting for the crust of bread which is denied to the American workmen. The trades-union, therefore, in an overstocked market, with the doors open for foreign immigration, is absolutely powerless. It is always powerless except in the single contingency of a very active demand, when it will not pay the owner to derange his business by a short stoppage.

But how often are we confronted with the other spectacle, of workmen striking to resist the reduction of wages made in consequence of an overstock of goods and failing utterly, as they must do, in the object they have in view. At the great strike in Pittsburgh last year, which lasted four months, the owners rejoiced at the stoppage, because they had a large surplus of goods on hand. The stoppage was a benefaction to the masters, and of course the trades-union failed.

I want the workmen of this country to comprehend this great fact. They have no means of bringing owners to terms except through their labor associations, and their labor associations fail every time when you have an overstocked market.

But we are told by the gentleman from Pennsylvania [MR. KELLEY] that overproduction is the inevitable result of the protective system, as I have shown, in a restricted market, where the surplus can find no outlet. . . .

Now, Mr. Chairman, I have shown, or tried to show, how futile in a restricted market is the system of association of labor, which is the only star of hope in the firmament of the laborers, and how impossible it is for it to succeed in this country, because manufactured surplus products, which compel stoppage or low wages, are forbidden by our protective laws to be carried to the open markets of the world.

Let us see how it is in Great Britain. I will now refer to the subject to which the gentleman from Pennsylvania [MR. KELLEY] called my attention and to which I promised consideration. The condition of Great Britain in the year 1824 was simply deplorable; starvation stalked throughout the land. It was the year when laborers, rendered desperate by want, rose in their might and, blinded to the fact that they were destroying their own means of livelihood, burned the wheat ricks of England. In that year Canning and Huskisson began the great work of clearing away the prohibitory and protective duties of Great Britain. They went slowly, but they went surely, to the end. They began with raw materials, they progressed to secondary products, and finally they swept away the whole mass of duties which impinged on manufactured goods. How fared it with the workmen of England? More wretched than the beasts of the field, Mr. Chairman, as they were when this reform began, every hour has witnessed amelioration in the condition of the wage-earning class of Great Britain. Every restriction removed, every prohibition annulled raised them in the scale of being.

My first visit to England was in 1844, just after the last of these protective duties had been removed, and just as Cobden and Bright were gaining the great victory which gave free food to the nation. I have gone to England since 1862 generally once in two years. The subject which has interested me most has been the condition of the European workmen. I never failed to mark in Great Britain a steady improvement. In 1867, when I wrote my report on the French exposition, which those gentlemen are so fond of quoting, I found the condition of the English workman better than that of the French or German, but not equal to the condition of the corresponding class in this country.

I believed that the difference was due to the tariff, and I said so. I have gone often since, and I have found the condition of the British laborer steadily improving in all that goes to make up the life of man. On the other hand, my business and inclination has enabled me to study the condition of American labor, and I confirm the testimony given before the Labor Committee of the Senate, that the condition of American labor has steadily gone down. It needed something to open my eyes, and unwelcome facts set me to thinking. But more than that, I am a manufacturer.

Mr. Chairman, I may be pardoned for some reference to myself. Others have had no hesitation in picking me out as an example to be reprobated; and one gentleman, or rather one member of this House—a member of the last House and a member of this one—went so far as to pry into my family affairs and to refer to my domestic concerns. What he said was absolutely false, as usually these criticisms have been. This incident, however, recalled the fact that I once believed that protection was necessary for the prosperity of my own business. I believed it and acted upon it. But when after forty years of close attention to business, with the use of abundant capital and without sacrifice to procure it, after having built up a great establishment which at least does not compare unfavorably with those of its kind, I discovered that not only were the workmen not better off by reason of protection, but that I was not better off. That if I had taken the money invested in that business and loaned it out at the current rate of interest on good security, which we will take to be 5 or 6 percent, my firm would have been richer today than we are out of the vast business we have been conducting.

Mr. Warner,[1] of Ohio. Suppose that all other manufacturers in this country had done the same thing, let me ask the gentleman what would be the condition of the loan market?

[1] Adoniram Judson Warner (1834-1910), a Democratic Representative from Ohio 1879-81 and 1883-87.

MR. HEWITT, of New York. I do not know what would be the condition of the loan market. But I do know that I have never found any
difficulty in getting people to take all the money in that way which was
offered to them.

MR. WARNER, of Ohio. And give good security?

MR. HEWITT, of New York. Yes, sir.

MR. WARNER, of Ohio. And at 5 percent interest?

MR. HEWITT, of New York. Yes.

MR. WARNER, of Ohio. Can you do that now?

MR. HEWITT, of New York. Certainly; and I will state to the gentleman that the banking firm of A. Corbin & Co. have an advertisement,
which I have seen within a few days in several journals, in which they
invite the public—and I give them the benefit of this notice for nothing
—invite the public to bring their money to them, for which they will
undertake in sums of any amount to give 7 and 8 percent interest on
loans in Iowa and other Western states. And they give the results of
some fifteen years' operation in the business, during which loans have
been made amounting to many millions of dollars, in which they show
that not a penny of loss has taken place. They invite the public to come
forward and bring in their means and dump it into their hoppers, for
which they promise a higher rate of interest than I have been able to
realize in my business.

MR. WARNER, of Ohio. Then that would go to show that some industries must be prospering in this country and are profitable.

MR. HEWITT, of New York. But it is not an evidence of prosperity
when a man is compelled to borrow money at 7 or 8 percent.

MR. WARNER, of Ohio. No; but it is an evidence of prosperity if
a man is able to borrow it and can give security at that high rate of
interest for it.

MR. HEWITT, of New York. He may be forced to pay a high rate
of interest by the exigencies of his situation. But I admit that they
can borrow it, and I want to make it possible for the farmers of this
country, if it be necessary, to be able to borrow money and pay good interest if his welfare is thereby advanced. But the reason why the farmer
was able to pay high interest is well known to the gentleman from
Ohio, and he knows as well that the causes which led to it are no longer
at work. From 1873 to 1879 there was an era of short crops all over
the world except in this country. Here we had abundant harvests and
there was an abundant market in Europe. The price of wheat went up
to $1.98 a bushel in New York city, and there came a flood of wealth
back from Europe into this country. And yet during all that time, with
the flood of wealth pouring in upon us, when we had the influence of a
high protective tariff, there never was, and I hope there never will be,
such an era of distress among the protected industries of the country as

existed at that time. They were all ruined and broken down. Two years ago in this House, when I elaborately discussed the causes which brought about the prosperity of the farmers, I pointed out that it was temporary, being due to this invasion of large amounts of money, stimulating new enterprises and opening new wheat fields. I predicted that the prosperity would come to an end as soon as Europe could get her supply of food from any other quarter. And it has come to an end, and today the farmer can not produce wheat at the prevailing price and pay his expenses. The only chance that is left for him is that manufactures shall be established in his neighborhood and give him thereby a market for his produce, saving the cost of transportation. But manufactures can not grow in a market already overstocked——

MR. WELLER.[1] Will the gentleman allow me to ask him a question?

MR. HEWITT, of New York. When I get through with the sentence which I have begun I will hear the gentleman's question.

MR. WELLER. It will not be apropos except at this point.

MR. HEWITT, of New York. Well, now, the gentleman has succeeded in interrupting the current of my thought. I must decline to yield for a question at present. I was saying that the farmers of this country can have but little hope for the future without manufactures, and that manufactures can not grow in an overstocked market.

There is only one way by which they can be reopened and enlarged, and that is to make a market for our manufactures in the open markets of the world. The gentleman from Maine [MR. DINGLEY] this morning referred to the fact that we buy more from Cuba and South America than we sell to them. He seemed to be ignorant of the fact that we sell more to England than we buy, and that we take the surplus which we sell to England, the money realized by it, and pay the debt for that which we buy in South America, in Mexico, and in Cuba. But if we could produce manufactured goods in competition with Great Britain there would be a change in the current of this business. As it now is, we sell food to Great Britain; Britain consumes the food making manufactures. The manufactures are exported to South America, and we pay for what we buy there by drafts on London against the food we have sold in England, and the account is balanced in London by the balances of trade between the respective countries. But let the manufacturers have a chance to go out and export the $100,000,000, of which the gentleman from Maine speaks, direct to South America and Cuba and Mexico, and we will get in exchange the commodities of those countries —in direct exchange; and we will thus build up the shipping business, which the gentleman so much desired to develop, and at the same time increase our manufactures and the demand for the farmer's produce.

[1] Luman Hamlin Weller (1833-1914), a Democratic member of Congress from Iowa 1883-85; identified with the Greenback movement in his state.

Now, Mr. Chairman, returning to the point where I was when I was interrupted: I wish to call attention to the proof that the condition of the British laborer has steadily improved under the operations of free trade. For this purpose I shall not resort to assertion; I shall bring proof. Mr. Robert Giffen is the secretary of the statistical department of the English Board of Trade and also the president of the London Statistical Society. He is the most eminent living authority on the subject of statistics. His diligence, his intelligence, and his rectitude have never been called in question, and they can not be questioned. Mr. Giffen, in his address before the society in November last, treated of the progress of the working classes of Great Britain in the last half century. I have procured this document, which I regard as the most important contribution to social statistics ever made in any country, to be republished in the *Popular Science Monthly* for the month of May, and I ask every gentleman to read it for himself. . . .

The title of the pamphlet to which I have referred is *The Progress of the Working-Classes in the Last Half Century*. I just now simply give the conclusion of Mr. Giffen. I shall be disposed to append more of this document to my speech unless the House should consider it an infraction of privilege.

From this it appears that the increase of what is known as working-class income in the aggregate is greater than that of any other class, being 160 per cent., while the return to capital and the return to what are called the capitalist classes, whether it is from capital proper or, as I maintain, a return only in the nature of wages, has only increased about 100 per cent., although capital itself has increased over 150 per cent. At the same time the capitalist classes themselves have greatly increased in number, so that the amount of capital possessed among them per head has only increased 15 per cent., notwithstanding the great increase in capital itself, and the average income per head can have hardly increased at all. On the other hand, as the masses of the nation, taking the United Kingdom altogether, have only increased about 30 per cent. since 1843, when these income tax figures begin, while their aggregate incomes have increased 160 per cent., it is explained how these incomes have gained, individually, about 100 per cent. as against hardly any increase at all in the incomes of what are called the capitalist classes on the average. Thus the rich have become more numerous, but not richer individually; the "poor" are, to some smaller extent, fewer; and those who remain "poor" are, individually, twice as well off on the average as they were fifty years ago. The "poor" have thus had almost all the benefit of the great material advance of the last fifty years.

We may now conclude this long inquiry. It has been shown directly, I believe, that, while the individual incomes of the working classes have largely increased, the prices of the main articles of their consumption have rather declined; and the inference as to their being much better off, which would be drawn from these facts, is fully supported by statistics showing a decline in the rate of mortality, an increase of the consumption of articles in general use, an improvement in general education, a diminution of crime and pauperism, a vast increase of the number of depositors in savings banks, and other evidences of general well-being. Finally, the increase of the return to capital has not been in any way in proportion, the yield on the same amount of capital being less than it was, and the capital itself being more diffused, while the remuneration of labor has enormously increased. The facts are what we should have expected from the conditions of production in recent years. Inventions having been multiplied and production having been increasingly efficient, while capital has been accumulated rapidly, it is the wages receivers who must have the benefit. The competition of capital keeps profits down to the lowest point, and workmen consequently get for themselves nearly the whole product of the aggregate industry of the country. It is interesting, nevertheless, to find that the facts correspond with what theory should lead us to anticipate.

All the statements of individual cases of misery made by the gentleman from Pennsylvania weigh nothing against this great conclusion of an investigation based upon facts running over a period of fifty years. If individual cases of misery were to be a test the gentleman from Pennsylvania [MR. KELLEY] has only to go to his own city, and I have only to go to mine. Sad it is to think that there is no large aggregation of people anywhere in the world where there is not great human misery. So far as this misery exists in England it is due only to one cause, intemperance, where money enough is expended each year in drink to provide for all its pauperism and misery. So far as it exists on the Continent of Europe—and it is greater in the protected countries than it is in England, as the result of my observation made in England, France, Germany, Turkey, and Italy last year; it is less in England because England has greater natural resources—but all over the Continent the cause is to be found in the great standing armies, which have converted Europe into an armed camp garrisoned by 2,000,000 of soldiers, who eat up the substance of the people. With my own eyes I have seen a woman cut up a dead carcass because her husband was in the army and would not return to his family for three years; that was in Austria. She did his work and did it well, too.

I have seen a woman and a dog harnessed to a cart drawing a drunken husband home from market to his house. Would I draw deductions from this, as the gentleman from Pennsylvania does from sporadic instances, that Austria, where I saw this sight, was, too, a country in which human happiness had ceased to exist? No, sir; if I want to know the condition of Austria I will take in the whole circle of its interests and its people, and I will draw my deductions from the incontrovertible evidence of large masses of facts.

In England these results thus given by Mr. Giffen have not been produced by free trade alone. I want the gentleman to understand this matter fully. The foundation was laid by free trade, but the result in its best estate was caused by trades-unions. Free trade made it possible for the trades-unions to organize and go to the masters and say, "Your contribution is capital, which is worth in business 5 or 10 per cent, as may be agreed; your other contribution is management and administration; that is worth a certain percentage, which is easily determined by the experience of the nation. The rest belongs to us, and we intend to have it." And they have got it. There is, however, one great deduction to which the British workman is subject, which does not apply to us, and that is the rent of the land, which is paid to the privileged classes and is the heritage of a past age and an obsolete system of government, when the nobles were responsible for the defense of the country. But under the beneficent action of free trade in food, which opens the granaries of the world to British markets, rent is falling, privilege is dying, and the progress toward equality before the law is making rapid and satisfactory progress. That England is not retrograding, but is steadily increasing her industry, is proved by the fact that her annual output of coal, which measures her productive power, increases year by year, and that last year it exceeded by over 6,000,000 tons the product of the year before. That the people are in good condition is proved by the "sugar test," which is the best measure of the comfort of the great mass of the people. In 1883 the sugar consumed in Great Britain and Ireland was 67.3 pounds per capita of population; in the German Empire it was 18.3 pounds; in France it was 27.2 pounds; in the United States it was 43.25 pounds.

In a strike which I witnessed on the Brighton Railway in England I had an interview with one of the chief officers of the great Association of Amalgamated Engineers. I asked him what was the limit of the wages which they expected to get from the railway. He said: "There is no limit; we intend to have all the net earnings of these railways, except a fair remuneration for the capital actually invested and fair salaries for those who administer them; and the only question with us is how to find out what the amount is, and we intend to have it." That great association contained as its members all the engineers of Great Britain, numbering many thousands. It has a great fund in its treasury of nearly a million of dollars, and it has had as much as a million and a half dollars at one time.

It selects one concern at a time and puts the men there employed upon a strike until their demands have been acceded to. The hours of labor have been cut down by this process to fifty-five hours per week, and the wages of labor have been largely increased, for no man can say them "nay" within the limits of right and justice which they strive to observe.

With this example other trades have organized, and these trades have confederated together and now constitute a great congress. They met in 1881 when I was in London, and the figures of that time are the latest that I happen to have. There were one hundred and fifty-seven delegates in that congress, representing a constituency of 463,899 members. They met there to consider what could be done to raise the average condition of the British workmen. Their deliberations were conducted with a calmness, with a courage, with an intelligence that would do honor to this House or to any other deliberative body in the world. They did not seek to attack capital. They have learned that capital is their best friend, but they intend to make it their servant, and they can make it their servant.

There is a steady increase in the growth and influence of this great organization, but what concerns me here is to define the significance of such organizations. The labor of Great Britain today is practically pooled for the purpose of securing out of the products of industry the full portion which ought to be alloted to labor after paying current rate of interest upon capital and a proper remuneration for management. This result they have been able to accomplish. The rate of wages has steadily tended upward in Great Britain, and although much time has been lost in disputes ending in strikes, the result of the organization has been to introduce arbitration between the masters and men, so that strikes are becoming the exception rather than the rule in trade disputes. In these arbitrations the masters and the workmen meet upon equal terms. The result is a better understanding of each other's rights, interests, and duties, and out of which is slowly growing, through the agency of co-operation, the association of the workmen with the owners in ownership and management of the property.

That process is only at its beginning, but, thank God, the day is at hand, and will surely come in my time I hope, when workmen themselves will be the owners of all the machinery upon which they expend their daily toil and shall themselves have whatever profits the God of Nature intended them to have as the fruit of their labor.

That process in England will precede its possibility in this country, but it will be there as a great example. In this country it can not begin until protection is broken down. I repeat that protection is in the nature of artificial friction causing so large a deduction from the earnings of labor as to prevent the accumulation of capital in the hands of workmen.

Hence I have changed my views. I have changed my views because I am a Democrat who believes that the welfare of the people is to be considered before the welfare of any single interest or of any single man.

Let us try to measure the limit to which these organizations will enable the workmen to progress in securing for himself the largest possible remuneration for his labor. We have seen that after paying capital the natural resources of the country will determine the rate of wages of its workmen when the markets of the world are opened for the free exchange of the fruits of his labor. Under natural laws they will be exchanged for the products of other countries where production is carried on under less favorable circumstances. The profits will therefore be the difference between the natural resources in the exchanging countries, and the whole of these profits belong and will surely come to the possession of the working classes unless they are obstructed artificially by the operation of law.

Hence Great Britain will exchange with all other countries, except the United States, at a rate which will enable her workmen to be better paid than the workmen of those countries, but the United States, having greater natural resources than Great Britain, will exchange with her and all the world upon still better terms. Hence our workmen under natural laws will be better paid than the workmen of Great Britain. But such a result is only possible with free trade, because the protective system prevents our products from going out into the markets of the world in free competition with those of Great Britain. Nor can the beneficent principle of association embodied in the trades-union system be available by the workmen of this country until they have free access to the open markets of the world by which alone they can avoid the paralysis of overproduction. I do not know that the manufacturer will gain by free trade; I do not know that the capitalist will gain by it; but I do know that the workman is suffering for the want of it, and that the improvement in his condition after it is achieved will be as marked and as satisfactory as that which has been accomplished in Great Britain during the last fifty years. And I know further that the workmen of this country will have no trouble to get their fair share of the profits of industry when they are put in the position, as now they are not, of making practical use of the principle of association, out of which in other departments have sprung the great triumphs of modern civilization.

To these conclusions I have been forced by my experience, by my observations carefully made at home and abroad, and by the conscientious study which I have given to the industrial and economic systems of other countries, and to the conclusions of the great thinkers of modern times. To one among these thinkers, Thorold Rogers, I commend the attention of the gentlemen who still believe in the efficacy of the protective system to promote the welfare of the wage-earning classes. His great treatise on *Work and Wages* has just appeared in England and in this country. He confirms in a most remarkable manner the conclusion which I have announced, that the wage-earning classes of the world have no hope except in freedom of trade and in the organization of the trades-unions and labor partnerships. In that admirable work he has developed the remarkable fact that the reward for labor in Great Britain has just recovered to the point which it had attained in the fifteenth century, when through the agencies of the guilds, which were labor partnerships, labor was far better paid than at any time in the history of the human race. The progress to this conclusion was in his mind slow, as it has been in mine. Nevertheless, in a paper which I submitted to the Church Congress in 1878, I announced this conclusion and discussed the probable results to society. This paper I shall append to these remarks in the Record.

The proposition can no longer be successfully disputed that for the welfare and improvement in the condition of the workers for wages the principle of association in labor partnerships or trades-unions is indispensable, and offers a solution of the perplexing problem of the proper relations of capital and labor. But before this great solvent for human suffering can be applied, industry must be relieved from its shackles, and its products be freed from obstructive duties, which add to the cost so as to prevent free exchange.

Mr. Chairman, how would I begin this great reform? How would I bring about this magnificent policy, this redemption of the sons of toil from the servitude of ages? I believe that the protective system must go, but it must go as it came, slowly, and by such wise and moderate steps as will commend themselves to the judgment of all fair-minded men.

To abolish protective duties at once would ruin me, it would ruin the manufacturers, it would dislocate the labor of this country now engaged in the protected manufactures. We have no right to inflict this wrong. Hence, with the views I entertain, I have not hesitated upon all occasions to confirm the statements of gentlemen upon the other side that this reform must be made slowly. I warn my friends upon this side not to proceed rashly. I warn them that any mistake they may make will be taken advantage of by the manufacturers to put down wages, and to persuade the workmen that we are their enemies, and not their friends.

There is only one method by which we can accomplish this great result. Remove duties where it is possible—and there is plenty of room —without injuring existing interests, and then the steady progress in the improvement of the condition of the working classes, especially in their regular employment, without loss of time, which is what they want now more than high wages—this steady progress will convince the working-men that we are on the right road; and particularly will it convince them when they find that in the day of profits their trades-unions will be powerful enough to demand a better and fairer share of the earnings of industry.

I would begin with the raw materials. Gentlemen on the other side are very fond of repeating that phrase. Let me tell them that they have a constituency behind them that wants raw materials just as much as I do. Let me tell them that the manufacturers of New England are today perishing for the want of raw materials.

And I know what I mean by "raw material." Gentlemen have chosen to pervert my definition of that phrase. I have defined it and I will define it again. For the purpose of tariff reform I mean by raw material those articles to which no process of manufacture has been applied.

MR. SPRINGER.[1] Or human labor.

MR. HEWITT, of New York. I do not say that. There are many raw materials which involve human labor; all of them, I believe, involve human labor. I would permit duties to begin when the process of manufacture has begun, not before. All the others I would put on the free list, and I would put on it such manufactured articles as we do not make in this country. Of these tin plates is the most striking example.

And I know nothing that would suffer unless it be the wool of my friend from Ohio [MR. CONVERSE]. I do not believe it will suffer, but there is one class of wool which might be put on the free list without any damage to the interest he represents. I mean carpet wools. Then I would limit duties. I would not have those excessive rates of duty which contradict the sense of justice of every man upon the Committee on Ways and Means. I would have rates beyond which no article on each schedule could go.

Then I would go before the people of the country and say: "We have begun the work of redemption; judge you 'the tree by its fruits.' Are you better employed? Have you steadier wages? Have you more of the comforts of life? If you have, then let us go on with the good work."

If it should turn out to be otherwise, then, Mr. Chairman, I would pause. I am not bigoted and prejudiced as once I was. I can be converted from opinions which I once held by the logic of facts and experience.

MR. BRUMM.[2] Will you allow me to ask a question? Your time is unlimited.

MR. HEWITT, of New York. But my voice unhappily is not.

MR. BRUMM. Only one question. Would the gentleman be in favor of repealing the conspiracy laws of this country?

MR. HEWITT, of New York. Absolutely.

MR. BRUMM. As they are in England?

MR. HEWITT, of New York. Absolutely. They are a disgrace to the statute book. I will go with the gentleman from Pennsylvania or anyone else to the very end in giving the laborer the same rights before the law that he has before his God. I would deprive the workingman of no right which is enjoyed by his employer, but I would not allow him to injure his employer or other workmen by intimidation or violence. My grievance against the protective system is that it robs him of at least half of

[1] William McKendree Springer (1836-1904), a Democratic Representative from Illinois 1875-95.
[2] Charles N. Brumm (1838-1917), a Republican Greenbacker in the House of Representatives from Pennsylvania 1881-89.

what he might have had and probably of two-thirds of what he will have when the era of free trade prevails throughout the universal globe, and men and brothers may make exchanges with each other as if they were all the subjects of one government and one law.

Believing as I do that we have reached an era of permanent low prices, which will greatly benefit the masses of the people if we accommodate ourselves to the necessities of the situation, nevertheless I would proceed slowly, especially at the beginning, toward their accomplishment. I would follow the great example set us by Great Britain, which in the legislation of the tariff of 1842 proceeded upon the doctrine: first, of freeing raw materials from duty; secondly, of a low rate of duty upon articles partially manufactured and of a higher rate of duty, there 20 per cent, but here necessarily higher upon completely manufactured articles. No interest would be injured by the application of these principles. The freeing of raw materials would be a benefit to every interest.

I have been reproached with desiring to get free iron ore on the ground that I am a buyer of it and use it in my business, but the fact is that I rarely buy foreign iron ore but am a miner and seller of American ore. I am fully protected against any differences in the cost of labor by the cost of transportation. I should be a gainer, however, by the larger market which would be secured to me if I could mix my ores freely with foreign ones. The result would enable us to produce cheaper iron, which would give new life to every branch of business in this country. The same statement is true as to the other ores of the metals. It is true as to ingot copper, which is a secondary product, for we are now able to export our copper in competition with all the world. The duty is a mere nullity and should be repealed, because if copper should rise in the markets of the world it would simply be a bonus paid out of the pockets of our consumers to a particular interest which has no need of it.

But, in view of the fact that public opinion is not yet well settled upon this question, and that the prejudices of the manufacturers and farmers and workmen are largely on the side of the protective system, I would not attempt to go as I have heretofore said, in advance of public opinion. I would begin at the foundation and by removal of duties from the materials which enter into the protected industries prepare a way for the gradual and final abolition of the duties upon the finished products. At every step of this process the condition of the workingmen of this country would improve, and when they once realize the beneficence of the progress toward free trade, the journey will be soon completed, and the United States will be emancipated from a system which is at war with the declaration of the preamble of the Constitution of the United States, which declares that it is designed "to secure the blessings of liberty to ourselves and our posterity."

The progress of the human race toward freedom has been slow and painful, but it has been sure and in accordance with a well-defined law, now clearly traceable, in the history of man. It began with the struggle for freedom of thought, for the attainment of which we have to thank the Greeks. Although during the long night of the Middle Ages the light of intellectual liberty paled and often took refuge in prisons and cloisters it was never extinguished but burned with new brilliancy in the era of the revival of learning. Today a man may freely think, write, and publish the results of thought without the fear of man, and, if he chose, without the fear of God.

The next step in the great procession of the ages was the achievement of religious freedom, asserted by Luther and sanctified by the blood of saints and martyrs. Liberty of conscience drove our fathers to the inhospitable wilds of America, where in its turn it gave birth to political freedom, the next creation in the Genesis of human liberty. The child grew, even in our free atmosphere, but slowly and only reached its full maturity when the proclamation of the martyred Lincoln gave political freedom to every human being, without regard to color, race, or previous condition, within the borders of our land.

Industrial freedom only remains to be secured in order to complete the glorious record of the advance of the human race from servitude to liberty. For such industrial freedom we have now entered upon the final struggle. To the student of history the result can not be doubtful. It may come by moderate reforms, as I hope, or it will come as comes the avalanche, overwhelming and crushing the obstacles in its path. It may be attained by reform, or it may come by revolution.

But when it is achieved the world will be lost in wonder at its beneficent results, in comparison with which the triumphs of intellectual, religious, and political liberty, which were its necessary progenitors, will be but as dust in the balance of advantage to the physical and social welfare of the families of men.

Let us try then to form some idea of what will be the actual condition of the human race, when the temple of freedom is thus completed with its final story of industrial liberty, to which it will be glory enough to have contributed a single stone, as I am striving this day to do.

The world will be filled with wealth, partly the accumulations of past ages, and more the product of the present age, when the genius of man has made him master of all the subtle forces of nature. Capital will be superabundant and therefore cheap. It will be like the living water which the prophet of God struck from the rock. But capital will then be the servant, and no longer the master, of labor. Labor will no longer be hired by capital, but will hire it. It will no longer work for wages but for profits, which will be proportioned to the natural resources of each country, without deduction for the support of special classes of men or for the advantage of special interests at the expense of the general welfare. All privilege will cease, and all men will be equal before the law, as they are before the Creator. They will differ only in physical and mental endowments, and each will be paid according to his work. Men will become more and more individualized, and the property of each will thus be better defined and scrupulously respected; but the divine law that "we shall love our neighbors as ourselves" will then receive a new significance, because the force and habit of association in great industrial enterprises, wherein men have a common interest, will teach them to bear each other's burthens, as well as to respect each other's rights.

In such a state of society there will be still rich and poor, there will still be good and bad, but with the law of justice all-powerful, and legalized robbery unknown, jealousies will disappear, charity will increase, and the world, ceasing to be a pandemonium in which men are struggling with each other like demons for the possession of property, will become a paradise in which the primal curse has been converted into a final blessing.

This is no dream of an enthusiast, for I am a plain man of business, nor is it an excursion into the realms of Utopia, for I have been trained to weigh and measure the results of human action. It is a sober deduction from the study of the operation of the principle of association, which has crowned this age with material achievements of stupendous grandeur and beneficence, which is invading and taking possession of every domain of human affairs. It has already begun to organize labor for its emancipation from the bondage of ages, and it will be found as easy of application and as fruitful of benefit, in this final field of action, as it has been triumphant and beneficent in other spheres of social development.

The Treasury Surplus and Honest Money

SPEECH IN THE HOUSE OF REPRESENTATIVES, JULY 14, 1886

[*The first two years of Grover Cleveland's first administration, 1885-86, found the silverites and inflationists still active. They had tried at the beginning of his term to commit him to free and unlimited coinage; Hewitt was one of the men instrumental in binding him to oppose it. The silverites particularly disliked the large surplus kept in the United States Treasury. Some argued that much money was locked up there which should be in free circulation. But it cannot be doubted that many were actuated by a desire to reduce the gold reserve to so low a figure that in some time of sharp financial distress it would be easy to thrust the United States off the gold standard— as it was almost thrust off in 1895. A joint resolution was offered in the early summer of 1886 to the effect that whenever the Treasury surplus should exceed $100,000,000, the Secretary of the Treasury should be required to apply such surplus, in sums of not less than $10,000,000 a month, to the redemption of United States bonds. Hewitt scented danger. In this masterly speech he argued the necessity of furnishing adequate protection to the gold standard.*]

MR. CHAIRMAN: I intended yesterday to have followed the chairman of the Committee on Ways and Means and to have explained at some length the reasons why I am opposed to this joint resolution. I found myself then unable to take up the discussion, and I regret to say that, as is apparent from the condition of my voice, I am less able today to go into any elaborate discussion of this very important matter. I must content myself, therefore, with the reasons which were given in the minority report which I had the honor to present. If I had anticipated my inability to discuss the matter here I would have asked to have had that report printed in the Record. As it is, if I find myself unable to proceed I shall incorporate the minority report as part of the remarks which I offer this morning.

One or two points, however, brought out by the discussion which has taken place, I may be permitted to notice at this time. One objection to the resolution has been met by the amendment offered by the gentleman from Illinois [MR. MORRISON [1]] this morning. As the resolution was

[1] William R. Morrison (1825-1909), a Democratic Representative from Illinois 1863-65, and 1873-87.

reported to the House, $29,000,000 of subsidiary coin would have been included in the Treasury balance, so that, as a matter of fact, the available balance under the resolution would have been reduced to $71,000,000. That defect is corrected by the amendment which the gentleman from Illinois has just offered.

Another objection which I hoped he would meet, and which I think must have escaped his notice, is probably based upon an inadvertence. The resolution provides that whenever the surplus in the Treasury exceeds $100,000,000, a call of ten millions of bonds shall be made. The effect would be that if this resolution were adopted, and if the surplus reached $101,000,000, a call would have to be made which would reduce the available surplus to ninety-one millions.

MR. MORRISON. No, no.

MR. HEWITT. I see that the chairman of the Committee on Ways and Means shakes his head and says "no, no," but this is a matter of language and construction, and I simply submit the question to the consideration of the House and of the gentleman himself, and suggest that, if he does not intend that effect, he had better modify the language of his resolution so as to provide that whenever the surplus reaches $110,000,000 there shall be a call of ten millions. That will place his intention beyond doubt.

The gentleman from Illinois in his report and in the remarks which he made yesterday bases his advocacy of this joint resolution upon the saving of the interest which it will effect. Assuming that $75,000,000 is the amount over $100,000,000 which under this resolution would have now to be paid out, the saving in interest would be about two and a quarter million dollars per annum. He also says that it will release from the Treasury $100,000,000, which hundred millions would go into the channels of trade and give employment to one hundred thousand men, and the gentleman from Tennessee added that it will thus support five hundred thousand people. The gentleman from Illinois [MR. MORRISON] is too well acquainted with the principles which govern business not to know that if this act should impair public confidence the saving of two and a quarter million of dollars would be a case of "saving at the spigot and losing at the bunghole." The disturbance of business would be so serious that a couple of millions of dollars would be of no consequence, and, in fact, would be daily lost in the commercial transactions of the country.

But as to employment, one hundred thousand men would be dismissed from employment on the very first day when the public should begin to realize that under the operation of this resolution the stability of the Treasury was impaired and its ability to meet its obligations was undermined. Therefore, such considerations as the saving of $2,000,000 a year or the possible employment of one hundred thousand men are trifling in comparison with the danger and disturbance which would result if the financial transactions of the Government were seriously interfered with by the operation of this resolution. But the gentleman is mistaken in supposing that the release of this money from the Treasury would set a single additional man to work, unless it be the men who would have to count the money when it came out of the Treasury.

There are today idle in the city of New York more than $75,000,000 of unemployed capital. If that capital could be made profitable, it would be employed tomorrow, and if this $75,000,000 comes from the Treasury of the United States, it will not be given to the men who are short of means and are seeking for capital; it will be paid to the bondholders, and the bondholders, who are supposed to be capitalists or to represent capitalists, will simply deposit the proceeds in a market already gorged with superabundant capital, and not a single additional human being will be employed in consequence of this release. I refer to these considerations now because they were not urged at the time the report was made but have been urged in debate here, and I think this the proper place to make answer to them.

Upon one or two other points brought out by the debate I wish to say a few words. My colleague from New York, who is also my colleague on the committee [MR. HISCOCK], has stated that the introduction of this resolution and the peculiar manner in which it has been brought before this House for discussion is a declaration of war on the part of the Democratic majority of the House against a Democratic administration. It must be conceded, I think, that this resolution is at war with the declared policy and practice of the administration.

I think this is not disputed on either side of the House. Hence, governed by the ordinary rules of party management, I was exceedingly anxious to avoid the discussion of the resolution; and I resisted the adoption of the amendment to the rules by which it was brought on. But I was reminded by what happened of the time when I used to recite "The boy stood on the burning deck, whence all but he had fled"; for I found that I was not only the only Democrat who voted against the resolution, but notwithstanding what my friend from Illinois says about New York men, I was the only member from the city of New York who resisted its consideration. Hence I suppose there are some occasions on which the New York men do not hold together on the money question. Perhaps it is best to have the discussion. I think it very likely they were right and that I was wrong in trying to resist the discussion; for in a country governed by public opinion it is well that every great question affecting the employments of the people should be ventilated here and elsewhere; and any attempt to repress the judgment of the people would in my opinion be an error.

Hence I do not consider that the action of the Committee of Ways and Means in reporting this resolution, or of the Committee on Rules in bringing it before the House, is a declaration of war against the administration. If, however, it should be adopted, I should regard it as a vote of want of confidence in the policy of the administration, which under other forms of government would lead to the resignation of the ministry and under our form of government would lead to a change in the practice of the administration, because the administration is governed by law, and law is expressed by the action of Congress when approved by the President.

The gentleman from New York [MR. HISCOCK [1]] seemed to think there was a pledge given in the Democratic platform for bringing this measure before Congress. As usual on that side of the House the Democratic platform has not been very carefully studied by the gentleman from New York. There is no such pledge in the platform; and there is not a syllable in it which indicates that any action ought to be taken by the Democratic House in order to bring down the surplus in the Treasury. There is a declaration that the surplus of taxation should be reduced, and there is an allegation that $100,000,000 could be taken from the taxes of the people and the Treasury still have ample means for carrying on its business. When that declaration was made it was true. The effort has been made to give effect to that declaration of the platform, and thus far it has failed. But the declaration on the money question was most explicit: "We believe in honest money, the gold and silver coinage of the Constitution, and a circulating medium convertible into such money without loss."

That is the only declaration contained in the platform on the subject of the money of the country. The gentleman from Illinois and I were concerned in the preparation of that declaration. Neither he nor I nor any other Democrat on the committee which reported that declaration dissented from a single word or line of it. The President of the United States,[2] when he accepted the nomination of his party, planted himself squarely upon the declarations of the platform. He went into no detail, but he accepted it in a broad and generous declaration; and I have reason to know that the President regards his promise to observe the declarations of the platform to be as binding upon his conscience and his action as is his oath to support the Constitution and maintain the laws of the country. He has never left us in any doubt as to how he construed that declaration of the platform. Prior to his inauguration, in the famous letter addressed to the gentleman from Ohio [MR. WARNER], who gave us yesterday such an able and bountiful exposition

[1] Frank Hiscock (1834-1914), a Republican Representative from New York 1877-87, and Senator 1887-93.

[2] That is, Grover Cleveland.

of the facts of the currency, he recites the condition of the Treasury and then uses this language:

> These being the facts of our present condition, our danger, and our duty to avert that danger, would seem to be plain. I hope that you concur with me and with the great majority of our fellow-citizens in deeming it most desirable at the present juncture to maintain and continue in use the mass of our gold coin as well as the mass of silver already coined. This is possible by a present suspension of the purchase and coinage of silver. I am not aware that any other method is possible. It is of momentous importance to prevent the two metals from parting company—to prevent the increasing displacement of gold by the increasing coinage of silver, to prevent the disuse of gold in the custom-houses of the United States in the daily business of the people, to prevent the ultimate expulsion of gold by silver. Such a financial crisis as these events would naturally precipitate, were it now to follow upon so long a period of commercial depression, would involve the people of every city and every State in the Union in prolonged and disastrous trouble. The revival of business enterprise and prosperity so ardently desired and apparently so near would be hopelessly postponed. Gold would be withdrawn to its hoarding places. An unprecedented contraction in the actual volume of our currency would speedily take place. Saddest of all, in every workshop, mill, factory, store, and on every railroad and car the wages of labor, already depressed, would suffer still further depression by a scaling down in the purchasing power of every so-called dollar paid into the hand of toil. From these impending calamities it is surely a most patriotic and grateful duty of the representatives of the people to deliver them.

This was the declaration of Grover Cleveland before he became President of the United States. When he became President he was confronted with the very difficulties which he had outlined in that letter to General Warner. The gold in the Treasury had been for many months gradually drifting away. Its place was being filled up with coined silver dollars. The last administration—and I speak now from the personal communication of the then Secretary of the Treasury, a man whose very able services to this country cannot be too highly appreciated—the then Secretary of the Treasury told me that the most he hoped to be able to do was to carry the Government over the 4th of March upon the basis of gold payments.

I have reason to know when the present administration came into power its first and chiefest concern was to avoid the danger which had been predicted by the Republican Secretary in his official statement and in his private communications. The amount of gold in the Treasury on the 4th of March, 1885, was $126,000,000. This was a much smaller sum than had usually been held in the Treasury in gold since the resumption of specie payment. It was steadily running down. The public confidence was gone. The hoarding of gold had begun—not by the mass of the people, not in stockings, not in secret hiding places, but by the masters of finance, the men whose business it is to handle millions and to prevent their deterioration; they began to prepare for the hour of danger and the collapse which they thought was impending.

I know three of the greatest institutions in the city of New York—

I shall not name them lest it might possibly bring down upon them the condemnation of those who are prejudiced against banks—but I know three institutions in the city of New York which had accumulated more than $25,000,000 of gold as a preparation for the collapse they thought was coming.

MR. BROWN,[1] of Pennsylvania. But which never came.

MR. HEWITT. It did not; thanks to Grover Cleveland and that superb management of the Secretary of the Treasury which has made the name of Daniel Manning famous throughout the financial world.

The first effort made was to strengthen the Treasury in gold, but unfortunately it was at the season of the year when gold shipments usually take place. The effort was a failure. The gold gradually ran down until on the 30th of June it fell to $120,000,000. An effort had been made by the Republican Secretary of the Treasury, I mean by the Secretary of the Treasury of the last administration, I do not use the word "Republican" in any party sense—an effort had been made to avoid this state of things by paying out silver certificates in the city of Boston. The result had been to bring on a feeling of profound distrust, and it was abandoned. The Treasury thought finally they ought not seek to force silver certificates on the unwilling creditors of the Government. They pursued the policy which had been from the foundation of the Government, except during the era of suspension of specie payments, its crowning glory; that is, to pay the creditor of the Government in any funds he might desire, and that all the money of the Government should be interchangeable and of equal value. Now, this money is not of equal intrinsic value. Gold is the unit of value, not merely by the statutes of the United States, but by the fact that it is the medium of exchange and payment throughout the civilized world. Everything else measures itself in commerce, in international transactions, by gold.

The money of the United States in like manner, whatever may be its intrinsic value, is necessarily thus measured. It consists partly of gold which is the unit value by law. It consists partly of paper which has no intrinsic value, but which derives its value from the fact the people may take it to the Treasury and get gold for it. It consists partly of silver, the intrinsic value of which today is 74 cents on the dollar, but which equally with the greenback passes for 100 cents on the dollar because the Government has provided a practical redemption for it in its taxes and custom-house duties.

It was this parity of value that the President of the United States and his Secretary of the Treasury determined to maintain at all hazards, and I have no doubt that if the emergency had arisen as mentioned by the gentleman from Illinois yesterday, making it necessary to sell United

[1] William Wallace Brown (1836-1926), a Republican Representative from Pennsylvania 1883-87.

States bonds, in order to put gold in the Treasury, that drastic and final remedy would have been applied. But by the most careful management the contingency was avoided.

If any gentleman doubts whether it existed or not, but I suppose none do doubt it, a resolution adopted at the New York clearing house on the 20th of July, 1885, by the associated banks of the city of New York will certainly clear up any doubt on the subject. This resolution contains the following:

NEW YORK CLEARING HOUSE,
New York, July 20, 1885.

At a meeting of the associated banks of this city, held on the 13th instant, the following resolutions were unanimously passed:

Whereas, after careful inquiry into the current operations of the United States Treasury, it is ascertained that with the continued purchase of two million silver bullion per month the probable receipts of gold currency will be insufficient to meet the demands upon it until the meeting of Congress in December next, but that the Secretary will be compelled to make his payments in silver dollars, which will become a most disturbing element in the daily business of the country: Therefore,

Resolved, That to avert this threatened danger, and in the confident belief that Congress will take early steps to prevent the deterioration of the present commercial standard of value, the banks hereby tender to the Government, from their gold reserves, the sum of $10,000,000 in exchange for that amount in fractional silver coin, or for such other currency as the clearing-house committee may approve, the same to be apportioned among banks in the clearing house respectively, pro rata of their deposits and gold reserve.

Resolved, That should this amount prove insufficient, a further sum, not to exceed ten millions, be offered, and that the banks of Philadelphia, Boston, Chicago, and other cities, be invited by the clearing-house committee to participate in carrying out the object of these resolutions.

The undersigned committee appointed under these resolutions respectfully invite your co-operation in securing the object in view. Since the resumption of coin payments on 1st January, 1879, the banks throughout the country, together with the Government itself, have practically maintained the gold standard then re-established, and the business of the nation has been carried on upon that basis in harmony with all the leading commercial nations of the world. The varied products of industry and the natural operations of its trade have since furnished this country with superabundant supplies of gold, so that the surplus money reserves held by all the banks now greatly exceed anything ever known in our history. With all these favorable financial conditions we are suddenly called upon to confront the fact that the resources of the Government have become unnaturally absorbed by the purchase of silver bullion converted into coined dollars of inferior value to such an extent as to constrain the officers of the Treasury to force them upon an unwilling people in payment for public dues, and these coins, or their representatives, now threaten to invade and poison all the channels of trade by being introduced as commercial equivalents into the clearing-houses of the country.

That is the recorded judgment of the best financial authorities of New York, and concurred in by bankers throughout the country.

These "financial men of New York" and their financial operations, various gentlemen are in the habit of criticizing severely. They are spoken of as persons without patriotism and with no regard for the general interests of the country. These men of New York occupy the positions which they hold by the divinest right—the right which comes from possessing knowledge and ability. They are gathered into New York from every state in this Union. The best brain of the country goes to New York. It is the best market for brains. They come from every portion of the habitable globe. They come with their knowledge of resources of this and of other countries. They have been trained in the school of experience. They are rich because they have made themselves rich. New York has not made them rich. New York has no power to make any man rich. New York has made many a man poor; but it can make no man rich. It is simply the center of the exchanges, as it is the headquarters of the financial ability of this continent. When you are sick you send for a doctor; when you are in litigation you send for a lawyer; when you are going to build a railway you send for an engineer; but when you are going to administer the finances of a great country what do you do? Three hundred and twenty-five gentlemen, of whom certainly not more than ten would pretend to run a bank, who would quote against most of us, "Fools rush in where angels fear to tread"— three hundred and twenty-five gentlemen sit down here and take up the most difficult and the most complicated problems of finance, and instead of legislating upon general principles come down to specific details, as is done in this resolution, directing the Secretary of the Treasury how much money he must keep in the Treasury and how much money he must let out, without any possible comprehension of the tendencies of the future, the possibilities of business, or the demands of foreign capitalists upon the reserve which they have invested in this country.

I contend and always have contended that it is a perversion of the functions of the Treasury to possess the power to make money easy or to make it tight at its pleasure. But it is no fault of this administration nor of the last administration that it possesses that power. It was the result of that conflict which overwhelmed in a common destruction both North and South so far as the finances of the country were concerned. The United States Treasury, from being a fiscal machine, as it was before the war, has now become a great bank; it is a bank of issue, a bank of deposit; it is a member of the clearinghouse. It could not disregard if it would the condition of the money market; because, suppose for a moment that the balance should run down in a time of great depression, when business was embarrassed; suppose it was necessary to re-enforce that balance in order to maintain the parity between the various kinds of money issued by the Treasury—suppose that should happen, where would the Government go to get its money? It would have either to go into the money centers and produce it by hypothecating, as this administration was compelled to do, a portion of its Treasury reserves in order to get gold, or else it would have to sell bonds in order to keep up the Treasury balances, either of which would withdraw from an already depleted money market an additional sum to be locked up in the Treasury, thereby increasing the stringency of the money market. The Government cannot strengthen itself in a close money market. It must keep strong. The gentlemen who advocate this proposition are fair-weather sailors.

Since the resumption of specie payments we have had a long era of easy money; and it has been an easy task in the main to keep the Treasury in a strong condition. It would be an easy task now, too, but for the fact that $2,800,000 of silver are poured into it monthly, which in effect must drive $2,800,000, either in greenbacks or in gold, out of the Treasury unless it is hoarded there.

Now I will tell the gentleman from Illinois who asked the question what was done with the proposition of the banks to which I referred. It would be unjust if I were to leave the House under the impression that this action of the banks was altogether without suggestion from some other quarter. No official application was made to them for help, but the situation was discussed and resulted in the offer on the part of the banks to furnish $10,000,000 and a further sum of ten millions if necessary. About six millions, or a little over six millions, was thus paid into the Treasury, when the balances began slowly to increase because public confidence was restored by the action of the banks and the evidence it afforded that the banks were prepared to make common cause with the Treasury and maintain payments upon a gold basis. Since that time the Treasury balance has increased in gold to one hundred and fifty-six millions, and this has been accomplished by a change in the system of payments by the Treasury.

They have paid out greenbacks freely. They have paid out gold freely when it was asked for. The result was the greenbacks and the gold have flowed back into the Treasury through the channels of taxation. When the attempt was made to force the silver certificates upon the public the receipts of the Government began rapidly to increase in silver certificates, because people always pay away first that in which they have least confidence. But the normal condition of things has now been restored, and the Treasury is in a comfortable position, and calls on bonds have been resumed to the fullest extent that in the judgment of those charged with this responsibility the Treasury can afford to go without disturbing the relation of convertibility of every class of money issued by the Government into every other class of money upon the basis of gold as the unit of value at 25.8 grains to the standard dollar.

Now, it is proposed to limit this discretion which has been exercised since the resumption of specie payments by the Treasury Department, and which has been exercised since the 4th of March, 1885, by a Democratic administration in a manner which has elicited the warmest encomiums, the highest admiration from all financial authorities at home and abroad. I forbear for even one minute to consider the motives which may be behind this movement. But I wish to say, inasmuch as my colleague from New York [MR. HISCOCK] made the charge that it was a movement on the part of the Democratic leaders against the administration—I wish to say just this, in view of the record of my friend from Illinois [MR. MORRISON], that such a supposition is simply impossible. For years he and I have stood shoulder to shoulder to maintain gold payments as the basis of the money of the United States.

Year after year he has gone home to his constituents, and has raised aloft the banner of honest money in a region of country where the heresy of fiat money was most prevalent, and almost alone he has made a gallant fight, and I shall be the last man ever to allow an imputation to be made on him that he is deliberately planning the destruction of that policy for which he has made sacrifices and which owes to him as much as to any living man the fact that we are on a gold basis today. I can not account for his action now on any other theory than this: He has discovered that a "fiscal distemper" has broken out. It was a sporadic case. But he had to pay attention to it and to study its symptoms. I am afraid that that sporadic case has become contagious, and all I can say of my friend from Illinois is, I account for his action on the ground that he has got the disease; but I predict that he will recover from it, for not to recover would be against the principles and practice of his life.

I do not expect that the other gentleman who co-operated with him will recover. I expect he will die of the disease. I do not expect to go to his funeral.

MR. RANDALL. I belong to a long-lived stock.

MR. HEWITT. I will be under the sod long before you.

MR. REED,[1] of Maine. That is merely an expectation born of hope.

MR. HEWITT. As to the third member of the committee, the Speaker, his good nature is proverbial. I have no doubt when he found that the two wings of the Democratic Party were flapping together for the first time this session he felt it was his duty to let them keep on flapping; and I suppose my friend from Pennsylvania [MR. RANDALL] when he referred to that fact had this matter in mind.

Now, Mr. Chairman, let us suppose that this resolution is put into operation; what will happen? In about five months we shall be brought back, so far as the gold in the Treasury is concerned, to the condition in which we were on the 4th of March, 1885. That was a condition of

---

[1] Thomas Brackett Reed (1839-1902), a Republican Representative from Maine, 1877-99, and famous as Speaker of the 51st, 54th, and 55th Congresses.

great alarm and distrust. In another month we would be ten millions worse off. In another month we should be further down. In seven months we should be down to the one hundred million limit. What happened then will happen again. This is a question of experience and authority. People's ideas of what they think will happen or what they would like to have happen amount to nothing against the actual lessons of experience and authority. We tried this experiment as far as we could try it. We got down to a limit of one hundred and twenty-six millions. The gold was hoarded. When we get back there or begin to go back there on the passage of this resolution it will be hoarded again. The result must inevitably be that the gold coin—five hundred and fifty millions I believe it is estimated to be; I refer all these matters to my learned friend from Ohio [Mr. WARNER]—five hundred and fifty millions must disappear from circulation; I will not say from the country; but it must disappear from circulation the moment a premium, however small, is once established between gold and the other money of the country.

Mr. WARNER, of Ohio. What effect will that have on the remaining volume of money?

Mr. HEWITT. The remaining volume of money will be reduced *pro tanto*.

Mr. WARNER, of Ohio. In value?

Mr. HEWITT. No; in quantity. The result of a sudden withdrawal from the channels of trade of a large amount of currency in use means the stoppage of business, not the fall in value of the remaining money. No; that will come later. But it means the stoppage of business for the want of the lubricating material for the machinery of business, which is money. A hundred thousand men are to be employed by the adoption of this resolution; a million of men will lose their daily employment the moment the gold is withdrawn from circulation.

Mr. BUTTERWORTH.[1] Will my friend permit me to ask him a question which is pertinent to what he has just suggested? If the $550,000,000 of gold hides itself away, will there not be a pressure upon this House to supply its place with a cheap currency printed at the Bureau of Engraving and Printing?

Mr. BRUMM. That "cheap currency" is at 5 percent premium now in England.

Mr. HEWITT. I said, in answer to the question of the gentleman from Ohio [Mr. WARNER], that the quantity of money would be reduced and that the wheels of business would be stopped; but in this country, governed by a people who have to earn their daily bread, the wheels of business will not be permitted to remain long idle, and, what-

1 Benjamin Butterworth (1837-98), a Republican Representative from Ohio 1879-83, and 1885-91.

ever may be the remedy—my friend from Illiniois will tell us that it would be the restoration of gold (I differ with him)—but whatever may be the remedy that is required to set those wheels in motion it will be adopted, and we who have brought on this mischief, including believers in the gold basis, will be powerless to resist the demand which will come here for further issues of paper money, and I venture to predict the form in which those issues will first be made.

The greenbacks are maintained at par upon a reserve varying from 30 to 40 percent. The reserve behind the silver certificates is today 74 percent, a most wasteful and unnecessary reserve from a financial point of view. The first proposition that will be made, to which no financial authority will be able to make answer, will be: "If 35 or 40 percent is a sufficient reserve let us double up the silver certificates upon the fund which is now in the Treasury." That will be the first step. The next step will be a demand for more greenbacks—not the greenback that saved the life of the nation, but a new kind of greenback to save the business and the industries of the nation. And under the decision of the Supreme Court I know of no answer which can be made by this House or by Congress in denial of that demand. Of the evils of such a state of things it is not necessary for me to speak. We go back to the basis of inconvertible paper money.

We deliberately adopt fiat money as the end of all this long struggle for a sound currency, and that, too, notwithstanding the pledge of the Democratic Party that "we believe in honest money, the gold and silver coinage of the Constitution, and a circulating medium convertible into such money without loss." That process is one which robs those who have accumulated property and who have loaned it out to borrowers of a portion of their property, how large a proportion I know not; but during the period when we were under suspension it robbed them at one time of 60 percent. It results in the transfer of the property of the country from the hands of those who have earned it and saved it into the pockets of the rich, the speculators, the masters of finance, many of them, most of them, perhaps, residing in my own city, and many of them in my own district.

I do not want to pile up these overgrown fortunes at the expense of the industry and the labor of the country. I do not wish to rob the widow and the orphan who have their savings deposited in savings-banks. I do not wish to take away from the man who has provided a life-insurance fund for his family half of what he supposed he had secured to them. Of course when we have passed through the valley of the shadow of death which once we traveled with tears and lamentations, made wiser by suffering, taught by bitter experience, we shall slowly retrace our steps to the basis of honest money, the money which the Democratic Party from the time of Jefferson and Gallatin to the present day have insisted is the only money for the people. The best money, the money which measures all other money in all other parts of the world, gold, is not too good for the working man, is not too good for the widow and the orphan, is not too good for the pensioner, is not too good for the citizen who wishes that justice shall be established and maintained in this land forever.

It is for this that the President has made this struggle. It is to fulfill his obligation to the party that put him in power; it is to comply with his oath to support the Constitution which alone permits the coinage of gold and silver; it is for this that he has resisted all pressure from all quarters to call bonds at a time when, as he has told us in his annual message, the calls would have compelled the two metals to part company. The policy of the administration is to keep gold and silver married, for better, for worse, one as good as the other, neither the better half of the other, but when the time comes that the choice must be made between them, the President of the United States will adhere, as he has promised and sworn to do, to that standard of value which pays debts in the value intended at the time the debts were contracted.

Now, Mr. Chairman, it may be said, in fact it has been said, that this is all very well to talk about, but that it will not happen. Sir, I am no prophet; I am not the son of a prophet; I am only an humble student of history and finance, trained in business, often brought face to face with questions of this kind, and therefore I can only bring to the House the measure of my own experience and knowledge, supplemented, however, by the knowledge and experience of those who are confessed to be the masters of the question. A hundred millions of dollars will, if this resolution be adopted, be the sole reserve for the redemption of the paper money of the United States. How much is there of this paper money? Three hundred and forty-six millions of greenbacks and three hundred and eleven millions of national-bank notes, making in round numbers $650,000,000, upon which $100,000,000 of reserve is about 15 percent.

To this is to be added the whole volume of silver money, now amounting to $234,000,000, and increasing at the rate of $3,000,000 per month, for the reason that not being of the intrinsic value of gold its parity can only be maintained by redemption out of the reserve fund.

That is your reserve. Let us see what we provided when we began to resume specie payments. When resumption took place there were $246,000,000 in the Treasury. We were told triumphantly yesterday that only $12,000 of greenbacks came in for redemption. Of course the quantity of notes coming in for redemption was inconsiderable, for the Treasury held gold enough to pay upon demand two-thirds of the entire amount outstanding. After the public had become accustomed to specie payments the gold balance in the Treasury was suffered slowly to run down until the average amount of gold in the Treasury varied from year to year between $140,000,000 and $150,000,000 free and clear of all demands.

Now remember this is fair weather. I do not hesitate to say that in a stormy time $140,000,000 or $150,000,000 is not a sufficient sum of itself to insure convertibility into gold for both the national-bank notes and the greenbacks. But in fair weather it is abundant. The effect of this resolution will be to bring on foul weather—a storm. Instead of being stronger we are weaker; instead of having furled our sails in advance, they are all spread to the wind, and the ship, rolling and tossing, will finally go down under the overpowering volume—I was going to say of wind, but currency when inflated and wind are correlative terms, and therefore I may say of currency which will be poured in for redemption.

I know the Government holds security in bonds for the national-bank notes. I know that the banks can redeem their notes in greenbacks. What will happen if the Government calls in its bonds and the national banks deposit greenbacks to cover their outstanding circulation? The greenbacks will be withdrawn from circulation; and then the difficulties of business will be increased tenfold, unless the Treasury does what I think it has no moral right to do, although it may have the legal right—unless it uses the trust fund deposited by the banks for the redemption of their currency and pays it out into the community, so that not only the national-bank notes but the greenbacks will be in circulation. But if the demand be for gold (and for gold it will be) the fact that both forms of currency are outstanding and the Government is then responsible for both will only increase the rush upon the Treasury for gold and sooner bring about collapse.

What do other countries do? The gentleman from Ohio gave us the facts and has spared me the necessity of repeating them. In England, with bank notes to the amount of £24,000,000 in circulation, and including those of the private banks—about £30,000,000 ($150,000,000)—the Bank of England never lets her specie get below £18,000,000. When that point is reached she raises the rate of interest and, as she has done within the last sixty days, restores the balance, until it is now over £20,000,000. In other words, with $150,000,000 in circulation, the bank is sure to keep $100,000,000 in hand ready to meet her notes, the reserve thus being 66⅔ percent.

But the gentleman from Ohio will tell us that this is a reserve to meet other obligations. So it is; but at the very worst period we have seen in the last twenty years the reserve of the Bank of England was 35½ percent in specie for every dollar of circulation and every dollar of deposits in her possession.

That is her practice. What is the practice of the Bank of France?

Today the Bank of France holds in round numbers over 90 percent of gold and silver in her vaults against the paper currency which is outstanding; and the Bank of France has behind her in addition the government of France. More than that, she has in circulation among her people the largest fund of gold and silver that exists in any nation of the world. Yet the gold and silver which the Bank of France keeps on hand is 90 percent of her paper money. The same thing substantially is true of the other great banking institutions—for instance, the Imperial Bank of Germany, though there the circumstances are somewhat different. But human experience has never contemplated the maintenance of specie payments in time of trouble upon a basis below 35 or 40 percent. . . .

I dissent from the report of the majority of the Committee on Ways and Means in favor of the joint resolution directing the payment of the surplus in the Treasury in excess of $100,000,000 on the public debt, because the effect of this resolution, if enacted into law, may be to reduce the balance in the Treasury available for the payment of its current indebtedness and for the redemption of the legal-tender notes below $100,000,000. It makes no provision for replenishing the Treasury when the available balance shall fall below $100,000,000. The question thus presented is whether, in view of the obligations and the functions of the Treasury as now defined by law, the proposed limitation upon the balance to be held for meeting the liabilities payable on demand is prudent and safe, with a due regard to the solemn pledge of the United States to redeem all its indebtedness in coin or its equivalent. I believe that such a limitation would be unwise, dangerous, and at variance with the experience alike of solvent nations and of sound financial institutions.

The ordinary disbursements of the Treasury may be roughly stated to amount to about $1,000,000 per day. To meet these disbursements it is necessary that a reasonable working balance should be kept on hand, because at times the current expenditures largely exceed the daily receipts. Careful business firms usually carry a balance equal to one month's disbursements. Measured by this standard, and a lower one can not be safely adopted, because the Secretary of the Treasury has no power to make temporary loans, the working balance in the Treasury should be about $30,000,000. That this amount is not too large will be apparent from the fact that in the Pension Bureau alone drafts for $10,000,000 were made on the 1st of March, and that the amount of future payments, under the Arrears Act, can not be definitely fixed for any specified date.

But, besides the current expenditures provided for by law, the United States has a totally distinct obligation to provide for a debt payable on demand, in the shape of $346,681,016 of legal-tender notes.

These notes form about one-half of the paper currency of the country. They constitute the final means of payment between individuals and of settlement in all the transactions of business. It is absolutely necessary, therefore, that the ability to redeem these notes in coin shall be at all times assured beyond peradventure. For this purpose there must always be retained in the Treasury a reasonable and adequate reserve of coin. The only question is as to the amount of coin which will constitute a reasonable and adequate reserve.

To determine this point we have no other guide but usage and experience. In the case of gold and silver certificates the Treasury keeps dollar for dollar, but in the case of the legal-tender notes it has not been usual to have at any time in the Treasury a reserve in coin exceeding one-half of the whole issue of such notes. When specie payments were resumed bonds of the United States were sold so as to provide a fund amounting to $95,500,000 in gold for the purpose of assuring the redemption of the notes, which, as the law then provided, were to be reduced by cancellation to $300,000,000. It was certainly not considered safe to begin resumption with less than one-third reserve, and, as a matter of fact, the available balance in the Treasury amounted to over 66⅔ percent.

At the present time, under the practice of the Treasury, claimed to be in accordance with the Bank Act of 1882, $100,000,000 in gold coin is set apart for the redemption of the legal-tender notes, being rather less than 29 percent. This reserve would be regarded by prudent bankers as a minimum amount in an easy money market, but if the financial prospects should be threatening, prudence would require that it should be enlarged and strengthened. The practice of the Treasury, under Secretary Sherman, who put the resumption act in operation, was not to allow the reserve to fall below 40 percent, and, all things considered, this is probably the smallest amount consistent with absolute safety. If this ratio be adopted, the amount of the reserve in coin would be $138,000,000. Adding this amount to the amount heretofore stated as a reasonable working balance, we have the sum of $168,000,000 as the minimum balance which the Treasury should carry in order to be in a condition of ease and safety. Any other conclusion is at variance with lessons of experience and the well-established rules for the safe conduct of business.

The main argument urged for infringing on this balance must be the saving in interest on $68,000,000, which, after allowing for the tax on bank circulation, is 2½ percent per annum, amounting to $1,700,000 annually. But it is to be remembered that the demand debt of the United States, represented by the legal-tender notes, bears no interest and that the gain in interest between the total amount and a proper reserve is over $4,000,000 per annum, so that the Government can well afford the outlay required to keep its finances in the strongest possible position and should certainly never approach the point where, under the law, it might become necessary to sell United States bonds in order to preserve specie payments. Such a contingency would not be an edifying spectacle to a people whose proud boast it is that in twenty years from the close of the war it has paid off more than one-half the public debt and reduced the burden of interest to one-third of its original amount. Certainly a policy so humiliating would be condemned by the people when its effects shall become apparent.

In all measures affecting the currency of the country the greatest care must be taken not to interfere with its flexibility. This essential attribute of a safe currency must reside somewhere, its exact depository depending upon the system of banking in operation. Under our system of national banks, in which the issue of notes is limited to 90 percent of the bonded debt deposited to secure the circulation, the only flexible agency resides in the Treasury, by virtue of the power now exercised by the Secretary to make calls for the redemption of the public debt. It is a grave question whether such power should ever be intrusted to the Government or to the discretion of any official. In other conservative commercial countries it has been conferred upon intermediate agencies, in direct communication with the business interests of the people. We have no such system, and hence the Treasury has been forced to become a member of the New York Clearing-House, which is the financial center of the exchanges of the country. The Treasury is thus practically engaged in the banking business, not only in the issue of currency, but in adapting its operations to the general requirements of trade.

Dangerous as this system is, it was the outgrowth of necessity, and until some other security beside the bonded debt of the United States is devised for the issue of bank currency, the power to come to the relief of the money market in times of stringency must reside in the Treasury. The remedy is not to destroy or impair the only flexible element of the existing system in the calls of bonds, but to divorce the Government altogether from the banking business, and bring it back to its ancient and only legitimate function of collecting its revenues in lawful money, and of making its disbursements out of the money thus collected in accordance with law. This result can only be reached by the payment of the demand notes of the United States, and substituting through the national banks, or some other fiscal agency, an issue of currency subject to adequate taxation, properly secured and automatic in its expansion and contraction, the redemption of which will belong to the agency of issue and not to the Government, whose only function will then be to see that the security is sufficient and the general administration is carried on in accordance with the well-settled principles of safe banking.

One other consideration may be presented as a fatal argument against the reduction of the Treasury balance to $100,000,000 in coin, necessary at all times to be kept for the redemption of the legal-tender notes. The ability of speculators to reduce this balance below $100,-000,000 by presenting demand notes for payment is obvious, and unless the expedient for replacing the amount by the sale of bonds be resorted to, the money market could be so manipulated as to impair confidence and bring about a general disaster, by which the operators for a fall would reap abundant profits at the expense of the legitimate business of the country. Within a very recent period, when the Treasury was plethoric with money but with an impaired gold balance, all the indications pointed to a great disturbance to be effected by the hoarding or exportation of gold. Very strenuous efforts and decided measures were required to prevent the catastrophe, which at any time may occur when the danger line is passed in the reduction of the gold balance below the minimum reserve originally provided for the resumption of specie payments.

Being clearly of opinion that the proposed resolution will neither be economical, so far as the Government is concerned, nor advantageous to the business interests of the country, but in fact extremely dangerous in times of recurring stringency in the money market, I recommend that it be laid upon the table.

The South and Sound Money

SPEECH TO THE SOUTHERN CLUB OF NEW YORK, FEBRUARY 22, 1894

[*This is an example of Hewitt's skill with the informal after-dinner speech. It was delivered at a time when Southern voters and Southern Congressmen had largely gone over to the free-silver cause; and while it is full of wit, it is also full of frank rebuke. Congress was bitterly at odds with President Cleveland. Southern and Western leaders were urging a bill to coin the seigniorage gained by the Treasury under the Sherman Silver-Purchase Act, a bill which Cleveland eventually vetoed. Led by David B. Hill, the Senate had just refused to confirm two excellent judicial appointments made by Cleveland. Hewitt seized the opportunity to tell the South just what he thought of its recreancy to principle.*]

MR. PRESIDENT AND GENTLEMEN: This is the first time in my life that I have ever experienced how cool it might be in a Southern atmosphere. I am not only called upon, apparently, to begin the performances, but having picked up this program, I find upon it: "The National Credit, the Foundation of Our Industries—the Hon. John G. Carlisle." [1] Now, if there is any man in the world who fills me with envy and whose place I would like to take on any public or private occasion, or in any other official position or otherwise, it is my old friend, John G. Carlisle. No one who has served with the Secretary of the Treasury in Congress as long as I did could fail to conceive the highest admiration for his extraordinary lucidity of intellect, his sound judgment upon all abstract questions, and his capacity to apply fundamental principles to concrete cases.

I think he came nearer to the nickel-in-the-slot mechanisms than I have ever known in my life—you drop the premises in at the top, and the conclusion will come out irresistibly at the bottom. If the premises should happen to be wrong, however, you may be sure that the conclusion will be equally wrong.

Mr. Carlisle never expected, I think, to stand at the foundation of public credit. While he would, from the nature of his training and his intellectual endowments, be naturally the friend of sound currency and of the maintenance of public credit at all hazards, still I think if he

[1] At this time Secretary of the Treasury.

had had the selection of the job which he was called upon to do he would have chosen some other line of business. But we will all agree that, coming without experience into his great office, and without the training which fits men ordinarily for the consideration of matters of finance and the maintenance of credit, he has come up to the exigencies of the situation with a calm courage and a determination to wipe out any prejudices that might have existed in the past, and any errors of practice or of judgment that might, in his previous career, have been calculated to influence his judgment—that he has met the demands of the situation with courage, with promptness, and, I am glad to say, up to this point with absolute success.

And let me say, gentlemen, that the occasion has been most critical. I doubt whether at any time in the history of the country an emergency has arisen where prompt and sound decision was so necessary as it was in reference to the recent loans rendered necessary in order to prevent the bankruptcy of the Government.

Mr. Carlisle has shown his eminent fitness for the position which he occupies, and we of New York owe to him a debt of gratitude for the work which he has done. We owe many debts of gratitude to men who have been born south of Mason and Dixon's line.

You celebrate tonight the birthday of the greatest of all Americans. He was a typical Southern man; he represented a condition of society; he was brought up in the midst of established institutions which have passed away. Whatever may be said in regard to the existence of slavery in any portion of the Union—and in his day it existed in all portions— whatever may be said of it in reference to the slave or to the whites, there is one thing perfectly certain—that there was trained up in the midst of slavery a ruling class whose business it was to rule, and who fitted themselves for government by study, by training and grave responsibilities.

And it is a remarkable thing, in turning back to the history of the revolution, that no man from the South ever failed, not merely in his duty, but in the successful discharge of the great responsibilities which were imposed upon the leaders in that great contest.

Southern men, as a rule, are accustomed to take responsibilities, and I have observed that when they come here to New York they take all the responsibilities that they can lay their hands on. I do not know how many little responsibilities they take—it was the big ones that I was talking about.

They came here at the close of the war, without money, without influence, without prestige of any kind, and yet today there is no profession which is not adorned by men of Southern birth. They sit here in New York upon the bench. They fill the pulpit. They decorate the medical profession. They are in every branch of business. They dominate the Chamber of Commerce, and even my good friend Mr. Inman has to restrain the impetuous ardor of the Rapid Transit Commission lest we should wake up some morning and find that we can get from the Harlem to the Battery in less than an hour and a half.

I beg my Southern friends not to go too fast. Give us a rest. It seems to me that it is a great commentary upon the catholicity of this city, upon the cosmopolitan character of New York, which, whether the North, or the East, or the West, or the South like it or not, is the Clearing House of the brains of the nation. Here is a free field. We ask not the place of a man's birth. The arena is open to all, and the man who survives is the fittest to survive.

If you gentlemen from the South have made any places in this community, it is because you proved your title, and you have shown your fitness to be the leaders in finance, in law, and in every branch of business to which you have seen fit to devote yourselves.

I sometimes think that perhaps what we have gained has been the loss of the section from which you came, for, comparing the men whom we see representing the South in public life with the race of giants who from the foundation of the Government to the breaking out of the war represented the Southern portions of this Union in the Senate and in the House, and applying the gauge of statesmanship which is only to be derived from the study of history, I am compelled to say that some great change has come over the South, either in the loss of its best men or in the devotion of its best men to other pursuits than those of statesmanship.

If I depart in any respect from the standard of good taste in what I have said or may say, set it down first to the fact that I am speaking without preparation and from my own heart, and possibly giving expression to opinions which, if I had more time to meditate, I might see fit to retain within my own mind.

But you must remember that this age had been an age of preparation for the solution of great problems affecting the destiny of this people and of every people. You must remember that the century which is now closing has been one in which the forces of nature have been developed beyond the wildest dreams of the most poetic imagination. You must remember that a great fund of wealth such as the world never saw in any previous period of its history has been accumulated and that the problem before us is no longer the problem of production so much as it is the problem of just distribution, and in order to settle that question, which is the great problem for the next century, the highest order of statesmanship, the profoundest knowledge, the most intimate acquaintance with the fundamental laws upon which society must rest, are requisite.

Do you see among your Southern Representatives many signs of such study of these grave questions which have been pending in Congress? One Southern man is battling today in Congress for something in which he profoundly believes, in whith he has absolute faith. He wants to coin the seigniorage.

He might as well try to coin a vacuum! And yet he honestly believes it—and the bulk of his supporters, the majority of his supporters, are Southern Representatives and some newly discovered specimens of politics, hitherto unknown in the history of the world, found out in the West.

Now, the subject for Mr. Carlisle was the public credit. Can you imagine any foundation for public credit that is not based upon intrinsic value? Is it possible, by taking thought, to add a cubit to your stature? And yet all the propositions which have been made in reference to finance, coming mostly from the South, with an occasional help from the West, have been based upon the idea that something can be created out of nothing.

The fallacy can be stated very briefly and very simply. The amount of silver bullion that goes into a silver dollar can be purchased for about eighty cents in gold. The government puts its stamp upon that amount of bullion, and it is called a dollar. The difference between the true value and the current value—I might say the sham value at which the dollar was coined—is what is called the seigniorage. Now, this sham and fraud is proposed to be coined into more money. And more than that, every dollar of silver that is in the Treasury is represented by a certificate for which the owner has a right to demand a dollar as good as the gold dollar. That is the law as well as the foundation of public credit. Now, if all the silver in the Treasury today was sold at its market value there would be a shortage of $100,000,000 in gold to redeem the silver certificates and the silver dollars.

I said he might as well attempt to coin a vacuum. It is worse than that, it is a negative quantity upon the side of the vacuum that he proposes to coin.

Gentlemen, public credit cannot be maintained unless you can teach your fellow citizens of the South that there is no royal road to value; it is the result of labor honestly expended and is measured by the current value of the article in the world and by no other possible standard.

Get your Southern Representatives to rise to the standard of those great men who, from the date of the Government down to 1860, stood in the Congress of the United States, not only as statesmen representing the whole country, and not a part of it but as men who understood that the fundamental principles of values and property were the creation of a higher power, which no man by act of Congress can undo or overturn.

I see that other Representatives of the South have succumbed to the fallacy that positions on the bench of the Supreme Court of the United States are local questions, to be settled by the demand of some local politician upon the President to consider how the appointment will affect his political prospects and his following in some remote part of the Union. I had supposed that the Supreme Bench represented the whole United States and that every Senator and every member of Congress and every citizen, whether in Congress or out of it, had a right to demand that the place should be filled without regard to party politics and without regard to locality; that the men who should sit on that bench should be above suspicion; men whose character, attainments, and reputation were such as to command universal respect, and that this great place was not to be made a football for ward politicians to kick about from one end of the state of New York, and from one end of the United States, to the other.

Go and tell your Southern Representatives that Calhoun and Benton and Crawford and Rives, and the other great men who for so many years represented them in the Senate of the United States would have abandoned even the high position of Senator and gone home in sackcloth and ashes rather than to have degraded the great commissions which they held from their states into the mere servitude of a politician without reputation, without character, and without right to speak for the state of New York.

I suppose that, as I am only a reminiscence and a back number, I can afford to speak. You gentlemen who are younger than I am—have you convictions and the courage of your convictions? Your people had them even when they went to the dread arbitrament of war and sacrificed all that they held dear—life, property, everything—for the principle in which they believed. Are you less brave now? Are you less ready for sacrifice now than you were thirty years ago when you went into the great conflict?

Unless the South has degenerated from the high standard of conscience on which they then acted—although, as you know, I believe it was a mistaken conscience—you owe it to yourselves, and the people of the South owe it to themselves, to express to their Senators the opinion which they held in regard to the recent rejection of fit and able men for the Supreme Bench of the United States.

I do not know that I have said all that Mr. Carlisle would have said. Mr. Carlisle would have said what I have said in much less time and with much more force. I know the man so well that I am trying to give a feeble interpretation to what would be his convictions, to what would be his sentiments if he were here to speak for himself.

The foundation of public credit rests primarily upon honesty and secondarily upon physical facts. In other words, a rich country can have a large revenue because it is rich; a poor country can have a poor revenue because it is poor. You have an example in comparing the United States with Italy. The United States can afford much; it is today the righest country in the world, and therefore it can afford to have the most substantial standard of value. And in all this country there is no portion more richly endowed than the South.

And now I come to the point which your President has said I ought to be able to talk about when I stated I had nothing to say. He said: "Yes, you know something about the resources of the South, and you can tell these gentlemen what a magnificent position they have and how the United States is enriched by the fact that it includes the Southern territory and did not lose it, as it had a mighty good chance of doing about thirty years ago."

You have in the South every element of wealth. The foundation of all industry and production is, as you know, force stored up in the coal mines. The most important application which you can make of force is to the manufacture of iron and steel. You have in the South not only the most abundant stores of these raw materials for industry and for the production of wealth, but you have them so related to each other as to make the South absolutely beyond rivalry or competition by any portion of the habitable globe.

And yet, with these great stores of iron ore, which can be mined cheaper than anywhere else in the world, and of coal, which can be produced in larger quantities than in any other portion of the globe, lying near together, you have Southern Representatives in the Lower House and you have Senators in the Upper House contending that the South will be ruined if coal and iron are put upon the free list. How it would be possible to damage the interests of any portion of the country which has the power to produce coal and iron ore cheaper than any other place on the globe—how it could damage such a section to make these articles free—passes my comprehension.

I have very large interests in coal and iron in other parts of the Union, and some in the South. I can readily understand and do understand—I have a painful experience of the fact—that the possessors of these very cheap natural agents in the South can do very great damage to my interests elsewhere, and they have done it.

They have ruined many branches of business in which I have been engaged heretofore, simply because they can produce cheaper than I can. What protection would I have in New Jersey or Pennsylvania against the production of Alabama or Tennessee? How, under the Constitution, can it be given me?

And yet the Representatives of this very section of the country, which is able to undersell not only every other portion of the United States in distant markets, but to produce iron at a lower cost than any other place on the habitable globe, stand up there and demand that there shall be protective duties imposed upon coal and iron ore. Protection to whom? Certainly not to the South. And if the Southern Representatives have got the idea that they are going to protect Pennsylvania and New Jersey by these duties, they have risen to a degree of magnanimity which is not common in this world.

I cite these things in a formal, spasmodic way, only for the purpose of impressing upon you the fact that the Representatives who sit in Congress from the South are not up to the standard either of the great men who formerly sat there, or to the demands of the situation and the knowledge of the facts of the case.

Now, can this be accounted for? I account for it in this way: At the close of the war everybody in the South was ruined. Every man who had any ability immediately betook himself to some kind of business by which he could support himself and his family. The men who had most brains got out of the South, and those who could not get out stayed and devoted themselves to the development of the resources of which I have spoken, except that some of them went into the business of building towns on paper with enormous success. Those who could not get away and could not make a living at home in any regular branch of business went into politics.

They were mostly men who had not been trained as their fathers had been. They had not gone to college and received that mental discipline which comes from the study of fundamental principles. They were trained on the field of battle—brave, gallant, noble men, ready to die for the South as they are now ready to die for the Union. But they were ignorant of the fundamental principles of government, they were ignorant of the conditions upon which the great commercial exchanges of the world are made, and they had no experience of the nature of money, except to find that it very soon reached the vanishing point when it was paid to them for their supply or their services on the field.

I have met many of these men. They are my personal friends. They are honest, they are truthful, they are gallant—but they are ignorant. There is no other word to be used for it. And this panic through which we have passed, this depression is the fruit, not of the Divine Providence, but is the result of gross, crass ignorance, and nothing else.

And the votes of the men of the South, almost in solid phalanx—I am glad to say there were exceptions—the votes of the men of the South gave us the silver bill; they gave us most of these measures which my friend Mr. Gordon will tell you he had to combat at every point, step by step, and which were passed against the opposition of all the experience and all the accumulated wisdom of mankind. They are the men who are responsible for this legislation and for this dreadful depression from which they have been the greatest sufferers.

This is the lesson that I should like to drive home into every Southern mind here tonight, and those with whom you are related in the South: that there is no enemy of the public welfare so great as the fool who rushes in where angels fear to tread.

Capital and Labor

The Mutual Relations of Capital and Labor

SPEECH AT THE CHURCH CONGRESS, CINCINNATI, OCTOBER 18, 1878

[*The long depression, 1873-79, was a period of great discontent among industrial workers in America. For twenty years Hewitt had given part of his scanty leisure to a study of the labor problem. He had testified on labor before a Parliamentary Commission in England in 1867; he had formed a large collection of books on the subject. In New Jersey Cooper & Hewitt were known as model employers. When the railroad riots of 1877 inspired the House of Representatives to appoint a committee to investigate the condition of labor, Hewitt was made chairman. He made careful preparations, induced many important men—capitalists, economists, union leaders—to testify and gave the House evidence filling more than a thousand printed pages. Circumstances did not permit him to finish an interpretive report which he expected to attach to this evidence. But he distilled his conclusions into this careful address to a religious congress, of which he distributed 250,000 copies within a few years. For the time, its demands for a true partnership of capital and labor, for the stimulation of profit-sharing and stock-distribution among employees, and for the establishment of social insurance, were decidedly liberal. These proposals and Hewitt's marked friendliness toward labor unions attracted much attention.*]

The three cardinal and unchangeable facts of humanity are the individual, the family, and society. There is and can be no other basis for government or religion. The fundamental characteristic of the individual is personal liberty; of the family, love; and of society, justice. Personal liberty implies equality of rights and contains the germ of individual property, while justice implies its equitable distribution; and this distribution can only rest upon the axiom, "to each according to his work." The problem, therefore, presented to systems of religion and schemes of government is, to make men who are equal in liberty —that is, in political rights and therefore entitled to the ownership of property—content with that inequality in its distribution which must inevitably result from the application of the law of justice.

In the solution of this problem, all the ancient religions and governments absolutely failed. Briefly summed up, their progress was either from equality of property under the patriarchal system, or from equality of political rights under the early and rude democracies, into despotism in which no rights were respected, involving the almost total destruction of civilization and ending in the long night of the Middle Ages. With the Christian religion and the governments which have been based upon it as a foundation, the results have been directly the reverse. Christianity co-ordinates the individual, the family, and society into one harmonious scheme. It addresses itself to the personal conscience only, and its whole scope and efficacy is toward the development of the individual in all directions—physical, intellectual, and moral and spiritual. But the necessity for association in order to achieve results is not merely enjoined but is the cardinal principle upon which the Church itself is constituted. Individualism and association thus go hand in hand in the march of progress; and it is a most suggestive fact that in ancient times no considerable development of industry was ever achieved, and the reason is that either the energies of the individual were deprived of free play, or society was so organized that men could not work together in peace and harmony.

Looking back over the eighteen centuries since the Christian doctrine was first preached, it is not difficult to discover the methods by which its results have been accomplished; but to one of the apostles looking forward into the centuries which have now passed it was impossible to comprehend or to predict by what means Christianity would work out its beneficent purpose. So, throughout the whole course of its history its most devoted adherents, its ablest expounders, have not only mostly failed to discover its drift but have frequently resisted its march of progress, as we now see, toward the successive steps by which it is developing itself into the fullness of its beneficence.

Let two illustrations suffice to prove this proposition. If individual liberty is to be maintained, then government must rest upon the consent of the governed. To this proposition is opposed the principle of the Divine right of kings to govern, and yet until within a century this theory was maintained by the ablest men in the Church. Nevertheless, the right of the people to govern themselves asserted itself by silent and irresistible progress, based upon the growing convictions of mankind, until at last the whole theory of a Divine right to govern was overthrown in a cataclysm of blood at the close of the last century.

And so with personal slavery. When Christ began to preach a large portion of the human race was in bondage. He incited no insurrections. On the contrary, he counselled obedience to the law. Nevertheless, he preached a doctrine which, of its own innate power, has sufficed, by slow and silent growth, to undermine the foundations upon which the right of property in man was upheld, and in our own day and generation the last stronghold surrendered; and henceforth the equality of men as to political rights will not be seriously controverted. And yet, during the eighteen hundred years which have been required for the accomplishment of this result of Christian doctrine, many of the ablest and best men in the Church resisted the operation of that silent law, which has at length secured to man the liberty with which Christ intended to make him free.

These primary steps in the Christian scheme—namely, the establishment of the right of men to govern themselves and to own and control the fruits of their own labor—may thus be said to have been only completed in our own day.

GROWTH OF WEALTH

With the recognition of these rights has come a vast increase in the amount of wealth, which it is the object of society to accumulate and distribute. This growth in wealth is, so far as we can judge, the direct result of the physical, political, and mental enfranchisement of man. His energies, now for the first time unshackled, have penetrated into the boundless storehouse of nature, captured the invisible forces which have heretofore guarded her treasures and subjugated them to the service of the human race. But whether it be due to this cause or not, it is a fact that the growth of wealth has been contemporaneous with the enlargement of personal freedom.

The question of the distribution and ownership of property has always been one of primary concern to the human race, but when property is suddenly and enormously increased in amount, the question assumes a proportionably increased importance and is surrounded with increased difficulties. Even if it be admitted that the existing system of distribution at any given time is equitable, it does not follow that upon a sudden development of wealth from new sources and by new agencies the old methods of distribution would continue to be just.

Hence controversies are inevitable. In ancient times these controversies resulted in intestine war and the destruction of government and society. In Christian times these controversies have not resulted in social disintegration, but, on the contrary, the social forces have been steadily developed and strengthened. The explanation of this difference is to be found in the fact that Christ based the organization of society upon the principle of justice, and whatever differences may have existed as to what justice requires, the conscience of society has come more and more to recognize the fact that it is to be done at whatever cost to vested interests, and the progress of society shows conclusively that there is a steady advance in the direction of justice.

LABOR AND WAGES

The difficulties of the situation are, however, enormously increased by the fact of the comparatively recent enfranchisement of so large a portion of the human race. They have achieved liberty, but they have not inherited property which is the fruit of liberty. The principles upon which they are to receive their share of the results of human effort have not only not been defined but they have only begun to receive attention. Until the modern development of industry the compensation of labor had but little reference to what the labor might produce. The slave, the serf, the bondsman, was fed and clothed, and when freed he inherited the custom of being fed and clothed. Hence what may be termed the "custom of wages" was based upon what the laborer required to keep him in a condition for efficient labor. Any thing beyond this limit he could get only from the conscience of his employer, or by the force of his own will. The power of isolated men to resist and overcome the force of custom is very slight. No radical, or even appreciable, change can be effected except by a union among those who believe themselves aggrieved. In other words, the principle of association must be invoked in order to produce any marked departure from prevailing practice.

THE CONFLICT

Given, then, a state of things in which the wealth was in the hands of one class, who necessarily became the employers of labor instead of being its owners; and the muscular power in the possession of another class, possessing nothing besides muscle, and who out of the common results of the employment of capital and labor obtained only a bare subsistence, notwithstanding it was apparent that there was a steady increase in the amount of wealth, which, instead of being equitably distributed, was all appropriated by the employing class—it was inevitable, as it was just, that a struggle should arise to enforce a different ratio of distribution.

What is known as the conflict between capital and labor has thus a natural origin, and so far from being a subject of regret, it is to be welcomed as evidence of a healthy and growing vital force in the organization of society. It is an effort to correct an abuse; for, however ready we may be to admit that there must be inequality in the distribution of property proportioned to the contribution of each individual to its accumulation, no one has ever pretended that the entire surplus should go to one class at the expense and to the deprivation of another class. I know that natural laws are relied upon by the economists to effect this distribution, and I am not prepared to say that these natural laws might not assert themselves by some other methods than those which we find adopted by the contending forces of society. My purpose is rather to show the way in which the problem is being solved and to insist upon it that this particular way is not to be resisted and objected to because the abstract thinkers of the world would prefer some other method.

STRIKES AND LOCKOUTS

What is the method of solution which we find in process of execution? The working classes think they do not receive their fair share of the proceeds of productive industry. As individuals they ask for more. The demand is refused. They combine; they call themselves a "Trades-Union." As a Union they ask for more. The demand is again refused. They decline to continue to labor; in other words, they strike. Capital ceases to earn profit, and labor ceases to earn wages. Capital can feed upon itself for a time. Labor cannot. The strike fails, and labor has made no progress in obtaining what it believes to be its just rights. Labor takes a lesson from capital. It saves money from its scanty earnings as a reserve fund to sustain itself while in a condition of strike. Then, when sufficiently strong, it repeats the experiment. Sometimes it is successful, and sometimes it is not. The reserve is generally exhausted before success is achieved, and labor falls back, sullen, defeated, but resolute. The lesson of association is not lost. The unions in different trades combine and make common cause with each other, and when one union goes into a strike, the others assist. Thus they become a great power; and capital at length comprehends that profit can no longer be realized except by the consent of labor, and labor comprehends that while it can deprive capital of profit, it can only do so through an amount of personal suffering which tries the human heart to its utmost capacity, because it addresses itself to that love which is the foundation of the human family and is a co-ordinating element in the constitution of society.

Up to this point the progress has only been attended with evil, just as the progress of mankind toward free government and toward the enfranchisement of men was by a pathway strewn with the wrecks of human hopes and marked by sacrifices and calamities which no pen can describe. But one good result has been achieved. Labor is thoroughly organized and marshalled on the one side, while capital is combined on the other; each powerful to destroy the other if they engage in conflict, but equally powerful to assist each other if they work together in harmony. The contending forces are thus in a condition to treat. The great result achieved is that capital is ready to discuss. It is not to be disguised that until labor presented itself in such an attitude as to compel a hearing capital was not willing to listen, but now it does listen. The results already attained are full of encouragement; the way to a condition of permanent peace appears to have been opened.

CONCILIATION AND ARBITRATION

The first step was taken about fifteen years ago, when the principle of conciliation was successfully adopted at Nottingham. Conciliation necessarily led to arbitration, and as the direct result of conciliation and arbitration the necessity for strikes has been very largely diminished, so that it may now be affirmed that while strikes still take place, they are the exception, and not the rule. Let it not be supposed, however, that conciliation and arbitration are other than transitional means for bringing about the ultimate relations of peace and harmony which must exist between capital and labor before the vast evils which accompany modern industry can be eliminated or materially circumscribed.

Before attempting to point out the road which the law of Christian progress seems to be taking in this direction, I desire to reinforce what I have already said in regard to the power of trades-unions, singly and in combination, by a few figures. The strongest of the trades-unions in England is the Amalgamated Society of Engineers. They were organized in 1851. They have passed through many strikes. Sometimes they have failed and sometimes they have succeeded. They began with an accumulated fund of £1,700. The growth of this fund has varied, as a matter of course, with the demands which have been made upon it to sustain the members of the union during a strike; but the practical result is that in 1876 the fund in hand amounted to over £275,000, and the number of members, which began with 11,617, had risen to 44,578. The Society of Boiler Makers and Shipbuilders in ten years have accumulated a fund of £45,000. The Society of Carpenters and Joiners in sixteen years have accumulated a fund of £74,000. At the General Trades-Union Congress, held at Leicester in 1877, one hundred and twelve of these Unions were represented, with a membership of 691,089 persons.

These figures make it apparent that a new power has entered into the industrial world which must be recognized. It is also apparent that this power can not be destroyed by force or violence unless society be destroyed with it. It must be heard. Its just demands must be heeded. This is the voice of reason as well as of religion.

WEALTH AND CAPITAL

What are these demands, and how far are they just? In order to answer this question we must penetrate a little deeper into the true nature of what is called the conflict between capital and labor, and we must define what we mean by capital. All wealth is not capital. So far as this discussion is concerned, and so far as regards the conflict of which we are speaking, capital may be defined to be that portion of the wealth of society which is employed in the work of production and distribution. Outside of this portion of human wealth there is a vast fund which is otherwise employed—in ministering to the wants, the luxuries, the tastes, the charities of mankind. Now when a strike takes place it is in fact a contest between the laborers, *and not labor,* on the one hand, and the employer, *and not capital,* upon the other hand. In fact, the employer is not always, nor indeed in the majority of cases is he, the owner of the capital which he uses. Sometimes he owns none of it. It may be all borrowed; and, as a matter of fact some of it, to the extent of the current wages due and unpaid, is always borrowed from the very men whom he employs. No conflict, therefore, between capital and labor ever really takes place, nor indeed is it possible for it to occur. Between the individual who labors and the fruits of his labor there can in the nature of things be no conflict. The very object of his labor is to acquire these fruits, which we call capital, and the possession of this capital is necessary for increasing the productiveness of his labor. If this be true of any one man, it is true of all the men who make up society. Therefore, whether the individual or society be considered, there is no antagonism and there can be no conflict between capital and labor. The utmost that can happen is that they each cease to earn anything. Great suffering always results to the laborers, and very often ruin to the employer; and yet so far as labor and capital are concerned, while they are paralyzed for the time being they are not capable of rendering anything to each other but benefit. Still, there *is* a conflict going on—a conflict which the employer, as a rule, is powerless to mitigate, and which may ruin him, although he be the owner of no capital. In other words, the employer is often the victim of circumstances over which he has no control and of an antagonism which he rarely understands.

What is it that labor really aims to accomplish? It is to transfer to itself a larger portion of the proceeds of the business. If it succeeds, this portion must be taken either from the capital itself or from the profits of the business which have heretofore been appropriated to capital. It cannot be taken from the capital without either impairing the ability of the employer to pay wages, or compelling him to suspend business altogether; in which event labor fails utterly to attain its object. If, therefore, a concession is made by the employer which impairs the capital and he continues business, the impairment must be filled up from some outside source, and that source can only be that portion of human wealth which was not previously employed in the work of production and distribution. If, on the other hand, the demand of labor is met out of the profits, then the amount conceded is taken from that portion which would have been transferred from capital to this outside fund. In either case, therefore, the result is to withdraw a portion of the outside fund not in use as capital and transfer it to labor. The conflict, then, is a struggle for the ownership, not of active capital, but of that portion of the wealth of society which is used for other than productive purposes. In its essence, therefore, the conflict is between *riches and poverty*, and is an attempt to change the existing ownership of wealth.

RICHES AND POVERTY

We are thus brought face to face with the great underlying question whether property is equitably distributed. What are the facts? We find society practically divided into four classes. First, the very rich, who live without labor upon the proceeds of realized property, with super-abundant means which they are free to employ either as capital in business or to minister to their own desires, whether commendable or censurable. Second, the great middle class, who know neither poverty nor great riches, who are as a rule engaged in useful employments, who have more or less of the comforts and luxuries of life, and who are above the reach of want. Third, the industrious working classes, who possess little property, but who gain a decent livelihood for themselves and their families by their daily labor. They may be said to be poor only in the sense that they are liable to be reduced to want by sickness or by the chances and changes of business depriving them of the opportunity to work. Fourth, the paupers, who neither work nor care to work.

If the first and fourth classes should cease to exist, humanity would not have cause to shed many tears. The problem, then, which society finds itself forced to solve, is engaged in solving, is the mode of getting rid of these two extreme classes without revolution and without injustice. The relations of the second and third classes would be readily adjusted, because the transition from one to the other is not only very easy, but very constant. The ties between them are often the ties of family. Their interests are identical, and their relations to each other are such as can be and are substantially regulated by the principles of justice. As between them, it is scarcely necessary to discuss the limitations of wealth. But when we come to consider the position of the very rich, we are met by the self-evident fact that they possess and control an amount of property which is far beyond the capacity of any class of human beings of their limited number to contribute by their own efforts to the sum total of human wealth. In fact the present possessors have rarely accumulated the fortunes which they control. The possession of superfluous riches will not stand the test of human justice; and in affirming this I only repeat the conclusions to which the greatest thinkers and the best men who have ever lived have invariably been driven. But even if it were not reinforced by such authority, it is in accordance with the whole spirit and temper of the teachings of Christ

Himself. He nowhere condemns the ownership of property. On the contrary, when He tells us that the poor we shall have always with us, He expressly recognizes that there will be inequalities in the ownership of property. He states it as a fact. But He nowhere says that we shall always have the rich with us, and the spiritual danger of great riches is repeatedly enforced.

I use the word "rich" as the Saviour used it—in the sense of the possession of superfluous wealth. I do not pretend to say what is superfluous. It is not necessary for this discussion, nor do I think it will ever come within the province of legislation to decide that question. I think it will be settled by the action of causes now in operation, by which a larger portion of the accumulated wealth of society will be transferred from the class of the very rich to the class of the industrious poor, and that the struggle which we call the conflict of capital and labor will slowly and surely effect this transfer by the gradual growth of a better understanding between employers and employed, out of which will gradually come a different ownership of capital from that which now obtains.

CHANGE OF OWNERSHIP

How can this change of ownership be effected? Already the employers and the employed meet upon the equal ground of open discussion. Already they endeavor to persuade each other to conciliate opposing interests. Failing in this, they arbitrate, and, in order that the arbitration may be just, the employers at length produce their books of account and submit their ability to pay to the decision of a fair tribunal. On the other hand, the workingmen are free to proclaim their grievances and to assert their rights. They submit them to the arbitrament of reason; they accept the award of the tribunal; and it is to their everlasting honor that in no single instance have they ever refused to abide by the award. Having got upon the common ground of free and open discussion, it is not a difficult step to reach the ground of joint ownership. As business is now organized, the workmen do not participate directly in the profits, but they have a first lien upon the profits; in other words, they must be paid before any surplus remains for capital. If they desire to participate in profits directly, this prior lien must be given up, and its abandonment will demand far greater intelligence on the part of the workingmen than they have yet displayed. But they are rapidly advancing in all the qualities which go to form the basis of intelligent action. Better elementary education and larger privileges in the exercise of the elective franchise, and the acquisition of political knowledge and sound economic principles through the agency of night colleges, mechanics' institutes, and workingmen's clubs will soon prepare the way which will lead them to make the temporary sacrifice required to effect the great change in their social status which must inevitably attend the ownership of capital.

I shall be told (and I fully appreciate the force of the objection) that there are great difficulties in the way of associating employees in the ownership of the business in which they labor. So long as human industry is mainly controlled by individuals or firms composed of individuals, and so long as the laws impose individual liability upon all the partners for the acts of any partner, it will be impossible to associate a miscellaneous mass of workmen in the ownership of the business. But in England the old legislation has been entirely reformed, with the view to admit of such joint ownership upon almost any terms that may be agreed upon. In this country we need additional legislation, but in both countries there is one fact which points the way to an easy solution of the whole question, and that fact is the enormous growth of corporations for the conduct of industrial enterprises.

CORPORATIONS

Here, again, I detect one of those unseen agencies which so often in the progress of Christian development have been opposed, deplored, condemned, by the best and wisest men, and yet go on gaining, in spite of opposition and resistance, until they absorb the whole field of action. Although it is not fifty years since the first industrial corporation was organized, today corporations control more than half, if not two-thirds, of the manufacturing business of the world. It may be therefore assumed that the corporative principle is a necessity for the development of society and for placing its products upon a basis of equitable division. To attack corporations, therefore, as is still the fashion, is, so far as I can see, to attack that phase of human organization which offers the best promise for the advancement of the working classes. Of course corporations are liable to abuses, and in the early stages of their existence they assume powers which they should never possess. They develop evils, just as strikes have produced great suffering, although the end is seen to have been beneficent. Such evils are incident to progress under all circumstances. The most conspicuous example is to be found in the introduction of machinery, which has conferred benefactions upon mankind quite beyond the possibility of estimate. With the growth of machinery has come the displacement of labor and the growth of pauperism, evils almost intolerable, and yet by no means comparable to the greater evils which would spring from the abolition of machinery, the result of which would be universal pauperism. Because new agencies produce evils, we must not lose sight of the greater good of which they are capable, and which in reality they accomplish. Now the corporate principle is the only one which admits of the association of labor and capital upon the basis of an ownership distributed among those who contribute either capital or labor. Such an ownership is indispensable not merely to harmony, but to the achievement of the largest possible results and the equitable distribution of the products of human industry.

JOINT OWNERSHIP

This division of ownership must, however, spring not from charity but from mutual interest. The present owners begin to see that profits are impossible on the existing system, and labor is becoming sufficiently intelligent to understand that it must rely for compensation upon what the business can afford to pay. But until labor becomes an owner it never will understand the capacity of the business to pay. Heretofore great fortunes have been achieved mostly by monopoly of some sort or other, but the days of monopoly are now numbered. Even secrets are no longer kept, and the monopoly of a secret is limited by the duration of the patent. The exact condition not only of any particular business but of business of all kinds is now generally understood and will become more and more the common property of society. In no respect is the influence of the press more potent than in this direction. Henceforth the great object to be aimed at in the industrial world is rather steadiness and stability of business than excessive or spasmodic profits. When those who labor also become interested as owners, it will be easy to adapt the business to the conditions required for steady work; and the habit of association not only between workmen and employers but between different organizations engaged in the same kinds of business will go far to mitigate the evils of the competitive system, by placing checks upon reckless production involving sales at a loss and by united efforts to extend the markets through the promotion of increased consumption. In fact, increased consumption will necessarily result from the greater intelligence and improved condition of the working classes. It is idle to deny that self-respect usually increases with the possession of property. Property is a humanizing and refining agency. Increased production means lower prices, and lower prices mean increased consumption; and thus there is an entire harmony between the two agencies which are most concerned in the improvement of the condition of mankind.

In order that this joint ownership may be brought about, it is necessary, first, that the employers shall see that it is to their advantage to encourage the workingmen to become interested directly in the business; and, secondly, that the workingmen shall take the necessary steps to become owners. This they can only do by *abstinence*, which is the parent of capital. They must save in order to have. Their capacity for saving is far greater than is generally supposed, even out of the scanty earnings which they receive in times of depression. It is a matter of record that in the Schulze-Delitzsch organizations in Germany the workingmen who have become the owners of those successful and wonderful institutions, founded on the principle of "self-help," saved out of their small gains as much as 40 percent for a series of years together; and when one reflects upon the vast expenditures of the working classes in all civilized countries for tobacco, liquor, and other indulgences, which, to say the least, are productive of no advantage to them, it is easy to see that in a single year a large fund could be accumulated for investment in business enterprises, and that in a generation the whole capital invested in industrial undertakings might be transferred to the wage-earning class.

THE MISSION OF THE CHURCH

How are these results to be hastened? That they will come in the ordinary course of society I do not doubt, any more than I doubt the fatherhood of God and the brotherhood of man. But the Church and its ministers, and above all its intelligent laymen engaged in affairs, can hasten the good time coming by efforts to enlighten both those who employ and those who are employed; to point out that though these are evil times, yet they are not so evil as the times which have gone before; that there has been a steady, irresistible, unmistakable progress in the amelioration of the condition of mankind and the relations of men to each other; that the industrial strife which has been so conspicuous in our day, instead of being an indication of the decay and disintegration of society, is the evidence of progress toward a better state of things; and that the questions presented, although difficult at first, grow clearer and clearer day by day and are advancing to a solution which should comfort the patriot, console the philanthropist, and encourage the Christian.

I am aware that the unrest and agitations which prevail throughout the Christian world have caused great anxiety and apprehension in the minds of good men, amounting almost to despair of the future of the human race. The growth of Communism is cited as a discouraging omen for the future; but I have said enough to show that Communism is not possible in the Christian scheme as it has been developing itself for the last eighteen centuries; that the growth has been altogether toward individualism, and, individualism being secured, toward that kind of association, and that kind only, which preserves the individual right to liberty and property. Some point with despair to the depressed condition of modern industry and conclude that the social structure is about to fall. They cite the excess of commodities which has been produced by the association of capital and labor, the lack of employment consequent thereon, and the widespread suffering which unquestionably prevails as evidence that civilization is a failure. The fact is, that the energies of men have been almost altogether directed to the work of production. They have heretofore had no occasion to consider the question of proper distribution. In the nature of things, the question of distribution cannot become pressing until there is a very great surplus of production to be divided. Society, in reference to commodities, is today in precisely the situation in which China and India find themselves in regard to food. There is a famine in portions of those countries, although there is a surplus of food in other portions adequate for entire relief. Between the two, however, there is no proper means of communication or distribution. This was formerly the case in Europe; but food famines in Europe are now unknown, because channels of communication have been opened in all directions, and today England imports two-thirds of all the food which she consumes and yet is under no apprehension for the future. So in regard to commodities there is an industrial famine prevailing in one portion of society, an absolute want and destitution of those very commodities which are in great excess in other portions of society. In other words, we have the very rich and the very poor. Surely if man is equal to the task of distributing food he is equal to the task of overcoming the causes which lead to such industrial famines. The work in either case is the same—that of distribution; and I have endeavored to show that this problem has already presented itself as the great question of the age and that it is in process of solution by the agencies of association between workmen and employers, to be carried farther into more intimate association as copartners not merely in production, but in the division of the proceeds of their joint labor.

The evils, therefore, under which the world suffers are incidental to its progress and in fact compel progress. Indeed, it would not be difficult to show that the evils in any one age are mainly produced by the remedies which society has adopted to cure the greater evils of a previous age. In other words, the evils are transitory, the benefits are permanent, and the result of the whole is to place humanity upon a higher plane of intelligence, justice, and consequent happiness.

CONCLUSIONS

The points which I have sought to enforce are:

That the great question now pending is the equitable ownership of property and that no ownership which does not conform to the principles of justice will be tolerated by society.

That the present distribution of wealth does not conform to the principles of justice.

That distribution has been undergoing a change during the whole Christian era, and that this change has been to distribute the ownership more and more over the great mass of society; in other words, that of all the wealth of the world there is a larger percentage today held by the majority of mankind than at any previous period in the history of the world.

That this progress toward a more equitable distribution must result in the diminution of great fortunes, the improved condition of the poorer classes, and the consequent extinction of pauperism.

That the conflict between capital and labor, which has assumed such prominence in our day, resulting in strikes, conciliation, and arbitration, is a healthful but transitional stage toward a more intimate and beneficent association of capital and labor through the corporative principle.

That in the nature of things it would seem that corporations must continue to grow and absorb the great bulk of the business of the world, but that these corporations will be organized upon a distribution of ownership among those who are engaged in them, so that in the end the business of the world will be conducted by men in association with each other, each being directly interested in the ownership of the enterprise in which he is engaged.

That the result of the better understanding thus produced will be such an economy in the work of production as to cheapen commodities and extend their consumption, whereby the condition of mankind will be greatly benefited, and the resources which are now utterly wasted in the strife between capital and labor, resulting in strikes and lockouts, may be appropriated toward the creation and maintenance of funds to insure the working classes against the temporary evils which are necessarily produced by the introduction of machinery and the dislocation of labor from causes over which they have no control; that society owes indemnity in such cases to the industrious poor, and that the principle of life insurance, adopted already by the British government, points out the method by which such indemnity may be provided, not only without imposing additional burthens upon the producing classes, but that such a provision will be a measure of positive economy, extinguishing pauperism and largely reducing the necessity for public charity.

I am not disturbed by the objection which will be made to some of my positions, that they are at war with the received principles of political economy. Political economy deals only with one side of human experience—the laws of the production and distribution of wealth. It is founded upon observation, experience, and reason. Just as Christianity has assumed various phases in different ages of the world, so political economy will vary in its conclusions with the changes of society. Christianity, addressing itself to the moral nature of man, is the prime mover in producing these changes. Political economy must, therefore, follow, and not lead, Christianity and will conform itself to the conclusions at which society arrives in its progress toward a permanent moral order. What that moral order will be no man can pretend to predict, but that there is a procession toward it, all men can see; and political economy takes its place among the elements which go to make up that procession, and its truths when finally ascertained and settled will be found to conform strictly to the higher laws which bind man to his Maker by the great bond of love.

Finally, there is one consideration which must never be lost sight of. If during the last hundred years there had been no industrial development, the questions which now stir society to its foundations would never have forced themselves on public attention. It is the marvelous improvement in the condition of the human race during the present century which has brought into prominence and created the necessity of dealing with the evils which in previous ages passed unnoticed or were accepted as inevitable. The very growth and abundance of wealth make the inequalities of its distribution more apparent. The standard of conscience has been raised with the standard of comfort. The conflicts between labor and capital are more intense because there is more to contend for. Privilege slowly but surely recedes before the advance of knowledge. The question, "By what right?" penetrates the very heart of power, and is no longer answered by the plea of tradition. Thus at length the way is opened for the amelioration of humanity by growth instead of by revolution, and henceforth society will take no steps backward. Moreover, we can see, it may be as "through a glass darkly," that the methods by which the possibility of peaceful progress has been reached are in accordance with a divine order, not to have been predicted, but to be clearly seen as it develops results, and points the way to new triumphs of justice. The soul of man is thus cheered with hope, and at the same time taught humility, as it is admitted to glimpses, dim and shadowy though they be, of the beneficent plan and purposes of Him who

> Moves in a mysterious way
> His wonders to perform.

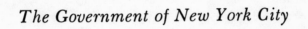

The Government of New York City

The Meaning of Brooklyn Bridge [1]

SPEECH AT THE OPENING OF BROOKLYN BRIDGE, MAY 24, 1883

[*The citizens of New York rightly considered the completion of Brooklyn Bridge a landmark in their history. It ranked with the Erie Canal, the Croton Aqueduct, and the Central Park as a public work which had contributed in a memorable way to the greatness of the city. Fifteen years of labor and ten millions of the taxpayers' money had gone into the structure. The plans drafted by John A. Roebling had received the approval of a municipal commission in 1869. Preliminary work at once began, and Roebling was making observations at the site when an injury to his foot resulted in lockjaw and death. His son Washington A. Roebling threw himself into the task of solving the many new problems which the huge structure involved. In 1872 he was taken unconscious from a caisson, and for most of the subsequent years he directed the work from his house in Brooklyn, which he was too ill to leave. President Arthur and Governor Cleveland came to New York for the formal opening. Hewitt had been chosen to make the principal address, and he gave to it as much time and pains as to any speech he ever wrote. In form and diction it is simplicity itself, but it expresses some searching ideas with memorable point and emphasis.*]

Two hundred and seventy years ago the good ship *Tiger,* commanded by Captain Adriaen Block, was burned to the water's edge, as she lay at anchor, just off the southern end of Manhattan Island. Her crew, thus forced into winter quarters, were the first white men who built and occupied a house on the land where New York now stands; "then," to quote the graphic language of Mrs. Lamb, in her history of the City,[2]

in primeval solitude, waiting till commerce should come and claim its own. Nature wore a hardy countenance, as wild and as untamed as the savage landholders. Manhattan's twenty-two thousand acres of rock, lake and rolling table land, rising at places to a height of one hundred and thirty-eight feet, were covered with sombre

---

[1] Reported in part only by the press; published in pamphlet form by the city.

[2] Martha J. Lamb (1829-93) published her *History of the City of New York. Its Origin, Rise, and Progress* in two large volumes, 1877-81; a work still standard.

forests, grassy knolls and dismal swamps. The trees were lofty; and old, decayed and withered limbs contrasted with the younger growth of branches; and wild flowers wasted their sweetness among the dead leaves and uncut herbage at their roots. The wanton grape vine swung carelessly from the topmost boughs of the oak and the sycamore; and blackberry and raspberry bushes, like a picket guard, presented a bold front in all possible avenues of approach. The entire surface of the island was bold and granitic, and in profile resembled the cartilaginous back of the sturgeon.

This primeval scene was the product of natural forces working through uncounted periods of time; the continent slowly rising and falling in the sea like the heaving breast of a world asleep; glaciers carving patiently through ages the deep estuaries; seasons innumerable clothing the hills with alternate bloom and decay.

The same sun shines today upon the same earth; yet how transformed! Could there be a more astounding exhibition of the power of man to change the face of nature than the panoramic view which presents itself to the spectator standing upon the crowning arch of the bridge whose completion we are here today to celebrate in the honored presence of the President of the United States, with their fifty millions; of the governor of the state of New York, with its five millions; and of the mayors of the two cities, aggregating over two million of inhabitants? In the place of stillness and solitude, the footsteps of these millions of human beings; instead of the smooth waters "unvexed by any keel," highways of commerce ablaze with the flags of all the nations; and where once was the green monotony of forested hills, the piled and towering splendors of a vast metropolis, the countless homes of industry, the echoing marts of trade, the gorgeous palaces of luxury, the silent and steadfast spires of worship!

To crown all, the work of separation wrought so surely, yet so slowly, by the hand of time, is now reversed in our own day, and "Manahatta" and "Seawanhaka" are joined again, as once they were before the dawn of life in the far azoic ages.

> It is done!
> Clang of bell and roar of gun
> Send the tidings up and down.
> How the belfries rock and reel!
> How the great guns, peal on peal,
> Fling the joy from town to town! [1]

"What hath God wrought!" were the words of wonder, which ushered into being the magnetic telegraph, the greatest marvel of the many marvelous inventions of the present century. It was the natural impulse of the pious maiden who chose this first message of reverence and awe to look to the Divine Power as the author of a new gospel. For it was the invisible, and not the visible, agency which addressed itself

[1] The opening stanza of J. G. Whittier's "Laus Deo."

to her perceptions. Neither the bare poles nor the slender wire, nor the magnetic battery, could suggest an adequate explanation of the extinction of time and space which was manifest to her senses, and she could only say, "What hath God wrought!"

But when we turn from the unsightly telegraph to the graceful structure at whose portal we stand, and when the airy outline of its curves of beauty, pendant between massive towers suggestive of art alone, is contrasted with the over-reaching vault of heaven above and the ever-moving flood of waters beneath, the work of omnipotent power, we are irresistibly moved to exclaim, What hath *man* wrought!

Man hath indeed wrought far more than strikes the eye in this daring undertaking, by the general judgment of engineers, without a rival among the wonders of human skill. It is not the work of any one man or of any one age. It is the result of the study, of the experience, and of the knowledge of many men in many ages. It is not merely a creation; it is a growth. It stands before us today as the sum and epitome of human knowledge; as the very heir of the ages; as the latest glory of centuries of patient observation, profound study and accumulated skill, gained, step by step, in the never-ending struggle of man to subdue the forces of nature to his control and use.

In no previous period of the world's history could this bridge have been built. Within the last hundred years the greater part of the knowledge necessary for its erection has been gained. Chemistry was not born until 1776, the year when political economy was ushered into the world by Adam Smith, and the Declaration of Independence was proclaimed by the Continental Congress, to be maintained at the point of the sword by George Washington. In the same year Watt produced his successful steam engine, and a century has not elapsed since the first specimen of his skill was erected on this continent. The law of gravitation was indeed known a hundred years ago, but the intricate laws of force, which now control the domain of industry, had not been developed by the study of physical science, and their practical applications have only been effectually accomplished within our own day, and indeed, some of the most important of them during the building of the bridge. For use in the caissons, the perfecting of the electric light came too late, though happily in season for the illumination of the finished work.

This construction has not only employed every abstract conclusion and formula of mathematics, whether derived from the study of the earth or the heavens, but the whole structure may be said to rest upon a mathematical foundation. The great discoveries of chemistry, showing the composition of water, the nature of gases, the properties of metals; the laws and processes of physics, from the strains and pressures of mighty masses, to the delicate vibrations of molecules, are all recorded here. Every department of human industry is represented, from the quarrying and the cutting of the stones, the mining and smelting of the ores, the conversion of iron into steel by the pneumatic process, to the final shaping of the masses of metal into useful forms, and its reduction into wire, so as to develop in the highest degree, the tensile strength which fits it for the work of suspension. Every tool which the ingenuity of man has invented, has somewhere, in some special detail, contributed its share in the accomplishment of the final result.

> Ah! what a wondrous thing it is
> To note how many wheels of toil
> One word, one thought can set in motion.

But without the most recent discoveries of science, which have enabled steel to be substituted for iron—applications made since the original plans of the bridge were devised—we should have had a structure fit, indeed, for use, but of such moderate capacity that we could not have justified the claim which we are now able to make, that the cities of New York and Brooklyn have constructed, and today rejoice in the possession of, the crowning glory of an age memorable for great industrial achievements.

This is not the proper occasion for describing the details of this undertaking. This grateful task will be performed by the engineer in the final report, with which every great work is properly committed to the judgment of posterity. But there are some lessons to be drawn from the line of thought I have followed, which may encourage and comfort us as to the destiny of man and the outcome of human progress.

What message, then, of hope and cheer does this achievement convey to those who would fain believe that love travels hand in hand with light along the rugged pathway of time? Have the discoveries of science, the triumphs of art, and the progress of civilization, which have made its accomplishment a possibility and a reality, promoted the welfare of mankind, and raised the great mass of the people to a higher plane of life?

This question can best be answered by comparing the compensation of the labor employed in the building of this bridge with the earnings of labor upon works of equal magnitude in ages gone by. The money expended for the work of construction proper on the bridge, exclusive of land damages and other outlays, such as interest, not entering into actual cost, is nine million ($9,000,000) dollars. This money has been distributed in numberless channels—for quarrying, for mining, for smelting, for fabricating the metals, for shaping the materials, and erecting the work, employing every kind and form of human labor. The wages paid at the bridge itself may be taken as the fair standard of the wages paid for the work done elsewhere. These wages are:

	Average Wages per Day
Laborers	$1.75
Blacksmiths	3.50–$4.00
Carpenters	3.00– 3.50
Masons and stonecutters	3.50– 4.00
Riggers	2.00– 2.50
Painters	2.00– 3.50

Taking all these kinds of labor into account, the wages paid for work on the bridge will thus average $2.50 per day.

Now if this work had been done at the time when the Pyramids were built, with the skill, appliances, and tools then in use, and if the money available for its execution had been limited to nine million ($9,000,000) dollars, the laborers employed would have received an average of not more than two cents per day, in money of the same purchasing power as the coin of the present era. In other words, the effect of the discoveries of new methods, tools, and laws of force has been to raise the wages of labor more than an hundredfold in the interval which has elapsed since the Pyramids were built. I shall not weaken the suggestive force of this statement by any comments upon its astounding evidence of progress, beyond the obvious corollary, that such a state of civilization as gave birth to the Pyramids would now be the signal for universal bloodshed, revolution, and anarchy. I do not underestimate the hardships borne by the labor of our time. They are, indeed, grievous, and to lighten them is, as it should be, the chief concern of statesmanship. But this comparison proves that through forty centuries, these hardships have been steadily diminished; that all the achievements of science, all the discoveries of art, all the inventions of genius, all the progress of civilization, tend by a higher and immutable law to the steady and certain amelioration of the condition of society. It shows that, notwithstanding the apparent growth of great fortunes, due to an era of unparalleled development, the distribution of the fruits of labor is approaching from age to age to more equitable conditions, and must, at last, reach the plane of absolute justice between man and man.

But this is not the only lesson to be drawn from such a comparison. The Pyramids were built by the sacrifices of the living for the dead. They served no useful purpose except to make odious to future generations the tyranny which degrades humanity to the level of the brute. In this age of the world such a waste of effort would not be tolerated. Today the expenditures of communities are directed to useful purposes. Except upon works designed for defense in time of war, the wealth of society is now mainly expended in opening channels of communication for the free play of commerce and the communion of the human race. An analysis of the distribution of the surplus earnings of man after providing food, shelter, and raiment shows that they are chiefly absorbed by railways, canals, ships, bridges, and telegraphs. In ancient times these objects of expenditure were scarcely known. Our bridge is one of the most conspicuous examples of this change in the social condition of the world and of the feeling of men. In the Middle Ages cities walled each other out, and the fetters of prejudice and tyranny held the energies of man in hopeless bondage. Today men and nations seek free intercourse with each other, and much of the force of the intellect and energy of the world is expended in breaking down the barriers established by nature or created by man to the solidarity of the human race.

And yet in view of this tendency, the most striking and characteristic feature of the nineteenth century, there still are those who believe and teach that obstruction is the creator of wealth; that the peoples can be made great and free by the erection of artificial barriers to the beneficent action of commerce and the unrestricted intercourse of men and nations with each other. If they are right, then this bridge is a colossal blunder and the doctrine which bids us to love our neighbors as ourselves is founded upon a misconception of the divine purpose.

But the bridge is more than an embodiment of the scientific knowledge of physical laws or a symbol of social tendencies. It is equally a monument to the moral qualities of the human soul. It could never have been built by mere knowledge and scientific skill alone. It required in addition, the infinite patience and unwearied courage by which great results are achieved. It demanded the endurance of heat, and cold, and physical distress. Its constructors have had to face death in its most repulsive form. Death, indeed, was the fate of its great projector, and dread disease the heritage of the greater engineer who has brought it to completion. The faith of the saint and the courage of the hero have been combined in the conception, the design, and the execution of this work.

Let us then record the names of the engineers and foremen who have thus made humanity itself their debtor, for a successful achievement, not the result of accident or of chance, but the fruit of design and of the consecration of all personal interest to the public weal. They are: John A. Roebling,[1] who conceived the project and formulated the plan of the bridge; Washington A. Roebling,[2] who, inheriting his father's genius

[1] John A. Roebling (1806-69) had been encouraged by Peter Cooper and Abram S. Hewitt in 1848 to remove his wire-rope factory from Saxonburg, Pa., to Trenton, N. J. There he obtained much of the iron for his wire cables and the other parts of his suspension bridges from the Cooper & Hewitt works; and he and Hewitt became warm friends.

[2] Washington Augustus Roebling (1837-1926) was the eldest son of John A. Roebling. The father died just as field work for the Brooklyn Bridge was beginning, and the son at once took his place as chief engineer.

and more than his father's knowledge and skill, has directed the execution of this great work from its inception to its completion, aided in the several departments by Charles C. Martin, Francis Collingwood, William H. Payne, George W. McNulty, Wilhelm Hilderbrand, Samuel R. Probasco as assistant engineers, and as foremen by E. F. Farrington, Arthur V. Abbott, William van der Bosch, Charles Young, and Harry Tupple, who, in apparently subordinate positions, have shown themselves peculiarly fitted to command, because they have known how to serve. But the record would·not be complete without reference to the unnamed men by whose unflinching courage, in the depths of the caissons, and upon the suspended wires, the work was carried on amid storms, and accidents, and dangers sufficient to appall the stoutest heart. To them we can only render the tribute which history accords to those who fight as privates in the battles of freedom, with all the more devotion and patriotism because their names will never be known by the world whose benefactors they are. One name, however, which may find no place in the official records, cannot be passed over here in silence. In ancient times when great works were constructed, a goddess was chosen, to whose tender care they were dedicated. Thus the ruins of the Acropolis today recall the name of Pallas Athene to an admiring world. In the Middle Ages, the blessing of some saint was invoked to protect from the rude attacks of the barbarians and the destructive hand of time the building erected by man's devotion to the worship of God. So, with this bridge will ever be coupled the thought of one, through the subtle alembic of whose brain and by whose facile fingers communication was maintained between the directing power of its construction and the obedient agencies of its execution. It is thus an everlasting monument to the self-sacrificing devotion of woman, and of her capacity for that higher education from which she has been too long debarred. The name of Mrs. Emily Warren Roebling will thus be inseparably associated with all that is admirable in human nature and with all that is wonderful in the constructive world of art.

This tribute to the engineers, however, would not be deserved if there is to be found any evidence of deception on their part in the origin of the work or any complicity with fraud in its execution and completion. It is this consideration which induced me to accept the unexpected invitation of the trustees to speak for the City of New York on the present occasion. When they thus honored me, they did not know that John A. Roebling addressed to me the letter in which he first suggested (and, so far as I am aware, he was the first engineer to suggest), the feasibility of a bridge between the two cities, so constructed as to preserve unimpaired the freedom of navigation. This letter, dated June 19, 1857, I caused to be printed in the *New York Journal of Commerce*, where it attracted great attention because it came from an engineer who had already demonstrated, by successfully building suspension bridges over the Schuylkill, the Ohio, and the Niagara rivers, that he spoke with the voice of experience and authority. This letter was the first step toward the construction of the work which, however, came about in a manner different from his expectations, and was finally completed on a plan more extensive than he had ventured to describe. It has been charged that the original estimates of cost have been far exceeded by the actual outlay. If this were true, the words of praise which I have uttered for the engineers who designed and executed this work ought rather to have been a sentence of censure and condemnation. Hence the invitation which came to me unsought, seemed rather to be an appeal from the grave for such vindication as it was within my power to make, and which could not come with equal force from any other quarter.

Engineers are of two kinds: the creative and the constructive. The power to conceive great works demands imagination and faith. The creative engineer, like the poet, is born, not made. If to the power to conceive, is added the ability to execute, then have we one of those rare geniuses who not only give a decided impulse to civilization but add new glory to humanity. Such men were Michael Angelo, Leonardo da Vinci, Watt, Wedgwood, Brunel, Stephenson, and Bessemer; and such a man was John A. Roebling. It was his striking peculiarity, that while his conceptions were bold and original, his execution was always exact and within the limits of cost which he assigned to the work of his brain. He had made bridges a study and had declared in favor of the suspension principle for heavy traffic, when the greatest living authorities had condemned it as costly and unsafe. When he undertook to build a suspension bridge for railway use, he did so in the face of the deliberate judgment of the profession that success would be impossible. Stephenson had condemned the suspension principle and approved the tubular girder for railway traffic. But it was the Nemesis of his fate, that when he came out to approve the location of the great tubular bridge at Montreal, he should pass over the Niagara River in a railway train on a suspension bridge, which he had declared to be an impracticable undertaking.

When Roebling suggested the bridge over the East River his ideas were limited to the demands of the time and controlled by the necessity for a profitable investment. He had no expectation that the two cities would embark in the enterprise. Indeed, in one of his letters so late as April 14, 1860, he says, "As to the corporations of New York and Brooklyn undertaking the job, no such hope may be entertained in our time." In eight years thereafter, these cities had undertaken the task upon a scale of expense far exceeding his original ideas of a structure, to be built exclusively by private capital for the sake of profit.

How came this miracle to pass? The war of the rebellion occurred, delaying for a time the further consideration of Roebling's ideas. This war accustomed the nation to expenditures on a scale of which it had no previous conception. It did more than expend large sums of money. Officials became corrupt and organized themselves for plunder. In the city of New York, especially, the government fell into the hands of a band of thieves, who engaged in a series of great and beneficial public works, not for the good they might do, but for the opportunity which they would afford to rob the public treasury. They erected courthouses and armories; they opened roads, boulevards, and parks; and they organized two of the grandest devices for transportation which the genius of man has ever conceived: a rapid transit railway for New York and a great highway between New York and Brooklyn. The bridge was commenced, but the ring was driven into exile by the force of public indignation, before the rapid transit scheme, since executed on a different route by private capital, was undertaken. The collapse of the ring brought the work on the bridge to a standstill.

It was a timely event. The patriotic New Yorker might well have exclaimed, just before this great deliverance, in the words of the Consul of ancient Rome in Macaulay's stirring poem,

> And if they once may win the bridge,
> What hope to save the town?

Meanwhile, the elder Roebling had died, leaving behind him his estimates and the general plans of the structure, to cost, independent of land damages and interest, about $7,000,000. This great work which, if not "conceived in sin," was "brought forth in iniquity," thus became the object of great suspicion and of a prejudice which has not been removed to this day. I know that to many I make a startling announcement, when I state the incontrovertible fact that no money was ever stolen by the ring from the funds of the bridge; that the whole money raised has been honestly expended; that the estimates for construction have not been materially exceeded; and that the excess of cost over the estimates is due to purchases of land which were never included in the estimates; to interest paid on the city subscriptions; to the cost of additional height and breadth of the bridge, and the increase in strength rendered necessary by a better comprehension of the volume of traffic between the two cities. The items covered by the original estimate of $7,000,000, have thus been raised to $9,000,000, so that $2,000,000 represents the addition to the original estimates.

For this excess, amounting to less than thirty percent, there is actual value in the bridge in dimension and strength, whereby its working capacity has been greatly increased. The carriage-ways, as originally designed, would have permitted only a single line of vehicles in each

304 The Meaning of Brooklyn Bridge

direction. The speed of the entire procession, more than a mile long, would therefore have been limited by the rate of the slowest; and every accident causing stoppage to a single cart, would have stopped everything behind it for an indefinite period. It is not too much to say that the removal of this objection, by widening the carriage-ways, has multiplied manifold the practical usefulness of the bridge.

The statement I have made is due to the memory not only of John A. Roebling but also of Henry C. Murphy,[1] that great man who devoted his last years to this enterprise; and who, having, like Moses, led the people through the toilsome way, was permitted only to look, but not to enter, upon the promised land.

This testimony is due also to the living trustees and to the engineers who have controlled and directed this large expenditure in the public service, the latter, in the conscientious discharge of professional duty; and the 'former, with no other object than the welfare of the public and without any other possible reward than the good opinion of their fellow citizens.

I do not make this statement without a full sense of the responsibility which it involves, and I realize that its accuracy will shortly be tested by the report of experts who are now examining the accounts. But it will be found that I have spoken the words of truth and soberness. When the ring absconded, I was asked by William C. Havemeyer, then the Mayor of New York, to become a trustee, in order to investigate the expenditures and to report as to the propriety of going on with the work. This duty was performed without fear or favor. The methods by which the Ring proposed to benefit themselves were clear enough, but its members fled before they succeeded in reimbursing themselves for the preliminary expenses which they had defrayed. With their flight a new era commenced, and during the three years when I acted as a trustee, I am sure that no fraud was committed and that none was possible. Since that time the Board has been controlled by trustees, some of whom are thorough experts in bridge building, and the others men of such high character that the suggestion of malpractice is improbable to absurdity.

The bridge has not only been honestly built, but it may be safely asserted that it could not now be duplicated at the same cost. Much money might, however, have been saved if the work had not been delayed through want of means and unnecessary obstacles interposed by mistaken public officials. Moreover, measured by its capacity and the

[1] Henry Cruse Murphy (1810-82), lawyer and political leader of Brooklyn, drafted and obtained the passage of the legislation required for the building of Brooklyn Bridge. He was president of the private company which launched the enterprise and also of the corporation which followed it. He labored valiantly to overcome all opposition to it.

limitations imposed on its construction by its relation to the interests of traffic and navigation, it is the cheapest structure ever erected by the genius of man. This will be made evident by a single comparison with the Britannia Tubular Bridge erected by Stephenson over the Menai Straits.[1] He adopted the tubular principle, because he believed that the suspension principle could not be made practical for railway traffic, although he had to deal with spans not greater than 470 feet. He built a structure that contained 10,540 tons of iron, and cost 601,000 pounds sterling, or about $3,000,000. Fortunately he has left a calculation on record as to the possible extension of the tubular girder, showing that it would reach the limits in which it could bear only its own weight (62,000 tons), at 1,570 feet. Now, for a span of 1,595½ feet, the Brooklyn Bridge contains but 6,740 tons of material, and will sustain seven times its own weight. Its cost is $9,000,000, whereas a tubular bridge for the same span would contain ten times the weight of metal, and though costing twice as much money, would be without the ability to do any useful work.

Roebling, therefore, solved the problem which had defied Stephenson; and upon his design has been built a successful structure, at half the cost of a tubular bridge that would have fallen when loaded in actual use. It is impossible to furnish any more striking proof of the genius which originated, and of the economy which constructed, this triumph of American engineering.

We have thus a monument to the public spirit of the two cities, created by an expenditure as honest and as economical as the management which gave us the Erie Canal, the Croton Aqueduct, and the Central Park. Otherwise, it would have been a monument to the eternal infamy of the trustees and of the engineers under whose supervision it has been erected, and this brings me to the final consideration which I feel constrained to offer on this point.

During all these years of trial and false report a great soul lay in the shadow of death, praying only to stay long enough for the completion of the work to which he had devoted his life. I say a great soul, for in the springtime of youth, with friends and fortune at his command, he gave himself to his country and for her sake braved death on many a well-fought battlefield. When restored to civil life his health was sacrificed to the duties which had devolved upon him, as the inheritor of his father's fame and the executor of his father's plans. Living only for honor and freed from the temptations of narrow means, how is it conceivable that such a man—whose approval was necessary to every expenditure—should, by conniving with jobbers, throw away

[1] The Menai Strait separates Anglesey from Carnarvonshire in North Wales. Robert Stephenson built the great railway bridge here, 1,841 feet long, for the L. M. S. Railroad, completing it in 1850. It still stands and does good service.

more than the life which was dear to him that he might fulfill his destiny, and leave to his children the heritage of a good name and the glory of a grand achievement? Well may this suffering hero quote the words of Hyperion:

Oh, I have looked with wonder upon those, who, in sorrow and privation, and bodily discomfort, and sickness, which is the shadow of death, have worked right on to the accomplishment of their great purposes; toiling much, enduring much, fulfilling much; and then, with shattered nerves, and sinews all unstrung, have laid themselves down in the grave, and slept the sleep of death, and the world talks of them while they sleep! And as in the sun's eclipse we can behold the great stars shining in the heavens, so in this life-eclipse have these men beheld the lights of the great eternity, burning solemnly and forever!

And now what is to be the outcome of this great expenditure upon the highway which unites the two cities, for which Dr. Storrs [1] and I have the honor to speak today? That Brooklyn will gain in numbers and in wealth with accelerated speed is a foregone conclusion. Whether this gain shall in any wise be at the expense of New York is a matter in regard to which the great metropolis does not concern herself. Her citizens are content with the knowledge that she exists and grows with the growth of the whole country, of whose progress and prosperity she is but the exponent and the index. Will the bridge lead, as has been forcibly suggested and in some quarters hopefully anticipated, to the further union of the two cities under one name and one government? This suggestion is in part sentimental and in part practical. So far as the union in name is concerned, it is scarcely worth consideration, for in any comparison which our national or local pride may institute between this metropolis and the other great cities of the world, its environment, whether in Long Island, Staten Island, or New Jersey wil always be included. In considering the population of London, no one ever separates the city proper from the surrounding parts. They are properly regarded as one homogeneous aggregation of human beings.

It is only when we come to consider the problem of governing great masses that the serious elements of the question present themselves, and [they] must be determined before a satisfactory answer can be given. The tendency of modern civilization is toward the concentration of population in dense masses. This is due to the higher and more diversified life which can be secured by association and co-operation on a large scale, affording not merely greater comfort and often luxury but actually distributing the fruits of labor on a more equitable basis than is possible in sparsely settled regions and among feeble communities. The great improvements of our day in labor-saving machinery and its appli-

---

[1] Richard Salter Storrs (1821-1900), a Congregational clergyman, was pastor of the Church of the Pilgrims, in Brooklyn, for more than fifty years. He was a leader in many forms of civic endeavor and the author of several historical works.

cation to agriculture enable the nation to be fed with a less percentage of its total force thus applied, and leave a larger margin of population free to engage in such other pursuits as are best carried on in large cities.

The disclosures of the last census prove the truth of this statement. At the first census in 1790 the population resident in cities was 3.3 percent of the total population. This percentage slowly gained at each successive census, until in 1840 it had reached 8.5 percent. In fifty years it had thus gained a little over 5 percent. But in 1850 it rose to 12.5 percent; in 1860 it was 16.1 percent; in 1870 it was 20.9 percent, having in this one decade gained as much as in the first fifty years of our political existence. In 1880 the population resident in cities was 22.5 percent of the whole population.

With this rapid growth of urban population have grown the contemporaneous complaints of corrupt administration and bad municipal government. The outcry may be said to be universal, for it comes from both sides of the Atlantic; and the complaints appear to be in direct proportion to the size of cities. It is obvious, therefore, that the knowledge of the art of local government has not kept pace with the growth of population. I am here by your favor to speak for the city of New York, and I should be the last person to throw any discredit on its fair fame; but I think I only give voice to the general feeling, when I say that the citizens of New York are satisfied neither with the structure of its government nor with its actual administration, even when it is in the hands of intelligent and honest officials. Dissatisfied as we are, no man has been able to devise a system which commends itself to the general approval, and it may be asserted that the remedy is not to be found in devices for any special machinery of government. Experiments without number have been tried, and suggestions in infinite variety have been offered, but today no man can say that we have approached any nearer to the idea of good government, which is demanded by the intelligence and the wants of the community.

If, therefore, New York has not yet learned to govern itself, how can it be expected to be better governed by adding half a million to its population, and a great territory to its area, unless it be with the idea that a "little leaven leaveneth the whole lump." Is Brooklyn that leaven? If not, and if possibly "the salt has lost its savor, wherewith shall it be salted?" Brooklyn is now struggling with this problem, it remains to be seen with what success; but meanwhile it is idle to consider the idea of getting rid of our common evils by adding them together.

Besides it is a fundamental axiom in politics, approved by the experience of older countries as well as of our own, that the sources of power should never be far removed from those who are to feel its exercise. It is the violation of this principle which produces chronic revolution in France and makes the British rule so obnoxious to the Irish people. This evil is happily avoided when a natural boundary circumscribes administration within narrow limits. While, therefore, we rejoice together at the new bond between New York and Brooklyn, we ought to rejoice the more that it destroys none of the conditions which permit each city to govern itself, but rather urges them to a generous rivalry in perfecting each its own government, recognizing the truth, that there is no true liberty without law, and that eternal vigilance, which is the only safeguard of liberty, can best be exercised within limited areas.

It would be a most fortunate conclusion, if the completion of this bridge should arouse public attention to the absolute necessity of good municipal government and recall the only principle upon which it can ever be successfully founded. There is reason to hope that this result will follow, because the erection of this structure shows how a problem analogous to that which confronts us in regard to the city government has been met and solved in the domain of physical science.

The men who controlled this enterprise at the outset were not all of the best type; some of them, as we have seen, were public jobbers. But they knew that they could not build a bridge, although they had no doubt of their ability to govern·a city. They thereupon proceeded to organize the knowledge which existed as to the construction of bridges; and they held the organization thus created responsible for results. Now, we know that it is at least as difficult to govern a city as to build a bridge, and yet, as citizens, we have deliberately allowed the ignorance of the community to be organized for its government, and we then complain that it is a failure. Until we imitate the example of the Ring and organize the intelligence of the community for its government, our complaint is childish and unreasonable. But we shall be told that there is no analogy between building a bridge and governing a city. Let us examine this objection. A city is made up of infinite interests. They vary from hour to hour, and conflict is the law of their being. Many of the elements of social life are what mathematicians term "variables of the independent order." The problem is, to reconcile these conflicting interests and variable elements into one organization which shall work without jar and allow each citizen to pursue his calling, if it be an honest one, in peace and quiet.

Now, turn to the bridge. It looks like a motionless mass of masonry and metal; but as a matter of fact it is instinct with motion. There is not a particle of matter in it which is at rest even for the minutest portion of time. It is an aggregation of unstable elements, changing with every change in the temperature and every movement of the heavenly bodies. The problem was, out of these unstable elements, to produce absolute stability; and it was this problem which the engineers, the organized intelligence, had to solve, or confess to inglorious failure. The problem has been solved. In the first construction of suspension bridges it was attempted to check, repress, and overcome their motion, and failure resulted. It was then seen that motion is the law of existence for suspension bridges, and provision was made for its free play. Then they became a success. The bridge before us elongates and contracts between the extremes of temperature from 14 to 16 inches; the vertical rise and fall in the center of the main span ranges between 2 ft., 3 ins., and 2 ft., 9 ins.; and before the suspenders were attached to the cable it actually revolved on its own axis through an arc of thirty degrees, when exposed to the sun shining upon it on one side. You do not perceive this motion, and you would know nothing about it unless you watched the gauges which record its movement.

Now if our political system were guided by organized intelligence, it would not seek to repress the free play of human interests and emotions, of human hopes and fears, but would make provision for their development and exercise, in accordance with the higher law of liberty and morality. A large portion of our vices and crimes are created either by law or its maladministration. These laws exist because organized ignorance, like a highwayman with a club, is permitted to stand in the way of wise legislation and honest administration and to demand satisfaction from the spoils of office and the profits of contracts. Of this state of affairs we complain, and on great occasions the community arises in its wrath and visits summary punishment on the offenders of the hour and then relapses into chronic grumbling until grievances sufficiently accumulate to stir it again to action.

What is the remedy for this state of affairs? Shall there be no more political parties, and shall we shatter the political machinery which, bad as it is, is far better than no machinery at all? Shall we embrace nihilism as our creed, because we have practical communism forced upon us as the consequence of jobbery and the imposition of unjust taxes?

No, let us rather learn the lesson of the bridge. Instead of attempting to restrict suffrage, let us try to educate the voters; instead of disbanding parties, let each citizen within the party always vote, but never for a man who is unfit to hold office. Thus parties, as well as voters, will be organized on the basis of intelligence.

But what man is fit to hold office? Only he who regards political office as a public trust, and not as a private perquisite to be used for the pecuniary advantage of himself or his family or even his party. Is there intelligence enough in these cities, if thus organized within the parties, to produce the result which we desire? Why, the overthrow of the Tweed ring was conclusive evidence of the preponderance of public

virtue in the city of New York. In no other country in the world and in
no other political system than one which provides for, and secures universal suffrage would such a sudden and peaceful revolution have been
possible. The demonstration of this fact was richly worth the twenty-five
or thirty millions of dollars which the thieves had stolen. Thereafter,
and thenceforth, there could be no doubt whether our city population,
heterogeneous as it is, contains within itself sufficient virtue for its own
preservation. Let it never be forgotten that the remedy is complete;
that it is ever present; that no man ought to be deprived of the opportunity of its exercise; and that, if it be exercised, the will of the community can never be paralyzed. Our safety and our success rest on the
ballot in the hands of freemen at the polls, deliberately deposited, never
for an unworthy man, but always with a profound sense of the responsibility which should govern every citizen in the exercise of this fundamental right.

If the lesson of the bridge, which I have thus sought to enforce, shall
revive the confidence of the people in their own power and induce them
to use it practically for the election to office of good men, clothed, as
were the engineers, with sufficient authority and held, as they were, to
corresponding responsibility for results, then indeed will its completion
be a public blessing, worthy of the new era of industrial development
in which it is our fortunate lot to live.

Great indeed has been our national progress. Perhaps we, who belong
to a commercial community, do not fully realize its significance and
promise. We buy and sell stocks, without stopping to think that they
represent the most astonishing achievements of enterprise and skill in
the magical extension of our vast railway system; we speculate in wheat,
without reflecting on the stupendous fact, that the plains of Dakota and
California are feeding hungry mouths in Europe; we hear that the
Treasury has made a call for bonds, and forget that the rapid extinction
of our national debt is a proof of our prosperity and patriotism as
wonderful to the world as was the power we exhibited in the struggle
which left that apparently crushing burden upon us. If, then, we deal
successfully with the evils which threaten our political life, who can
venture to predict the limits of our future wealth and glory—wealth
that shall enrich all; glory that shall be no selfish heritage, but the
blessing of mankind. Beyond all legends of oriental treasure, beyond all
dreams of the Golden Age, will be the splendor, and majesty, and happiness of the free people dwelling upon this fair domain; when fulfilling
the promise of the ages and the hopes of humanity, they shall have
learned how to make equitable distribution among themselves of the
fruits of their common labor. Then indeed will be realized by a
waiting world, the youthful vision of our own Bryant:

Here the free spirit of mankind at length,
Throws its last fetters off; and who shall place
A limit to the giant's untamed strength,
Or curb its swiftness in the forward race!
Far, like the comet's way through infinite space,
Stretches the long untraveled path of light
Into the depths of ages; we may trace
Distant, the brightening glory of its flight,
Till the receding rays are lost to human sight.

At the ocean gateway of such a nation, well may stand the stately figure of "Liberty enlightening the World;" and, in hope and faith, as well as gratitude, we write upon the towers of our beautiful bridge, to be illuminated by her electric ray, the words of exultation, *Finis coronat opus.*

Education

Liberty, Learning, and Property [1]

DEDICATION OF THE NEW BUILDINGS OF COLUMBIA UNIVERSITY,
MORNINGSIDE HEIGHTS, MAY 2, 1896

[*Hewitt was always a loyal alumnus of Columbia University. He was a warm friend of three successive presidents—Frederick A. P. Barnard, Seth Low, and Nicholas Murray Butler; he was chairman of the trustees of Barnard College for many years; and in 1901 he became a trustee of Columbia itself. Twice he made an earnest effort to bring about a union between Columbia and Cooper Union. It was natural that when the new site on Morningside was dedicated he should be chosen as the orator of the day. Part of his address was devoted to a delineation of the importance of Columbia's rôle in the history of New York City. But the more important part was a refreshingly plain-spoken reminder to wealth of its social and cultural duties. The year was 1896; Bryan and the agrarian discontent he represented were soon to be arrayed against McKinley and his stand-pat supporters; most addresses made by orthodox Eastern leaders to Eastern audiences dwelt with the rights and immunities of property rather than with its obligations. But Hewitt declared that "the time has come for a new and nobler civilization," and painted a glowing picture of what New York might be when "the wealth which has accumulated in this city by the joint association of its people, and to which every human being contributes by his industry, shall come to be regarded as a sacred trust to be administered in the public interest for works of beneficence to all."*]

This occasion and these impressive ceremonies are intended to recognize the trinity of religion, learning, and patriotism. It is most fitting that such a conjunction should be celebrated on these Morningside Heights, consecrated by the blood of heroes in a conflict which first showed the ability of the Continental militia to hold their own against trained British soldiers whose valor had been proved on many a hard-fought field. It is meet and right that the ministers of the churches which were associated in the foundation of King's College, and that the Bishop and other clergy of the noble Cathedral which hard by is slowly

[1] Published in pamphlet form by Columbia University.

rearing its majestic proportions to Heaven, should lend to this occasion the benediction of their presence and their prayers. It accords with the fitness of things that the presidents and faculties of the great sister institutions of learning, which are the pride of the closing, and the hope of the coming century, are here to rejoice with Columbia in the day of her rejoicing and to renew with her the pledge to train up a free people in the virtue and knowledge on which their liberties depend. It is well for the Governor and the regents of the University of the great State of New York, by whose wise and timely legislation Columbia College was reorganized and endowed with an estate, which enables it at this late day to realize the expectations of the far-seeing legislators who declared that she was to become "the mother of a university," to witness the fulfillment of the prophecy of the fathers, on a scale of grandeur beyond the dreams of the most sanguine friends of sound learning. But above all, the presence of the Mayor of New York and of the members of the Corporation, its aldermen and commonalty, in this great audience assembled, is proof of the deep and abiding interest which the city has in the final dwelling place of an institution which, as I shall hope to show, has contributed largely to its growth, is the most striking monument of its progress, and must be its guide in the development which promises to make it chief among the cities of the world.

Such a rare concurrence of piety, learning, wisdom, and authority indicates that this occasion has a significance which demands and justifies an explanation, familiar as it must necessarily be to the students of history and to the friends of education, but necessary in order to comprehend the genesis and the mission of the new university, destined to radiate its influence for good in all time to come from these buildings which we are here to dedicate to the service of God and man. Let it be remembered, however, that we are here not to dedicate buildings alone but also to dedicate to the responsibilities and duties of advancing civilization the wealth, the energies, and the potentialities of the millions of men who will in the ages to come constitute the population gathered around this center of light and learning.

It is well that these ceremonies have been inaugurated by unfurling the national flag, which is the emblem of the sovereignty of the people. In every clime and under every form of government the flag represents the principle of loyalty to the constituted authority. Patriotism is not peculiar to any land nor to any people but is the property of humanity wherever organized society exists. But with us the flag has a special significance. It represents not merely love of country but something more. It is not only the ensign of the whole people, but it is the evidence of the liberty of the citizen, without which the stars and stripes would be for him but a badge of slavery. We are accustomed to speak of our Government as an "indestructible union of indestructible states," and in one sense this is a true definition, but in a larger spirit the Republic is rather to be regarded as an aggregation of units, every one of which is an independent citizen with equal rights and correlative duties.

But whence is the citizen to derive his knowledge of the nature of his rights, and how is he to rise to the full measure of the performance of his duties? Political knowledge is not a natural endowment. It is the growth of painful experience and the outcome of training through ages of effort and sacrifice. The history of the world is the record of its acquisition. In its range are included the lessons of every age and every nation. Heroes and saints, statesmen and demagogues, tyrants and traitors have alike made their contributions to its evolution. The silent masses of the people have suffered and died in order that humanity might at length achieve freedom. There is not a region on this great globe which has not made its mark upon the final record which we call civilization.

But among all the peoples of the world, to none has the opportunity been so propitious for waging the conflict between right and wrong, for carrying on the struggle between ignorance and knowledge as in this land of ours, which seems to have been reserved under the providence of God for settlement by men who were dominated by a single idea, for which they were prepared to sacrifice home and comfort and wealth and all that men usually hold dear. The idea of personal liberty, which elsewhere was an abstraction, was made a reality in a new land, and the only land in which no aristocracy had ever existed and privilege was unknown. They were enthusiasts who came to a region where there were no prejudices to encounter, no abuses to overcome, no traditions to fetter the free spirit of man. While they claimed the right to worship God according to the dictates of conscience, they held this right always subordinated to the individual liberty of the citizen. In whatever else they may have differed among themselves or with their neighbors, civil liberty was never in question, and its rights were asserted whenever and wherever assailed by kings, governors, or parliaments. They regarded liberty as an end, and not as a means. "To secure it, to enjoy it and to diffuse it was the main object of all their social arrangements and of all their political struggles. They held it to be the inalienable prerogative of man, which he had no right to barter away for himself, and still less for his children. It was a sacred deposit, and the love of it was the main instinct engraven in their hearts." These pioneers of freedom understood that without education liberty would perish from the land in which they had sought refuge. They were not numerous, but they were as prolific as they were earnest, self-reliant, and independent. It is estimated that the three millions who inhabited the British colonies which joined in the Revolution were descended from less than one hundred thousand immigrants, nearly all of whom could read and write, and some of whom were very learned men and statesmen of the highest order. They realized the value and necessity of education in order to preserve the liberty which they sought in a new world, and which they were prepared to defend at the peril of life and fortune. Hence they founded schools and colleges, even before they had acquired the primary comforts of civilization. Whatever else their children might lack, they were to be instructed in the knowledge of their political rights and their religious duties. Hence from the first religion and education were the inseparable guardians of liberty, equality, and property. These three primary elements of the social organization were never separated and indeed never separable in the minds of the exceptional men who laid the foundations of the Republic upon the inalienable rights of man. They justly held that private property was the concrete expression of liberty and that any interference with property was an attack upon individual liberty. They believed that all men had an equal right to acquire and hold property, but they recognized that this very equality of opportunity would necessarily involve inequalities of possession, due to capacity, thrift, and energy. Thus were developed communities of freemen, in which each man was master of himself, equal to every other man before the law, and recognizing no claim upon his property to which he had not assented as the price of the maintenance of order and the dispensation of justice.

While the love of liberty and its dependence upon education were recognized in all of the thirteen colonies, Massachusetts founded Harvard College one hundred years, Connecticut founded Yale fifty years, and Virginia founded William and Mary sixty years before New York had made any provision for higher education. Her youth were thus forced (reluctantly, perhaps, but probably to their gain) to resort for education to these institutions, which were afterward denounced by the enemies of freedom as "nests of sedition." It is provided in the will of the father of a patriot whose fame constitutes one of the chief glories of our college [1] that his son should never "be sent to the colony of Connecticut for his education, lest he should imbibe in his youth that low craft and cunning which they disguise under the sanctified garb of religion."

And yet, to the cadet of a New York family, graduated at Yale, we owe the fundamental condition in the charter of King's College, granted in 1754, that no tests shall "exclude any person of any religious denomination whatever from equal liberty and advantages of education." [2]

[1] The will was made by Robert R. Livingston (1718-75) and the son was Chancellor Robert R. Livingston (1746-1813), a graduate of King's College in 1765.

[2] William Livingston, a graduate of Yale in 1741, as a young lawyer in New York established in 1752 a weekly journal called the *Independent Reflector*. It took a

Moreover, in the long and bitter controversy which preceded the granting of the charter, the principle was laid down for the first time in the colonies that it was the duty of the state to provide for the education of all its children, free from the control of sectarian religious influence. The ideas thus propounded by William Livingston, the statesman and patriot, have all been incorporated into the legislation of the several states of the Union, and at length in the new constitution of the State of New York it is made a fundamental provision that no public money shall ever be appropriated to any educational institution under the control of any religious denomination.

The delay in the establishment of an institution for higher learning in New York was due, however, not so much to indifference or to opposition, as to the extraordinary variety in the nationality and religious belief of its inhabitants. Unlike New England, it was not homogeneous in creed or in race. It is said that eighteen different languages were spoken in the colony, and there were certainly thirteen different churches in the city of New York prior to the Revolution. When, however, at length the college came to be chartered, the leading denominations were all represented in the Board of Trustees, and so far as instruction was concerned, unlike the colleges of New England, it was absolutely unsectarian. Nevertheless, King's College was the special care of the Church of England, and its site was the gift of Trinity Church upon condition that its president should always be a communicant of the Church of England.[1] If, however, it were thus expected that its graduates would be less devoted to the principles of individual liberty and the right of self-government, its promoters made a grievous mistake, for in the controversies which were soon to ensue between the colonies and the mother country, there were no more earnest advocates of the doctrine inherited from their Dutch, as well as from their English ancestry, that taxation should not be imposed without consent and without representation. It was the lucid and cogent argument of these patriots which called forth the eloquent eulogium of the elder Pitt that they occupied the very first rank among logicians and statesmen. Even the large land holders of the State of New York were on the side of free government. Between them and the patriots of New England in the long struggle for liberty and equality there was entire sympathy of

prominent part in the discussion over the religious qualifications for the Board of Trustees of King's College. Seven of the trustees were, by the act of November, 1751, to be of the Church of England, two of the Dutch Reformed Church, and one of the Presbyterian Church. Livingston himself was chosen as the Presbyterian member.

[1] Trinity Church in May, 1755, conveyed to King's College the land enclosed by Church, Barclay, and Murray Streets and the Hudson River. It stipulated not only that the president should always be a member of the Church of England, as Mr. Hewitt says, but that the liturgy of the church should always be used in the service of the college. Beyond this there was no condition or stipulation of a religious nature.

feeling and harmony of action. The contest was conducted in the main by college-bred men in all the colonies, while in the rank and file of the army there was scarcely a man who had not received a good common-school education. The feeling of equality which thus prevailed universally was not without its drawbacks when it became necessary to introduce military discipline. Here, upon the very ground where we stand, it was complained that each soldier seemed to regard himself as responsible for the issue of the battle, and followed the dictates of his own judgment rather than the orders of his superior officer. Washington, after the conflict was over, gave expression to his annoyance by the issue of a general order which expressly enjoined the necessity of obeying orders without assuming to question their wisdom. Nowhere and at no time during the struggle for independence was the fundamental idea of political equality ever forgotten, and when success was finally achieved, in every document which has been preserved, the blessings of liberty are declared to be the end and object of all the sacrifices of life and fortune which the struggle involved.

In this struggle the sons of our college bore a conspicuous and noble share. They were in fact not many in number but of unusual parts and probably better trained in sound learning, especially in the classics, than their compatriots from the other colonies. The first president of the college, Samuel Johnson, was a man of great piety and learning, the friend and companion of Berkeley, and the correspondent of his illustrious namesake, the lexicographer.[1] In view of what our college is now doing and what it hopes to accomplish, it may be well to put on record here the aims which Dr. Johnson proposed to himself in the conduct of the institution which he had undertaken to organize:

A serious, *virtuous and industrious* course of life being first provided for, it is further the design of this college to instruct and perfect the youth in the learned languages and in the arts of reasoning exactly, of writing correctly, and speaking eloquently; and in the arts of numbering and measuring, of surveying and navigation, of geography and history, of husbandry, commerce and government; and in the knowledge of all nature in the heavens above us and in the air, water and earth around us, and the various kinds of meteors, stones, mines and minerals, plants and animals, and of everything useful for the comfort, the convenience and elegance of life in the chief manufactures relating to any of these things. And finally to lead them from the study of nature to the knowledge of themselves and of the God of Nature and their duty to Him, themselves and one another, and everything that can contribute to their true happiness both here and hereafter.

I think it will be conceded that if our university shall be able to cover this ground and to accomplish the results expected to be produced by

[1] Dr. Samuel Johnson (1696-1772), a native of Guilford, Conn., and a graduate of Yale, was brought from his parish at Stratford in 1755 to take charge of the infant King's College. He was a friend of Bishop Berkeley and Benjamin Franklin, the holder of a doctorate of divinity from Oxford, and a man of great learning and piety. In 1763 he retired, and Myles Cooper became the second president.

the college course, no just criticism or complaint will ever be made by the most ardent friend of education.

Certain it is that the scheme outlined in the original circular was carefully followed for more than one hundred years, during which the standard of scholarship was always of a high order, and the cultivation of morality and honor was maintained as the primary object of education.

If, as I have said, the leaders in the struggle for independence were college-bred men, the foundation of the Government and the formation of the Constitution was pre-eminently their work. Of the fifty-five members of the Constitutional Convention of 1787 nine were graduates of Princeton, four of Yale, three of Harvard, two of Columbia, one of Pennsylvania, seven of William and Mary, and six of foreign colleges. The small number from Columbia was due to the fact that New York sent but three delegates to the Convention, but its two sons, Alexander Hamilton and Gouverneur Morris, were with Madison and afterwards with Jay in the "Federalist," the very bulwarks of that instrument which is acknowledged to be the most wonderful and successful political achievement ever devised by the wit of man. It is a mistake, however, to suppose that the Constitution was the application of a preconceived theory of government. It was, in fact, only the deliberate and inevitable expression of the ideas and experience of a people who had settled in the wilderness in order to enjoy social and religious liberty. They had fought and suffered for individual liberty, for equality before the law, and for the rights of property which they would not permit to be diminished even by taxation for public purposes without their own consent. The Constitution aimed, therefore, to secure to the individual citizen the right to labor in his own way, security for the property thus acquired, and absolute equality before the law. The essence of the Constitution is to be found in the declaration that "No man shall be deprived of life, liberty or property without due process of law." To make this declaration effective, the States were prohibited from passing "any law impairing the validity of contracts." Inasmuch as all contracts relating to property are practically solvable in money, the right "to coin money and regulate the value thereof is reserved to the Federal Government, while the States are forbidden to make anything but gold or silver a legal tender for the payment of debts." A supreme and unique tribunal is created to protect the citizen in his rights of person and property, and a National Government established which deals directly with the individual citizen and guarantees him in the enjoyment of these fundamental rights. Thus the whole history of our people culminates in the fruition of the idea which led to the settlement of the country, produced the War of Independence and created the Constitution, the individual right to liberty, and the equality of citizens before the law.

If the construction of the Constitution was thus a triumph of patriotism over what appeared to be insuperable difficulties, its ratification by the States was only achieved by memorable efforts of wisdom and statesmanship. The battle was really fought out in the State of New York, where Hamilton, Jay, Morris, and Livingston, who were the sons of our alma mater, overcame the opposition of Clinton,[1] whose sturdy patriotism and great services to the cause of liberty made him a formidable foe. While the decision was still in doubt the impatient people of this city determined to celebrate the ratification of the Constitution, which was secured by the adhesion of the State of New Hampshire before the New York Convention could be induced to act. In the procession, which was the first of many memorable celebrations of a similar character, the professors and students of Columbia College took a conspicuous part. On the banner under which they marched were inscribed the words: "Science and Liberty mutually support and adorn each other." The author of this legend (certainly not remarkable for classic grace) could by no possibility have anticipated the potentialities for New York which were involved in these simple words. Liberty was indeed secured by the Constitution just ratified, but science was in its cradle. The principle of gravitation had been discovered, and the composition of air and water had recently been disclosed, but the application of this knowledge had not yet been made in America. Not a single steam engine had been erected on the continent, and beyond the rude application of a few water powers, all forms of industry were still carried on by hand. But the country was a land of unbounded resources, and its inhabitants, animated by individual energy and protected by law, were well prepared to undertake the conquest of a continent and to develop its possibilities of wealth. The free spirit of the nation was thus loosened at the very juncture when science entered upon the career of discovery and development which has crowded the nineteenth century with great achievements and produced a sum of wealth far exceeding all the results of the eighteen preceding centuries of the Christian era. No pen can describe, no imagination can conceive the material triumphs of which this generation has been the witness and the partaker.

The favorable geographical position of New York gave it the natural primacy in this development, and its sons were not slow to see and to take advantage of its opportunity. DeWitt Clinton, the first graduate of Columbia College after the Revolution, created the Erie Canal, by which the wealth of the great West was opened up and poured into the

---

[1] George Clinton (1739-1812), Revolutionary general and first governor of the State of New York.

lap of New York. Robert R. Livingston (another graduate), the great chancellor who administered to Washington the oath of office, recognizing the genius of Fulton, supplied the means which made steam navigation a success. John Stevens, an alumnus of Columbia College, gave us the railway and the screw propeller, which have revolutionized transportation by land and by sea and enabled us to feed the teeming millions of Europe. Thus were supplied the stimulus which has made the century now closing a very carnival of enterprise, and an uninterrupted triumph of science and industry.

But in order that the results of genius and energy may be made beneficial to society, the protection afforded by government and by law must be assured. This work fell to the lot of James Kent, appointed in 1793 Professor of Law in Columbia College. His lectures to the students, afterwards expanded into his *Commentaries on American Law,* have had a deeper and more lasting influence in the formation of the national character than any secular book of the century. The rapid growth of wealth tends to undermine that respect for the rights of property which were imbedded in the Constitution, and hence the timely exposition of the great chancellor, followed, as it was, by the exhaustive commentaries of Mr. Justice Story, became the inspiration of the conservative legislation which has characterized all the States of the Union and produced that respect for law which is the most striking trait of our people, and which preserved the Federal Union in its time of peril.

Enough has been said to show not only that Columbia College has thus contributed its full share to the creation of the free Government, which is our chief glory, but that in the marvelous material development which has taken place under its influence and protection, the achievements of her sons have been of transcendent value. They have certainly made New York the largest and richest city on the Western continent, with possibilities of progress which promise to make it the metropolis of the world. With this conclusion we might rest the case of Columbia College in the consciousness that her past is at least secure. But this occasion takes note of the past only as the pioneer of the present and the promise of the future.

A nation is not great because it is rich, any more than a man is a hero because he is a millionaire. The question is not how much riches we have accumulated but what we are doing with them. Is this great store of wealth being used merely for the acquisition of more wealth and for the satisfaction of material wants and pleasures, or does a fair share of it go to the gratification of the spiritual needs of humanity and for its elevation into a higher and purer atmosphere?

These questions cannot be answered without a few words upon the nature and origin of the wealth which we find concentrated in the city of New York. Broadly it may be stated to be of two kinds—the one altogether material, in the form of commodities, houses and other visible property in which the value is due to the expenditure of labor and skill upon raw material; the other element of wealth is invisible and conventional, but none the less possessing commercial value because the world is willing to pay for genius, taste, beauty, and potential utility. The most important form of this invisible value resides in that increment in the selling price of land, which comes from the mere presence and aggregation of population. It is estimated that one-half of the assessed value of real estate in the city of New York is of this conventional nature. Its evolution in this country is phenomenal, and it goes on steadily advancing because of the unceasing growth in urban population. When the Government was founded about 3 percent of the people resided in towns. Today over one-third of the nation is dwelling in cities containing more than ten thousand people. The land which then was unsaleable and was often abandoned to the tax gatherer, has become a source of wealth even where no structures have ever been erected on its surface. This increase in value, not due to any effort on the part of the owner, inures under our system of property solely to his benefit. It could not be otherwise without violating the principle of individual liberty on which our political system is based. The law imposes no obligation upon this form of property except the payment of taxes according to a general and uniform rate upon all property. And yet there is a feeling in the public mind that value created by the general effort has in morals attached to it certain obligations of trust, which do not inhere in other property produced by the labor and capital employed in the walks of industry and of commerce. In the city of New York, where the unearned increment has been most marked and can be most easily studied, it is interesting to observe how under natural laws, without the intervention of legislation, a very large portion of this increase has already been devoted to public use. Most of the large estates which, at the time of the founding of the College, extended uninterruptedly from its site on Murray Street to the limits of Manhattan Island, have already passed from the families of their original owners and are now distributed among the community at large. The exceptions are today mostly devoted to public uses. Thus the King's farm, under the ownership of Trinity Church, is altogether used for religious and charitable objects. The same statement holds good of the property of the Dutch Church, of the New York Hospital, of the Sailors' Snug Harbor, and largely of the Lenox [1] estate. The city of

[1] That is, the estate of James Lenox (1800-1880); he founded the Lenox Library, now part of the New York Public Library, and gave generously to the Presbyterian Church and Presbyterian Hospital, and to the College of New Jersey. His father Robert Lenox, a Scot by birth, had owned a thirty-acre tract on Manhattan Island.

New York is itself the greatest beneficiary of this principle, because it is the largest handholder within its limits and possesses a vast amount of other property and of franchises incident to property, the proceeds of which all go into the public treasury. Its other possessions have been secured by taxes levied mainly on real estate, which by the rise in value has been enabled to stand the heavy assessments for streets, parks, schoolhouses, and the other necessary adjuncts of municipal life. Careful investigation will, I am convinced, prove that the total amount, which may be fairly regarded as due to the unearned increment of real estate, is represented substantially by the aggregate value of the property devoted to the public use, either under the direct control of the municipality or in the numerous public institutions administered by trustees for the general benefit. The unearned increment, therefore, so often the subject of inconsiderate denunciation, is rather to be regarded as the equivalent of outlays made in the public interest, and as the measure as well as the means of development into a higher municipal life, due to a healthy growth in civilization. While it may appear that in a few striking instances, an excessive proportion of this fund has been secured to private ownership, the opportunity thus afforded to intelligent and conscientious capitalists to execute works of great public utility, which might otherwise be impossible or too long deferred, more than compensates for any temporary drawbacks incident to the personal control of large possessions, subjected as they always must be to the salutary influence of public opinion.

But Columbia College is perhaps the most prominent example of the beneficent operation of the natural tendency by which the unearned increment sooner or later is devoted to the public welfare. Its original buildings were erected by the proceeds of two lotteries authorized by the state and by modest contributions from the enlightened friends of education at home and abroad. Its site consisted of about six acres of land, the gift of Trinity Church, which held the King's farm in trust for the promotion of religion and learning. Its value in 1754 was estimated by President Johnson at $16,000. In 1814 the state of New York, desirous to rid itself of the burthen of the Botanic Garden (which had been founded by Dr. Hosack,[1] one of the most enlightened sons of Columbia), transferred to the latter the fee of about sixteen acres of unproductive land in the vicinity of what is now 50th Street and Fifth Avenue, estimated at the time to be worth about $20,000. These parcels of land now constitute the source from which the permanent revenue of the institution is derived. They are estimated to be worth twelve millions of dollars, and yield at the present time an annual revenue of

[1] David Hosack (1769-1835), the son of one of General Amherst's soldiers, was educated at Columbia College and Princeton, and after receiving his medical degree in Philadelphia, held the professorship of botany and materia medica in Columbia.

$400,000. This property practically enables higher education to be sup-
plied at about one-half the actual cost of its provision. Thus Columbia
College is not merely a great educational agency, in which New York
takes special pride because it is the product and evidence of its growth,
but it is also a standing monument to the wisdom of our political
system, founded on individual liberty and the security of property.

While this process of incrementation was thus slowly but surely
progressing, it must be conceded that Columbia College, in common
with the other institutions of learning throughout the country, fell into
a condition of comparative stagnation, in marked contrast with the
activity in the material and industrial world. It continued, indeed, to
perform its original work of educating Christian gentlemen—men, who,
as Herodotus says, "could ride and shoot and tell the truth," and whose
influence in the community tended to promote conservative action and
to mitigate the demoralizing influence of the mere pursuit of wealth.
The trustees of the college, upon whose roll for a century appear the
names of the foremost citizens of this state, were at no time insensible
to the desirability of extending its educational advantages so as to bear
some adequate proportion to the growth of the city in population and
enterprise. In 1810, in accordance with an able report presented by
Rufus King, in which the primary principle of all sound education was
declared to be "the evolution of faculty and the formation of habit,"
changes were made in the curriculum and in the discipline of the institution, which, however, failed to enlarge the demand for its privileges.
In 1854, when the old college site became available for revenue, a comprehensive university scheme was devised by a committee of the trustees,
chief among whom was Dr. Henry James Anderson [1] (of sweet and
precious memory to the alumni of his time), which was justly regarded
as the beginning of a new era in the educational history of the United
States. Although this scheme was not at the time made operative, it
resulted in securing for Columbia College the services of President
Barnard, under whose enlightened administration the initial steps leading to the present university development were taken. There is nothing
more touching in the long history of the college than the devotion by
President Barnard of his modest fortune to the execution of the plans
which he had never ceased to urge for university extension and to which
he had consecrated his life and given the results of his ripe experience
and vast resources of learning.

But the efforts of the colleges everywhere, even if they had been
endowed (as they were not) with ample means, would have failed in

[1] Dr. Anderson (1799-1875) was professor of mathematics, analytical mechanics,
and physical astronomy in Columbia College 1825-43. Hewitt had been one of his
most brilliant students and as a young man had filled Dr. Anderson's place during
a temporary absence.

view of the fact that the demand for instruction in the liberal arts had actually fallen off in this country, in consequence of the diversion into industrial pursuits of the most promising and intelligent young men, to whom the rewards of business were more attractive than the delights of learning. It is a remarkable fact that from the beginning of the century down to the conclusion of the late Civil War, there was an actual decline in the number of students who graduated at the various colleges in proportion to the whole population. In other words, while the country was growing in wealth, the conservative influence of sound learning was steadily diminishing, with the depressing results which are manifest today in every department of public life, in the halls of legislation, and in the sensational character of the public press.

The natural balance between the ethical and material elements of civilization has thus been deranged, and in the city of New York this dislocation is far greater than in any other portion of the land, because there is a greater disparity of wealth on the one side and poverty on the other, due largely to the vast influx of foreigners, many of them illiterate, who have been landed chiefly in this port. While the general average of wealth has more than doubled in fifty years, indicating a vast improvement in the condition of the people at large, there has been a differentiation between the two extremes of the scale—the very poor and the very rich—without a precedent in the history of society and accompanied by an accumulation of disturbing questions which unless wisely dealt with threaten an aggravation of discontent dangerous to social order.

Perhaps the most conspicuous feature of the time is the remarkable manner in which competition, heretofore regarded as the prime element of progress, is being checked and curbed by the principle of association. We have been made very familiar by the great extension of corporations during the last half century, with the beneficent results which spring from associated action. But of late the principle of combination has taken on a new and strange development, under which corporations are associated together for the purpose of controlling production and regulating prices. Contemporaneous with this new development, and, indeed, anterior to it, combinations of workmen have been formed to regulate wages and to determine who shall be permitted to labor in the walks of industry. The individual liberty of the citizen has thus been attacked on the one hand by trusts, and on the other hand by trades-unions with an exhibition of power which threatens its very existence, and which, if finally triumphant, would overthrow the fundamental principle upon which our free Government was founded.

The same tendency toward the restriction of the liberty of the citizen can be detected in our recent politics. We have been taught, and have always believed, that free government could only be based upon the representative system, and yet of late it is manifest that this system fails in its aims and its results. The representative is no longer the choice of the people, but is the product of elaborate machinery, managed by men who devote themselves to politics in order to gain a livelihood. The will of the people no longer finds expression except when it happens to accord with the interests of the leaders who have practically put universal suffrage into commission.

We have been accustomed to rely in this country upon the public press for guidance and for the dissemination of sound principles in morals and politics. Indeed, the press has been regarded as the very palladium of liberty, and yet within our day sensationalism has largely taken the place of reasonable discussion, and far too many of the metropolitan newspapers seem to have substituted greed for love of truth, and profit for the dignity of leadership.

Foreign immigration, which during the earlier part of the century was encouraged as a necessary means of development, and which in fact has largely contributed to the rapid growth of the country, has become a dangerous element, because much of it is now illiterate and of a character not easily assimilated into the general mass of the people. The magnitude of the danger may be inferred from the fact that we have received 18,000,000 of foreigners in the last twenty-five years too many of whom are not in sympathy with our institutions and cannot discharge the ordinary duties of the citizen. Again, the franchise has been diluted in the Southern states with illiteracy to such an extent as to compel objectionable methods of interference in order to preserve society from peril, if not from ruin. The rights and duties of the suffrage are therefore undergoing a new discussion, the outcome of which is involved in great uncertainty. It may be predicted, however, that if limitations shall be prescribed they are more likely to be imposed upon the rich than upon the poor.

Crime also is thought to be on the increase and to grow faster than the population. This ominous exception to the general experience of civilized nations in modern times shows that there is a radical and dangerous defect in our social system, to which the serious attention of the legislators might well be transferred from the contentions of foreign nations, in which we have but a sentimental interest.

Another manifestation of the time is the frequent and extensive dislocation of labor in all branches of industry, by which numbers of deserving persons are suddenly deprived of the means of livelihood. This is no place to discuss how far this condition is due to unwise legislation, but the fact is to be noted that at no time in the history of the country has there been such general discontent among the working classes as there is today in the presence of superfluous wealth controlled by a small number of individuals.

Although these are indeed serious evils, fraught with great peril to our republican institutions, there is not one of them which would not yield to the magic touch of knowledge and patriotism. Beset with difficulty as the task may be, and novel as some of the problems unquestionably are, they are not more formidable than those which were successfully solved by the great men of the Revolution and the framers of the Constitution. In the great crisis of the Civil War, and in the work of the reconstruction of the Union, involving the restoration of a sound financial system, statesmen were found equal to the responsibilities they were compelled to carry. Even the disputed Presidential succession, in our own day, was decided in a spirit of patriotism which called forth the plaudits of the world.

While we strive to take courage from these proofs that the heart of the people is still sound, we are dismayed by the existence of a Congress which stands dazed by the complexities of the tariff and is in doubt whether there is a standard of value. Under the operation of the new constitution expressly amended to secure for the State of New York a reform in the civil service and to protect its citizens from the politicians, we are forced to recognize the supremacy of an autocrat unknown to the law and holding no commission from the people.

These are depressing facts, which might well make us despair of the Republic if we could not detect in many quarters, and especially from the possessors of the great wealth, which is to some extent responsible for the decay of statesmanship, the evidence of a reaction as healthy as it is reassuring. Thoughtful men, everywhere and in every rank of society, have come to the conclusion that the main cause of the degeneration of which we complain, is to be found in lack of knowledge, not merely among the politicians, but among the people at large. Hence, there is a general demand for education, not such as suffices merely for the performance of the ordinary duties of life and the conduct of industrial enterprises, but of a higher order, plainly required for the successful administration of public affairs and calculated to raise the standard of intelligence and morals.

The feeling is rapidly spreading that the time has come for a new and nobler civilization. A spiritual wave like that which produced the crusades, erected the cathedrals and the universities in the Middle Ages, or the later movement which culminated in the Renaissance and in the Reformation is plainly in sight and ready to usher in the advent of the next century, when the question will be, not as in the eighteenth century, "What are the rights of man?" or in the nineteenth century, "How these rights are to be made available for the production of wealth?" but rather what is the duty of society in regard to the use of wealth which has thus been created.

Already we can see the effect of this coming movement. In the present generation there has been a sudden and wonderful outbreak among rich men to endow higher institutions of learning, which they instinctively recognize as the true saviours of society. Not only have large benefactions been made to the existing colleges by which Harvard and Yale and Princeton and Columbia have been converted into true universities, but new universities have been munificently endowed by Cornell, Johns Hopkins, Rockefeller, and Stanford, thus perfecting the chain of higher learning from the Atlantic to the Pacific Ocean. The smaller colleges and the technical schools have not been overlooked in this avalanche of munificence, but its characteristic feature is the recognition that something higher and nobler is needed in order to save the coming century from the materializing influence of the great increase of wealth in the nineteenth century. It is a confession that the mere knowledge of facts is not sufficient for the elevation of character, but that the ethical and spiritual side of man's nature needs the nutriment which can only be supplied by scholars and teachers who devote their lives to the pursuit of truth without regard to its material rewards.

These considerations, which are true of the country at large, apply with peculiar force to Columbia College, which in the nature of things must become the foremost university, of the foremost city, of the foremost state, of the foremost country in the world. What opportunity, what possibility, what duty is implied in these simple words? How the souls of its faculty and its trustees must be inspired by the greatness of the undertaking! Confided to their hands is a vast fund, contributed not by individuals, but the product solely of the growth of New York. They must and do recognize, therefore, that its first duty is to the city by whose progress it has been thus enriched.

A city is not great because it contains many dwellings and covers much territory. Its greatness does not consist in mere numbers and in commerce. Its eminence is determined by the character of its civilization and by its provision for the material, intellectual, and spiritual wants of its citizens. Life, liberty, and property must be secured, order maintained, and the law enforced. The best system and appliances of education must be provided for its children; there must be adequate means of recreation from infancy to old age; the young must be trained to habits of obedience and diligence; outlets must be provided for their physical energies, and the spectacle of young men growing up without occupation must be removed from the conscience of the community, which is violated when there is no opportunity to learn mechanical trades—the natural outlet for their physical and mental powers. The population must be properly housed, perfect sanitary conditions must prevail, the standard of living must be raised, and parks and pleasure grounds provided on a scale which will enable every dweller in the city to exclaim:

I care not, Fortune, what you me deny,
You cannot rob me of free Nature's grace.

Schools for commercial and technical education must be provided at night, so that artisans of talent and ambition may have the opportunity to develop natural capacity to its full extent; the evil influence of demoralizing resorts must be counteracted by the opening of museums of art, science, and industry, so that the population may become familiar with the highest types of beauty and the results of genius; free libraries and reading rooms must be provided on a scale demanded by the intellectual wants of an intelligent population; such provision should be made for the sick and poor that there will be no excuse for the presence in its avenues of tramps and beggars; its streets should be well paved and clean; transit should be speedy and cheap, and, above all, the churches should be conducted in a spirit so liberal as not merely to cultivate the religious instincts of men but to exert a spiritual influence upon the rising generation through social organizations intended to amuse, instruct, and refine.

Such will be the great city of the future, and such a city New York will be if the Columbia University, whose new birth we celebrate today, shall be enabled to perform its mission as the teacher and exponent of the best results of civilization. It is evident, however, that New York is in a formative condition and has not yet attained to the ideals of municipal excellence. It seemed to realize its imperial destiny when, in 1837, it introduced an adequate water supply. In 1854 it recognized its coming greatness by the creation of the Central Park; it was an inspiration of municipal genius when the Museums of Art and Natural History were founded upon a basis which secured the co-operation of enlightened and munificent citizens in providing admirable collections in the buildings erected by the city. The same policy will now give to New York the great free library which has been rendered possible by the private beneficence of Astor, Lenox, and Tilden, whose endowments should be devoted solely to the increase of its collections and the expenses of administration. In fulfillment of the great ideals which have thus been slowly developed the city is now preparing to expend vast sums on speedways, docks, new means of transit, new and better schools, small parks and playgrounds in the older and more crowded portions of the city, and in diversions of a healthful kind demanded for the comfort, recreation, and elevation of the masses of the people. It need not be feared that too much money will be invested in this direction if the works are wisely planned and honestly executed. The lessons of the Civil War taught the people of this country that its resources are practically exhaustless when expenditures are made for the benefit of the whole community.

I have been moved to make this plea for individual liberty and private property because Columbia College by its origin, its history, and its traditions stands, and ought to stand, for them as a sure defense; and from the unique manner in which its endowment has been provided should be a perpetual inspiration for the highest development of municipal spirit, as lofty as that which in the days of Pericles made Athens "the eye of Greece" and by a sublime exhibition of civic genius crowned its Acropolis with the peerless temple of the Goddess of Wisdom, before which the world still bows with admiring recognition. To educate the citizen, to place before him the highest ideals of duty, and to stimulate him to the stern performance of the obligations which rest upon him as partaker in mind, body, and estate of the inestimable benefits of good government ought to be the chief aim of the university, which from this day will be the most conspicuous and powerful institution in this great city. Here will be treasured the best memories of unselfish sacrifice and heroic achievement; here will be recorded all the failures as well as the triumphs of civic statesmanship; here social problems will be discussed and solved through its affiliated institutions, which will reach every household and every citizen. The children in the kindergartens, the boys and girls in the schools, the workmen in the shops, the clerks in the marts of commerce, the merchants and the manufacturers in their offices, the professional men in their studies, all will come under its influence. The efforts of the community will thus be co-ordinated for progress and for evolution into a higher and better environment. Every agency for instruction, for culture, and for refinement will be systematically employed in the development of a nobler civic life; and, above all, the wealth which has accumulated in this city by the joint association of its people, and to which every human being contributes by his industry, will come to be regarded as a sacred trust to be administered in the public interest for works of beneficence to all. The petty jealousies between the classes will steadily disappear, and it will be demonstrated that democracy and liberty are co-existing and inseparable factors in the largest and best development of civilization.

The trustees of the college have shown themselves to be fully conscious at all times of the obligation which rests upon them in the administration of the great trust confided to their keeping. From the humble beginning in 1754, with seven students and two instructors, with an income so modest for nearly a century as to limit the instruction of the college to such branches as were necessary to educate Christian gentlemen, the college under the wise guidance of President Barnard and President Low has been developed into a university which, during the last year gave instruction to nineteen hundred and seventy-three students, enlisted the services of two hundred and sixty-five teachers, and expended a revenue of over $750,000. It now undertakes to provide instruction in all departments of human learning required for the highest development of modern life. The old academic training is preserved for those who wish to lay the foundations of a scholarly education, fitting them for the study of the learned professions or for the pursuit of a literary career. Its schools of science qualify the engineers who are to become the captains of modern industry, or to pass their lives in the study of natural phenomena; its school of medicine, with its affiliated hospitals in connection with which the names of Sloane, Vanderbilt, and Kissam will ever be held in grateful remembrance, provides the best instruction for alleviating the physical sufferings of the race, and the sanitary knowledge necessary to prevent the spread of disease; its school of law graduates the men who are to protect, enlarge, and defend the civil rights of a free people and to develop jurists who will have the knowledge, courage, and honesty to maintain the law and administer justice without fear and without favor.

But, above all, and crowning all, is the school of political science, whose province it is to investigate the principles of justice, the elementary conditions and customs of the social organization, and the history and the results of their influence in the development of civilization, and the progress of man from a state of barbarism to the infinite refinements and culture of modern life. Herein Columbia College has realized the ideals of Jefferson for the university to which he gave the ripe experience and the affectionate devotion of his old age. It has given effect to the hopes of Washington, who in his first message delivered to Congress in this city, in his correspondence and in his last will, gave voice to the purpose which was near his heart, of founding an institution in which the principles of free government might be taught to specially selected students, who would thus be qualified for public office in the same manner as the Academy at West Point educated officers for the military service of the country. Already in issues of great moment the influence of Columbia University has done much to dispel error, to promote a better understanding between nations, and to avoid complications which might otherwise have resulted in actual hostilities.

Such is the university which the Legislature of New York in 1784 foreshadowed, when it declared that Columbia College was to be the mother under whose fostering care the educational system of the state would be made worthy of the great people who had pledged every dollar of its property for the education of every child within its domain.

But, as it is with the city which has given birth and wealth to this chief monument of its prosperity and glory, so the University stands only upon the threshold of a great career. Already it has outgrown the provision which a decade ago was supposed to be adequate for all possible requirements. By the general concurrence of its trustees, its faculty and its alumni, and with the approval of the city and of the state, it is to be transferred to these historic heights, surrounded by a vision of beauty which satisfies the ideals of the poet, the patriot, and the scholar. Here, then, is to be forever the center of the intellectual life of the city—the citadel of last defense against the perils of ignorance, of superstition, and of false doctrine. Here, buttressed by the noblest cathedral of our age, by institutions of charity and learning, and especially by Barnard College, in which if the rich people of New York do their duty the women of the future will be admitted to equal educational privileges with their brothers, the university buildings will forever under the flag of freedom be an unassailable bulwark of sound learning, and the gateway to universal knowledge.

If, then, the university has a duty to the city which it is striving to perform, have the citizens of New York no corresponding duty to discharge in providing it with the halls and buildings in which this beneficent work is henceforth to be carried on? If its vast endowment is to be sacredly applied, as it should be, to defray the cost of instruction and administration, ought not the rich citizens of New York, whose wealth has been derived from the same source and by virtue of the same law of increment which has given to Columbia College this endowment, be emulous to apply their surplus riches to the building of the structures and to the provision of the appliances for higher education on a scale adequate to meet the ever-increasing demands of modern civilization? Large gifts have already been made by the alumni, by the Fayerweather estate, and by public-spirited citizens for the purchase of the new site. Seth Low, its honored president, inspired by filial piety and by public spirit, has given the great sum of money required for the construction of the library, around which all the other departments of the university must necessarily be grouped. William C. Schermerhorn, the chairman of its Board of Trustees, whose long life of usefulness in this city has only been equaled by his modesty, has set the example of appropriating a portion of one of the large fortunes which have been created by the growth of the city to the erection of a hall of physical science, whose developments day by day are awakening an astonished world to new possibilities of discovery tending to the prevention and cure of disease, the increase of the general welfare, and to the final triumph of mind over matter.

While these lines are being penned, another family, among whose members are distinguished graduates from Columbia, have provided the means for erecting the great building devoted to chemical science and art, which will for all time commemorate the source from which the prosperity of the descendants of Frederick Christian Havemeyer has been derived. For the naming of the remaining halls to be constructed, there will undoubtedly be a generous rivalry among the families whose names are connected with the early history of New York and whose descendants have been enriched by its growth. In this country patents of nobility are wisely prohibited, but a title to immortality is surely within the reach of those to whom the trustees may finally award the privilege and the glory of erecting any one of these buildings. One college hall, however, the trustees have wisely reserved for the alumni to build by contributions, large or small, as a memorial to the living and dead sons of Columbia, whose names shall be inscribed upon tablets to be placed in the great hall of the building. In the entire history of Columbia College the number of its graduates has not been large, but in point of character, ability, and achievement the roll of honor is illustrious. Hereafter, when the university shall number its sons by hundreds of thousands, every one of these early names will have an interest for future generations, especially when they suggest the ties of family and excite the pride of an honorable ancestry. In the coming competition, which I foresee, it is to be hoped that the trustees will be very cautious in admitting to the company of the immortals whose names these great halls shall bear any one which may not hereafter revive the memory of an honorable and useful career in the acquisition of fortune. Thus Columbia will stand not only for what is pure in thought and action, but will be a perpetual incentive to virtue, public spirit, noble aspirations, and successful achievement.

Although our system of government was intended by its founders to restrain the democratic spirit from hasty action, nevertheless political power has been steadily transferred from the few to the many, until at length the will of the majority may be said to be supreme, except for the barriers which are provided by the Constitution of the United States and by the conviction of the people that their own liberties depend upon the protection afforded to private property—the essence of individual liberty. There is, therefore, in this country but little jealousy of great fortunes. The cry of the demagogue against their possession finds small sympathy in the masses of the people, who understand that these fortunes usually represent value which has not been taken from the general wealth, but has not infrequently been contributed to it by the energy, the enterprise, and the sound judgment of their creators. The existence of great fortunes, however, gives a corresponding opportunity for usefulness. Fortunately, by the laws of nature wealth can only be made productive to its owner by such uses as are productive to the community. If this were not so the general fund would cease to grow and progress would come to a halt. Public opinion more and more demands that great fortunes should be administered in a large and liberal spirit. Otherwise their possessors fall into general and just contempt. Although the universities where sound economic doctrines will be taught and disseminated may be relied upon to prevent the practical confiscation of private property, the mental condition of that man who is willing to share in the beneficial results of this defense to which he makes no contribution is not to be envied.

The masses of the people have never demanded equality of fortune, and indeed understand it to be impossible; but they have always insisted, and will always insist, upon equality of opportunity. With free schools and universal education, with opportunities for the youth of exceptional ability in the ranks of the rich or the poor to secure the benefits of the highest instruction, the approaches of communism need never be feared. Equality of opportunity insures the ultimate distribution of wealth upon just conditions and within reasonable periods of time. If this were not so, society would be justified in demanding a reorganization upon more equitable lines. But this demand will not be made so long as provision exists for the general diffusion of knowledge and the acquisition of that higher learning which is essential to the stability and development of civil institutions.

Social reforms never come from below. They originate in the trained intellect of scholars and in the inspirations of genius in an atmosphere favorable to their reception. Slowly but surely great ideas descend and penetrate the mass of the people. The current belief of today was the scientific discovery of yesterday, while the evil of one age is very often due to reforms instituted in a previous age, and yet the underlying principles of truth and justice never change. The guardianship of these principles resides in the higher institutions of learning, and their application to the changing conditions of society depends upon teachers and scholars who devote their lives to the investigation of truth, regardless of the material results of their labor.

In this country the democracy, whose power will never grow less, will tolerate no violation of its ideals. But these ideals may be either true or false. They may lead to the ruin of society, as they did in the French Revolution, or they may raise it to new standards of justice and happiness. The outcome will depend on how far the public will is guided by the knowledge of sound principles. This knowledge cannot be acquired in the common schools. Even if every child is instructed in the rudiments of education, the limitations of age and of the time which can be devoted to elementary learning, do not admit of the intellectual and moral training necessary in dealing with great questions of public policy. It is true that in rare instances men like Benjamin Franklin, Roger Sherman, and George Washington, who were not college bred, appear upon the stage of public life and take their place among the leaders of thought and action. But they were men of great natural powers, which had been developed by extraordinary opportunities and responsibilities in early life, serving thus to prove the rule that thorough training and large experience in public affairs are prerequisites to successful administration.

Upon the university, then, we must build the foundations of our municipal glory and greatness. It will not lack the means of usefulness nor the opportunity of expanding its influence when the rich men of our city realize the opportunity it affords for making the millions which they control fulfill the duty imposed by the possession of wealth, and by which alone its possession can be justified. If liberty, science, property, and labor are to continue to work together in the future as in the past for the advancement of civilization, the institutions of higher learning must be extended to the limits of their possibilities. So far as the city of New York is concerned the Columbia University must be made the fountainhead of knowledge, the center from which will flow the conservative and recuperative principles of social progress. In association with all other beneficent influences it must be made to reach every household and to come into touch with every citizen. Against its walls the waves of communism and anarchy will then beat in vain. The city which is its home will feel its influence in every profession, in the walks of business, in its public institutions, in the conduct of its churches, in the execution and administration of the great undertakings which will be demanded by its continued growth. Its citizens will come to its halls for instruction, for guidance, for inspiration, and as they approach the portal of a higher municipal life and are confirmed in nobler aims, they will feel the force of the prophetic motto of King's College, the mother of the Columbia University in the City of New York, *In lumine tuo videbimus lumen.*

The Last Commencement Address at Cooper Union [1]

MAY 31, 1902

[*Of all his many activities, Hewitt put more devotion into his work for Cooper Union than anything else. He had done more than anyone else to advise Peter Cooper in its establishment; the charter of the Union as adopted by the Legislature in 1859 was drafted in his handwriting; he was one of the original trustees and as secretary conducted the first registration. During a long generation he was executive head of the Union, and he gave it as much attention as an ordinary college president gives his college. The inadequacy of the endowment, to which at first few contributed save members of the Cooper-Hewitt family, troubled him to the very end of the nineteenth century. Then the generosity of two of his friends, Andrew Carnegie and H. H. Rogers, wrought an abrupt transformation. The annual report for 1901 showed an endowment of less than a million; that for 1902 showed an endowment of more than $2,100,000. After its years of struggle and pinching, Hewitt saw the Union placed in a position to meet the demands of a far larger body of aspiring young men and women. The complete story of this sudden step forward and Hewitt's hopes for the results that would follow are given in this his latest important speech—but a speech still full of ardor.*]

For forty-three blessed years it has been my privilege to present, on behalf of the trustees, the report of the operations of the Cooper Union. I have never had the report read, but usually talked to the audience here assembled in a confidential sort of way, pointing out various matters which I thought might interest us as members of one family, all devoted to one great object: the diffusion of knowledge through the Cooper Union. Usually I have had no difficulty in selecting the topic upon which I desired to talk. It was generally a statement that the income of the Institution was entirely inadequate to meet the demands made by the public for its privileges; that we wanted more money; that we wanted more room; that we wanted to get rid of the tenants; that we wanted more funds to pay more teachers and to let in more of the public until every foot of space, from this floor where we are

[1] Published in the annual report of the Union, 1903.

assembled tonight right up to the roof, should be entirely devoted to the purpose for which Mr. Cooper designed it, namely, the free education of the masses of the people of the city of New York who desired not only to be self-supporting, but to aid others in the course of time in getting an honest livelihood.

The greater part of these forty-three years this appeal seemed to fall upon deaf ears. Very few persons gave us anything, and although the amounts, when they were given, were perhaps considerable in themselves, yet they were totally inadequate to carry out the plans which we had in view. In other words, my task was like the wail of Jeremiah, and I confess that I did not expect to live to see the great object which the trustees had in hand—had in view—of freeing this institution from its secular uses and devoting it entirely to educational purposes—confess I did not expect to live to see the time when it should be accomplished. But we have struck what my young friend the valedictorian calls a volcano, and we have done what I think he will find it rather difficult to do with his volcano. Ours is a financial volcano, and we have appropriated what was discharged with a facility and a success that we think thoroughly commendable.

If you had at hand a report of last year, you would find that our endowment fund then amounted to nine hundred and fifty-eight thousand dollars. By the report which the treasurer has just presented to you, our Endowment Fund now amounts to two million one hundred and thirteen thousand three hundred and fifty dollars and thirty cents, being an increase during the year, in round numbers, of twelve hundred thousand dollars. I really do not want to take up your time, but this is such an extraordinary event, and the results of it are so far-reaching, that I think I will have to ask your indulgence while I go into a little history of the Cooper Union. Mr. Cooper was a poor boy, born of good Revolutionary stock, but like most of the patriots of that time he had a good deal more patriotism than money. He began life as an apprentice. There were no schools in New York in those days—no night schools. He was very anxious to get on, but there was no place where he could obtain an education. He had no money with which to pay a teacher. So he had to get what knowledge he could get by himself, and, as I have often heard him say, by the light of the single tallow candle which his means made him able to get; and that every night he passed his time trying to acquire some knowledge which would be of use to him in the battle of life. This made a great impression on him, and he determined that the reproach of New York, of its lack of means for free education, should be removed.

This occurred about the beginning of the last century, in 1804 or 1805, and he set himself to work, alone, without friends, without suggestions from any quarter, to get money enough together to open what he called a night school, for at that time there was not a single free night school in New York City. This was the purpose of his life. He never lost sight of it; and I will tell you this—I tell these young men and women here, this story particularly in order that they may see how a noble purpose formed by even the most friendless boy may result in course of time in great benefits to society. And so he pursued his course. He was, of course, a man of great natural ability and great strength of character. I have often heard him say that the first thing a young man should do was to save a little money; that no man could succeed in life who did not begin by saving; and that when a man had saved a little money and had acquired some property he was pretty sure then to make a good citizen. So in the institution which he proposed to found, he never lost sight of the fact that he wanted to inculcate thrift—he wanted to teach industry—he wanted the lesson of saving to be learned—and he left the rest to the conscience of the good citizens he knew would be produced by such lessons. And as he provided for the kind of education which these young gentlemen have had, he said that of all the things to be taught in the Cooper Union, the preeminent one must be the art—the science, as he called it—of good government. He did not mean by this merely the teachings of political economy or political science, but an inculcation of the principle, that men "shall do unto each other as they would have others do unto them."

The time came when he had accumulated money enough to begin to build a building. His original idea of a night school was of a rather moderate character, but it very soon enlarged itself until at last, having selected this site, on which he had carried on business for some years, he was able to buy the whole block, and he proceeded to erect this building. He knew, when he undertook this task, that his means would not suffice for more than the erection of the building, and he was determined not to incur any debts. When he called the trustees together to receive the property at his hands, he said to them, "Here is this building. I want it appropriated as soon as possible to the education of the young men and young women of New York City, and appropriated to *free* education. There must be no fee paid in the Cooper Union, for education ought to be as free as air and water." He said,

I have given practically all the property that I can control to build this building, and here is thirty thousand dollars more which I have left over, with which you can furnish the apparatus required, and for carrying on the work of instruction. I have called this building the Union for the Advancement of Science and Art. Against my wishes and against my will the Legislature have, unfortunately, attached to it the name of Cooper. I did not want my name attached to the Union. I wanted this to be a union of all well-disposed people in New York who are willing to contribute to carry out the work of free education in the building I have created. But the use of this name will inevitably, to some extent, interfere with my views for that purpose, and hence you will have to rent as much as is necessary of this building in order to maintain the classes and the reading-room.

Under those circumstances, forty-three years ago, the trustees entered upon their task. From the very outset the demands upon the institution for admission to it were far greater than the income which they could possibly derive from the rented portions of the building. Hence the great object of these trustees was to secure an endowment fund; and Mr. Cooper before his death was able to provide two hundred thousand dollars, the income from which he thought would be able to pay the running expenses of the building and keep it in order, but would not, of course, pay the expenses of instruction. He said to the trustees: "I hope, before you die, the day will come when some one will give money enough to free this institution from the incumbrance of tenants, and devote it entirely to the work of free education."

Up to the time of his death very little money had been contributed; but soon after his death, the family of his younger brother, Mr. William Cooper, who had obtained a fortune in connection with Mr. Cooper,[1] gave in successive gifts, owing to the death of successive members of the family, the sum of three hundred and forty thousand dollars. Those of you who have been in the institution for any length of time will remember that this happened about five years ago, and was immediately followed by the enlargement of the classes in the rooms in the two floors above this. That was the first considerable sum of money the trustees had received, and it did not come until thirty years after the building had been established. In giving an account of this transaction in the report of that year, it was mentioned that this sum would enable the extension of the work, but it was also stated that it was entirely inadequate to gain the great object which we all had in view, of ridding the building of tenants, and an appeal was made to the public to gain money, but none came.

But this appeal came to the notice of Mr. Carnegie, who was a great admirer of Mr. Cooper, and he has never tired of saying that Mr. Cooper's example had been of great help to him and had given him great inspiration in the use of his money in advancing public education. He wrote to me that he wanted in some way to manifest his admiration for Mr. Cooper and his sympathy for our efforts in enlarging the institution. The amount he offered to give us was one hundred thousand dollars. In reply to this offer I mentioned to Mr. Carnegie that we were very glad to get it, and that it would be the beginning of a fund that would be sufficient in the course of time to keep the whole institution.

[1] As manager of Peter Cooper's extensive glue works in Brooklyn; long a rolling stone, William Cooper came to rest very lucratively in this berth.

He said in reply: "I did not understand the case. Let me give three hundred thousand dollars."

"Yes," I replied, "three hundred thousand dollars, with three hundred thousand dollars more added to it, will enable us to begin to take possession of the greater part of the building—of all the building except the stores—and to widen the scope of the scheme of education."

Later Mr. Carnegie offered to give three hundred thousand dollars more. And this reminds me of President Lincoln during the war times, when he was always asking for three hundred thousand more. It had previously been arranged by Mr. Peter Cooper's descendants that a trust fund of three hundred and fifty thousand dollars created by him for the benefit of his grandchildren and the residuary interest of his children of two hundred and fifty thousand dollars in the property subject to the trust, should come to the institution on the deaths of the members of the family as they occurred. It was now arranged that the whole property should be transferred to the institution at once to meet Mr. Carnegie's gifts, so that in the month of January last, between this six hundred thousand dollars and Mr. Carnegie's two gifts of three hundred thousand dollars each, there was an increase in the amount of the endowment fund of twelve hundred thousand dollars over what it was before Mr. Carnegie gave his first three hundred thousand.[1]

On the strength of this gift I thought I saw the way clear to notify the tenants to quit the stores, and most of them have moved out, all but two, who have leases which will not be terminated until next year. We will then have possession of the floor above, and practically the whole floor will be made into a great physical laboratory.

But this would not be sufficient. The scale on which the operation of the institution was to be carried on would require another sum of money, and I was speculating in my own mind where the next three hundred thousand dollars would come from. You can imagine my astonishment at what followed. A gentleman whom I have long known—a gentleman who had never manifested any special interest in the Cooper Union—called at my house, and after chatting pleasantly on various subjects, and after having had a little cup of tea with me, as he was just going away he said: "By the way, I have got something for you; a little gift for Cooper Union;" and to my intense astonishment he handed me two hundred and fifty thousand dollars.[2] I confess that

[1] Mr. Carnegie stipulated that his gift of $600,000 should be matched by an equal gift on the part of the Cooper-Hewitt family. At great hardship to the family, the trust arrangement was broken and property which included the site of the Chrysler Building was sold to raise the sum.

[2] The generous donor was H. H. Rogers, who expressly stated that he gave the money out of admiration for Mr. Hewitt and because he had satisfied himself that nowhere was money so efficiently used as at Cooper Union. After careful inquiry he had learned that the per capita cost of an excellent education there was less than in any other institution.

I have not recovered. I cannot realize it, that for forty odd years we have been struggling with this problem, with a sort of vague hope that in some way or other the answer would come from some quarter or other—I cannot realize that it has been answered. There was an arrangement which Mr. Edward Cooper and I had made with our respective families by which we knew that ultimately six hundred thousand dollars would come to the institution, so as to at least replace the rents which would be lost. But we had gone on for forty years considering this matter, and every trustee doing what he could to make the position more tolerable. Let me say that three of us of the original trustees, Mr. Cooper, Mr. Parsons, and myself, are still living. There were originally five trustees, and three of them are still alive. To them he gave this charge, that they should see to it, if they could, that this institution should be made free from every occupation except that of the distribution of knowledge. Mr. Parsons is not here tonight. For forty odd years he has gratuitously attended to all the legal business of this institution, and that in itself is no small undertaking. And besides this he has contributed to the endowment fund—he has given twenty thousand dollars to the endowment fund in order to manifest his interest in the institution.

And here we are, with an income of not less than ninety thousand dollars—possibly it may amount to a hundred thousand dollars—sufficient to pay the expenses of this institution according to the original plans of Mr. Cooper, made nearly a hundred years ago; yes, quite a hundred years ago, when he was a poor boy, working as an apprentice, and followed during his long lifetime of ninety-three years; followed by his children since his death and prior to his death for forty years, and before his immediate family has passed away this great undertaking had been accomplished.

Now, young gentlemen, I want you to see and to learn that a noble resolution, once formed and resolutely adhered to from generation to generation, will ultimately work out its destiny and secure its triumph. That is the great moral lesson which this institution has taught, and while I do not underestimate the value of the technical and scientific instruction which has been given by this institution, let me say that the moral lesson afforded by the Cooper Union in the story as I have told it to you, the moral lesson is one of the greatest I have ever known, or ever expect to know, in the history of man.

You may ask me if the days of miracles have really passed, for this seems like some miracle, that the Cooper Union should have achieved this result. I will tell you how it was expected to be achieved. Mr. Cooper said that of course in the course of a hundred years there would be a great many graduates of the institution, alumni. "The day will come," he said, "when they, these graduates, will rally around this

institution, and if the plans I have formed can be executed in no other
way, they will see that my plans are executed. Now, in forty years I
have been waiting for these alumni, but they did not pan out. But in
many respects this has been a very remarkable year, for about two
months ago I received a letter from Mr. Elmer E. Garnsey, in which
he says:

April 8th, 1902.

HON. ABRAM S. HEWITT,

My Dear Sir:—I thank you for your kind letter of the 4th inst., and for your
approval of my suggestion, made through Mr. R. Swain Gifford.

I shall take an early opportunity of arranging with him to accept your very
courteous invitation to meet, at your house, the ladies who have founded the Museum
of Decorative Art; and later, I shall be glad to re-visit the Night Classes in Art, and
to report to the Trustees anything that may occur to me, worthy their consideration.

I am glad that my little contribution may be kept separate from the general
funds of the Union, and the foundation may bear my name, or not, as you may
consider wise and proper. My whole desire is to express in some degree, my appreciation of what Cooper Union and its great founder have done for me, in a manner
that shall have the approval of those who have so splendidly carried on the work
begun by Peter Cooper, and at the same time be of benefit to those who are studying
and working to improve themselves, in their leisure hours. For the establishment of
the fund, I enclose, to your order, my cheque for one thousand dollars, and beg
to remain, sir,

Sincerely yours,
ELMER E. GARNSEY.

I read that letter because it is the first contribution in money we
have ever received from an alumnus.

Then, a few days ago—it was received too late to put in this year's
report—I got this letter:

May 26th, 1902.

HON. ABRAM S. HEWITT,

Dear Sir:—It gives me great happiness to enclose you herewith, check for $5,000
to be used by the Board of Trustees as they deem best.

The education which I received at Cooper Union, fitted me for the practice of
civil engineering, in such a thorough and practical manner, that it was my good
fortune to occupy positions of responsibility at an earlier age than I have known
graduates of other technical schools to attain, with the result that I can make this
contribution now anticipating to further aid my Alma Mater in a far greater degree
some time in the not very distant future.

Trusting that your Board will do me the great honor of accepting this check,
and assuring you that no one appreciates more than I do the great sacrifices of
Peter Cooper, his family and associates in the founding of Cooper Union and the
carrying on of its great work with such constant and increasing success, I am, with
all best wishes for Cooper Union and yourselves,

Most faithfully yours,
JOHN F. O'ROURKE.

Mr. O'Rourke stands today at the head of the constructive engineers
in the United States. His success has been phenomenal. He is the inventor of the system which is used in all the skyscrapers, these tall

buildings, of placing the foundations on pneumatic caissons. Every one of these buildings has to use Mr. O'Rourke's system, and he tells me that for every foundation which he puts in in the future he expects to make a further contribution to the Cooper Union.

They say that misfortunes never come single, but in our case I am very glad to say that good fortune never comes alone. I received a letter from the town of Krakow in Poland some weeks ago, announcing that a Mr. Felix Kucielski had died and left the sum of five thousand dollars to the Cooper Union. I did not attach much importance to it until I got a notice from the Austrian consul in New York that there were five thousand dollars awaiting us in Krakow, Poland, which we could get as soon as we sent the proper vouchers and identifications for its collection. I suppose that this gentleman must at some time have been in New York and have had some knowledge of the Cooper Union, for I cannot imagine how any one away off in Poland could make such an endowment unless that had been the case.[1]

Young gentlemen, wherever you may go, wherever your work may take you, whether to Kamchatka or to Martinique—I want you to remember that Cooper Union is quite ready to receive contributions from every habitable part of the world.

Now, a word or two more. I will be merciful, for it is too bad to take up so much of your time. I may be saying so much on account of your applause. I have not always had so much applause given me in the course of my lifetime. They say "Old men dream dreams." Well, Dr. Slicer says that it is the young men who dream. And the dream that I dreamed forty years or more ago has tonight come true. "Old men see visions." I think I am right, but it may be that I have reversed the Scriptures. The clergymen are so busy these days with controversies about what they do believe and what the Scriptures really do mean, that we poor laymen have to get along as best we can by ourselves in making quotations. I am an old man, and I see a vision of the future. The Cooper Union is now complete. It is a finished institution, although, as a matter of course, we can spend a great deal more money when it is sent to us. But it can run from this day forward on the resources which it has acquired. But I should be sorry to see that the Cooper Union was going to stop with this building or the work it is doing here. The work which we have undertaken to do is to teach the scientific principles which underlie the arts of the country. We never undertook to teach the trades. We never intend to teach what are known as the constructive trades. But there are established in Germany, England, and to some extent, in France, industries which are not extensively carried on in the United States, although we have the richest

[1] This paragraph differs somewhat from the corresponding paragraph in the reported speech.

country in the world. These trades are what are known as the handicrafts. They deal with the application of the arts to the finer classes of constructive work and materials, the textiles, gold, silver, and the metals, the manufacture of instruments of precision, and a high order of mechanical work. Work of this class we chiefly import, as a rule, for not many Americans are art workers of that kind. To carry out this work we require a good deal of money and a good deal of space. That is the second chapter in the history of the Cooper Union. The present trustees have no hope of being able to execute this object in their lifetime. They but look forward to these handicrafts. In Paris at the present time there are ninety schools which are giving instruction in art industry.

Now we have located in this neighborhood the armory of the sixty-ninth regiment, which is soon to be vacated. This armory belongs to the city, and if the city would turn it over to us after it is vacated, for the establishment of these classes of handicraft work, I am very sure, from what I now know, that I can secure an endowment sufficient to carry on the work. This would cost the city nothing, and there would be no burden on the city for keeping it up. The city would merely appropriate the armory for the work in the same way that they have appropriated land and buildings for the establishment of the Museum of Art and the Museum of Natural History.

By the time our new laboratory is done the Astor Library will be vacant. The building in itself is of no value except as a library, and we need it for a library. It is admirably designed for this purpose, and is admirably located for the extension of the work of this institution, and in proximity to this building, where the work of administration would have to be carried on. The most economical use to which it could be put would be to turn it over to Cooper Union, as otherwise it would be of no value except for the value of the land. Now, I hope it will enter into the heart of someone, after I am dead and gone—though I do not object if they do it while I am alive—to add to the Cooper Union one or both of these great buildings for the extension of the work we are carrying on here. We could then remove our reading room and library to the Astor Library, and that space could be devoted to the Art Museum, which I think is getting to be one of the most instructive additions to the education of New York.

If Dr. Slicer [1] had not told me it is the old men who have visions, I should think that I was a young man. Perhaps it was after all not a mistake but a twist of the tongue. I am in my eightieth year. I am seeing visions because I am so much younger than some of less years than are mine, because I am still young and fresh. If so, I shall be quite glad to live to see any extensions to the Cooper Union which may be possible.

[1] Dr. Slicer had made the opening prayer.

In conclusion let me again quote the Scriptures, and say for the trustees that we have "fought the good fight. We have finished our course with joy." And for myself, since I have got in the quotation line, I think I am quite prepared to say: "Lord, now lettest Thou Thy servant depart in peace, for mine eyes have seen Thy salvation."

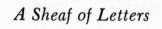

A Sheaf of Letters

A Sheaf of Letters

[Throughout early and middle life Hewitt was too busy a man to write many discursive and chatty letters. His correspondence was large, but it was almost wholly concerned with business and politics and was crisp, curt, and confined to the matter in hand. But after his retirement from the mayoralty his letters became longer, more general in content, and more interesting. Some of his most pungent expressions of opinion are to be found in them, and they give a unique view of his restless, energetic, incisive, determined personality. It would be possible to compile an interesting volume from them. This brief selection, however, will suffice to indicate Hewitt's many-sided interests, his broad and liberal point of view, his unfailing shrewdness, and his high regard for principle.]

To S. H. Smith, September 7, 1888 [1]

Your letter of the 6th instant probably refers to an interview which I had more than a year ago with a committee of the Knights of Labor, who called upon me in reference to certain suggestions which they had to make in regard to the management of the business of Cooper & Hewitt at Trenton. In the course of the conversation I told them I would be very glad indeed to turn the works over to the workmen if they would pay interest upon the floating capital and nothing at all upon the cost of the plant until some profits were made. Since that time, the works have been conducted at a loss of over a hundred thousand dollars for the year ending June 30th last; so that, if the men had accepted my offer, Cooper & Hewitt would have been better off to the extent of the loss which has been incurred. The practical result of the business has been that we have paid to the workmen the entire earnings of the works plus $100,000. Of course this cannot go on; but it gives one instance in which the workmen have been kept employed, not only without any profit, but with a positive loss, to the owner. Of course I should be glad to make an arrangement to transfer the works to the workmen on the terms which I offered last year.

1 Of Jersey City, New Jersey.

To Daniel Connolly, September 25, 1888 [1]

The *Pilot* may not intend to do me injustice, but it is evident that its editor is so full of prejudice that he does it in spite of his good intentions. You ask me to state what the facts are in reference to the decoration of the City Hall with flags on the occasion of Queen Victoria's Jubilee celebration. These facts are perfectly well known to the public. I was requested to direct the flags to be displayed on the City Hall, on St. Patrick's Day, the 17th day of March, and particularly the Irish flag. I declined on that occasion to allow any other flags to be unfurled except the American flags, and these flags were displayed as requested. A similar request was made to me on the occasion of the Queen's Jubilee, except that the British flag was substituted for the Irish flag. I declined to allow the British flag to be displayed, but directed the American flags to be unfurled, just as I did on the occasion of St. Patrick's Day; and I then laid down the rule that whenever requested by any respectable body of my fellow citizens to display the American flag I would do so, but that I would never permit any foreign flag to float over the City Hall while I was Mayor of the City. This rule has been rigidly adhered to, and was applied alike when requested by my Irish fellow citizens as when I was appealed to by my English fellow citizens to allow other than the American flags to be displayed.

To J. Herbert Phillips, March 18, 1891 [2]

Your letter of the 14th inst. affords much food for reflection. For a long time I have been considering the position in which the country finds itself, practically dominated in all the large cities by foreigners instead of being governed by Americans. A striking illustration of this state of things is afforded by the recent events in New Orleans.[3] I fear that the example thus set will not be without imitation in other parts of the country. I do not wonder that native born Americans are restive when they find themselves governed instead of governing in the land of their birth. Besides, the influence of the foreign element is not in harmony with our institutions and the theory of our government. There can be no doubt that church influence is more powerful in some of our great cities than the convictions of either party.

The result of popular elections is determined by the interests of

[1] Editor of a Catholic publication in New York.

[2] Of Chicago, Illinois.

[3] The chief of police in New Orleans had been murdered, apparently by Italians connected with the Mafia. Nine Italians were tried for the crime. When they were acquitted or remanded to another trial, a citizens' committee called upon the people, who suspected bribery, to prevent a miscarriage of justice. A mob took the Italians from jail and lynched them.

particular religious creeds rather than consideration of public welfare. Moreover, the machinery of politics enables the minority to govern the majority. Our system of government was never framed with reference to the large influx from foreign countries, and it is a remarkable fact that in the period extending from the adoption of the Constitution down to the administration of James Monroe in 1820 less than 50,000 foreigners came to the United States. Up to a period beginning about fifty years ago the country was essentially occupied and governed by those who were born within its confines. I think it is not exaggerating the situation now to say that the country is governed by men who were born in other lands, and certainly is so governed if we include the children of foreigners who vote.

I am at a loss to know what course ought to be taken under the circumstances, but I have generalized somewhat to the conclusion that foreigners should be prohibited from holding office of any kind whatever. I think this will be found to be a much more effective remedy than restricting the right of suffrage. It is simple, and can be made effective by act of Congress, certainly as to all future naturalizations if it cannot be made applicable to those who are already citizens.

I suppose, however, that the mere declaration of this remedy would produce very great excitement, and the dangers to the advocates of the limitation of office to American-born citizens would be very serious. I am not prepared to make any recommendation on the subject, nor am I willing at present to write any letter for publication. This letter is for your personal and private use, and not for publication or circulation. It is rather intended as tentative to see how it will strike you, but I am not myself clear that the proposed limitation as to office could be enacted even if we should think it wise to make the attempt.

To Philip Williams, August 24, 1891 [1]

I am very well aware that the interference of an outsider (even though he be an old friend) in family affairs is to be deprecated, and is generally regarded as an impertinence. You will, I am sure, acquit me of any disposition to meddle with matters which do not concern me, when I say that I have very carefully reflected upon the circumstances which lead me to write this letter, and I feel that not to present the matter to your notice would be a failure of duty on my part to an old friend and an unfortunate young man. Your nephew, the son of my old friend Walter Williams, came over with Mrs. Hewitt and my family in the steamship *Umbria* about six weeks since. I was very glad to see him, and as in duty bound, my family received him as they would one of my own children, and we tried to make him feel at home with us. We could not

[1] An ironmaster friend, Harborough Hall, Kidderminster, England.

help seeing that the young man was in a great state of depression, due, perhaps, to failing health or to the circumstances which induced him to leave England. We gave him such sympathy as we could, and gradually it became known to us that the young man was in a very false position—without money and without the confidence of the relatives who should be his best friends. I did not know the circumstances which led him to leave England at this time, but it seemed to me that his proper place was at home and not here. I would very willingly have found some employment for him, but he had received no training which would fit him for the active competition of American life. Besides, as the only young man in your family, he naturally has expectations which can be better realized on your side than in this country. So far as I could judge, he is a very amiable person, with good manners, but without much force of character. With good surroundings and in a tolerably independent position I have no doubt that he would do credit to his family and the position to which he is born. As it is, he is depressed and cannot do himself justice, and it seemed to me that he would probably sink into an early grave unless he is buoyed up by the sustaining action of the members of his family. You are the head of the family, and he tells me that you have always been kind to him and provided him with his passage out and back, and with the little money which he brought with him. I venture, therefore, to suggest that you take the matter in hand and see that this young man is not allowed to sink into utter despair. The kindest thing you could do would be to let him have employment at the iron works in some subordinate position where he can feel that there is a prospect of advancement. A reasonable allowance in money, regularly paid to him, would undoubtedly develop his self-respect, and I think would fit him to occupy the position which his family would like him to fill when he gets to be older and shall have greater responsibilities. . . .

I can only ask you to make allowance for the feelings which have induced me to write this letter. I can assure you that I address you with great reluctance, but I have done precisely what I would like any friend of mine to do if my own son were concerned. . . .

To E. Ray Stevens, January 23, 1893 [1]

Your favor of the 20th inst. is received. You ask me to specify at least one instance in New York in which a private concern, having control either of the street railways or of the gas works, have been the cause of corruption. I reply that in the well known case of Jacob Sharp and the Broadway Railroad grant it was proven that several hundred thousand dollars had been used to corrupt the Board of Aldermen.

[1] Of Madison, Wisconsin.

Sharp was tried and convicted, but died before he was sent to the State prison. Several members of the Board of Aldermen were tried, convicted and sent to prison, and one of them has just served out his term of five years. This case is comparatively recent, but in the time of Tweed it was clearly shown that every franchise was purchased by bribery or granted for political or personal reasons.

2nd. You ask whether I think a greater interest would be excited in the public mind if the ownership of these works were vested in the city. I cannot answer this question, because so long as the taxes are light and no frauds are developed, the public here seem to care very little about the municipal government. The city of New York owns at least $300,000,000 worth of public property, but this vast amount does not seem to have excited the interest necessary to protect them from spoliation or peculation.

3rd. You ask whether private ownership or public ownership of the same industries permits greater influences for corruption. Inasmuch as I have always favored the ownership of public franchises by the city, and the operation of these franchises for limited terms by private companies, I cannot give any direct answer to your inquiry, but I think there would be no end to the corruption if the city both owned and operated the street railways and the works for supplying light.

4th. You ask whether the civil service of New York grows better year by year. I reply that when the civil service regulations are honestly administered, the civil service improves. I cannot give you any opinion as to the manner of administration at present, but I observe that only the adherents of Tammany Hall seem to be able to get office.

To M. E. Ingalls, June 28, 1893 [1]

On the receipt of your last letter I sent a copy of it to Mr. Page for his opinion as to whether it would warrant us in proceeding further with the plan of making an opening on the Gauley River. I am now in receipt of his answer and find that he does not approve of the idea of a

[1] M. E. Ingalls was an officer of the Chesapeake & Ohio Railroad; W. N. Page was manager of Hewitt's large coal holdings in West Virginia. Hewitt was anxious not to develop this property except under conditions which would enable him to build up model workingmen's communities. He instructed Page not to hire immigrants from Eastern Europe, but to confine the force to those with an American standard of living. He wrote also: "I hope in the improvements which you make that you will always bear in mind the general plan of having comfortable residences for our employees, and that you will so arrange the location of the houses as to ensure good drainage and, if possible, garden spots for each house. I should like, if the property will warrant, as it seems it will do, to have Anstead regarded as a model mining town. . . . I cannot too strongly impress you with the idea that we are very averse to making profits or dividends at the expense of the comfort, morality, and happiness of the employee."

new traffic area applicable to the region where our property is situated. He thinks it will be a damage to us which would be fatal, adding practically 10 cents per ton to the cost of transportation to our only market, which must be in the West, and amounting to the practical confiscation of the little profit we now get upon the coal we are already mining.

Unless the railroad company can see its way clear to enable us to make money, we have no motive to invest capital, and we prefer the present situation as it is to any suggestion which will deprive us of any portion of the remuneration which we now get from the business. I presume that a conference between you and Mr. Page will lead to some understanding, but, as at present advised, I feel compelled to instruct him to abandon all efforts to develop our lands on the Gauley River. Perhaps I am in error in supposing that you contemplate any change of rates upon the coal which we are now mining, but if you do contemplate it, I trust you will give us a hearing before making any change which would destroy the value of our property. You will readily perceive that the arbitrary power of railroad companies to interfere with the profits of business is one of the reasons, probably the main one, why capital is so slow to put itself in the power of the transportation companies. In a recent investment under consideration by parties in this city, it was laid down as a fundamental principle that the money must not be spent upon any locality which would put the investors in the power of any transportation company, and hence it was finally concluded to place the works upon tidewater. I think this fact explains how it is that capital is reluctant to leave the vicinity of New York and other tidewater cities.

To George Gunton, July 8, 1893 [1]

In response to your request for my opinion as to what Congress should do when it meets in extra session on the 7th of August next, I reply briefly:

FIRST. It should pass a joint resolution empowering the President in his discretion to suspend the further purchase of silver under the Sherman Act.

SECOND. The Speaker should constitute the Committee on Ways and Means, the Committee on Banking and Currency, and the Committee on Coinage, Weights and Measures; and the House should instruct these committees to report at an adjourned session in October next the measures necessary for the reformation of the tariff and the revision of an elastic system of currency suited to the varying conditions of

---

[1] George Gunton (1845-1919), born in England, was long prominent in the United States as an editor of labor publications, and an economist. At this time he was editing the *Social Economist*, which he had established in 1891.

business in this country. In this system all dependence upon the Government for the supply of currency should be absent, except so far as may be necessary to secure uniformity of value in the currency to be issued.

THIRD. It will be necessary to deal with the question of the coinage of silver, but whatever is done, the present unit of value, which is the gold dollar, containing $25\frac{3}{10}$ grains gold $\frac{9}{10}$ fine, should be preserved, and all silver dollars which may have been coined or may hereafter be coined at any different ratio of value, should be redeemable in gold dollars of the standard weight and fineness. If this view be adhered to, I do not see how it is possible to authorize the free coinage of silver at any ratio whatever, but it is possible to coin silver dollars at any ratio, provided the Government does not undertake the redemption in gold nor prohibit the use of such dollars in discharge of contracts made between parties for payment of obligations in silver dollars.

Where no specific metal is specified in contract, gold dollars alone should be legal tender, as there cannot be in the nature of things two varying standards of value.

To Representative William L. Wilson, October 31, 1893 [1]

The newspapers say (and they are probably right for once) that you have prepared a draft of the proposed tariff bill. I suppose this means that the Democratic majority have such a bill under consideration. If so, it would save time if the metal schedule could be sent to me, confidentially. I am aware that these matters cannot be disclosed to the public, and I have no doubt that the members of the committee will consider me to be trusted so far as the draft is concerned. I find in getting ready to send you the proposed schedule, that I have all the data from which I prepared the metal schedule for the Morrison Bill, subsequently incorporated, with a few changes, into the Mills Bill. It will therefore be easy for me to compare the draft proposed by the committee with the work heretofore done and to recommend such modifications as the changed conditions of the trade will warrant.

I suppose that you have not forgotten that in my tariff speech in 1883 I laid down the principles upon which tariff reform should rest. So far as I know, the scheme proposed was new. The principle was subsequently incorporated in the Democratic platform of 1884, the tariff portion of which I wrote, and re-adopted in 1888, and reported to the convention by the committee in 1892, but, unfortunately, as I think, overruled by the convention. Very great reductions on rates can

1 William Lyne Wilson, who had entered Congress from West Virginia in 1883, was at this time chairman of the Ways and Means Committee of the House, and preparing what became known as the Wilson Tariff Bill. He later became Postmaster-General under Cleveland. Hewitt had known him well in the House.

be made in the bill which you will bring in, but one principle will have to be carefully considered by the committee, and which will be overlooked unless someone very familiar with the history of the iron business is taken into your counsel. The *ad valorem* principle as a revenue basis is correct, but it must be applied with reference to the peculiarities of each branch of industry. Assuming that a revenue duty of 30 percent is necessary to supply the wants of the Government, the amount will be collected with certainty on articles which do not fluctuate much in price. Iron and steel are not such articles, but if you will look at the diagram of prices in the address which I send to you by this mail, you will see that the fluctuations are enormous, and that an *ad valorem* rate would, when the prices are very low, yield but little revenue, and equally when prices are very high, would yield none, because there would be no importations. It is therefore necessary to adopt the average price as the basis for duty and assess the *ad valorem* revenue duty upon this average price and to put the duty in a specific form. This has been the result of experience in all countries. The duties are then necessarily specific as a rule, although there are some branches of the business in which an *ad valorem* is the most convenient and on the whole the most satisfactory. Wire is an example of this class of product, and there are other commodities which may be treated in the same manner.

It is for this reason that I would like to have the draft of the proposed schedule, as it will shorten and simplify my work very much and enable me to give the committee the information which it ought to have before the bill is actually reported to the House.

To William L. Wilson, November 15, 1893

I am sorry you cannot send me, in strict confidence, the sketch of the metal schedule, because it would save both you and me time and trouble, but it is very easy for me to give you the basis on which I think the Committee ought to proceed.

Iron ore and coal should of course be on the free list. I say this notwithstanding the fact that I am very largely interested in iron ore mines and in coal mines, both anthracite and bituminous, upon the Atlantic Slope. They have nothing to fear from foreign competition. The ores are kept low in price by the competition from Lake Superior, for which there can be no protection and no remedy. We can mine ores in New Jersey and along the Coast generally for less money than the freight from any foreign country. As to coal, I notice that your West Virginia friends think they cannot get along without protection. I am largely interested in coal property in West Virginia, the cost of mining which is actually less than the present duty upon bituminous coal.

The only reason why they want the duty is to make New England pay the penalty for being far away from the coal, which of itself is all the burthen New England can bear.

Ore and coal being free, the duty on pig iron should be fixed at $3 per ton. I would make it less but for one reason: that pig iron comes in ballast from England to such an extent as practically to place the English furnaces in better shape to take possession of our markets on the Coast than if they were on our side of the Atlantic. Even at $3, there will be considerable competition between foreign and American pig on the seaboard, and on the Western Coast I think the foreigners will get the market, but I cannot see why the Pacific industry should be taxed in order that other industries, thousands of miles away, should be made to flourish.

Steel ingots and steel billets, out of which a great many articles are made in this country, should be subject to a duty of $4 per ton, the additional dollar over pig being sufficient to cover any cost in the difference of labor. It is in fact doubtful whether we really pay more per ton for work done on this side than they do in England; but Carroll Wright can give you exact information on that subject.

A fair competition in rails would be produced by a duty of $6 per ton; but for the Western markets no duty at all would be required.

On beams and girders, of which I have long been a maker, but whose manufacture I propose to abandon because we are driven out of business by Western competition, and not by foreign products, I would place a duty of a half a cent per pound. The reason why this duty should be higher than the duty on rails is because of the very great waste in cutting beams, and the infinite variety of lengths and sizes that must be made to meet the demand. In making rails the rolls run often for weeks together without any change upon the same pattern, but in making beams and girders, the rolls are often changed several times a day, because the orders are necessarily irregular in quantity and for many different lengths and sizes.

I make no recommendations now in regard to bar iron, wire rods, and a great variety of other forms of iron, because I think this can be more readily done after you send me the schedule submitted to the Committee.

You will perceive that I am not an extremist in my ideas of duty. In fact, I have long thought that the iron trade would have been in a far better condition if we had never had any duties at all, but in view of public opinion and the enormous influence exercised by the iron-masters, I would concede moderate duties, sufficient to overcome the extra cost due to the difference in the wages of labor.

I send you another copy of my address made in 1890, appended to which you will find the diagrams referred to in my previous letter.

If I were able to come to Washington, I could save you a lot of trouble, but I will defer any attempt to do so until you begin to get ready to fight the battle for revenue reform. At present I am not well enough to leave home, but if I can contrive to spend a few days in Washington, I shall be very glad to do so.

To Sir Lowthian Bell, January 4, 1896 [1]

I am very much rejoiced to get your letter of the 20th ult. and to assure you of the pleasure it gives me to hear of your restoration to as good health as you have reason to expect at your advanced age. You will remember that you were ill when I was in the north of England toward the end of July last, and that I made an effort to see you, but unfortunately you had left Scarborough. . . .

The complication in which we are involved in regard to Venezuela is most deplorable. Intelligent men here do not approve of the language used by the President in his message, although the feeling is very general, nay, almost universal, that Great Britain ought to have submitted the question to arbitration and thus avoid a ground of dispute in regard to which England herself has little interest. There can be no objection whatever in determining the respective rights of Guiana and Venezuela, and it seems absurd that out of a dispute over a region which both countries ought to be glad to get rid of should arise a conflict between the two branches of the Anglo-Saxon race, upon whose peaceful relations depends the progress of mankind.

Inasmuch as you seem to think that an avowal from me might be desirable, I enclose a slip from the New York *Tribune* which promptly published my views at the time of the delivery of the message. I have thought it better to refrain from any criticism of the President, but inasmuch as the Chamber of Commerce proposed to hold a meeting, at which there might have been a regrettable explosion of feeling, I prepared the report of the committee, of which I also enclose a copy. My object was to pour oil upon the troubled waters. Of course it was necessary in criticizing the President's language to give expression to the feeling which exists here in favor of the Monroe Doctrine, although we all know that it was not intended for any such emergency as the present and forms no part of the code of international law. The fact, however, is certain that instead of the Monroe Doctrine we have learned to substitute what may be known as the American Doctrine, and it is

[1] Sir Lowthian Bell was an eminent British ironmaster and a close friend of Hewitt. This letter of course refers to the famous Venezuela message which Cleveland sent to Congress in December, 1895, recommending peremptory American action to determine the true boundary between British Guiana and Venezuela; a message which Hewitt sharply condemned.

that the Western Continent shall be sooner or later governed by its own inhabitants, without any control of the European powers. This result will come to pass during the next century, and many causes of difference will thus be eliminated with the Eastern Hemisphere. I do not believe that the peace will be broken, but I am quite sure that Great Britain will find it, for its interest in some way or other either to settle the question with Venezuela by negotiation or by a reference of the question in dispute to arbitration, to which, for the life of me, I have not been able to find any objection.

To Richard H. Edmonds, September 17, 1896 [1]

I have to thank you sincerely for sending me a copy of your pamphlet entitled, "A few Facts for the Consideration of the People of the South and West." I have read it with great interest and satisfaction. It is admirable in statement and conclusive in argument. I do not see how any fair minded man can, after considering the facts recited in your statement, believe for one moment that what is called the demonetization of silver in 1873 has had the slightest influence upon the depression in business which prevails throughout the country. This depression, is fully accounted for by the unprecedented increase in the products of the mining and manufacturing interests of the country in the decade between 1880 and 1890. The productive power of the nation has been increased beyond all precedent and all prophecy. The machinery of consumption and distribution could not possibly keep pace with such an enormous increase in production. Your statement of the facts amounts to a demonstration that silver has had nothing to do with the demoralized condition of business, and you have shown beyond cavil that a process of readjustment is going on which will inevitably restore the balance between production and consumption unless it be retarded by the false doctrines enunciated in the Chicago platform.

In confirmation of your statement that many old industries have been injured, even ruined, by the development of new and better methods and of cheaper sources of supply for raw material, I may add that during the fifty years of my connection with the iron and steel business I have seen many prosperous establishments brought to ruin by the competition with other establishments having newer and better machinery and cheaper sources of supply for raw material. The great works with which I am connected have been rebuilt three times, and yet today they are idle because the competition of Lake Superior in the North, and of Tennessee and Alabama in the South, based upon better and cheaper supplies of ore and fuel, has made it impossible to con-

[1] Mr. Edmonds was editor of the *Manufacturers' Record*, then recently established in Baltimore as a journal devoted chiefly to the business interests of the South.

tinue the business with any hope of success. The works are idle and capital to the extent of three millions of dollars has been practically destroyed. I do not believe that a single workman in the establishment is so ignorant as to attribute this result to silver legislation or to the lack of it. It is due to progress and to natural laws which intelligent men recognize as governing the business of the world.

I do not see how in any way the argument can be better stated than you have done it. You have rendered a very great service to the cause of truth and to the best interests of the country, which, in spite of the drawbacks it has had to encounter, and of the errors which have misled so many estimable voters, is making steady strides towards the readjustment which will restore confidence, and finally place the country upon the basis of enduring prosperity. I cannot believe for one moment that the nominees of the sham Democratic party at Chicago can be elected, but if such a result should come to pass, the men who have ignorantly brought about the result would be the first to shrink in dismay and despair from the disastrous consequences of their success.

So far as the Southern states are concerned, it is very difficult for any one in the North to understand how they can expect to profit by the destruction of capital and the depreciation of the currency. Ever since the close of the Civil War I have given my best efforts, and used what capital I could command towards the development of Southern industry, and I have always, when I had opportunity, endeavored to point out to my Southern friends the mistake which some of them have made, in attacking the foundations of public credit and the condition of confidence under which private capital can be secured for investment in new enterprises. While the whole country is dependent upon a stable currency based upon the best standard of value, which is gold, the South in particular has a greater interest in maintaining the highest standard of honor and good faith in public and private transactions.

To Henry L. Pierce, October 6, 1896 [1]

I would not presume to write to you if I had not heard that you had under consideration the best way for insuring the defeat of Bryan and the pernicious doctrine which he represents. My own conclusion is that the ticket nominated by the National Democracy will, if properly pushed in the Middle Western states, insure their electoral vote to McKinley. I was at first opposed to the nomination of this ticket, but from information which I have received and from subsequent reflection I am fully satisfied as to its necessity and wisdom. I am therefore doing

[1] Henry L. Pierce (1825-96) was a Democratic Representative in Congress from Massachusetts, 1893-97, and twice mayor of Boston. In 1896 he was a Gold Democrat.

all in my power to raise the funds required for an efficient campaign, under the management of the National Committee, of which Mr. Bynum is the chairman. Between that committee and the Republican committee there is entire harmony of action, and they both realize that they are working to the common end of defeating the effort which is made to array the poor against the rich. Under these circumstances perhaps you will think it advisable to help me in the effort to sustain the National movement. If so I will either receive or convey any subscription which you may see fit to make to the committee. You will of course understand that I do not appeal to you on personal grounds, although, recalling our friendly intercourse, I should not hesitate to do so if I felt that any personal appeal was necessary. You understand these matters as well as any man in the country, and I have too often experienced your liberality not to know that I should restrain rather than urge your generous action. I have not had the pleasure of seeing you for many years, but I hope before we leave this sphere of action that we may meet again. Meanwhile I am . . .

To George Foster Peabody, October 8, 1896 [1]

In accordance with the request contained in your letter of this date I have mailed to Don M. Dickinson my check for $20,000. In my note to Mr. Canda last evening I told him that I had secured $6,000, making the total amount in my possession actually $65,000, with a promise of $1,000 additional. Today I have received no reply from Mr. Pierce, nor from Mr. Ottendorfer,[2] from whom I expected to get a subscription. In regard to Major Byrne, it is perfectly true that I had a conversation with him yesterday. He seemed then to know of the fund and wished to learn whether any of it could be applied to the Honest Money League. I told him that it had been raised for Michigan, Indiana, and Kentucky, and that not a dollar of it could be turned over to him, but that the Republican committee had promised to take care of his arrangements. I cautioned him against speaking of the matter to others, but I may have been to blame for having spoken of it at all.

1 George Foster Peabody, born in Georgia in 1852, and prominent as a banker in New York, was enlisted this year in the Gold Democratic Party; in 1904-05 he was Treasurer of the Democratic National Committee.
2 Don M. Dickinson (1846-1917) of Michigan was Postmaster-General in Cleveland's first term, and prominent in the Gold Democratic Party in 1896; Oswald Ottendorfer, the influential owner and editor of the *Staats-Zeitung* in New York, was likewise prominent; and Charles J. Canda of New York was Treasurer of the Gold Democratic organization. Mr. Hewitt was the principal liaison officer between the Gold Democratic and Republican parties, which acted in close coöperation.

To Senator Donelson Caffery, April 17, 1897 [1]

Some weeks ago a friend of yours, whose name has slipped my memory, asked me to furnish him with some information in regard to tariff legislation. His request was rather vague, but I got together such information as I happened to have accessible and sent it to him, and I believe it has been forwarded to you. It consisted mainly of copies of my own speeches upon the tariff and of a letter which I had addressed to Mr. Dingley in regard to the duty upon iron ore. It occurs to me, however, that the whole matter may be very briefly summed up in a few propositions, which perhaps it may be convenient for you to have:

FIRST. The productive power of this country is now so great that in all staple articles we produce much more than we can consume, and therefore can expect no relief from the existing stagnation due to an overstocked market until we can sell our surplus products in the open markets of the world.

Second. The aim therefore of all tariff legislation should be to enlarge our foreign markets and to remove any obstacles which may exist interfering with our ability to meet the prices of foreign competitors.

Third. The cost of our products depends upon the value of the raw materials, the price paid for labor, and the interest upon capital. If raw materials are made dearer by legislation we cannot compete in the open markets of the world, unless we reduce the wages of labor or the interest on capital. As you know the rate of interest is now lower than it has been ever in the history of the world. There is no margin for further reduction in this direction. The removal of duties from raw materials will effect an economy to the producer. We shall have to reduce wages if we put duties on raw materials. In other words, the effect of duties on raw materials is to reduce the wages of labor.

To sum up the matter, the disease from which we are suffering can only be cured by widening the foreign markets for our goods. The laws of nature have asserted themselves even against the protective duties which have heretofore existed on raw materials, and we have secured an extension of our foreign markets, but unfortunately at the expense of the wages paid to the working man. The only service that Congress can render to the industries of the country now suffering from stagnation due to over production is to remove and not to impose duties upon any of the materials which enter into the products which we desire to sell abroad.

---

[1] Donelson Caffery (1835-1906) was United States Senator from Louisiana from 1892 to 1901 and as such a spokesman for the sugar-growing interests of his state. He had indirectly approached Mr. Hewitt for information to be used in the debates upon the Dingley Tariff Bill.

To Senator J. L. McLaurin, June 23, 1897 [1]

My old friend, Henry H. Smith, formerly the Journal Clerk of the House, has kindly sent me a copy of the *Congressional Record* for Thursday, June 17th, in which he calls my attention to some remarks of yours in reference to "free raw materials," which otherwise I would not have seen, as I am no longer compelled to wade through the dreary pages of Congressional debate. I am usually content, moreover, to pass by without notice any reference to my public career, but in this instance, it is a great satisfaction for me to find that you have carefully and judicially investigated the history of the doctrine of free raw materials in connection with the Democratic platform. So far as I know, your statement is absolutely correct, that I was the first person who brought before Congress and the Democratic Party the policy of relieving raw materials from duties of any kind, and in order that there might be no misapprehension, I defined "raw materials to be all materials which had not been subjected to any process of manufacture," and in them I included "all waste products, fit only to be remanufactured." It is also true that the leaders of the party in the House, Messrs. Morrison, Carlisle, Mills, and Tucker, did not at the time accept my views as representing the principles of the Democratic Party. Nevertheless at a later period they all came to believe in them and to advocate them. I cannot agree with you that this doctrine was not incorporated in the Democratic platform of 1884. It was my privilege to draft the financial plank in that platform as well as to write many more of its declarations. You very properly say that the reference to raw materials is somewhat indirect, but this declaration was made in the form in which it exists, because it was not deemed expedient by the committee to place it among the propositions included in the tariff plank. Nevertheless, from 1884 the debates in the House and before the people show clearly that the doctrine of free raw materials had come to form one of the fundamental principles upon which the political contests were carried on. You are quite right in saying that President Cleveland adopted this policy, and in accordance with the general views of the leaders of the party, the schedules of the Mills Bill were practically copied from the draft of a previous bill which I had introduced into the House, and which was referred to the Committee on Ways and Means.

I have therefore to thank you for making my true position known in reference to this important doctrine, without the adoption of which in tariff legislation there cannot be any permanent return to prosperity. The bill now pending before the Senate is drawn in absolute negation to the doctrine of free raw materials. I have no doubt that it will be

---

[1] John Lowndes McLaurin served as Senator from South Carolina, 1897-1903.

enacted into a law, and I predict that the depression which now exists will be intensified until the whole revenue legislation of the country is reformed upon the basis of free raw materials.

In one respect only I feel aggrieved by your remarks. You quote from a speech of Mr. Townsend of Ohio [1] in reply to my speech of 1882, in which he attributes to me selfish motives in proposing and advocating free raw materials. In this he did me very great injustice, which he afterward was led to acknowledge, for it so happened at the time of my speech I was probably the largest owner of iron mines and miner of iron ores in the United States. My interests were in the Lake Superior region, in New York, in New Jersey, in Pennsylvania, in Virginia, in West Virginia, in Tennessee, and in Alabama, in all of which states I was the owner and worker of iron mines. If therefore the policy were a selfish one it can only be so considered on the ground that I believed the iron business, in which I was engaged, would be benefited and not injured by free raw iron ore. This in fact was my conviction and upon which I acted, not only with reference to the business in which I was interested, but in reference to every other business which depended upon imported raw materials. I am sorry therefore to notice the remark that you were "thus led to suspect the doctrine of free raw material originated with Mr. Hewitt and that his motives were somewhat selfish." I am not conscious of ever having in my public career acted upon selfish motives, but in this particular case, as you will readily perceive from my interest in iron mines, I was acting against the general conviction of my fellow ironmasters. . . .

To Senator J. L. McLaurin, June 30, 1897

I did not asknowledge the receipt of your friendly letter, because I wished first to read carefully your tariff speech in the House in March last. I have now carefully perused it, and I can say frankly that it confirms the high estimate which I had formed of your intellectual honesty and your ability to deal with economic questions.

It is the work, however, of a trained logician and of a well read lawyer. From your standpoint and your premises, your conclusions are amply justified. What you lack, however, is a knowledge of the actual conditions of business and the developers of the industrial world.

If your experience had been of a more practical nature I feel quite certain that your conclusions would have corresponded with the declarations contained in my speech on the "Emancipation of Labor," which I enclosed to you in my last letter. I invite you to read the Appendix on page 22, being a letter to the Albany *Argus*, dated December 26th, 1883.

[1] Amos Townsend (1821-1905), Representative from Ohio 1877-83 and long a Republican leader in Cleveland, O.

The lapse of fourteen years has not materially changed the present conditions from those which prevailed at that time, while the experience of the interval fully demonstrates the truth of the statements which were then made. Your error lies in confining the work of production and distribution to this country. You have not sufficiently considered the fact that we now produce a surplus of every staple article and of very many manufactured products. Low prices prevail here because the domestic market will not take the goods. The only solution of the difficulty is to sell our surplus products in foreign markets, and there is no reason why we should not take the position now occupied by Great Britain in the open markets of the world. We have cheaper food, more efficient labor, and more varied natural productions. The only reason why we do not drive Great Britain out of the open markets of the world is that we cannot sell our goods as cheaply as she can.

Great Britain has free raw materials. We have taxed raw materials. The amount of the tax handicaps us in every way and it can only be met by a corresponding deduction from the wages of labor.

Hence a tax on raw materials, so far from protecting labor, involves a distinct reduction in its compensation. Such a reduction is naturally and properly resisted by the trade unions, but the result is that large numbers of workmen can find no employment, and honest laborers are converted into tramps. I pray you to give careful consideration to this view which I know to be absolutely correct. And I pray you to do so, especially because I foresee that you will exercise a powerful influence in establishing the tariff legislation in the future, and therefore upon the destinies of this country. You have a great opportunity for good, and your speech convinces me that you will follow your convictions wherever they may lead. My only object in writing this letter is to try to put you on the right track. Personally I have no interest to serve. My day of usefulness, whatever it may have been, is past.

I am not engaged in any business which can be benefited by protective duties, although I am bound to confess that I would share in the general prosperity which would come from the removal of all restrictive impediments to free trade. As to my last letter, it was like this one, written without any idea of having it published. Nevertheless, if you think it will serve any good purpose you are quite welcome to put it in the *Record*, although the disclaimer which it contains has appeared already in some form or other two or three times in the proceedings of Congress.

To the Rev. Henry M. Field, July 7, 1897 [1]

I have to thank you very much for the advance sheets of the chapter in the life of your brother Dudley, relating to the Electoral Commission. There is nothing in the statement made by you in which exception can be taken, and the opinions expressed therein are certainly beyond dispute at this late day. There is much, however, that might be added, if it were consistent with your plans, but I infer that other subjects are much more important in making the record of his long and honorable career. I may however properly mention one fact with which you may not be familiar. At the close of the electoral struggle in 1877 your brother and I came to the conclusion that the fraud had been made effective by the use of the troops at the polls, then authorized by law. We concluded that this violation of the principles of constitutional government ought to be redressed.

I asked him to prepare the way by writing some articles on the subject. Thereupon he contributed two articles to the *Albany Law Journal,* which are models of sound principle and of able discussion. With this ammunition I attached to the Army Appropriation Bill, of which I had charge in the 45th Congress, a provision repealing the power which then existed to detail U. S. troops to keep order at the polls. The records will show that the discussion occupied much of the time of the second session of Congress, and that at length a final adjournment took place without passing the appropriation bill—an event very unusual in the history of legislation.

The point of difference was the clause in reference to the use of the troops at the polls insisted upon by a Democratic House and rejected by a Republican Senate. President Hayes called an extra session of the 46th Congress, when the Army Appropriation Bill was passed, containing the proposed clause which had been the cause of its rejection in the previous Congress. Thus, although your brother was neither in the 45th Congress, nor the 46th, his work was made effective. I was naturally the spokesman in the 45th Congress, and I suppose I ought to be credited with the success of this legislation which resulted in free elections, where previously there had been coercion and intimidation on the part of the administration. I do not know whether you will care to refer to this matter, but if you do, you will have to read the discussions in the 45th and 46th Congress, which you will find under the head of Army Appropriation Bill.

I am glad to learn that we may hope to have a visit from you at Ringwood, thus renewing the pleasant memories of a time when you

[1] Dr. Field (1822-1907), author and Presbyterian clergyman, was long owner and editor of the *Evangelist* in New York; he was a brother of Cyrus W. and David Dudley Field. Mr. Hewitt knew all three well, and Cyrus W. Field was long his close neighbor.

and I were both much younger and when we learned to know and respect each other's motives and actions.

To R. D. Haislip, June 16, 1898 [1]

I acknowledge the receipt of your letter of the 14th inst. merely as a matter of courtesy, since you have been good enough to enlarge upon the subject to which I have given a great deal of attention. As you are probably aware, for many years, both in Congress and out of it, I have endeavored to keep my Southern friends within the lines of sound doctrine in regard to financial questions. Such leading men as Randolph Tucker, of Virginia, and Benjamin Hill, of Georgia, of course required no instructions. There were many others, however, with honest intentions who were misled by the accidents of the times and by their sympathy with those who had lost all in the Civil War. As long as I remained in Congress the Democratic Party was practically kept within the traces, but afterward it went wild and culminated in the Chicago platform on which Bryan made his campaign.

I have followed the work of the Baltimore *Record* with great sympathy and interest, and have endeavored to strengthen the hands of Mr. Edmonds in every way, as he will tell you. I am now, however, too far advanced in years to continue the work with any vigor, although I will never lack interest in the subject.

In one of my speeches, which I will try to mail to you, I pointed out as far as I was able the beneficent influence of corporations upon the development of the country, but more particularly their value as defenders of the rights of property and of individual liberty. It is curious that the mass of the people of this country should fail to recognize their best friends, because corporations have been the only barrier between the despotism of ignorance and the invasion of the rights of property. Doubtless they abuse their privileges at times, but they alone have the ability and the courage to resist attack, and they are doing the work which was done by Jefferson and Madison in the early years of the Republic. I can only wish you success in the efforts you are making to promote sound public opinion, and I can assure you that no man can render greater service in his day and generation.

To Colonel Thomas T. Crittenden, June 8, 1900 [2]

It was a genuine surprise as well as a great pleasure for me to get your letter of the 3d of May, which has been upon my desk ever since,

---

[1] Mr. Haislip was editor of the Staunton (Va.) *Daily News.*

[2] Thomas Theodore Crittenden (1832-1909), a nephew of Senator John J. Crittenden, was a Democratic Representative in Congress from Missouri, 1873-75 and 1877-79; later, in 1881-85, he was Governor of Missouri.

awaiting a favorable opportunity for me to acknowledge its receipt. I thank you very much for the kindly feeling which you still entertain toward a colleague with whom you were sometimes, but not often, in difference. You left upon my memory only the most pleasant impression, and I have often hoped that you would come to New York and make me a visit, if in the summer time, to my home at Ringwood, New Jersey. Perhaps you will be here this summer with some of your family, and you may be sure of a warm welcome both from Mrs. Hewitt and myself.

I remember very well the incident to which you refer, when I had a colloquy with you during the extemporaneous speech on the currency question. I think your friendly interjections are all recorded in the *Record,* which, however, I have not seen for some years. You did not know, however, the circumstances under which the speech was delivered. It was not a written speech, nor had I any brief even of what I intended to say. I had arranged with Gen. Garfield to discuss the subject in the morning hour, and he was to take the hour at night. I agreed to present the resumption of specie payments in France as an object lesson, and he undertook to deal with the conditions in this country. We had a conference in the Library and went over the points of the discussion. The next morning, however, he asked me if I would let him speak in the morning session, as he had another engagement leaving the night session to me. I agreed as a matter of course and was very much astonished when he took the floor to find that he discussed the French question which had been reserved for me and avoided altogether the question of domestic finance. In other words, he stole my thunder, and as he did not give me his brief, I was left to do the best I could on the spur of the moment. Probably I gained by the exchange and the exigency of the occasion. Nevertheless, it was a trying position, from which I was somewhat relieved by the evident interest which you showed in my treatment of the question.

The outlook for the Democratic Party is, of course, very gloomy. In fact, there is no such party. It was captured by the Populists and the old-fashioned Democrats are left in a hole, from which they cannot emerge with any hope of success. I voted for McKinley, and rather than see Bryan elected I will vote for him again, although I have nothing in common with his economic views and think he is a trimmer on all great questions. Nevertheless, the peril of a depreciated currency overrides every other consideration in my mind. We have now got upon a firm basis, and if no disturbance in the standard of value takes place, we have before us a career of unexampled prosperity. All progress means better conditions for the working people. They are today better paid than at any previous era in the history of the race. They have more comforts and they have more power, which I am sorry to say they are not always using wisely. The great enemy of progress is ignorance. When the workmen become more enlightened, many of the present dangers will disappear.

To the editor of the New York Sun, January 5, 1901

You have rendered an inestimable service to the people of New York by the publication in the *Evening Sun* of Friday, January 4th, of a thorough, though revolting, account of the moral condition of the region east of the Bowery, known as the "Red Light District." I only know one man in New York who could have prepared this article.[1] If I am right in my conjecture he has established a new claim to our gratitude for this addition to his former publications in regard to the Tenement House System of New York. I venture to hope that you will give this article wider circulation by reprinting it in your morning edition. It ought to reach the notice and the conscience of every self-respecting citizen of New York. It reveals a condition which cannot be allowed to continue unless we are prepared to abnegate our duties as men and as citizens. There should be no delay in bringing this deplorable condition of affairs to a speedy termination, and it should be made impossible ever to see a resurrection.

The gravity of the situation was not, however, unknown to anyone who has had occasion to visit the district referred to and to study and to witness the exhibition of vice, which was not even concealed by any respect for decency. Hence when I was asked to make a brief address at the Annual Meeting of the Educational Alliance, and afterward at the public meeting held at the Chamber of Commerce building and later at the services at the Pro-Cathedral, I felt constrained to violate the rule which forbids a veteran "To lag superfluous on the stage." [2] The remarks which I made were not well reported, and hence they did not receive the approval of the *Sun*. Some of my statements were entirely misrepresented, and the main point of my address at the Pro-Cathedral, where no reporter was present, was entirely missed by the well-meaning person who gave a summary of my remarks to the press. I did not condemn the pursuit of business and the acquisition of wealth. I did not intimate that the rich men of New York were not freely giving to works of charity. On the contrary, I bore testimony to their munificent liberality.

[1] Mr. Hewitt referred to Jacob Riis, with whom he had been closely associated in establishing small parks in New York City. Riis was long a reporter for the *Evening Sun.*

[2] Mr. Hewitt's speech at the Pro-Cathedral in Stanton Street in 1900, at a meeting to raise funds for slum work, is summarized in Nevins, *Abram S. Hewitt, with Some Account of Peter Cooper,* 596.

I did, however, condemn the pursuit of wealth as a final end, and I urged upon rich men to expend a larger portion of their profits in rectifying the evil conditions which had been produced in the course of the acquisition of these properties. I stated that the importance of an improvement of the environment of the working classes of the city could not be overestimated. I stated that a very much larger amount must be expended in educational and social movements than had heretofore been done. I think it is the duty of the rich men to do this work voluntarily, but if it is not done I think it is the duty of the city, as a community, to undertake some of the improvements which are so imperatively demanded for public safety and common decency. You stated in one of the articles I refer to that millions of money will be available when proper opportunities for expenditure are pointed out, and you ask me to indicate in what direction these millions can be advantageously expended. This is a reasonable request, with which I think I am bound to comply.

By common consent the region referred to is criminally overcrowded. The tenement system, which prevails in that part of the city, has been condemned by every association which has ever made any investigation of the subject. When I was Mayor I secured the first report upon the subject, the result of which was the passage of the Small Park Act and the cleaning out of the intolerable nuisances which prevail in what was called the Mulberry Bend. Under the Small Park Act it was intended that the city should expend a million of dollars per annum, which was supposed to supply one new park each year. If this duty had been performed many of the evils which have now become intolerable, would have been abated. The tenement house system, however, would not thus have been improved. The only method ever pointed out for curing this evil is the demolition of the present houses and the reconstruction of buildings furnished with modern sanitary appliances and a proper amount of air and space.

I have no hesitation in saying, therefore, that any rich man in New York, who wishes to render the community a public service, can find an outlet for all his available means in the reconstruction of tenements on the East Side, preferably block by block, if sufficient money can be got. This duty will be cheerfully performed by the City & Suburban Building Association, already organized, and ready to expend any amount of money which may be supplied. It is under the best possible management, and its stockholders are among the most reputable citizens of New York. The money thus expended will not be money given away. It can be made to pay a revenue of 5 percent per annum and yet furnish decent accommodations for half the present rental which is paid by the unfortunate dwellers of the East Side. I consider tenement house reconstruction to be the emergent duty of New York, and if the money shall not be forthcoming by private subscription or by private effort I think the city will be justified and ought to undertake the work in the same manner as the County Council is now doing in London.

If the above suggestion does not form a sufficient outlet for the countless millions of which you speak, I venture to call the attention of the rich to the necessity of adding to the funds of the New York Kindergarten Association, which has struggled for many years to take the little children from the streets and give them at least a chance to grow into promising boys and girls. Several hundred thousand dollars a year could be profitably expended in this direction. Besides instruction and recreation the children should be supplied with at least one good nourishing meal during school hours.

When the children are thus cared for, provision should be made for the care of respectable old men and women who are no longer able to earn their own living. There are several homes for old people in New York, some nonsectarian, and others connected with the various religious denominations. They are all full. They are clamoring for more money in order to enlarge their accommodations. I think that five million dollars could be at once profitably devoted to aiding the various societies which have undertaken, and are performing, the duties which belong to society at large.

I have thus indicated three directions in which large amounts of money can be well expended and in which the organizations already exist, under competent management, to expend wisely any money which may be confided to their administration. I refrain from recommending any of the various educational movements because I think the directions which I have indicated above will absorb all the money which will probably be available, notwithstanding your assurance that the amount is unlimited.

You state that lawyers are constantly in trouble with their clients because they cannot advise proper directions in which to distribute the fortunes of testators who desire to benefit the public. I am amazed at this statement. In the Directory of the Charity Organization Society will be found the names of more than one hundred associations in this city whose usefulness is acknowledged and whose lack of means is regularly set forth. In fact, the intending testator can hardly go amiss, and I think a study of the wills which have been probated during the last five years in this city show that the testators have been at no loss to find worthy recipients of their bounty.

To the editor of the New York Sun, January 9, 1901

We seem to be in agreement that the congested and lamentable condition of the tenement house district of New York demands not only serious attention but proper and effective measures for its reformation. In response to your suggestion that I should point out how the rich men of New York could contribute most effectively to this desirable end, I recommended that they should use more of their means in enterprises which would improve the environment of the masses of the people. Knowing very well the difficulty of inaugurating the measures which I recommended, I pointed out that responsible incorporated bodies already existed, charged with the duty of giving instruction to the children, of providing homes for the aged, and of replacing pestiferous tenements with improved dwellings. I also stated that the money could be used in the latter direction so as to earn 5 percent and still supply decent accommodations, with all the sanitary appliances required, at about half the cost of the present rents paid by the occupants of the tenement district. To this suggestion you reply that any scheme which offers to pay 5 percent will not lack capital in this city, provided the honesty of the management is assured. In this position you are correct. You will be glad to see by the report of the City & Suburban Homes Company, of which I enclose a copy, that all the capital which they have asked for up to this time has been freely subscribed. The first million was oversubscribed. The second addition to the capital of $500,000, announced recently, is already in process of voluntary subscription by parties who are seeking to combine a reasonable investment with a public benefit. The company does not seek from the public capital which can be profitably expended in rebuilding the tenement house region. They are prepared, however, to administer all the money which may be offered to them and I am informed by the president that my estimate of one hundred millions of dollars for the whole undertaking is not too large and that his company now see their way clear to expend at least half that amount, not of course all at once but by additions to the improved dwellings which they have already erected both upon the East and West sides of the city. The way is open, therefore, for any rich man who can spare money for this purpose to place it where it will yield a sufficient return and at the same time remove the reproach which all good citizens feel when they see how the working classes of this city are housed. One of your correspondents very properly states the difficulty of providing homes for the occupants of the houses which are thus torn down. The process will be gradual and not more probably than a thousand tenants would be displaced at any one time.

In this connection it may be well for me to state that in devising the Rapid Transit system, now in process of execution, I had in view and clearly described in my message the advantage which it would offer for distributing the working population over a wider area. The scheme, as you know, looks to the return of the whole system to the city at the end of fifty years, free and clear of all indebtedness. No sinking fund will then be required, and the cost of transportation can be reduced from five to three cents, which of itself relieves the problem of housing the working people of New York from most of its difficulties. In other words, a very much larger area will be available for use in this direction, and the environment of the outlying regions will be much more favorable to their sanitary condition.

I forbear to give you the names of the directors of the City & Suburban Homes Company, but they are among the most responsible and energetic business men in this city. They have made no parade of their work, but it is certainly progressing in a manner which is full of encouragement to its projectors and to the people of New York who feel that the fundamental principle of any permanent reformation in the physical and moral condition of the congested districts must rest upon the creation of improved and decent dwellings. The difficulties, which you suggest in regard to the management and to keeping the houses clean and in good order, were not found to exist. They have many hundreds of tenants who cheerfully comply with the rules, and a careful supervision is kept up as to every apartment in order that they do not fall below the standard. . . . I pray you not to imagine that I do not see all the difficulties connected with the administration of charity and especially in the use of large means for the public good. Having spent a lifetime in the study of the question, I can say positively that I would have no difficulty whatever in recommending useful, and even moderately remunerative, investments for very large amounts of money. In doing this, I am fully aware that money ought not to be used to pauperize any portion of the community, and the example of some of our rich men, who have been giving large sums of money for educational purposes upon condition that the community shall raise an equal amount, is most highly to be commended. I think the past five years is very full of encouragement for an improved social condition in this country everywhere. In New York unfortunately we have allowed one evil to outrun the remedies which ought to be applied. It will take us many years to remedy the evil of congested population, but the completion of the Rapid Transit system will be a great step toward its solution.

In the meantime one of your correspondents is quite right in saying that many of the evils complained of exist only because they are tolerated by the police, and that an enforcement of existing laws, under a conscientious administration of the city government, would in a very short time put a totally different face upon the deplorable exhibition of vice and immorality which you have so fully described in the *Evening Sun.*

To Stuyvesant Fish, February 8, 1901 [1]

As I have already told you, I am very much obliged to you for remembering me in connection with the Fiftieth Anniversary of the granting of the charter of the Illinois Central Railroad Company. I regret that I cannot attend the dinner, and still more that I do not find the time to write such a letter as I feel the occasion demands.

I do not know who originated the scheme upon which the charter was granted and the land grant was made by the United States to the State of Illinois. It was, however, a stroke of genius. The situation was peculiar. The State of Illinois was but sparsely settled, and only where there were means of communication with the outer world. The great central portion of the state was practically unoccupied. It consisted of a vast prairie of fertile land; and, in the southern part, of timber lands, in some portions underlaid with coal. The whole of this vast territory was inaccessible. The lands were open to purchasers under the Homestead Act at one dollar and twenty-five cents per acre, but very few settlers appeared, and the state gained very slowly in population and wealth. It occurred to someone that if the Government would grant the alternate sections of land and double the price of the remaining sections, it would lose no money, but, on the contrary, would gain a large revenue from the early sale of the lands, which otherwise would be indefinitely postponed. It was believed that with the land grant of the alternate sections, amounting to two million, six hundred thousand acres, means could be raised to build the road, and that when built the rapid settlement of the country would make it at first self-sustaining, and in time a profitable investment. On this theory capital was to be solicited, so that the original payment upon the stock need not exceed 10 percent, and all the money required for building the road could then be raised upon construction bonds, which would ultimately be paid off by the sales of land received from the general Government. The state of Illinois protected itself by a reservation of 7 percent of the gross earnings, in lieu of all taxation. This latter feature was unique and shows the wisdom of the statesmen who drew up the charter and who arranged for the transfer of the land grant from the state to the railroad company.

My knowledge of the undertaking began with the formation of the company, of which my friend, Robert Schuyler, was the first president, and the engineer selected was Col. Roswell B. Mason, whom I had

---

[1] Stuyvesant Fish (1851-1923) was a son of the eminent Hamilton Fish; in 1887 he became president of the Illinois Central Railroad, and held that post for more than twenty years, being forced out because of his courageous stand in 1906 against the scandalous misconduct of officers of the Mutual Life Insurance Company, of which he was a trustee.

known in connection with New England railways. The Board of Directors was probably the most substantial that had ever been got together for a public enterprise on the American continent. The leading merchants and bankers of New York were on the board, the stock was promptly subscribed and the initial payment of 10 percent in cash was made. No one expected that any more payments would ever be required.

As a matter of fact, none were required until misfortune overtook Robert Schuyler, who was the soul of the enterprise. The directors were thrown into great confusion by the unexpected resignation of all his trusts. A financial panic ensued, in which it seemed as if the whole enterprise would be wrecked. It took great courage on the part of the directors who decided to remain in the company and of the new associates whom they selected to execute the enterprise. Chief among the latter were William H. Osborn and John A. Griswold, both of whom were connected with original members of the board. Some of them remained, and to Jonathan Sturgis, J. N. A. Allsop, and Leroy M. Wiley in particular the very greatest credit is due for their tenacity of purpose, their confidence in the ultimate success of the company, and for the liberal manner in which they pledged their private fortunes to the execution of the original plan. It became necessary, however, to make further calls upon the capital stock, and ultimately the whole amount was called in, causing the stock to depreciate in the market to a mere fraction of the amount of money actually paid for it. I think it necessary to refer to this, because when I was in Congress Judge Holman was very fond of asserting that the stock of the company had cost its holders nothing, and that the Government was therefore justified in requiring that the mails and transportation should be made free for all public purposes.

The fact is that among all the Western railroads, I should think the Illinois Central is probably the only one in which the stock was ever paid for in cash, in which no bonuses were ever given to anyone for underwriting its securities, and no sacrifices of ultimate profits made for the purpose of raising capital. In the panic of 1857 the road passed into the hands of receivers, Mr. Frederick Schuchardt and Mr. Edward Cooper of New York. Both of these gentlemen declined all compensation, but finally accepted a remuneration of two thousand dollars, each, to be invested in a souvenir of the arduous labor which they performed. With the recovery of confidence the road was restored to the trustees, and during the eighteen years with which I was connected with it, its affairs were administered with great energy, intelligence, economy, and a due regard for the public interest.

On the whole, looking back, I do not believe that any enterprise ever undertaken in the United States can show such a record of self-sacrificing devotion on the part of the directors and the officers of the company, and of results based upon the actual expenditure of the money without the infusion of water, as it is called, of any kind into its stock or its securities.

The subsequent success of the company under your wise and vigilant administration is a matter of general congratulation, but in your jubilation it would be wrong if you were to overlook the services which were rendered by Mr. Osborn, Col. Mason, John M. Douglas, J. N. Perkins, and others who were prominently connected with the management of its affairs. "They builded wiser than they knew," and the best part of their labor consists in the fact that it has inured to the development of a great state, the enlargement of the resources of the United States, and the general advantage of the whole world.

I think I may properly add that I was one of the persons called in to act as a director in the reorganization of the board in 1854 and that I continued in the board until 1872. My term of service covered eighteen years, during which time the road was completed, the finances of the company put in excellent order, and the preliminary arrangements made for the extension of the lines to the Gulf of Mexico on the south and to the Missouri River on the west. In fact, the directors even contemplated the possibility of a line to the Pacific Ocean, and I was concerned as one of the original projectors of the Dubuque and Pacific R. R. Co., as it was at first called, now controlled and operated by your company. Other organizations, however, took up the land grants for the Pacific lines, with which the Illinois Central has a connection quite as advantageous as if its own line has been extended to the ocean.

As I believe I am the oldest living ex-director, it may be proper to add that none of us received any compensation for our services, and that at the last meeting which I attended, prior to my resignation, the sum of five dollars in gold was given to each director as a souvenir. This coin, the only compensation which I received for my services and devotion to the public good, is treasured by my family as a memento, and the share of stock, which I originally purchased in order to qualify me as a director, still remains in my possession as a reminder of the greatest and most difficult enterprise with which I have ever been connected.

To Andrew Carnegie, June 11, 1901

While you were making your splendid speech on Wednesday last at the Chamber of Commerce banquet, I was trying to enforce the lesson of your career and that of Mr. Cooper [1] at the Commencement of the Cooper Union which was held on the same evening. I intended to send you a stenographic copy of my extempory remarks, with a full ex-

[1] Peter Cooper, founder of Cooper Union.

planation of the condition of affairs which are discussed in the *Annual Report*, copies of which have been mailed to you and Mrs. Carnegie. Yesterday, however, there appeared in the *Herald* and I am told in the *World* and the *Journal* a statement in regard to your intention to give a large sum of money to the Cooper Union for the completion of its plans and to cover the expense of carrying on the work on a much larger scale. I enclose the clipping from the *Herald* which contains these statements. I need scarcely say that I was extremely annoyed, and I did not hesitate to express my opinion of such unscrupulous journals to the *Herald* reporter and to the other reporters who came to see me. I enclose a copy of the correction which has been made, very grudgingly, as you will see, in the *Herald*. I also enclose a cutting from the *Times* of this morning, which states more explicitly the contradiction which I felt constrained to make. The *Times* man goes too far, however, when he says that I have no expectation of any further gifts from you. You have at various times mentioned to me your intentions. I have at all times disclaimed any desire to secure further endowment until you and Mrs. Carnegie have made a study of the institution. Of course whenever you want to do anything, the trustees will be only too glad to complete the scheme which was originally prepared for the Cooper Union and to appropriate the entire building to free education. No one, however, connected with the institution, and least of all myself, desires to foreclose your judgment, or to put you in a position where you are committed to do anything more than shall seem good to you after a study of the situation.

Having said thus much, it is proper for me now to add that we feel that the final devotion of the building to its public uses should be no longer delayed. Hence Mr. Cooper [1] and I have decided to make all the changes that will ultimately be required. We are of course prepared to pay for what we undertake to do. More money will be required to occupy the additional space and to pay for the enlarged instruction. I have never for a moment doubted that when you deem it necessary you would gladly appropriate some portion of the means which you are distributing with such a lavish hand to the extension and completion of the Cooper Union work. In other words, I know how anxious you are to use your means in directions where it will not be possible to pauperize the community, and in which the results heretofore achieved have been found to be beneficial.

I still hope that we shall get the Armory building, when a very great extension will be possible, but that is a matter for future action, and it may not be accomplished until after I have passed away.

It can safely be left, however, in the hands of the trustees, of whom

[1] That is, Mr. Edward Cooper, son of Peter Cooper, brother-in-law of Mr. Hewitt, and ex-mayor of the city.

you and Mr. Cutting and Mr. Parsons [1] will necessarily be the controlling powers after Mr. Cooper and I have ceased from our labors.

Your gift to Scotland excites universal interest and admiration. My only criticism is, and I think I made it in my address, that if the Scotchmen are made more advanced than they have proved themselves to be in the past, they will own the earth and our Jewish friends will have to retire to Palestine for a scanty living.

Cadwalader [2] tells me that the library authorities have come to an understanding with the city authorities in regard to the new libraries here. This is very encouraging, and shows that your judgment was correct as to what was required to perfect the library system in New York city.

It is not impossible that I may give up my objection to leaving home, because Mrs. Hewitt and my daughters are extremely anxious to make a trip to Europe this year. Of course I would be glad to come, and above all to make you a visit at Skibo if my physical infirmities would permit. As they are, however, I cannot leave home without considerable risk, and hence I may not feel able to go abroad. If I should do so, however, I will let you know, and you may be sure that if we are well enough we will taste your bread and salt at Skibo, where oatmeal is served out freely to all comers.

To Dr. George L. Miller, June 21, 1901

I have read your communication to the Utica *Observer* with very great interest, and I need scarcely add that I am very grateful for the appreciation which you have always shown and continued to manifest in my public career. While I have never been able to subscribe to your high estimate of my capacity, I have always felt that you understood better than anyone else the methods which governed me in the discharge of my public duties. My relations with Mr. Tilden were of course very intimate and at times aggravating. It has often been said that in Washington at the close of the Electoral Commission debate I acted contrary to his wishes. This I have always denied, because there was not the slightest foundation for such a charge. I came to New York expressly on the Saturday prior to the final vote for the purpose of getting his views on the subject, and I told him, in the presence of Clarkson N. Potter,[3] that the Democratic majority were prepared to follow his decision in the matter, whatever it might be. They would either approve

[1] R. Fulton Cutting and John E. Parsons, trustees of Cooper Union.

[2] John L. Cadwalader, the well-known New York attorney; Assistant Secretary of State under Hamilton Fish.

[3] Clarkson Nott Potter (1825-82) was Democratic Representative from New York City, 1869-75 and 1877-79.

or reject the Commission Bill as he might finally decide was best to be done. We could get no decision from him, and finally when I left him I told him distinctly that unless I heard to the contrary I would assume that he was in favor of the passage of the bill. I never had one syllable from him indicating any opposition to the bill, but I had telegrams asking for delay. Of course delay was impossible, but I did succeed in getting the final vote postponed for one day in order that Pelton might come to New York and bring back his final decision. Pelton, on his return, told us to go ahead and pass the bill, and we did so, supposing that he spoke for Mr. Tilden. I have no reason to doubt that Pelton acted in good faith, but it is quite certain that Mr. Tilden himself never expressed any dissent, either to Randall or myself, from the action proposed to be taken by the Democratic majority.

Moreover, I see now very clearly that we did the right thing. We saved the country from civil war and possibly from an administration which might have been as disastrous as a civil war.

You are quite right in regard to Hayes, He was not elected to the office and his conduct in securing it was that of a traitor. When he passed under the guidance of Evarts, he tried to be fair, and the four years of his administration was a period practically of rest for the country, which it sadly needed. I never spoke to Mr. Hayes, and I had a great contempt for the methods by which he secured the office. Nevertheless, I think his administration was creditable to all concerned and was far better than four years of unrest which we should undoubtedly have had if Tilden had occupied the office of President. Sometimes we are disposed to doubt the guilding will of Providence in the history of mankind, but looking over the ground I feel that there never was in the history of the world an occasion where the interposition of a Higher Power was more manifest and more productive of good to the welfare of an entire country.

To a committee in the Bronx, July 15, 1901

I am in receipt of your letter of the 8th inst. in reference to the name of the high school nearly or quite completed in the Borough of the Bronx. I regret very much to learn that a difference of opinion exists as to the proper name for this new addition to the facilities for higher education in the city of New York. The only embarrassment, however, arises from the fact that the Board of Education in June, 1900, decided to call the building "The Peter Cooper High School." This action was taken without any consultation with the family of the late Peter Cooper, and when communicated to them was naturally regarded as an honor which they were in no position to decline, and which they

---

1 Colonel William T. Pelton, Tilden's nephew.

also regarded as the greatest tribute which had been paid by his fellow citizens to the memory of Mr. Cooper. No intimation was given that there was any difference of opinion as to the propriety of this action. From time to time, however, I have noticed paragraphs in the newspapers stating that the people of the Bronx desire that the name shall in some way perpetuate the memory of the Morris family, who for two centuries had been identified with Westchester County and whose eminence in all the walks of life had conferred honor upon the State of New York.

Until the receipt of your letter, however, the matter was never brought to the notice of the family of Mr. Cooper. You may be sure that they are extremely unwilling to be in the position of accepting an honor which in the public judgment ought, under the circumstances, to have been awarded to another family. They recognize the entire propriety of the title of "The Morris High School," which is proposed by your committees to be given to this school. There is no more eminent family in the State of New York and none which has rendered greater services to the people of this city and this state than the several generations of the Morris family, who for two hundred years have been identified with every movement for the development of the state and the creation of the free government under which we live. Mr. Cooper would if he were alive be the first man to urge the association of the name of the Morris family with any public building which might be established in the territory with which they were identified and more highly distinguished than any other family in that portion of the city.

The only difficulty would seem to arise from the action of the Board of Education and the acceptance by the family of Mr. Cooper of the honor which they proposed to confer. I can perfectly well understand that the members of the Board of Education feel great delicacy in making the change, which the people of the Bronx seem universally to desire. I write this letter therefore for the purpose of enabling you to say to the Board of Education that the family of Mr. Cooper will not feel in the slightest degree disturbed by the change of name to "The Morris High School," but on the contrary they desire me to express their entire sympathy with the people of the Borough of the Bronx in their wish to preserve for all time to come, and especially in the minds of the youth of the region, the memories which cluster round the name of Morris, and particularly attach to Gouverneur Morris.

To the Rev. Dr. John P. Peters, September 16, 1901 [1]

Although I am overwhelmed with accumulated work, I hasten to acknowledge the receipt of your letter of the 13th inst., which has just reached me today. I have not changed my opinion of the propriety of taking part in the Hearst Syndicate. What Hearst wants is the recognition of such men as Bishop Potter and you and others who have agreed to co-operate. He would print the Bible in chapters, if it were necessary to secure the implied endorsement for the *Journal* of men of high character. The Devil took the Saviour up in a high mountain, but He was superior to all temptation. No doubt Hearst would agree to any line of policy marked out by Bishop Potter if he could only get him to associate on terms of familiar intimacy, or become the patron of some one of his innumerable schemes for the benefit of mankind.

I return herewith the extracts from my address. I have no wish now to add anything for the simple reason that the death of the President and the collapse of the steel strike would have very great influence upon any further discussion. I will not be tempted to touch either the *Journal* or Mr. Hearst for any possible prospect of advantage in other directions, and so far as any permission is implied in what I have heretofore written to use my name in connection with the syndicate, I now withdraw it. You can make whatever extracts you see fit from the address, and you can credit them to me, but you must not state that it is done with my approval.

I shall be at Ringwood on Thursday next, but probably you will then be in New York. I shall also be there on Saturday. On either day I shall hope to see you at lunch, and then we can discuss the whole matter fully, but the more I reflect on the subject, the more I am satisfied that such traitors to humanity as Hearst should be excluded from all association, direct or indirect, with Christian gentlemen.

To C. V. Fairchild, Jr., October 9, 1901

I am in receipt of your letter of the 1st inst. asking me to furnish you with information which will be regarded as interesting in reference to the original construction of the street railways in the city of New York. I do not know that anything that I may have to say will be regarded as of general interest, but it is a fact that all the grants originally made for the Second, Third, Sixth, and Eighth Avenue lines were offered without cost to Cooper & Hewitt, who at that time were the owners of the iron works at Trenton, where special rails had been

[1] Dr. John Punnett Peters (1852-1921), Episcopal clergyman, became rector of St. Michael's Church in New York in 1893. As an officer of the Riverside and Morningside Heights Association he waged a long struggle against commercialized vice.

made for years. The late Peter Cooper was at that time the controlling power in our firm, although he was not a member of it. It had been his policy all his life to refrain from having any interests in grants made by the city of New York for public improvements. He was a man of great public spirit and, as all the world now knows, of singular disinterestedness of character. He was not willing that either he or the members of his family should be placed in the false position of being charged in the future as having profited by public grants. Other parties finally availed themselves of the opportunity offered to us. Our connection with the enterprise was therefore limited to the manufacture of the rails, which was conducted at Trenton for all the lines above referred to, and later for the Ninth Avenue Line. The original groove rail was designed by me. The center bearing rail, subsequently used, was also designed by me, the object being to prevent trucks from traveling in the groove.

After the construction of these railroads had commenced, there was great pressure to secure the rails, and the price, which was originally about $65 per ton, was advanced to $90 per ton, which was the price paid by the Second Avenue R. R. Co. for their rails. In these days of cheap steel these prices will seem to be very high, but at that time and in the state of the iron business they did not yield more than a fair profit.

The late George Law, who associated with him Oliver Charlick, constructed the Eighth and Ninth Avenue Lines, and showed much foresight in reference to the investment, which he personally superintended. The cars did not differ materially from those which have been used during the whole term of the existence of these railroads. They were smaller at first and were, I think, all constructed by John Stephenson.

I think the roads all paid from the start, except possibly the Second Avenue Line, which for a considerable time had a struggle against serious difficulties.

I do not think that there is anything else of interest connected with the matter except to call your attention to the fact that these grants originally went abegging and the companies who took them up certainly did not at the outset find that they had secured very profitable investments. The growth of population, however, was rapid, and undoubtedly greatly promoted by the construction of these roads, which, so far as their extensions to the northward were concerned, were always made in advance of the actual existence of paying traffic. I think the early builders of these roads are entitled to grateful recollection, because at the time they were supposed to take a considerable risk measured by the volume of the business as it then existed. They were men of much foresight, however, and the final results certainly justified their confidence in the success of the railways.

To Milton H. Northrup, October 9, 1901 [1]

I have just read your narrative in the *Century* of the events which preceded the formation of the Electoral Commission. I regard it as a very valuable contribution to the history of a measure which I think in the future will be regarded as solving a critical problem in free government. Your statement is absolutely impartial, and I do not see that anyone can criticize any portion of the narrative. There are some things, however, which you did not know, and which you could not use if you did know. For example, you could not know that Senator Conkling and I, as representatives of the great commercial interests of the State of New York, agreed from the beginning that we would perfect a measure and would from time to time make such concessions as might become necessary in the course of the discussion. If you will read over your own statement you will see how he and I at critical junctures interposed to remove difficulties or suggest alternative provisions. I think it is but fair to say that the commission would never have reached a conclusion but for this understanding, and I also think I am justified in adding that the conclusion arrived at by the committee was more favorable to the Democratic than to the Republican success. You very rightly say that the Davis incident was like the explosion of a bomb shell. What you say about my countenance is doubtless true, for I felt that the battle was lost. Of course I never knew the influence which was brought to bear to secure the election of Judge Davis to the Senate, but I am convinced that the Republicans took the necessary steps to secure the votes in the Illinois Legislature by promises or payments which were equivalent to a purchase.

It is quite true that I have always regarded any result as better than no decision. Time has proved the correctness of my position, but the allegation that at any time I acted contrary to the wishes of Tilden, or that I did not communicate to him every step of the negotiation, is absolutely untrue. He knew all that I knew, and if he did not approve the action of the commission he certainly never disapproved it. Moreover, before the final vote in the House was taken, his nephew, Pelton, who had been sent to New York for the purpose, came back and reported by word of mouth that Mr. Tilden was satisfied with the Electoral Commission bill and desired its passage. His statement may not have been true, but I have never seen any reason to doubt it.

[1] Mr. Northrup was secretary of the House Committee appointed late in 1876 to act with a Senate Committee in erecting a tribunal to settle the disputed election. In October, 1901, he published in the *Century Magazine* an article entitled "A Grave Crisis in American History."

To Theodore Roosevelt, October 15, 1901

On coming to town from Ringwood I find your unexpected letter of the 10th inst. I am very much surprised that, amid the overwhelming work of your great office, it has occurred to you to think of me, and I am more touched than I can describe by your evident desire to remove from my mind any impression which may have existed on either side that there had been any strain upon the old friendship which from boyhood was so pleasant an experience to your father and to me. We were indeed friends, and as you speak of good citizenship, I think I may say without vanity that we lived up, as far as we could, to the same ideals of patriotic duty. In you personally I always felt the warmest interest, and it was a real grief to me when, by the stress of political exigencies, we drifted, so to speak, somewhat apart. Nevertheless, I have followed your career with affectionate sympathy, but I did not feel at liberty to tell you how much I shared in your ambitions and in your efforts to do your full duty in every position to which you have been called. Your life has been a romance and your present position is one of which many have dreamed, but which has come to you as it would seem by the order of Providence. I can only assure you of my profound interest in all that you may do, and I am sure that your own desire to do your full duty is not greater than mine that you shall succeed.

I know that you must be absorbed in the considerations of public questions, and among them in the reciprocity policy, which President McKinley endorsed, although in the House of Representatives he was very much opposed to it. It occurs to me to send you with this note a copy of a speech on the subject which I made in the House in 1886 before Mr. Blaine had made his famous declaration in favor of reciprocity. I took so much trouble with this performance that I think it may interest you, and if it should do so, I will be glad to address to you a further communication on the subject. I only refrain from doing so now because I think it very likely that you have no time to give to the question at present, but I am sure that during your term of office you will have to deal with it in a decisive manner.

My family all join me in the expression of their sincere good will. My daughters and sons have always felt a most tender regard for your family, and they have often expressed regret that circumstances had caused us to drift somewhat apart. You may be sure, however, that if any one of them can do anything to strengthen your hands or make life more pleasant, they will consider it a privilege. Perhaps some day you and Mrs. Roosevelt will steal away from the glare of public life and give us a day or two at Ringwood, so that Mrs. Hewitt and I may renew before we go hence the warm friendship which always prevailed between the families of Peter Cooper and Cornelius Roosevelt.

Asking you to excuse the length of this note, and assuring you that I shall not as long as I live forget the feeling which prompted you at this time to express your friendship for me and mine, I remain sincerely and gratefully your friend.

To V. Henry Rothschild, October 23, 1901 [1]

Your letter of the 18th inst. presents a problem which has heretofore puzzled many people, and for which no solution has yet been found. My impression is that neither of the plans suggested by you will effect the desired reform. My own rule is to have nothing to do with sensational papers. I neither buy them, nor read them. nor advertise in them. I can readily understand, however, that others may not be so situated as to take an independent course. What I meant in my remarks at the Chamber of Commerce was that the great commercial and financial houses should withdraw their advertisements, without which the yellow journals would perish. I do not think, however, that they would be inclined to join a league for that purpose. It must be a matter of conscience with each individual person.

The suggestion that respectable newspapers should be furnished free to the masses of the people would scarcely accomplish the object. Many of them are quite unable to understand such disquisitions as appear in the *Evening Post,* the *Times,* and the *Tribune.* When Tweed abandoned Tammany Hall, Governor Tilden and many of his friends took possession and tried to convert the organization into a purely Democratic organization. They found to their disgust that the people who support Tammany Hall did not want to be reformed. They did not want the government of the people, but they wanted the government of a boss. The boss soon appeared in the person of John Kelly,[2] and the rest of us had to retire. This is the difficulty which confronts any attempt to supply the working people with a higher grade of reading. They don't want it, and they will have nothing to do with it. The yellow journals exist because there is a demand for them. The only remedy is better education, especially of the ethical kind. If Dr. Adler [3] could have his way the rising generation would not tolerate such trash as is now delivered to them.

I am sorry that I cannot suggest anything of a practical nature.

[1] Mr. Rothschild's letter has disappeared, and the editor is unable to discover any facts relating to him or to his proposals.

[2] John Kelly (1821-86), who was Representative in Congress from New York 1855-58 and sheriff of the city and county of New York 1859-69 and 1865-67, became head of Tammany Hall soon after the deposition of Tweed and remained there till his death.

[3] Felix Adler, founder of the New York Society for Ethical Culture.

In the meantime you and I will have to do what we can to elevate the masses and to prevent as far as possible the contamination and pollution produced by bad literature.

To the Rev. A. E. Hoffman, November 26, 1901 [1]

You will pardon this note from me in view of the special knowledge which I happen to have of the history of the Bryan Collection of paintings, now the property of the New York Historical Society. This collection was originally in the Cooper Union building, where I had abundant opportunity to examine it and to be assured of its very great value. It would have remained in the Cooper Union if there had been proper accommodation for a gallery of pictures. By my advice, it was finally presented to the New York Historical Society.

My daughters, who have received a careful artistic education, regard the collection as more valuable than any other in the city of New York. They have reported to me from time to time that the pictures are simply being destroyed by neglect, and they have often asked me whether I could not do something to preserve them from ruin. Today they have handed me the enclosed article printed some time ago by Mr. Charles Dowdeswell, and they assure me that his statements are entirely trustworthy and ought to attract serious and prompt attention.

Under these circumstances I venture to suggest that you shall take steps to have the pictures carefully cared for and the necessary repairs and alterations made by competent hands. No doubt this will cost money, but I am sure that when your leading members understand the pressing necessity of the case, the means will be forthcoming. Personally I should be glad to subscribe one hundred dollars toward the fund required.

I may add in conclusion that when I became mayor I found that the very valuable historical pictures belonging to the city were in the same deplorable condition. One of my first official acts was to employ competent experts to save the pictures from destruction. I doubt whether I have ever performed a public duty more valuable to the community, although I did not even allow the matter to be mentioned in the newspapers.

Apologizing for this intrusion, which is dictated solely by a sense of duty and of public spirit, I am, as always

[1] President of the New York Historical Society.

To President Theodore Roosevelt, December 5, 1901

Mr. Andrew Carnegie and Dr. Gilman [1] called upon me this morning for the purpose of considering an endowment which Mr. Carnegie proposes to make for the promotion of knowledge in this country. I need not recount the general features of the plan, which has been submitted to you and which I understand received your approval. I am glad of this, because for many years persistent efforts have been made to establish at Washington a great university in accordance with the well known suggestions of President Washington.

I had occasion, when I was in Congress, to make a very careful examination of this question, and I came to the conclusion that a national university at the capital would not be the best application of the money required for its foundation and maintenance. On the other hand, the legislation of the last Congress, providing for a commission to utilize the agencies now existing at Washington for the spread of knowledge, appeared to me to be a very wise policy fraught with benefits which can hardly be properly anticipated or estimated.

The scheme which Mr. Carnegie has formulated is in entire harmony with the ideas which led to the formation of the commission. It will put ample funds, to be used in connection with the various institutions at Washington, under the control of a Board of Trustees representing the intelligence of the country and adequate to the need, which undoubtedly exists, of supplementary aid to the work of the great universities fortunately diffused throughout the country and not concentrated in a single locality.

It is of course not possible to discuss the matter in much detail, especially as Mr. Carnegie desired me to send you this letter by today's mail. I can only briefly say that in my judgment the wise use of the great fund which he proposes to give to the United States will serve to co-ordinate the work of the great universities and enable them to engage in original research under the direction of the men who are most fitted to conduct each particular branch of investigation.

I hope, therefore, you will see your way clear to recommend to Congress the acceptance of the munificent gift which Mr. Carnegie proposes to make. Its proper use will certainly tend to make the capital of the country a great intellectual center and fulfill the objects which Washington must have had in view when he recommended the foundation of a national university. Conditions have so changed since this recommendation was made that I feel quite sure that if the Father of His Country were still living, he would recognize the greater advantages

[1] Daniel Coit Gilman (1831-1908) had resigned the presidency of Johns Hopkins University in 1901, and became head of the Carnegie Institution of Washington, 1901-3, to organize its activities.

of a central organization, working in harmony with all the other educational forces which the last century have produced in this favored land.

It seems to me that Mr. Carnegie's idea is in marvelous accordance with the spirit of the age and meets the demand coming up from all quarters for specialized knowledge in the new fields of scientific and intellectual effort which will determine the destinies of the Twentieth Century.

To F. F. Burgin, December 20, 1901 [1]

In reply to your letter of the 19th inst., I am free to say that the tariff needs revision. This revision, in order to be intelligent, must be preceded by an exhaustive inquiry into the condition of every branch of manufacture and its relation to the export and import trade of the country. No committee of Congress can by any possibility make such an investigation, and therefore a commission should be entrusted with the work and report to Congress before any legislation is initiated.

I do not think that a permanent commission will be necessary, but there ought in the Treasury Department to exist a permanent Board of Customs, where the necessary information can be accumulated and made available to all inquirers, whether in Congress or out of it. The Statistical Bureau furnishes in the main the necessary information so far as figures are concerned, but it has no jurisdiction over grievances of any kind and no power of investigation. The Board of Customs ought to be charged with the duty in order that the new conditions which are constantly developed by the growth of the country may have proper consideration and any evils which may result may be promptly removed.

To John B. Pine, December 20, 1901 [2]

I have not made any formal acknowledgment to your letter of the 2nd inst., in which you notify me that I have been elected as a Trustee of Columbia University, although I have had some correspondence with you and other Trustees in reference to the advisability, in view of my advanced age, of assuming new duties which I probably cannot discharge to my own satisfaction and to the advantage of the University in whose usefulness and prosperity we all feel so deep an interest. If I were to consult my own judgment alone I certainly would feel constrained to decline the honor, which I fully appreciate, and for which

[1] Managing editor of the New York *Commercial.*

[2] John B. Pine (1857-1922) was a distinguished New York attorney, active in civic affairs; as a member of the board of trustees of Columbia University, in 1891 he was chiefly instrumental in fixing upon the new site on Morningside Heights.

I desire to make my acknowledgment to the Trustees. It appears, however, from the letters which I have received from friends of many years standing and whose opinion ought to control my decision, that my accession to the Board will be regarded as an advantage to the institution, even though I may not be able to render efficient services.

Under the circumstances, with some reluctance, but with great satisfaction in becoming associated with members of the Board, who have by their unselfish labors converted the college into a university of the first rank, I have concluded not to decline the election.

To George W. Ochs, December 24, 1901 [1]

I am sorry to refuse, but I do not wish any portion of my letter to be published. The condition of the Democratic Party is simply deplorable. In fact it was dissolved when Bryan was nominated on the Chicago Platform. The principles, however, of the Democratic Party survive, and so far as I can see are being acted upon substantially by the Republican administration, except in the matter of the tariff, and there, as you know, was always a great divergence of opinion among the Democrats leading to compromises in the platform, which were scarcely in accordance with the fundamental principles of the organization. Moreover, the course of President Cleveland prevented any reunion of the divergent elements, and although I do not regard him as the author of the ruin of the party, I think he contributed very largely to its disintegration. I am too old to take part in any new movement, but I feel sure that the new questions, which confront us with the new century, will be met in the same spirit of resolute patriotism as preserved the Union and prevented a collision at the time of the disputed election to the Presidency. The only serious danger ahead of us is to be found in the labor question. The good sense of our people will surely solve the problem in a way that will admit of the continued growth and prosperity of the country.

To Charles R. Miller, January 14, 1902 [2]

The writer of the interesting editorial article in your issue of today, entitled "A College for Arts and Crafts," does not seem to be aware of the fact that such a museum as he desires to see established has been created during the past five years in the Cooper Union building, where it is open to the public at all times. It is already sufficiently large to meet the existing demands for artistic instruction in industrial direc-

[1] Mr. Ochs (1861-1931) later changed his name to George Washington Ochs Oakes; a brother of Adolph S. Ochs, he was for a time publisher and general manager of the Philadelphia *Public Ledger*, and later editor of *Current History*, in New York.

[2] Charles Ransom Miller (1849-1922) was editor of the New York *Times* from 1893 until his death.

tions, but under the intelligent management of the ladies who have it in charge its growth promises to be very rapid. The munificent gift of Mr. J. Pierpont Morgan of three collections of medieval stuffs has made the museum one of the richest in the world in that direction. These collections are being rapidly prepared for exhibition, and as soon as the cases are ready they will be open to public view, where they will excite general interest.

The object of this note, however, is to call attention to the existence of the museum, which appears to be but little known among the classes who are likely to profit by its study. Every facility exists in the way of classification, reference books and appliances for the proper study of the subject. The number of visitors, however, is surprisingly small, although every effort has been made to bring it to the notice of art students and industrial workers. Two classes have already been formed, one in the daytime and one at night, for the study of the best styles of art as applied to decoration.

Perhaps I ought to add that the art classes, both by day and by night, giving instruction to about fifteen hundred pupils, have for more than forty years formed the basis for the establishment of such a college as you describe. Attempts have been made at various times to form classes in special directions, but from the difficulty of procuring teachers and the want of sufficient endowment, this part of the work cannot be said to have been successful. The trustees of the Cooper Union, however, are ready now, as they have been in the past, to establish such classes, whenever the teachers can be procured and the endowment is furnished sufficient to make the instruction free to all, as it is in every other department of the institution.

To John E. Parsons, January 23, 1902

Yesterday Mr. Carnegie delivered to Mr. Cooper $300,000 of the same issue of railroad bonds as the previous $300,000. So far as Mr. Carnegie is concerned, the transaction is closed. It remains, however, for Mr. Cooper and myself to comply with our part of the agreement, which is to have the Lexington Ave. property conveyed to the Cooper Union free and clear of all liens and encumbrances whatsoever. We have arranged with our children to sign any releases which may be necessary and the trustees will execute any deed of transfer which you may advise to be prepared. I think it is desirable to have the transaction closed as soon as possible to avoid accident.

I need not tell you what a great relief all this unexpected solution gives to my mind. From this time forward we shall be fairly independent, but it will take some time to carry out all the plans which I have formed for the entire occupation of the building. To no one are we so much indebted as to you for the final outcome of Mr. Carnegie's benefaction.

To Andrew Carnegie, January 23, 1902

The three hundred thousand dollars of bonds were duly delivered by Mr. Franke to Mr. Cooper yesterday and are now in the box of the Cooper Union in the safe deposit vaults of the Mercantile Trust Co. Mr. Parsons has been instructed and is drawing up the papers by which the final transfer of the Lexington Ave. property shall be made to the Cooper Union free and clear of all liens and encumbrances whatsoever. We have arranged with our children to surrender their annuities at once, so that the Cooper Union comes into the absolute possession of a property for which $600,000 has been offered and which yields an income of twenty-five thousand dollars per annum. When the taxes are remitted, as they will be, the income will be over thirty thousand dollars, corresponding identically with the income of your munificent benefaction.

I cannot convey to you any idea of the relief which this transaction has afforded to my mind. For half a century I have been striving to secure the means to carry out the plans which I formulated originally for Mr. Cooper. Slowly, and sometimes in great perplexity, we have extended our operations until now I think we have the best organization for the practical instruction of artisans and working men which can be found in this, or any other, country. The new income will enable us to occupy the entire building or nearly so, and to pay the additional compensation which ought long since to have been paid to our teachers. We shall greatly enlarge the Physical Laboratories, so that next year we will be able to relieve the pressure which has overtasked our resources in the line of electrical instruction.

You have done a great thing for New York, but I can assure you it is a much greater thing for me personally to be permitted to see the realization of all my hopes in connection with the Cooper Union. But for your unexpected intervention these hopes could not have been realized in my lifetime. I feel now free to give you all the service of which I am capable in the execution of your national benefaction. When we go to Washington I will tell you a good deal more about my efforts in the direction of original research. I think you have done a great deal more than you can possibly realize for the advancement of science and the good of mankind. The possibilities are infinite. I can only hope that you will live long enough to see some of the great results which will be achieved. I cannot expect to see them, but I can at least help in pointing out what I believe to be the true method of procedure and this is what I want to talk to you about.

To H. H. Rogers, February 5, 1902 [1]

I have received your brief but suggestive letter of the 4th inst., and I have deposited the check for $250,000 in the Morton Trust Company to my credit as trustee pending the investment of the money, in regard to which I will venture to ask the benefit of your advice.

I have never seen a more eloquent document. The money does indeed "talk" and tells me that the hopes and labors of half a century in behalf of the Cooper Union have been brought to a happy issue. Your generosity coming so soon after the gift of Mr. Carnegie and of the children and grandchildren of Peter Cooper completes the fund which I had hoped to secure before my departure hence.

Mr. Cooper was able to erect and pay for the building, but his means did not permit him to give it an adequate endowment. For nearly fifty years the trustees have been confronted with a pressure for the privileges of the institution which they had not adequate means to meet. Up to this time Mr. Cooper's family have contributed about a million and a half of dollars in actual cash in order that his intentions might be carried into effect. Our great effort has been to free the building from tenants and to devote the entire space to the work of free instruction. Your gift enables us to accomplish this purpose and therefore crowns the enterprise with success.

I appreciate your reluctance to have your name known as the donor, but the gift will have to be acknowledged, and in time, certainly after we have passed away, if not before, your foundation ought to be designated by your name as all other gifts to the institution have been up to this time.

The trustees had their regular monthly meeting last night. You can imagine their surprise and their gratification, and they all join with me in extending their thanks to the unknown giver of so great an amount. The other trustees are Mr. Edward Cooper, Mr. John E. Parsons, Mr. R. Fulton Cutting, and Mr. Andrew Carnegie. None of them know from whom the gift comes, but at the proper time and before I go hence I hope you will not object to my communicating to them in confidence the author of this great benefaction.

I note that your letter conveys to me your "warmest regards." I need scarcely say how much I am gratified by this assurance and how fully they are reciprocated. For many years I have been, at some distance, impressed with the wonderful ability with which you have managed the great interests confided to your care and, as you know, so far as my modest connection with them is concerned you have had not merely my confidence but my gratitude.

[1] Henry Huttleston Rogers (1840-1909), capitalist, and for many years one of the directing heads of the Standard Oil interests, had just made the before-mentioned gift to Cooper Union.

To Nicholas Murray Butler, February 7, 1902

It is quite certain that you have fulfilled Mr. Carnegie's injunction to prepare a comprehensive scheme of benefaction. You make no mis-take in supposing that I am ready to co-operate with you in every proper way to secure the amount you desire. I have already spoken to Mr. Carnegie on the subject of the university, but he has always said that he was not prepared to take up that question at the present time. He has also stated that he is prepared to give a large amount for some object which may, after examination, address itself to his favorable judg-ment. I shall rejoice if he shall see his way clear to give you ten million of dollars, which seemed to be the sum which he was contemplating as a gift in some new direction.

I notice the list which you add to your letter of persons likely to give money to the university. I know that Mr. Baker [1] and Mr. . . . are abundantly able to give, but I know nothing of their disposition. Mrs. Clark [2] is a personal friend and she has at times given modest contribu-tions in various directions upon my suggestion. She has never intimated, however, any purpose of devoting a large sum of money to any specific object. There can be no objection to bringing the matter to her notice, but I do not anticipate that she will look upon the application with much favor.

I know Mr. Harriman [3] but slightly. He is supposed to have made a great deal of money. He is a man of large views and might possibly undertake some one of the specific objects enumerated in your list. He is certainly worth trying.

I also know Mr. Berwind but have never had any conversation with him in regard to the duties of wealth. I have only a passing acquaint-ance with Mr. J. Henry Smith. He is a man with a great deal of money and may possibly desire to use some of it for educational purposes.

Mr. Thomas F. Ryan is a rich man of very liberal ideas. He is, how-ever, a Roman Catholic and will naturally desire to make his gifts to the various institutions established by his church and which certainly need large contributions.

Considering the whole matter, I should think your best chance lies with Mr. Carnegie if he shall once make up his mind to consider uni-versities as proper objects for his bounty.

Of one thing I am sure. The money will certainly come to the university, but I hope you will not be compelled, as I have been in the Cooper Union, to wander forty years in the Wilderness before reaching the Promised Land.

[1] George F. Baker.
[2] Mrs. William A. Clark.
[3] Edward H. Harriman.

To Wolcott Gibbs, February 20, 1902 [1]

I am sorry to learn that you cannot come to the breakfast which a few of us are going to give to Prince Henry and to which we have invited the leading men in science and industry in this country. The pleasant task of selecting the scientific men was assigned to me. Certainly I put your name at the end of the list as the oldest and the most eminent scientist in this country. It will not be possible to fill your place, but many younger men will undoubtedly be ambitious to occupy it.

In regard to the Cooper Institute, I have indeed accomplished the great object of my life by securing endowment sufficient to devote it, from foundation to roof, to the work of free scientific education for those who have to earn their living as wage earners. I left college with this idea. I found Mr. Cooper by accident. He had a similar purpose in his mind. Together we have worked out the problem at a cost of about three millions of dollars. We have all had to make sacrifices, and it may interest you to know that my own contributions have exceeded three hundred thousand dollars. Mrs. Hewitt has given a similar amount, and our old classmate, Edward Cooper, has contributed at least five hundred thousand dollars.

We are greatly gratified, but more surprised, at the help we have recently received from other people. Carnegie has given six hundred thousand dollars, and an anonymous donor two hundred and fifty thousand dollars. Our income will amount to about one hundred thousand dollars a year. It is not sufficient for all that we want to do, but it will enable us to get rid of the necessity of renting any portion of the building. We are not able to pay adequate salaries to the teachers. Perhaps before I die we may from some other source get enough money to meet this necessity.

I wish I could show you our new chemical laboratory. It is very practical and it is filled with young men (about one hundred and sixty in number) who are doing excellent practical work.

I suppose you have noticed my connection with the Carnegie Institution, for which he has given ten millions of dollars. I was forced into this position, but I did not feel at liberty to decline Carnegie's request, in view of what he had done for the Cooper Union. Perhaps I may be of some use in directing the expenditure of the money, but I would greatly have preferred that the National Academy of Sciences should have been charged with this duty, and I gave this advice to Carnegie. We have several members of the academy, but I think the responsibility should have been placed in the whole body. This would have given distinct

[1] Oliver Wolcott Gibbs (1822-1908), the eminent chemist, was a founder and former president of the National Academy of Sciences.

direction to their study and a fund sufficient to accomplish valuable results. So long as I have any influence, however, the wishes of the academy will be controlling with me. . . .

It is more than sixty years since we parted at old Columbia. What an era it has been! We shall pass out from a different world from that which we entered when we were boys. Is it better or worse?

To Joseph M. Rogers, February 24, 1902

I have delayed replying to your letter of the 13th inst. until I could have time to consult some of the documents bearing upon the questions which you put to me. Some of them I can answer categorically, but there are others which would require considerable elucidation.

Your first question relates to Senator Hoar's statement that Mr. Blaine inspired the McCrary resolution. On this subject I have no knowledge whatever. I never heard that Mr. Blaine made the suggestion, but the records show that he voted against the Electoral Commission Bill. I think, therefore, if Senator Hoar made such a statement, it is a mistake.

Second. You ask whether the suggestion that four judges should select the fifth judge was not originated by me. To this I answer that it was so made after consultation with Mr. Tilden and with his approval. Mr. Tilden, however, objected to the selection of any judge by lot, as was originally suggested. Hence the confusion in the record, but the final form which it took removed the objections which he had made to previous suggestions.

Third. You ask whether in my opinion the two committees could have agreed to any bill unless it had been originally expected that Judge Davis would have been the fifteenth member of the Commission. It is, of course, impossible for me or anyone else to say what the committee might have done in some other contingency, but it was with the distinct understanding on the part of the Democrats that Judge Davis would be selected as the fifteenth member of the Commission. I have always believed that his transfer from the bench to the Senate was the result of a bargain, to which of course Judge Davis himself must have given his tacit assent. I do not believe, however, that he originated the movement. It was a device of the Republicans to get him out of the way, and it succeeded.

Fourth. You state that I disavowed the position of being the representative of Mr. Tilden in reference to the action taken by the Houses of Congress upon the Commission Bill. This is true to the extent that I considered it my duty, as a representative of the people, to be superior to my political and personal relations with Mr. Tilden. Nevertheless, nothing was done from first to last without having been submitted to Mr. Tilden, and nothing was done which was disapproved by him. On the contrary, in the final form which the bill took, Mr. Randall and I were assured by Col. Pelton, who had been sent to New York for the purpose, that the bill was satisfactory to Mr. Tilden and he desired his friends to vote for it.

Fifth. You refer to a conversation which took place between Mr. Bigelow and Mr. Tilden in reference to the purchase of the vote of a justice of the Supreme Court for two hundred thousand dollars, and you say that he quotes from one of my speeches, wherein it is intimated that the commission was sold. I desire to make an emphatic denial that I ever heard of any attempt to purchase the vote of any member of the commission for money, and I never made any intimation that the judgment of the commission was sold. The quotation which you refer to from my speech relates to the action of the Returning Board in Louisiana. I stated publicly in the House that the vote of the Returning Board was offered to me for two hundred thousand dollars and that I declined to buy it. I know further that attempts were made in other quarters to dispose of the vote of the Returning Board, that negotiations actually took place sufficient to satisfy the parties that the vote could be bought, and then the matter fell through in consequence of Mr. Tilden refusing to be a party to any such purchase.

Sixth. You ask me whether the election of Davis to the Senate affected many votes either way in the House. I can only express the opinion that no votes were affected in the House by the action of Judge Davis.

Seventh. You ask me whether I think personally that the action of Mr. Randall during the last three days saved the situation against the evident determination to filibuster and prevent final action. I reply that the action of Mr. Randall undoubtedly tended to secure the completion of the count and in fact did secure it. His action, however, was made after consultation with me, and we agreed upon every step of it. He held the House during the discussion on the Vermont return by distinct agreement with me, in order to give the representatives from Louisiana time to make their bargain with the Republicans who represented Hayes in the Wormley conference. When these representatives declared themslves satisfied, the count proceeded and was completed in accordance with the arrangement between Mr. Randall and myself.

Eighth. You ask me whether if the filibuster policy had succeeded two presidents would have been inaugurated on the fifth of March. This is a hypothetical question, to which I do not think it necessary to make any answer. I think, however, that the House would have declared Mr. Tilden to have been elected President, as in fact they did do by the resolution which they adopted on the last day of the session. What the consequences would have been is simply a matter of conjecture, in which at present I do not propose to indulge.

Having thus given as definite an answer as I can to your questions, I have come to the conclusion that you cannot fully understand the situation unless you should have access to the statement which I have prepared to be published after my death. If therefore you will come to New York at your convenience, giving me proper notice, I will allow you to read the manuscript.

To John Bigelow, March 31, 1902

I do not take much interest in ex-Presidents. I have no objection, however, to their being punished for their sins by being condemned to imprisonment for life in the Senate. It is rather suggestive of punishment after death, which I am willing to leave to a higher power. From my observation I should think that an ex-President in the Senate would be regarded by the other Senators very much as Aristotle was by the Ancient Greeks. It will probably end in a dose of hemlock.

I congratulate you on retaining your interest in public affairs. I confess that I feel very little responsibility for what is going on about me. I know that this is the evidence of decay, but age will tell.

To the Rev. John P. Peters, April 11, 1902

Any use which you may make of my views upon the capital and labor question will be acceptable to me. All that I objected to was any connection with the *Journal*,[1] that is to say, by my own consent.

I heartily sympathize with you in the regret that we were not able to meet last summer, and as you are going abroad that we shall not see each other this year. Perhaps it will be the last opportunity. I am reconciled, however, by the consideration that I have lived long enough to see all the plans which I had devised for the Cooper Union brought to a successful termination. I never expected to see the actual realization of the original idea that the entire building should be devoted to free education. We have, however, money enough now to see our way to this end, and we have hope of additional money in the future sufficient for any possible enlargement in the building as it now stands.

The imposition of the Carnegie trust was entirely unexpected. I am too old for such responsibility, but Mr. Carnegie insisted that I should at least see that the institution was properly organized. It has required much time and labor, but I think I begin to see how great results may be achieved from the expenditure of the income, five hundred thousand dollars per annum for the promotion of knowledge.

I am now busy with the disposition of about four millions of dollars, which have been confided to me for the benefit of the sick respectable poor in this city. If you have any suggestions to make as to the best mode of using the income, which will be from $100,000 to $120,000 per annum, I will be glad to have them. The idea of the donor is to provide hospital service for the respectable poor who are not able to pay. Ultimately a building will be erected, but at present my suggestion to him is to use the income in paying for the hospital accommodations which may be required and for the relief of the families whose bread winner is thus disabled. I propose to make provision for the support of those who have been discharged until they can get into remunerative employment.

If in your experience any special need has come to your notice I think I can make provision for it in the trust deed which I am now having prepared.

To John B. Pine, April 14, 1902

Although I was very reluctant to do so, I have spent an hour with Mr. Carnegie this morning. I pointed out to him, doubtless imperfectly, the requirements of the university and especially called his attention to the provision of sufficient land for its growth. I suggested that the installation of President Butler would be a very pertinent occasion to make the announcement. I am sorry to state that the suggestion was not received with any favor. Moreover, I think I can say that whatever he may do in the future, he has no present intention of making any gift to Columbia. He considers that he has got to the end of his donations for the present year. Incidentally he said that he would not select any university for special recommendation. He regarded the endowment of the Carnegie Institution as the full and reasonable response to any obligation which rested upon him in the direction of higher education.

If, therefore, the land is to be secured it must be through some other source. I ventured to suggest that he might buy it and hold it until the university could get subscriptions from other sources. This suggestion, however, he declined to entertain. Perhaps he is right, because when it was known that he had provided the means no one would probably contribute for the purpose.

To Mr. Goddard, April 24, 1902 [2]

Your letter of the 22d inst. would not require any reply, but for the unconscious injustice which you do to Mr. Carnegie and to Mr. Rockefeller by your closing remark. I have had much to do with these

[1] William Randolph Hearst's New York *Journal*.
[2] This correspondent is not identifiable.

gentlemen, and I can assure you that they never concern themselves about the benefactions of other people. They are only concerned that their own gifts shall not do mischief, and I have never known in all my life two men who gave more conscientious labor to the difficult task which Providence has placed upon their consciences. Neither of them ever make any condition that others should give, except in Mr. Rockefeller's case, where he has only done so upon the urgent request that he shall make a condition. In the case of Barnard College he simply offered to give as much as other people would give, but placed the limit for $200,000 for his benefaction. When it was found that $50,000 more might be raised, he promptly added this amount to his gift. I cannot conceive how men can be more generous and more alive to the duties imposed by wealth.

Probably I did not make myself understood in regard to appropriations for memorials. I have made many such appropriations in my lifetime, but I have so little time and means left at my disposal that for the rest of my life I propose to use what I have for the living and not for the dead.

To Nicholas Murray Butler, April 28, 1902

I am very much honored, as well as gratified, by your invitation to meet Lord Kelvin at dinner on the 9th prox. As you know, I have been compelled for a considerable time to decline all invitations to go out at night. My reason is that I am not reasonably certain of being well enough to keep an appointment made in the future, as my condition varies very much from day to day. I was therefore about to decline with thanks your hospitality and deprive myself of the pleasure of meeting Lord Kelvin, when it occurred to me that I might accept the invitation with a condition attached to it, that if I found myself unable to come, I may if you are willing substitute my son Cooper,[1] whose studies are all in Lord Kelvin's domain of science. They are to meet at Cooper's laboratory on the 5th of May, when the light will be fully explained to Lord Kelvin. At present Cooper intends to sail with him on the same ship, although he may be prevented. If therefore he should be substituted for me, it would be pleasant for both parties, but it may not suit your convenience. What I desire to avoid is the embarrassment of an empty place at the last moment. I would not venture to suggest an alternative, if I did not suppose Cooper would be better suited to the occasion than I shall be, with my scientific knowledge reduced to a reminiscence.

1 Peter Cooper Hewitt (1861-1921), scientist and inventor, best known as the discoverer of the mercury vapor lamp.

To John T. Doyle, April 28, 1902 [1]

Columbia University, as you have learned, is now a great institution, standing where the old Bloomingdale Asylum for so many years had its site. A new president was inaugurated last week, Dr. Butler, a man eminently fitted for the position. The President of the United States came to the function, and to me was assigned the duty of bringing him up to the university and taking him back again to his aunt's house. I have known him from childhood. He thinks he is strenuous, but I find him to be very emotional. I have no doubt he is patriotic, but he is also ambitious. He enjoyed the plaudits of the crowd in a manner that would have done credit to a small boy. He is unquestionably a man of force and of a certain kind of ability. I should be sorry, however, to entrust him with the conduct of a great enterprise. He lacks the solidity of character which the Chief Executive of a great Government ought to have. No one can predict what he will do in any given emergency. He is, however, open to advice, provided it is given before the act is committed. Fortunately, thus far he has had to originate no new policy. Whether he inherited one which will be beneficial is questionable. He seems to be loyally carrying out the policy indicated in McKinley's last speech. He is fortunate in holding office during an era of unexampled prosperity. If it should continue to the end of his term, he may be re-elected by the votes of what we used to call "the common people." He will certainly not have the support of the capitalists. They are afraid of him and justly so. He develops some of the traits of a demagogue, and if it should turn out to be a popular course, he will develop more of them. Meanwhile the activity of business is phenomenal, and there is nothing in sight at present to indicate that there is any reaction near at hand.

To Dr. Henry M. Leipziger, May 7, 1902 [2]

The article in the *Evening Post* entitled "Free Lecture Movement" did not escape my notice at the time of its publication. I have therefore called your attention to the fact that the free lecture system did not originate with the Board of Education. It was undertaken more than forty years ago by the Cooper Union, and until the last five years the

[1] John Thomas Doyle, secretary of the United States Civil Service Commission for many years beginning with 1886, and long prominent in the movement for civil service reform.

[2] Henry Marcus Leipziger (1854-1917), who was born in England and came to America in early life, became Assistant Superintendent of the New York Schools in 1891; as such, he devised plans for a system of evening lectures to be given in school centers. It soon grew into one of the largest organized lecture systems of the country; Leipziger called it "The People's University."

lectures were carried on exclusively under my direction. Knowing the value of this instruction to the public when I became Mayor I suggested to Mr. O'Brien that he should make application for an appropriation for the establishment of these lectures by the Board of Education. He promptly acceded to the request, the appropriation was made, and you were appointed superintendent. It is a mistake therefore for you to assume to have been either the author or the father of this system. I care very little for any personal credit which may attach to the origin of this valuable addition to the system of public education. I cannot, however, allow statements which have been repeatedly made, and which I have endeavored heretofore to correct by correspondence with you, to be repeated without putting in a distinct protest against the claim that the system was originated either by you or by the Board of Education.

To Dr. Henry S. Pritchett, June 4, 1902 [1]

Your letter presents a very embarrassing question. The Executive Committee have not yet arrived at any such conclusion as would enable me to express an opinion as to the future management of the institution. A great deal of quiet thinking has been going on, which will result in the course of time unquestionably in a definite organization for research, somewhat after the model of the Royal Institution. I explained to you very fully all that had occurred in regard to the direction of the institution, and I also had a very full conversation with Mr. Carnegie on the subject. In the present state of the affair, no one I think could venture to make a prediction as to the outcome. Personally I should be glad if you should be identified with the management in a satisfactory manner, but, as I have explained to you, there has been great reluctance to make definite commitments. I can only say that I do not know of anyone into whose hands I would so cheerfully confide the administration of the trust as to yours.

I know that Dr. Gilman [2] does not expect to be charged permanently with this responsibility, but until he shall return from Europe and express some positive opinion after having studied the whole situation, I do not see how anyone can give a definite answer to your inquiry. Dr. Gilman will doubtless have a distinct recommendation to submit to the trustees. As to his own position I am at a loss to conjecture how it can

[1] Dr. Henry S. Pritchett was at this time president of the Massachusetts Institute of Technology, but in 1906 became president of the Carnegie Foundation for the Advancement of Teaching.

[2] Daniel Coit Gilman, who as before mentioned was president of the Carnegie Institution in Washington. Mr. Hewitt was one of the trustees of the Carnegie Institution.

be harmonized with the practical direction of the work. With a president qualified to carry into effect a policy carefully elaborated in advance, and with a director and a secretary working in harmony with each other, I can foresee good results. Up to this time, however, nothing has been developed, which enables me either to give you advice or to predict what is going to happen. I wish I were not too old to take a more active part in the development, which is to come, but the fact is that I am now worn out, and hence I am the more anxious to have a man in the prime of life at the head of the institution. If you were there I would be satisfied, but whether you will be asked to take the position is more than I can predict.

To Dr. Felix Adler, June 5, 1902

As you know, we have been long desirous that the Cooper Union should have a systematic course of lectures on political and social ethics, to be delivered one night in the week between November and May. Knowing how busy you are I have refrained from bringing the matter to your notice, except in the conversation I once had with you at my house on the subject. I am glad to learn that you have accepted the Professorship at the university, requiring you to deliver such a course of lectures for the next three years. It occurs to me that as you have to make the preparation, it would not tax you too much to undertake to deliver one lecture a week in the evening at the Cooper Union on the same subject. Of course we shall expect to pay a reasonable compensation, although naturally we are constrained by the income of the institution. I think, however, that we could arrange to pay twenty or twenty-five dollars per lecture, or say about $500 for the entire course covering six months.

I make this suggestion with considerable diffidence, because I know that the compensation is altogether inadequate, but I regard the work as more important to the public than that which you have undertaken at the university. In the latter case you reach scholars and your work undoubtedly will have permanent results. We need, however, more than that in order to get at the masses as soon as possible. The Cooper Union audiences are made up of the best element among the working classes. The result of your teaching ought to be immediate, and in the present state of public opinion on the subject of duty we cannot afford to wait.

Kindly let me know whether you can entertain the suggestion, and if you are inclined to consider it and to take up the matter with me, I will be glad to make an appointment either at my house or elsewhere as may best suit your convenience.

Index